Beyond Deterrence

Beyond Deterrence

The Political Economy
of Nuclear Weapons

Frank L. Gertcher
and William J. Weida

Westview Press
BOULDER, SAN FRANCISCO, & LONDON

Copyright © 1990 by Westview Press, Inc.

Published in 1990 in the United States of America by Westview Press, Inc., 5500 Central Avenue, Boulder, Colorado 80301, and in the United Kingdom by Westview Press, Inc., 13 Brunswick Centre, London WC1N 1AF, England

Library of Congress Cataloging-in-Publication Data
Gertcher, Frank L.
  Beyond deterrence: the political economy of nuclear weapons/Frank
L. Gertcher, William J. Weida.
    p. cm.
  Includes bibliographical references.
  ISBN 0-8133-0477-6
  1. United States—Military policy. 2. Nuclear weapons—United
States. 3. Nuclear weapons—Economic aspects—United States.
4. Military policy. 5. Nuclear weapons. 6. Nuclear weapons—
Economic aspects. 7. United States—Armed Forces—Appropriations
and expenditures. I. Weida, William J. II. Title.
UA23.G554 1990
355.02′17—dc20   89-29126
                                                                                       CIP

Printed and bound in the United States of America

⊗   The paper used in this publication meets the requirements of the American National Standard
     for Permanence of Paper for Printed Library Materials Z39.48-1984.

10   9   8   7   6   5   4   3   2   1

CONTENTS

TABLES AND FIGURES

Figures

PREFACE

Beyond Deterrence explains the role of military, political and economic incentives in perpetuating the continued growth of worldwide nuclear arsenals. The book begins by identifying nuclear threats as perceived by both U.S. and Soviet military planners. It then discusses the economic and political incentives that result in a continuing demand for additional nuclear weapon production.

This book also provides a comprehensive, worldwide inventory of nuclear arms and a discussion of nuclear production facilities to define the dimensions of the current supply of nuclear weapons. It then shows how this supply has proliferated to create potential nuclear powers among several less developed nations and how the supply of usable weapons may be altered by the development of defenses to counter certain nuclear threats.

In addition, the book explores a wide range of internal and external factors that have created the demand for nuclear weapons. Internal factors cover a spectrum of motivations from local and regional economic stimulation to international considerations involving both resource allocation and military and political commitments. External motivations arising from competition to develop modern ballistic missile, air defense, and command and control systems are discussed as further elements that may alter the demand for new or additional nuclear weapons. Finally, the book outlines the likely effects of economic constraints and arms control agreements on the ability of nuclear powers to reduce the number of nuclear weapons.

Beyond Deterrence is designed for serious students of defense policy and economics, for defense planners and for people who wish to increase their understanding of the political economy of nuclear weapon production and proliferation. Students may wish to seek additional details in the references cited in the notes at the end of each chapter. The more casual reader may prefer to spend less time on the technical details in favor of a more general review of the analyses and the conclusions. In either case, *Beyond Deterrence* provides the reader with a bridge between the theoretical world of economic efficiency and the politically motivated world of nuclear defense planning.

Frank L. Gertcher
William J. Weida

ACKNOWLEDGMENTS

We are grateful to the many individuals who aided in the preparation of *Beyond Deterrence.* We especially want to thank Peter W. Kracht and Susan L. McEachern at Westview Press for their encouragement and administrative guidance, and our colleagues within R&D Associates and within the Department of Economics and Business, Colorado College, for their help in obtaining source materials and their insightful reviews and comments. Finally, we want to thank our wives, Judy and Betty, for their encouragement and for listening patiently over the past two years to periodic lectures on the nature of the nuclear threat and the prospects for deterrence as we approach the twenty-first century.

Although every effort was made to eliminate errors in the book, we recognize that some may have slipped through. For these we take full responsibility, and we encourage readers to correspond with us concerning corrections and suggestions for improvements.

F.L.G.
W.J.W.

PART ONE

Nuclear Dilemmas

1

Introduction

Politics, Economics and Nuclear Weapons

In a political economy context, this book explains the results of decisions by the governments of the United States, the Soviet Union, and other nations to develop modern nuclear weapons and defense systems. It begins by identifying nuclear threats as perceived by military planners. It continues with discussions of strategic defenses, the demand for nuclear weapons, budgets, opportunity costs, spinoffs, domestic and international economic aspects, arms control, and prospects for the future.

The discussions throughout this book deal with the possibility of nuclear war. A close examination of the continuing development of nuclear weapons and delivery systems in the Soviet Union, the United States, and other nations reveals that military preparations for nuclear war are ceaseless, and these preparations appear insensitive to the terrible consequences that would result if such a war occurred.

Yet in our over 27 years of association with the U.S. Department of Defense, we have not found any decision maker who would relish the thought of using nuclear weapons to demolish a perceived enemy. Like most civilians, most military decision makers appear genuinely appalled at the thought of what could happen if the present state of nuclear deterrence fails. It is likely that similar feelings of restraint and concern exist among people in the governments of other major nations that have nuclear weapons.

The incentives that perpetuate the growth of nuclear arsenals are not altogether military. They include numerous political and economic factors and substantial constituencies that benefit from nuclear weapons development, deployment, and maintenance.

The role of military, political and economic incentives in perpetuating the continued growth of worldwide nuclear arsenals provides the theme for this book. Perhaps, if enough readers develop an understanding of these incentives, they may collectively find ways to break the pattern of nuclear weapons accumulation, and by democratic processes and negotiations, enhance the prospects for the continued existence of our civilization.

This introductory chapter establishes the framework for subsequent chapters by providing an overview of the current military balance between the East, led by the Soviet Union, and the West, led by the United States. It also outlines the problem of nuclear weapons proliferation, the potential for nuclear terrorism, and current U.S. and Soviet nuclear defense capabilities. Throughout the chapter, important military, political, and economic incentives are introduced that have influenced the development and the extent of worldwide nuclear arsenals.

Nuclear Deterrence

For over two decades, the U.S. strategy for deterring nuclear war has been to aim nuclear warheads at military, industrial, and other high value targets in the Soviet Union. Under this strategy, deterrence is based on the idea that the U.S. should have enough nuclear forces so that some would survive a Soviet attack. These surviving forces must be capable of inflicting a level of damage on the Soviet Union that would be unacceptable to the Soviet leadership.

The direct benefits of deterrence are difficult to measure. They could be measured in terms of the 'benefits' of avoiding the costs that would be incurred as a result of a nuclear war. However, such benefits involve avoiding human and other losses that cannot be adequately measured in dollars. Indirect benefits from the production and maintenance of deterrent forces are easier to measure. These benefits include regional economic gains, employment, domestic political power, and other non-military benefits. Indirect benefits have little to do with deterrence or other possible military purposes of nuclear weapons, but the evidence indicates that they have often influenced the allocation of resources to deterrent forces.

Resource allocation patterns for deterrent forces evolved from a complex set of conditions over four decades. These patterns are unlikely to change in any meaningful way until something alters the fundamental situation we now have. As long as offensive nuclear forces remain central to U.S. and Soviet planning, the military establishments of these two nations and their allies will remain essentially unchanged, and resource allocation patterns for military forces will also remain unchanged.

Before the United States, the Soviet Union, and other nations can move beyond a political dependence on offensive nuclear forces, there must be incentives to reduce the capabilities of these forces. At the present time, there appear to be only two likely ways that such changes could occur: either the major nuclear powers must arrive at some form of nuclear disarmament, or they must perfect systems of defensive weapons similar to those proposed under the U.S. Strategic Defense and Air Defense Initiatives.

In this sense, the concepts of nuclear disarmament and strategic defense are on convergent courses. If either or both could be successfully implemented, the perceived requirement for offensive nuclear forces might disappear. It is important to note, however, that removing the perceived requirements for nuclear forces does not necessarily imply peace. It only suggests that warfare would probably be pursued on other levels.

Evolving from a dependence on nuclear forces for deterrence to a dependence on disarmament agreements and strategic defense involves the following complex issues:

- Would nuclear disarmament and strategic defense preserve the 'pure public good' elements of deterrence currently provided by nuclear weapons?[1]
- If the superpowers and their allies implemented strategic defenses, could one side overwhelm the defenses of the other by building vast numbers of offensive nuclear weapons and delivery systems?
- What constitutes a level of nuclear disarmament sufficient to allow military forces to be substantially restructured?
- If both strategic and tactical nuclear weapons are eliminated, what would happen to the current levels of non-nuclear forces?
- Would non-nuclear forces provide an effective deterrent? What are the roles of chemical or biological agents in non-nuclear deterrence?
- Would military or civilian Institutions contribute to 'inertia' that would oppose nuclear disarmament and or strategic defenses?

The Superpowers

Evolutionary changes, if they occur, must begin with the current strategic balance between major powers with nuclear weapons. In the United States, the perceived threat of the Soviet Union has dominated the development of U.S. defense policies since about 1949. The Soviet Union has built, and is continuing to build, an enormous strategic offensive nuclear capability that includes about 1,418 land-based intercontinental ballistic missiles, over 145 strategic bombers, 62 ballistic missile submarines, and at least 10,580 strategic nuclear warheads. Soviet strategic forces are augmented with more than 13,600 non-strategic nuclear warheads, 50,000 tanks, approximately 260 attack submarines, more than 8,400 tactical combat aircraft, over 28,200 artillery units, four naval aircraft carriers, two helicopter carriers, about 75 other combat surface ships, and over 5,300,000 military personnel.[2]

U.S. offensive strategic forces include about 990 land-based intercontinental ballistic missiles, 240 strategic bombers, 36 ballistic missile submarines, and about 10,550 strategic nuclear warheads. U.S. strategic forces are augmented with more than 13,000 non-strategic nuclear warheads, about

11,700 tanks, about 100 attack submarines, 3,600 tactical combat aircraft, over 2,750 artillery units, 14 navy aircraft carriers, about 553 other combat surface ships, and over 2,150,000 military personnel.[3]

Although numbers of weapons, warheads, equipment, and troops provide a rough indication of the relative strengths of Soviet and U.S. military forces, they do not account for qualitative, deployment, and strategy differences. These differences are explored in later chapters. For now, it is important to recognize that these differences could easily be decisive in determining the outcome of any major conflict.

The Soviet Threat

Soviet nuclear warheads can be delivered to targets in the United States by ballistic missiles launched from the Soviet homeland, from ballistic missile submarines, and by atmospheric vehicles such as bombers and cruise missiles. Nuclear detonations could devastate U.S. military forces, industrial complexes, and population centers. At the present time, a major attack by the Soviet Union could result in over 6,500 megatons of nuclear detonations within the United States within a matter of a few days or weeks, depending on the attack scenario.[4]

Although the Soviet leadership has periodically expressed a preference for attaining its objectives by means short of war, Soviet military doctrine states that global war and, in particular, global nuclear war, is possible, and that direct conflict with the U.S. would probably escalate to this level.

In this event, their global war aims are to protect what they consider to be their highest valued assets, which include the leaders of the Communist Party, Soviet military forces and industrial complexes, and the Soviet people, in that order.[5]

Thus, the Soviet Union would seek to:

- Ensure continued Communist Party control over the Soviet Government, the military, the internal security forces, and the population.
- Ensure the survival of the Soviet scientific and technical elite and other essential personnel.
- Provide for the continued viability of the Soviet political-military economic system.
- Limit the losses to the general population of the Soviet Union.
- Repair damage and organize recovery.

In addition, their doctrine states that they would seek to:

- Defeat NATO forces, occupy NATO countries, and use Europe's economic assets to assist Soviet recovery.

- Neutralize the United States and China by disorganizing and destroying their military forces, industrial bases, and if necessary, large portions of their respective populations.
- Dominate the post-war world in which 'socialism' will have replaced 'imperialism' as the basic political-economic system in all nations.[6]

Soviet military doctrine includes a preference for a preemptive strike to catch U.S. retaliatory forces on the ground. During a period of imminent hostilities, Soviet doctrine indicates that they would use their sophisticated intelligence network to discern imminent attack, and they would employ their extensive command and control communications network to rapidly launch and coordinate a preemptive strike against targets in the United States, Western Europe, and China.

If a preemptive strike is not possible, the next preferred option is to launch under attack. To support this, they have established both satellite and terrestrial ballistic missile warning systems and an extensive atmospheric surveillance system. They frequently run military exercises to practice launching weapons under stringent time constraints.

Their least favored situation is to launch a follow-on strike after enemy warheads have hit Soviet soil. To prepare for this possibility, they have invested heavily to protect their command and control communications networks, offensive weapon systems, and other military forces from the effects of nuclear detonations.

Finally, Soviet doctrine clearly indicates a belief that a nuclear war with the United States could be protracted. As a result, they pay considerable attention to war reserves and to protection for key people and equipment. Indeed, the Soviet Union's ballistic missile and air defense systems are the most massive in the world. They include active defenses such as a ballistic missile defense near Moscow, modern interceptor aircraft, surface-to-air missiles, and passive defenses such as surveillance and warning systems, underground bunkers, electronic countermeasures, and civil defenses.[7]

Opposing Alliances

An overview of the nuclear threat to the United States would not be complete without mention of the Soviet threat to U.S. allies, particularly those in NATO. Since 1949, the NATO alliance has relied—with varying emphasis—on the U.S. strategic nuclear arsenal as the ultimate deterrent to Warsaw Pact aggression. A similar reliance on the U.S. nuclear umbrella exists for Japan and other nations in the Pacific basin and certain nations in the Middle East, including Israel.

Since the inception of NATO, the standard military wisdom in the West has been that Warsaw Pact armies so outnumber and outgun NATO conventional forces that only nuclear arms could restore the balance. "Every year," according to recently retired NATO Supreme Commander General Bernard Rogers, "we find that the gap continues to widen." While at NATO, Rogers warned that "within days" of a Warsaw Pact invasion, he would be forced to seek permission to use tactical nuclear weapons to halt an otherwise unstoppable advance.[8]

This conventional forces 'gap' provides the primary basis for NATO's current reliance on nuclear weapons, including those controlled by the United States and the United Kingdom, and under certain conditions, the independent nuclear force maintained by France. This reliance has allowed NATO to hold down its spending on conventional forces, partially because nuclear weapons provide much more firepower per dollar spent than conventional weapons.

NATO fears of conventional force vulnerability are largely based on paper comparisons of tanks, troops, aircraft, artillery and other weapons. According to U.S. estimates, the Warsaw Pact has about 32,000 tanks, 2,700,000 troops, 6,310 aircraft, and 23,000 artillery units in place in Eastern Europe.[9]

In addition to the strategic nuclear forces outlined earlier, Warsaw Pact conventional forces are augmented by Soviet nonstrategic and battlefield nuclear forces. Although these receive less attention than the strategic variety, they are more likely to be used first in any East-West confrontation.

Nonstrategic nuclear forces employ various types of weapons for battlefield missions: surface-to-surface, surface-to-air, and air-to-surface missiles; nuclear bombs; atomic land mines; as well as nuclear artillery shells. The Soviets have over 6,979 nonstrategic warheads dedicated to Europe, with yields ranging from one megaton (warheads for SS-4 missiles) down to one kiloton (nuclear artillery shells). Most of these are deployed in the Soviet Union or in eastern Europe. These land-based warheads are supplemented by Soviet naval forces, which have an additional 2,469 warheads, ranging from 500 kilotons down to 1 kiloton. These are deployed on Soviet surface ships and attack submarines.[10]

An increasing number of nonstrategic nuclear weapons are 'crossover systems:' highly mobile, long-range, and usable in more than one theater of war or even for strategic strikes. Such systems include intermediate range ballistic missiles, many types of naval nuclear weapons, as well as cruise missiles and land-based aircraft.

The Soviet triple-warhead SS-20 intermediate range ballistic missile falls into the crossover category. Prior to the U.S.-Soviet treaty on Intermediate Nuclear Forces (INF) in 1988, two-thirds of the 441 SS-20 launchers were deployed in the Western Soviet Union, and one-third were in the Far East. The SS-20 has a 150 kiloton yield, 5,000 kilometer range, and moderate accuracy. It is capable of striking virtually any target in Asia, the Middle East, North Africa, and Europe.

In addition to the SS-20, the Soviets have 224 older SS-4s deployed in the western Soviet Union. These have single one-megaton warheads, a range of 2,000 kilometers, and are capable of hitting fixed, unhardened military targets, cities, and industrial complexes in Europe and the Middle East. The Soviets also have over 1,558 medium and short range missiles of various types with single warheads, and an unknown number of SS-NX-21 sea-launched cruise missiles. These missiles extend the striking range of Soviet naval forces to 3,000 kilometers.

The Soviet medium-range bomber force consists of 350 Badger, Blinder, and Backfire aircraft. These can carry nuclear bombs or air-to-surface missiles, but the precise number of warheads allocated for these aircraft is unknown. All of the bombers are assigned to bases within the Soviet Union, except for one Badger unit in Vietnam. The Soviets also have 2,545 tactical fighter aircraft, many of which probably have nuclear weapon roles. Most of these are deployed in the Soviet Union, Czechoslovakia, East Germany, Hungary, and Poland.[11]

Soviet forces in Europe are supplemented by the forces of other Warsaw Pact nations. However, these allies have only conventional weapons. The Soviets have reserved their nuclear warheads strictly for their own forces, partly out of concern over unauthorized use during a period of heightened East-West tensions, and partly out of fear that their erstwhile allies might use such weapons against the Soviet Union during a major European conflict.

Warsaw Pact forces are opposed by NATO forces that have 19,600 tanks, 2,100,000 troops, 3,260 aircraft, and 14,200 artillery units in Western Europe. These are supported by U.S., British, and French nonstrategic and battlefield nuclear forces. In addition, they are supported by substantial U.S. reinforcements that would be available within a few days, by the U.S. commitment to use its strategic nuclear forces in the event of a Warsaw Pact attack on NATO nations, and further, by British and French strategic nuclear forces.[12]

U.S. nonstrategic nuclear forces include a variety of nuclear weapons for battlefield missions: surface-to-surface, surface-to-air, and air-to-surface missiles; nuclear bombs; atomic land mines, and nuclear artillery shells. The U.S. has about 8,250 nonstrategic warheads with yields ranging from 400 kilotons (warheads for Pershing missiles) down to less than one kiloton (nuclear artillery shells). Over 7,542 of these warheads are deployed in western Europe. They are supplemented by U.S. naval forces, which have an additional 2,900 or more warheads, ranging from 150 kilotons down to one kiloton. These are deployed worldwide on U.S. surface ships and attack submarines. Of these warheads, over 700 are deployed aboard U.S. ships in seas adjacent to Europe.

Prior to the INF treaty, the U.S. counterpart to the Soviet SS-20 was the Pershing II ballistic missile. In 1987, the U.S. had 108 Pershings in Western Europe. These weapons, with warheads of 40 to 400 kilotons and a range of about 1,790 kilometers, are highly accurate and can destroy hardened military targets.

Prior to the INF treaty, the U.S. also had 464 ground-launched cruise missiles deployed in five NATO countries and a wide variety of tactical nuclear aircraft with nuclear bombs. The cruise missiles have 150 to 200 kiloton warheads and a range of about 2,500 kilometers. They are also highly accurate and can destroy hardened targets.

The deployment and armament of tactical aircraft were not affected by the INF treaty. These aircraft are armed with some 3,800 nuclear bombs: 1,700 are deployed in Europe, 130 in the Pacific, and 720 are aboard aircraft carriers at sea. These aircraft are supplemented by 250 F-111 bombers with an additional 600 nuclear bombs. At any given time, about 150 of the F-111s are deployed to two forward bases in Britain, and the remainder are in the continental United States.

Finally, the U.S. has a large assortment of nuclear artillery shells for battlefield use. Stockpiles of these weapons are deployed throughout Western Europe, with large quantities of reserves in the continental U.S.[13]

Unlike the Soviet Union, the U.S. has designated a large number of nuclear bombs and artillery shells for use by its European allies. Although these weapons are kept under tight U.S. control and cannot be released to the NATO allies without a Presidential order, they are integrated into allied war plans and would probably be used by U.S. allies to oppose a massive Soviet attack.

Conditions for the Use of Nuclear Weapons

Soviet military doctrine calls for swift victory in the critical European 'central zone' before the West's economic might and overall manpower advantage could be fully mobilized. Of the total Warsaw Pact force, 14,000 tanks, 998,000 troops, 3,420 aircraft, and 6,900 artillery units are located in the central zone. This includes deployments in East Germany and parts of Czechoslovakia and Poland. NATO has 9,700 tanks, 1,010,000 troops, 2,395 aircraft, and 3,400 artillery units in the central zone, which includes deployments primarily in West Germany.[14]

Thus, a tally of combat ready forces in the central zone gives the Warsaw Pact just under one million troops, slightly fewer than the number deployed by NATO. The Warsaw Pact does have a substantial zone advantage in tanks—14,000 to NATO's 9,700—but that edge is smaller than the difference for Europe as a whole.

As a result, "the Soviets cannot be confident of winning, even with a blitzkrieg," according to former U.S. Defense Secretary Harold Brown. And if Soviet leaders take into account the possibility that a successful attack might trigger a full-scale nuclear conflict, then an assault in the central zone appears even less attractive.[15]

Rather than accept a defeat in Europe, the U.S. has pledged to use its strategic nuclear forces against the Warsaw Pact, if a conflict in Europe escalated beyond a certain point. At times, the U.S. has threatened to use these weapons early in any war, even if the initial attack was not nuclear. At other times, the U.S. has pledged to use them if NATO found itself incapable of mounting a serious conventional defense against a conventional Warsaw Pact attack. But at all times, the U.S. has maintained that it would respond to a nuclear attack in Europe with nuclear weapons; the nature and degree of the retaliation would depend on the nature and degree of Warsaw Pact use of such weapons.

The NATO dependence on a U.S. 'nuclear guarantee' has had long-lasting consequences. Most important, it has made the reliability of this pledge a central issue of alliance security. However, the reliability of the U.S. pledge has been difficult to insure. There is a chronic fear within the alliance that the United States might commit its allies to a nuclear war they neither want nor, given their proximity and vulnerability to Soviet nuclear attack, could survive. On the other hand, there is also a fear, exacerbated by the 1987–1988 Gorbachev initiatives that the U.S. would sign a nuclear disarmament pact with the Soviets that would cast doubt on the nuclear guarantee, and therefore lessen its deterrent effect. Finally, the allies have periodically expressed doubts that the U.S. would actually use nuclear weapons in defense of NATO and risk a subsequent Soviet nuclear attack on the U.S. homeland.

The Gorbachev initiatives led to the INF treaty that calls for dismantling certain missiles in Europe. On the Soviet side, the treaty called for dismantling 693 missiles, including 441 Soviet SS-20s, 112 SS-4s, 120 SS-12s and SS-22s, and 20 SS-23s. In return, the U.S. agreed to dismantle 332 missiles, including 108 Pershing IIs and 224 ground launched cruise missiles.[16]

Although most observers view the agreement as historic, it covers less than five percent of the world's nuclear weapons. Further, the NATO allies, particularly the United Kingdom and West Germany, have expressed concerns that the U.S.-Soviet agreement to begin reduction of nuclear weapons in Europe could lead to a Soviet dominance due to their overwhelming superiority in conventional forces.

In spite of reservations in NATO and in the U.S. Congress, the treaty was ratified by the U.S. Senate in May 1988. As a British Foreign Office official stated in September 1987, "We don't think this ushers in Utopia and it's instantly a wonderful world, the end of weapons and war as we know it, but if you take arms control as a whole, it's the beginning of the beginning."[17]

Other U.S. alliances also depend, to some extent, on a nuclear guarantee similar to the one given to NATO. Japan, other allies in the Pacific basin, and certain allies in the Middle East, including Israel, are of particular interest. In general, U.S. policy has consistently stated that any use of nuclear weapons by the Soviet Union in regions of interest to the U.S. would risk U.S. nuclear retaliation which, in turn, implies grave risks of a subsequent Soviet nuclear attack against the United States.

While scholars continue to debate the nature of Soviet motives and international objectives, recent arms reduction proposals to the West by Gorbachev have heightened the controversy surrounding Soviet intentions. However, U.S. political leaders have developed U.S. defense policies based on observed facts concerning Soviet military capabilities rather than on theories of Soviet motivations.

Other Nuclear Nations

The United States and the Soviet Union are not the only nations that have nuclear weapons. The United Kingdom, France, and China are all avowed members of the nuclear weapons club. Other nations, including India, Pakistan, Argentina, Brazil, Egypt, Iraq, Israel, Libya, South Africa, South Korea, and Taiwan, may have the potential to develop nuclear weapons in five years or less from the beginning of a concerted effort to do so. Some of these nations, including China, have had policies that have been opposed to the interests of the United States, and have, from time to time, used or threatened to use military force to achieve these policies. Others, like Israel and South Africa, may already have weapons or the capability to assemble weapons within a very short time period.[18]

The United Kingdom and France have traditionally regarded the United States as a staunch ally. But they also recognize that complete identity of interests between sovereign states cannot be assumed at all times, especially when national survival may be at stake. Despite strenuous Soviet attempts in recent years to persuade NATO and the world in general that the British and French nuclear arsenals should be regarded merely as extensions of U.S. nuclear forces, both the United Kingdom and France have refused to accept the proposition that they are not independent nuclear powers.

Both British and French nuclear forces are credible deterrents. If the Soviet Union launched an attack on either nation, the subsequent response by British or French forces could inflict damage so great on Soviet cities and industrial complexes that the costs to the Soviets would probably outweigh the benefits.

The British currently have four strategic nuclear-powered ballistic missile submarines, each carrying sixteen Polaris missiles (1988). Thus, British submarines have the capability to deliver 64 nuclear warheads on Soviet targets. In the mid-1990s, the British will begin to deploy new submarines to replace its aging Polaris force. The new submarines will be armed with

U.S. Trident II missiles (but with British nuclear warheads). Thus, a force of four or five new British submarines will carry some 512 to 640 multiple independently targetable reentry vehicle (MIRV) nuclear warheads.

The British also have a fighter-bomber force capable of striking targets in the Soviet Union. Currently, about 300 British-made nuclear warheads are carried on about 200 nuclear-capable aircraft of three types: Jaguar, Buccaneer, and Tornado. These aircraft are stationed at four air bases in Britain and two in West Germany, the only permanent British overseas nuclear weapons bases. In 1988, the current Buccaneers and Jaguars are being replaced by a force of about 220 new Tornados. In addition, the British have nuclear-armed Sea Harriers on three aircraft carriers. This force is capable of delivering about 30 nuclear warheads on targets within a range of about 450 miles.[19]

The French have a mixed force of land-based ballistic missiles, nuclear-powered ballistic missile submarines, and nuclear-capable aircraft. The landbased missile force consists of 18 intermediate-range ballistic missiles, each with a single warhead. The French Force Oceanique Strategique includes five older nuclear-powered ballistic missile submarines, each armed with sixteen single-warhead missiles. A sixth submarine became operational in 1985 with a new missile, the M4, which carries six warheads. By 1992, the French will load the M4 into four of their six existing submarines. The M4 program will expand the French submarine force from today's 80 warheads to 496 warheads. France is also developing a fully MIRVed M5 missile and plans to build a seventh submarine, of a new design, to join the fleet in the mid 1990s.

France has four squadrons of about 34 Mirage IVA bombers in its Strategic Air Force. These aircraft are armed with about 75 nuclear bombs, and are deployed at four main and five dispersal bases located in France. The Mirage IVAs will be replaced by new Mirage IVPs by the mid-1990s. The French strategic bomber force is supplemented with 75 shorter-range Jaguar and Mirage IIIE fighterbombers, armed with about 85 nuclear bombs, and 36 Super Etendards deployed on aircraft carriers with about 40 nuclear bombs total.

The French are in the process of modernizing each element of its 'triad' of land, sea, and aircraft nuclear forces. By the mid-1990s, France will be able to strike over 500 targets in the Soviet Union with nuclear warheads.[20]

The maintenance of a truly independent nuclear capability presents problems for medium powers such as the United Kingdom and France. For example, a situation could arise where the Soviet Union felt able to threaten the United Kingdom or France in isolation without fear of involvement by the United States. Under such circumstances, small deterrent forces, even those based on a few nuclear-powered submarines, might be vulnerable to attack (a Soviet preemptive strike, Soviet use of attack submarines, etc.).

The problem of vulnerability and the limited political utility of independent nuclear options have induced the British to coordinate their nuclear strategy with the United States. Britain has committed its nuclear forces to NATO and allowed its weapons to be integrated within the U.S. strategic nuclear war plan, called the SIOP (Single Integrated Operations Plan).

France, on the other hand, took a divergent approach by leaving the NATO military structure in 1966, and it currently maintains a nuclear capability independent of American strategy. However, an imminent conflict between NATO and the Warsaw Pact would probably induce cooperation between France and other NATO members in the execution of nuclear war plans.

On the other side of the world, China has a conventional military force that includes about 10,500 tanks, 3,150,000 troops, some 4,700 combat aircraft, and 11,800 artillery units. China also has an operational nuclear capability, with warheads that can be delivered by land-based ballistic missiles (the CSS 1,2,3 and 4), by aircraft (the Chinese versions of the Soviet Tupolev TU-16 and TU-4 bombers), and by submarine-based ballistic missiles (a Han-class submarine fitted with missile tubes).

China's handful of CSS-3 (intermediate range) and CSS-4 (intercontinental range) missiles are capable of delivering perhaps as many as 10 to 15 warheads. It also has a force of about 125–185 nuclear-capable short-range missiles (CSS-1 and 2).

In addition, China has about 80–90 TU-16 long-range and 30–40 TU-4 medium range bombers, capable of delivering perhaps as many as 50 nuclear bombs. It also has one submarine capable of carrying six missiles. However, it is not known whether the Chinese have any operational missiles for their submarine.[21]

China has well-known ideological and territorial differences with the Soviet Union that are complemented by traditional border disputes inherited by the Soviets from Tsarist Russia: the Great North-East area, ceded to Russia in portions during 1858 and 1860; the Great North-West area, ceded to Russia in 1864; the Pamirs, allocated to Russia by a secret protocol with the United Kingdom in 1896; and more recently, Inner Mongolia, absorbed by the Soviet Union in 1944. It is therefore understandable that the Chinese would develop nuclear weapons as an effective means of striking deep into the territory of the Soviet Union.

Reliability problems, combined with the relatively small numbers of warheads and delivery systems, lead most Western military analysts to consider China's nuclear force more of a symbolic threat to the West than a major concern. However, China is more than a symbolic threat to the Soviet Union, as the Soviets acknowledge by their deployment of considerable nuclear and conventional forces in eastern Russia, with weapons aimed at Chinese military installations and cities.

China is not the only 'third world' country that has a nuclear weapon capability. In 1974, India exploded a nuclear device that used reprocessed plutonium from one of its nuclear reactors. This reactor was ostensibly designed for the peaceful generation of electrical energy. Although India has stated that it does not intend to develop nuclear weapons, it clearly has the potential to do so.

India's nuclear capability has caused a great deal of consternation on the part of Pakistan, India's traditional opponent in several border wars over the past 40 years. Pakistan has indicated that it has the capability to quickly assemble nuclear warheads for use against India. While these two nations are not likely to directly threaten the United States, the Soviet Union, or their respective allies, any conflict involving nuclear weapons could have political repercussions that could cause superpower confrontation.[22.]

It is widely accepted by military analysts that a number of other countries are on the threshold of developing nuclear weapons. Some of these nations are suspected of having clandestinely developed small stockpiles of fission-based nuclear bombs deliverable by aircraft. Aside from India and Pakistan, Israel and South Africa are suspected of having already developed a nuclear weapon capability, either without conducting tests or by having successfully accomplished tests without being detected. This latter prospect seems unlikely however, because such tests would probably have been detected by the extensive seismic and satellite detection systems deployed by the United States and the Soviet Union.

Many near-nuclear states are in regions of endemic political instability: Israel, Egypt, Iraq and Libya in the Middle East; Brazil and Argentina in South America; Taiwan and South Korea in East Asia; South Africa; and India and Pakistan in Southern Asia. In each of these areas, there are clearly identifiable and persistent sources of domestic instability and/or inter-nation conflict.

The evolving problems of nuclear proliferation are explored in greater detail in subsequent chapters. For now, it is important to note that the possession of nuclear weapons by nations that have a recent history of conflict adds to the risk of at least a regional nuclear war.

Proliferation can also involve subnational groups. For example, it is possible that a terrorist organization could pose a nuclear threat of some form in the future. Although the level of terrorist activity changes from year to year, the trend over the last 15 years has been unmistakably upward. As the number of incidents has increased, terrorism has also become more severe. Terrorists have acquired new capabilities and demonstrated a greater willingness to kill. Perhaps even more disturbing, a number of governments have become their accomplices. This is especially true in the Middle East (Libya, Iran, etc.).

To date, no terrorist group is known to have acquired a nuclear explosive device, although there have been several incidents related to possible theft attempts directed at American nuclear weapons storage sites in Europe.[23] Thus, in the future, the possibility of a successful attempt cannot be overlooked. A nuclear device could be obtained by a raid on one of the thousands of warhead stockpiles throughout the world, by hijacking a ship or aircraft that carries nuclear weapons, or by obtaining fissionable materials and building a nuclear explosive device. If some group obtained such a device, it could be delivered by a variety of simple systems: a ship entering a harbor, a truck on the highway, a civilian aircraft, etc. Terrorists have shown a willingness and ability to conduct suicide missions in the past, so the delivery system need only provide one-way transportation.

Although the use of nuclear explosives poses the most serious terrorist threat, there are lesser, but substantial dangers associated with other nuclear materials. For example, nuclear power plants could be sabotaged, causing widespread radioactivity, or radioactive waste could be hijacked on its way to a disposal site and used to contaminate water supplies or other elements of the environment.

This does not imply that a government need only maintain defensive mechanisms. Imaginative offensive strategies could include forging international agreements, developing intelligence and surveillance networks, international pursuit of fugitive terrorists, or a policy of attacking terrorist training camps and bases in those countries that provide such facilities. However, experience with non-nuclear terrorist incidents has shown that the probability of a decisive offensive victory over a small and elusive terrorist enemy is relatively low. Thus, improved defensive measures are likely to be more effective in the long run.[24]

The problem of inadequate safeguards is highlighted by actual incidents involving loss or diversion of weapon-related nuclear materials. In August 1977, several members of the U.S. Congress called for investigations following the release of a government report that indicated that nuclear fuel plants could not account for over 8,000 pounds of uranium and plutonium that had disappeared since World War II. Although the report stressed that there was no evidence of theft, the agencies involved clearly had failed to keep track of fissionable materials that could be used to make nuclear explosive devices.[25]

Terrorists could also gain a nuclear capability by sabotaging nuclear reactor facilities. Although steps appear to have been taken in the United States during the past few years to diminish the vulnerability of nuclear power plants, sabotage is still conceivable, with results that could dwarf the problems that occurred at the Soviet plant in Chernobyl in 1986.[26]

Although the Soviet nuclear threat and problems of nuclear proliferation overshadow the potential problem of nuclear terrorism, it is clearly possible for a terrorist related nuclear incident to cause substantial devastation and loss of life, both in the U.S. and in other countries. That a nuclear terrorist incident has not yet happened may be more a result of the fact that no known concerted effort has been mounted by a terrorist group, rather than by the ironclad nature of U.S. and other defenses against such an occurrence.

U.S. Defense Policy

Even with the evolutionary nature of the Soviet threat, the problems of nuclear proliferation, and the potential threat from nuclear terrorists, the fundamental goal of U.S. national security policy has remained essentially unchanged since the end of World War II. This goal is to preserve the independence, institutions, territory, and worldwide interests of the United States and to shape an international order in which U.S. institutions and freedoms can survive and prosper. The policy objectives to support this goal are:

- To deter military attack or coercion by the Soviet Union and its allies against the United States, its allies, and other friendly countries.
- In the event of an attack, to deny enemy objectives and to bring a rapid end to the conflict on terms favorable to U.S. interests.
- To promote meaningful and verifiable mutual reductions in nuclear and conventional forces through negotiations with the Soviet Union and the Warsaw Pact.
- To inhibit the expansion of Soviet control and military presence and to induce the Soviet Union to withdraw from countries where it has imposed and maintains its presence by force of arms.
- To strengthen NATO and U.S. capabilities to deter or defeat the threat posed by Soviet and Warsaw Pact forces.
- To maintain the security of U.S. sea-lanes and the supply of essential resources from other countries.
- To foster the security of allies and friendly nations throughout the world.[27]

Although these broad policy objectives provide a basis for a U.S. defense establishment, they do not specify the nature of the forces that must evolve to deter the Soviet nuclear threat and other threats that change over time. For example, the United States could rely on improved strategic retaliatory forces to deter a Soviet nuclear attack, or it could develop new ballistic missile and air defenses to stop incoming Soviet nuclear warheads before they reach their intended targets. The choice of one, the other, or a mix of these or other alternatives involves both economic and political decisions. Further, decision makers are uncertain about Soviet intentions, the reliability of weapon systems, the nature, location, and timing of a nuclear or conventional attack, and so on.

Deterrence and Strategic Defense

In discussing deterrence, it is important to keep in mind that "the power to deter is the power to deter a particular adversary in a particular situation."[28] However, the basic elements of deterrence do not change with circumstance. Three basic questions about the elements of deterrence are pertinent:

The first question is: "How can deterrence be obtained?" Basically, deterrence can be obtained through two mechanisms:

- Threaten punitive retaliation—This mechanism involves the maintenance of a deterrent force capable of holding at risk things of value to a potential adversary.
- Deny enemy objectives—Here, a nation maintains the ability to defeat enemy purposes, thereby removing the motivation for aggression.

The second question is: "What contributes to the quality of deterrence?" There are three factors:

- Capability: Forces must be able to carry out an intended strategy.
- Credibility: The forces must be visible and perceived to be effective. Further, the result of the use of force must not threaten such devastating effects that its use is unlikely. This latter result is known as the self-deterrence problem.
- Mutual Perceptions: An adversary nation must perceive the value placed on the issues at stake or it might miscalculate the will of the deterring nation to use force on behalf of these issues.

The third essential question is "Does the mechanism of deterrence enhance stability?" To do this, the mechanism of deterrence must demonstrate:

- Crisis stability: The incentives for the use of force in situations of extreme tension must not become imperative.
- Arms race stability: Given the U.S. commitment to protect its interests, the incentives for arms race competition should be minimized.[29]

Arms race stability, per se, might be difficult to achieve, given the current state of U.S.-Soviet relations. However, one hope of U.S. defense system upgrades and the diplomatic initiatives of the Reagan administration is that superpower competition might be funnelled into non-nuclear or other more crisis-stable forms.

The Evolution of U.S. Defense Strategy

For the past 40 years, the primary goal of U.S. defense strategy with regard to the Soviet threat has been deterrence. However, the strategy itself has undergone considerable evolution. At this point, it is useful to outline two important landmarks in this process. The first is the strategy of Mutual Assured Destruction (MAD), because it is thought to be U.S. strategy by much of the public, and because it gave birth to the Anti-Ballistic Missile (ABM) treaty. The second is the current U.S. declaratory strategy, which is the countervailing strategy of the Carter Administration, as modified by the Reagan Administration.

Mutual Assured Destruction (MAD), the declaratory strategy of the Kennedy and the Johnson administrations, defined the purpose of U.S. offensive nuclear weapons to be "readiness at any time before, during, or after a Soviet attack to destroy the Soviet Union as a functioning society."[30] This strategy required that the U.S. maintain a deterrent force of offensive nuclear weapons that satisfied only three conditions:

- The force must be powerful enough to destroy Soviet urban society.
- The weapons must be inaccurate enough not to threaten Soviet strategic weapons.
- The weapons must be invulnerable enough to survive a Soviet attack.

Proponents of MAD argued that stable deterrence exists if these conditions are satisfied and if the Soviets maintain a similar force. Since both U.S. and Soviet cities are at risk, stability will be maintained during a crisis because neither side can remove the risk by striking first. Arms race stability exists because an offensive nuclear weapons buildup, at least of the inaccurate type, cannot place strategic nuclear forces at risk. This philosophy has been identified with minimum deterrence since, if one believes its tenets, a relatively small number of large nuclear warheads can achieve stability.

However, MAD is not and never was the sole basis of U.S. operational strategy. Some counterforce targeting was always present in the Strategic Integrated Operations Plan (SIOP) for two reasons. First, destroying the Soviet civilian population in retribution for a deterrence failure would be, for the U.S., a psychologically difficult and morally abhorrent thing to do. Therefore, there has always been serious doubt that such an action would actually be taken by a U.S. President, particularly since it would probably result in subsequent Soviet strikes and massive destruction of the U.S. civilian population. Second, to be effective, a deterrent force must place at risk the highest valued assets in the adversary nation. It is now widely believed that the Soviet leadership places top priority on the survival of its military and civilian control functions rather than the survival of its civilian population. Finally, and perhaps most important, for MAD to work, both nations must accept it and design their strategic forces accordingly. The Soviets have never shown any inclination to accept the assumptions inherent in MAD. Instead, they have built a nuclear warfighting capability that is inconsistent with such a philosophy. For these reasons, MAD was widely discussed, but it never became the basis of U.S. operational strategy.[31]

The present U.S. countervailing strategy is designed to deter the Soviet leadership from either limited or all-out nuclear attacks by maintaining U.S. forces, command and control communications, and intelligence assets capable of denying the Soviets the achievement of their objectives at any level of conflict, or by inflicting costs upon them exceeding any of their anticipated gains. Thus, a countervailing strategy requires U.S. forces that can fight effectively at each rung on the conflict escalation ladder and that are able to endure repeated nuclear exchanges over an extended period of time. The force levels for this strategy far exceed the levels required for a MAD strategy.

The countervailing strategy is based on the view that the most effective way to deter a Soviet nuclear attack is to maintain escalation dominance, and to target those assets that the Soviet leadership values most. Thus, it puts in jeopardy the Politburo's political and military control assets, their nuclear and conventional military forces, Soviet defense industries, and the lives of Soviet leaders.[32]

Deterrence under this strategy is based on the ideas that the defender could inflict an unacceptable level of damage on the attacker and that Soviet leaders would be most deterred by the threat of military defeat, by the potential loss of control at home, and by the threat of U.S. 'decapitation' strikes against Soviet leaders. Thus, even if Soviet leaders were willing to sacrifice large numbers of their own people in war, they would still have a political and personal stake in seeing that no conflict occurred.[33] In addition, current U.S. strategy seeks to extend deterrence to Soviet-Warsaw Pact aggression in Europe by linking such aggression, whether nuclear or non-nuclear, to U.S. strategic nuclear systems. This linkage is accomplished by stationing U.S. nuclear and nonnuclear forces on the European continent. According to advocates, such deployments provide the capability to defeat aggression, the credibility that the U.S. will defend its allies, and they clearly establish the level of importance that the U.S. places on its allied relationships.

Thus the countervailing strategy of the Carter, Reagan and Bush Ad-ministrations allows the U.S. to use the deployment and threat of its offensive nuclear forces to deter a wide spectrum of conflicts.[34] In contrast to MAD, which gave the President an 'on-off switch,' a countervailing strategy provides the U.S. national leadership with a spectrum of responses. It at once calls into play both mechanisms of deterrence: punishment and denial of victory. While the use of two deterrence mechanisms requires additional nuclear forces compared to MAD, it also results in a force structure that exploits distinctive Soviet vulnerabilities. As such, it represents an evolution from the societal punishment theory of nuclear deterrence (MAD), to a theory which is (somewhat inaccurately) called a warfighting strategy although it has as its ultimate aim the destruction of the warfighting capabilities and coercive control mechanisms of the Soviet Union. Although collateral damage from actual implementation of a countervailing strategy might result in a human cost indistinguishable from that of MAD, it does seek to bring moral precepts and strategic reality to the nuclear conflict arena.

Proponents of the U.S. countervailing strategy and its forerunners point to over 40 years of major conflict avoidance between the superpowers as evidence of its success. In spite of this, and in spite of the more sophisticated basis of the countervailing strategy compared to MAD, the current strategy has been seriously questioned in terms of mechanism, capability, credibility, and stability. For example, critics claim that the current strategy implements only one mechanism of deterrence, i.e., that of punishment. The threat of offensive retaliation does not necessarily deny the enemy its objectives.[35]

Critics also question the credibility of the current strategy. Even if a U.S. countervailing strategy could inflict unacceptable damage to the Soviet Union, it neglects the problem of self-deterrence, i.e., a U.S. President might have inhibitions against unleashing a major nuclear retaliatory strike because the result would be massive casualties among the Soviet population, and because the Soviets might unleash further strikes against the U.S. population. This is a particularly serious problem for the case of deterrence against the Soviets if they invaded Europe.[36]

Critics also say that a countervailing strategy is hampered by technical limitations concerning the ability of U.S. warheads to destroy hardened Soviet targets. To achieve such a capability, the U.S would have to spend considerable funds for offensive weapon systems improvements. Such funding has been difficult to obtain from Congress during the Carter, Reagan and Bush Administrations.[37]

Critics also point out that Soviet technical advances make the survival of existing U.S. offensive forces during a Soviet first strike less likely. These same technical advances increase the probability of a Soviet decapitation strike against the U.S. National Command Authorities (NCA) and command and control communications networks. Thus, even if sufficient U.S. forces survived, it might be difficult to orchestrate a meaningful retaliatory strike. However, neither of these criticisms could be addressed without significant increases in nuclear defenses.[38]

Further, the combination of the Soviet preemptive strike preference with the U.S. countervailing strategy is thought to be crisis unstable. In a crisis situation, there is considerable pressure for the Soviets to launch a first strike in order to catch U.S. forces on the ground. Finally, the current U.S.

and Soviet strategies create pressures to produce additional nuclear forces and to endure the escalating costs associated with the accumulation of more accurate and sophisticated nuclear weapons.[39]

After a decade of quiescence, these issues led to a re-emergence of the ballistic missile defense debate in 1981–83. Causes of this re-emergence include:

- Concern over the lack of defenses against tactical missiles in Europe brought about by the Soviet introduction of SS-20 missiles in the region and the U.S. countermove of introducing Pershing IIs and GLCMs.
- Allegations of Soviet violations of the Anti-Ballistic Missile Treaty and the possibility of a Soviet renunciation of the treaty.
- Strategic parity made policy makers more attentive to opportunities at the strategic margin where even a limited ballistic missile defense might make a difference in the outcome of a nuclear conflict.
- The buildup of a Soviet nuclear warfighting capability caused U.S. strategists to consider warfighting concepts that called for offensive and defensive U.S. forces and that created possible roles for less than perfect defenses against incoming nuclear warheads.
- The inability to develop survivable basing modes for the MX missile and the increasing vulnerability of the current U.S. Minuteman missile force caused U.S. analysts to reconsider alternative ABM systems to enhance missile force survivability.
- Disenchantment among conservative elements in the Reagan Administration with traditional arms control negotiations raised questions concerning the moral basis of the ABM Treaty—a treaty that allows destruction of populations and denies the right of self-defense.
- Concern that the lack of even rudimentary space and ballistic missile defenses and limited air defenses leaves the United States vulnerable to accidental launch, to devastation by an insane sub commander, blackmail, coercion, or devastation at the hands of nuclear terrorists.[40]

Current U.S. and Soviet Nuclear Defenses

From the 1950s to 1983, the U.S. defense against the perceived Soviet strategic nuclear threat was based on the deterrence value of U.S. offensive nuclear weapons and the ability to defend against Soviet aircraft that carry nuclear bombs. However, since the mid-1960s, the Soviet Union has developed and deployed large numbers of increasingly sophisticated air, land and submarine based nuclear missiles.

In the absence of arms control agreements, missiles, not aircraft with bombs, will continue to present the major nuclear threat to the United States for the next two decades or so. To alleviate this threat, the Reagan

Administration embarked on the Strategic Defense Initiative and other programs (the Air Defense Initiative) to upgrade U.S. defenses against space, ballistic missile, and atmospheric nuclear threats.

Over the past three decades, the defense of the North American continent against Soviet strategic nuclear forces has been the responsibility of the North American Aerospace Defense Command (NORAD). This command includes both U.S. and Canadian forces. If a nuclear conflict should occur, current NORAD defenses would provide little more than warning that a ballistic missile attack was on the way and would alert National Command Authorities in time to launch U.S. retaliatory forces.

NORAD's primary attack warning, attack assessment, and command and control center is the Cheyenne Mountain Complex (CMC), which is buried deep under a mountain near Colorado Springs, Colorado. The CMC includes processing centers for data from sensors that can detect Soviet ballistic missiles and other sensors that can detect bombers, and to a certain extent, cruise missiles. These sensors are deployed on the ground, in the air, and in space.

Command and control communications networks connect the CMC with seven Regional Operations Control Centers (ROCCs) and selected sensors, including certain space-based sensors, 20 terrestrial space warning sensors, 11 ballistic missile warning sites, and up to eight E-3 Airborne Warning and Control aircraft. In turn, the ROCCs communicate with 139 microwave radar sites, 15 U.S. fighter-interceptor squadrons, and one Canadian fighter-interceptor squadron.[41]

With the exception of a small number of Canadian ground-to-air anti-aircraft missiles, fighter-interceptor squadrons provide the only current active defense against Soviet nuclear threats. Neither the U.S. nor Canada has a current capability to destroy incoming Soviet ballistic missiles or their deployed nuclear warheads.

With the possible exception of the CMC, none of the fixed terrestrial command centers, sensors, or air bases are considered capable of surviving a major Soviet nuclear attack. For example, the ROCCs were designed as 'soft' peacetime air sovereignty systems. Part of the rationale for this design is that neither the ground-based radars nor the communications supporting the ROCCs are considered survivable in a nuclear war environment.[42]

During and after a major nuclear attack, NORAD expects to rely heavily on relatively survivable mobile units for command and control of surviving defense forces. These mobile units include terrestrial command centers deployed on trucks and airborne command posts. These units are linked by survivable satellite communications (Milstar, DSCS-III, etc.), the Ground-wave Emergency Network (GWEN), and other radio links that have some survival capability. Surviving fighter-interceptors would be dispersed to secondary military and civilian airfields.[43]

On the other side, the Soviets have pursued wide-ranging programs in a determined effort to blunt the effects of any attack on the Soviet Union. These programs reflect Soviet military doctrine, which calls for equal attention to defensive as well as offensive capabilities.

As early as 1965, the Soviets were writing about space and ballistic missile defense systems, which they described as vital components of their strategic defense. The main purpose of a space defense system is to destroy enemy military space systems in orbit. The principal means of destruction, currently undergoing tests, involves special aircraft and space vehicles controlled either from the ground or by crews on board a space vehicle. In addition, the Soviets are developing a ground-based laser for use against low orbit satellites. For ballistic missiles, the Soviet Union also currently has the world's only operational antiballistic missile defense system. This system, deployed primarily around Moscow, has been continually improved over the past two decades.

In addition to its space and ballistic missile defenses, the Soviet Union has an operational air defense system that dwarfs the air defense system of the United States. The Soviet system employs a large number of interceptor aircraft, ground based anti-aircraft missiles and artillery, command centers, radars, and communications networks to protect territory, military forces, and other key assets throughout the Soviet Union.

Finally, the Soviet Union has a passive defense program that includes structural hardening of facilities to protect important political, economic, and military leaders. This program also includes civil defense measures designed to insure the survival of Soviet workers during and after a protracted nuclear conflict.

Soviet writings on the nature of war suggest that strategic defenses will be expanded to include defenses against cruise missiles and precision-guided conventional munitions that could be targeted against Soviet strategic forces in any protracted conventional war. As a result of this view of conventional war, fought under the constant threat of escalation to the use of nuclear weapons, the Soviets are likely to continue to enlarge their strategic defenses beyond the extensive systems that exist today. Both current and expected future developments in Soviet strategic defenses are explored in more detail in subsequent chapters.[44]

U.S. Nuclear Defense Evolution

Pressures for a ballistic missile defense would not have caused an official resurgence of interest were it not for the fact that recent advances in technology hold out for the first time in history the technical possibility to develop effective defenses against incoming ballistic missiles and warheads. Thus, in 1983, President Reagan directed an intensive study to describe a research program that would develop technically feasible defenses against ballistic missiles and to assess the implications of such a program for the prevention of nuclear war, deterrence of conventional aggression, and the enhancement of prospects for successful arms control negotiations.[45]

The subsequent study concluded that advanced defensive technologies might offer the potential to significantly reduce the military utility of a Soviet preemptive attack on the U.S. and its allies. Further, the study outlined a research program that could clarify future technical options for a ballistic missile defense program.

If a comprehensive defense against ballistic missiles proves feasible in terms of technology, cost, and political determination, such a defense might provide incentives for the reduction of offensive nuclear forces. To implement such a research program, now known as the Strategic Defense Initiative (SDI), President Reagan established the SDI Office (SDIO) directly under the Secretary of Defense. The primary purpose of this office is to direct the research and development program, whose specific objectives include the elimination of the threat of ballistic missile attacks on U.S. assets, and to counter the possibility of the Soviet development of additional ballistic missile defenses. Another program, similar in intent to the SDI, was set in motion in 1985 to upgrade U.S. air defenses (the Air Defense Initiative). This program is directed by the Air Force Systems Command, Electronics Systems Division, and various laboratories located at the Rome Air Development Center (RADC).

Finally, the U.S. has initiated programs to upgrade the protection systems for its nuclear weapon storage sites. These programs are designed to defend the sites against espionage and terrorist attacks. One such program, begun in the wake of the terrorist attack at the 1972 Olympic Games, cost about 340 million dollars and was completed in 1981. It involved hardening storage facilities against the effects of conventional explosives, improved lighting, and more stringent standards for reaction forces.[46]

In addition, the U.S. Department of Defense maintains task forces for counterterrorist emergencies. These forces have been approved by the Joint Chiefs of Staff for missions that could involve the recovery, neutralization or destruction of stolen nuclear weapons. The present configuration of U.S. military forces with counterterrorist capabilities includes selected U.S. Army Ranger Battalions; U.S. Marine Corps Battalion Landing Teams and Amphibious Units; U.S. Army Special Forces; a U.S. Marine Reconnaissance Company; U.S. Navy Sea, Air, Land (SEAL) Platoons; and U.S. Air Force support teams.[47]

Defenses against nuclear weapons can alter deterrence in at least two ways. First, they can protect the offensive nuclear forces of the defended country. Second, defenses can reduce the number of enemy warheads that reach military and civilian targets in defended areas. Both could alter the demand for nuclear warheads in the defended country. From a planner's point of view, a dollar or ruble spent on defense could replace a dollar or ruble spent on offense, since both contribute to deterrence. As long as the amount of deterrence gained per dollar or ruble spent on defense exceeds the amount of deterrence gained per dollar or ruble spent on offense, the incentive will be to substitute defense for offense, holding the level of deterrence constant.

Subsequent chapters provide additional details on new U.S. and Soviet defense programs. Each of these programs will have an evolutionary effect on the nature of deterrence and the incentives for adding to or subtracting from current stockpiles of nuclear weapons. For now, the reader should be aware that new strategic defense objectives have been formulated, the technology programs are in place, and the search for new nuclear defense systems has already begun.

Prospects for the Future

Nuclear weapons have consistently posed a paradox for U.S. defense policy. In the hands of the U.S. and in the service of U.S. alliances, nuclear weapons are considered to be a powerful force for deterring Soviet aggression. In the hands of the Soviet Union and other potential enemies, they are considered to be a threat to the survival of the U.S., its allies, and U.S. interests. Since the beginning of the nuclear era, U.S. strategic thought has stressed the imperative of deterring nuclear war by threatening retaliation in kind should an adversary use nuclear weapons. But at the same time, U.S. defense policy has continued to rely on U.S. nuclear weapons to help deter conventional attack, primarily because larger conventional forces are far more expensive than nuclear forces, and neither the U.S. nor its allies, apparently, are willing to spend larger sums on defense.

While the threat of nuclear retaliation has long played an important role in U.S. post–World War II strategy, efforts to defend against nuclear attack were not stressed from the late 1960s through 1983. In 1960, the U.S. Department of Defense spent as much on active defenses against Soviet strategic bombers as on its own offensive nuclear forces. But ten years later, this spending was directed overwhelmingly in favor of offensive forces. The idea that the United States should dismantle active defenses against nuclear attack gained some acceptance in government circles because of the growth in Soviet missile forces and the difficulties of defending against Soviet missile attack with the technologies of the 1960s and 70s. It was not until 1983 that U.S. efforts on strategic defense began to again assume a high priority. At that time, President Reagan launched the Strategic Defense Initiative. A similar research and development effort was started in 1985 to upgrade U.S. air defenses.[48]

For both the U.S. and the Soviet Union, the rationale for strategic space, missile, and air defenses is quite simple: either nation would be better off if it could destroy incoming nuclear warheads. Further, should deterrence fail, strategic defenses would enhance the survivability of offensive retaliatory forces. As a result, strategic defenses, according to advocates, also have deterrence value. For example, from the point of view of the Soviet Union, effective U.S. defenses would tend to reduce the expected benefits and raise the costs associated with a Soviet attack. Also from the Soviet point of view, an effective U.S. strategic defense would provide the U.S. with incentives for a first strike against the Soviet Union. The pros and cons of these arguments are explored in more detail in subsequent chapters.

In sum, the functions of U.S. strategic offensive forces, if deterrence fails, are to survive an initial Soviet attack and to then devastate the military forces and support activities of the Soviet Union and its allies. The functions of nuclear defensive forces include intelligence, threat assessment, surveillance of potentially hostile forces, engagement of hostile forces, battle management, command and control of defense forces, and reconstitution of surviving defense forces as a nuclear battle progresses.

In the absence of meaningful disarmament treaties, U.S. military planners want to update offensive deterrent forces and nuclear defense systems to counter threats from Soviet ballistic missiles, atmospheric vehicles, and space vehicles. Upgraded forces are also wanted for lesser nuclear threats, including nuclear-equipped terrorists. If improved U.S. offensive and defensive forces are to be employed against evolving Soviet and other nuclear threats, the U.S. will have to expend enormous amounts of money for the development, deployment and life cycle support of modern systems over the next several decades.

Evidence indicates that domestic political and economic criteria have often played decisive roles in the development of present nuclear deterrent and defensive systems. For example, the economic effects associated with the development of SDI and many other strategic systems have assumed substantial importance in gaining Congressional approval and funding. As a result, the worth of such programs is often measured in terms of money, jobs and technology development in key Congressional districts instead of the potential contributions to defense.

Based on our research and involvement with the U.S. Department of Defense over the past 27 years, we have concluded that the U.S. political system and the defense industrial base often respond to pressures and incentives that result in less than optimal military performance and greater than necessary costs. How this has come about, the nature of possible improvements, and the prospects for nuclear deterrence and defense in the future are explored in subsequent chapters.

Notes

1. Deterrence is often cited as the public good provided by national defense. By definition, no one can be excluded from the benefits of a pure public good, whether or not that person shares in its cost. Also, an additional person may benefit from a public good without adding to its cost. In the event of war, the situation is not so clearly defined. For example, young men have typically become the 'cannon fodder' of past wars. They have therefore been excluded from the benefits of defense. Also, a government may have ideas about 'acceptable losses' of territory, portions of populations, etc., during a defense of the nation. The benefits of defense may therefore be unevenly shared, depending on the territory, population group, etc. Thus, deterrence is a pure public good so long as it does not fail.

2. See Weinberger, Caspar W., *Annual Report to the Congress, Fiscal Year 1988*, U.S. Government Printing Office, Washington, D.C., January 12, 1987, 25–40; also see Weinberger, *Soviet Military Power*, U.S. Government Printing Office, Washington, D.C., March, 1987.

3. Weinberger, Caspar W., *Annual Report to the Congress, Fiscal Year 1988*. Other sources are given in Chapter 2, Tables 2.1 through 2.5.

4. Chant, C., and Hogg, I., *Nuclear War in the 1980's?* Harper and Row Publishers, New York, 1983, 27.

5. Yegorov, et al., *Soviet Military Thought*, No. 2., Moscow, 1973; also see Weinberger, *Soviet Military Power*, 1987, 15.

6. Leites, Nathan, *Soviet Style in War*, RAND, Santa Monica, CA, 1982, 371–380; also see Weinberger, *Soviet Military Power*, 1987, 15–18.

7. Leites, Nathan, *Soviet Style in War*, 367–380.

8. "Battle of the Bean Counters," *Time Magazine*, June 15, 1987, 33.

9. Ibid.; also see Weinberger, *Soviet Military Power*, 1987.

10. Arkin, W.M., and Fieldhouse, R.W., *Nuclear Battlefields: Global Links in the Arms Race*, Ballinger Publishing Company, New York, 1985, 54–59.

11. Ibid, also see Weinberger, *Soviet Military Power*, 1987.

12. Weinberger, *Annual Report to the Congress, Fiscal Year 1988*, 29–31; also see Arkin and Fieldhouse, *Nuclear Battlefields: Global Links in the Arms Race*.

13. Arkin and Fieldhouse, *Nuclear Battlefields: Global Links in the Arms Race*, 54–63.

14. "Battle of the Bean Counters."

15. Ibid.

16. "Reagan, Gorbachev Plan to Hold Summit," *Gazette Telegraph*, Colorado Springs, CO, September 19, 1987.

17. Ibid.

18. Chant and Hogg, *Nuclear War in the 1980's?* 56–63.

19. Arkin and Fieldhouse, *Nuclear Battlefields: Global Links in the Arms Race*, 37–63.

20. Ibid.

21. Ibid.

22. Chant and Hogg, *Nuclear War in the 1980's?* 56–63.

23. Beres, L.R., *Terrorism and Global Security: The Nuclear Threat*, Westview Press, Boulder, CO, 1979, 1–63.

24. Jenkins, B.M., "A Strategy for Combating Terrorism," an occasional paper, RAND, Santa Monica, CA, May 1981; also see Bass, G., Jenkins, B., et al., *Options for U.S. Policy on Terrorism*, RAND, Santa Monica, CA, July 1981.

25. Beres, *Terrorism and Global Security: The Nuclear Threat*, 1–63.

26. Ibid.

27. Weinberger, *Annual Report to the Congress, Fiscal Year 1988*, 42; also see Weinberger, Caspar W., *Annual Report to the Congress, Fiscal Year 1984*, U.S. Government Printing Office, Washington, D.C., January 1, 1983, 16.

28. Sloss, L., "The Strategist Perspective," in *Ballistic Missile Defense*, Carter, A., and Schwartz, D., ed., the Brookings Institution, Washington, D.C. 1984, 24–48.

29. Ibid., 24–48.

30. Dyson, Freeman., *Weapons and Hope*, Harper and Row Publishers, New York, 240.

31. Builder, C., and Graubard, M., *The International Law of Armed Conflict: Implications for the Concept of Mutual Assured Destruction*, RAND, Santa Monica, CA, January, 1982, 45–46.

32. Weinberger, *Annual Report to the Congress, Fiscal Year 1984*, 15–16.

33. Payne, K., *Laser Weapons in Space: Policy and Doctrine*, a Westview Replica edition, Boulder, CO, August 1983, 168–169.

34. Weinberger, *Annual Report to the Congress, Fiscal Year 1984*, 15–16.

35. Hyland, W.G., *Soviet-American Relations: A New Cold War?* RAND, Santa Monica, CA, May 1981, 63–73.

36. Ibid., 67; also see Podhoretz, "The Present Danger," *Commentary*, Volume 69, No. 3., March 1980, 39.

37. Weinberger, *Annual Report to the Congress, Fiscal Year 1984*, 51–58.

38. Weinberger, Caspar W., *Soviet Military Power*, U.S. Government Printing Office, Washington, D.C., March 1983, 27–31.

39. Ibid., 21–22.

40. Carter and Schwartz, *Ballistic Missile Defense*, 36–37, 46–48.

41. North American Aerospace Defense Command, *Pocket Information Handbook*, prepared by the Directorate of Cost and Management Analysis, DCS Comptroller, Peterson Air Force Base, Colorado Springs, CO, October 1984.

42. Blair, Bruce, *Strategic Command and Control: Redefining the Nuclear Threat*, The Brookings Institution, Washington, D.C., 1985, 109–110 and 234–280.

43. Arkin and Fieldhouse, *Nuclear Battlefields: Global Links in the Arms Race*, 14, 31–32, 80, 87, and 121.

44. Weinberger, *Soviet Military Power*, 1987, 45–61.

45. The concept of a total defense of the U.S. population against a massive Soviet ballistic missile attack has, for the most part, been abandoned by the Department of Defense in favor of a more conservative defense of U.S. ICBM fields and other elements of U.S. strategic retaliatory forces. Some systems for such a defense have already been demonstrated. See Weinberger, Caspar W., *Annual Report to the Congress, Fiscal Year 1985*, U.S. Government Printing Office, Washington, D.C., January 1984.

46. Beres, L.R., *Terrorism and Global Security: The Nuclear Threat*, 17.

47. Beres, *Terrorism and Global Security: The Nuclear Threat*, 16. Also see remarks by John Glenn, U.S. Senator, Thomas J. O'Brien, Director of Security Plans and Programs, Department of Defense, and Donald M. Kerr, Acting Assistant Secretary for Defense Programs, Department of Energy; *Hearings*, March 23, 1978, 319–323; also see Beres, *Terrorism and Global Security: The Nuclear Threat*, 16–17 and 138.

48. Weinberger, *Soviet Military Power*, 1987, 45–61.

2

The Strategic Balance

Setting the Framework

This chapter compares the strategic nuclear capabilities of the United States and the Soviet Union. It also compares the nuclear and conventional force capabilities of the NATO and Warsaw Pact alliances. Finally, brief references are made to forces in other regions of potential U.S.-Soviet nuclear confrontation.

As with the comparisons generated by other analysts, some subjective decisions were made concerning the nature of the comparisons and how to interpret the available data. To limit bias, we have cited more than one generally available source for each set of data. These sources are, of course, complemented by our personal knowledge gained during our long association with the U.S. Department of Defense.

Although this discussion focuses primarily on the strategic nuclear balance, it does not ignore the role of conventional forces. Indeed, recent agreements between the United States and the Soviet Union (1988) concerning reductions of Intermediate Nuclear Forces (INF) in Europe have caused concern over the perceived numerical superiority of Warsaw Pact conventional forces compared to their NATO counterparts. For example, one view holds that substantial reductions in NATO nuclear capability would increase the probability of a successful attack by Warsaw Pact conventional forces. An opposing view holds that balanced reductions in European-based nuclear weapons would tend to reduce the 'balance of terror' in Europe, and lessen the likelihood of nuclear war.[1]

However, if a comparison is made solely between military forces, the choice of what items should be compared may be difficult and somewhat subjective. For example, a particular assessment may involve consideration of one, several, or many kinds of military forces: strategic nuclear, tactical nuclear, conventional or maritime. Even quantitative comparisons involve decisions by the analyst on whether the comparison should be regional or global, whether to include total inventories or only those items that are actually deployed and ready for immediate use. Also, dual-use systems, such as artillery units that are capable of firing both nuclear and conventional munitions, present further counting problems. Finally, an analyst could compare the weapon systems of each side (e.g., tanks versus tanks, attack aircraft versus attack aircraft, etc.), or compare the systems of one side with the counter-systems of the opposing side (e.g., tanks versus anti-tank weapons, attack aircraft versus air defenses, etc.).

For these reasons, most analysts recognize that numbers of weapons and troops alone do not necessarily reflect military capabilities. Therefore, the comparisons in this chapter also take into account demographic and economic measures and certain qualitative aspects related to the military forces being compared. Such measures include: Gross National Product (GNP), population, annual military expenditures, technological capabilities, and system performance factors.

For example, GNP serves as a useful standard for measuring potential military capabilities. Also, the percent of GNP expended to provide and maintain military forces indicates the priority for these forces granted by the society to which they belong. For the United States, this expenditure was about $297 billion (Total Obligation Authority) in Fiscal Year 1987, which accounted for about six percent of the U.S. GNP. By comparison, the Soviet defense budget had approximately the same dollar value, however, it accounted for between 12–17 percent of Soviet GNP.[2]

After an appropriate framework has been established and data have been gathered, these data must be analyzed and presented in ways that permit meaningful comparisons. Comparisons can range from categorization and aggregation of data to calculations of outcomes of hypothetical armed conflicts for a range of scenarios. While these 'war games' can be quite sophisticated, involving skilled and experienced participants, each method of comparison involves judgements and interpretations, each has inherent strengths and weaknesses, and each can provide useful insights. While no single comparison can accurately and confidently predict the outcome of an armed conflict, the process of comparison itself contributes to an understanding of the likely balance of power in a variety of potential conflict situations.

From the above discussion, it is clear that reasonable persons may disagree on the relevance of certain comparisons, and ultimately, on which nation or alliance would prevail over others should a conflict occur. More importantly for U.S. and Soviet politicians and decision makers, reasonable persons will also disagree on whether or not their forces are adequate to deter the opposition from actions that may be detrimental to each country's national security and other interests.

Recent Trends in Weapon Acquisition

Over the past decade, U.S. and Soviet modernization programs have resulted in the development and deployment of new generations of more capable offensive nuclear forces on land, under the sea, in the air, and potentially in space. For example, the Soviets have developed a new single-warhead, road-mobile SS-25 Intercontinental Ballistic Missile (ICBM), and are now deploying the multiple-warhead SS-X-24 ICBM. On the other side, the United States is developing the single-warhead road-mobile Small ICBM, and is deploying the multiple-warhead MX ICBM. Both sides are also upgrading their ballistic missile submarine forces and their aging manned bomber fleets.[3]

In conjunction with these modernization programs for offensive systems, both sides continue to increase their active and passive defenses in an attempt to blunt the effects of a possible nuclear attack from the opposing side. For example, the Soviets have hardened ICBM silos and command and control facilities against blast and other nuclear effects, and have enhanced their already extensive civil defenses. On the other side, the U.S. has hardened missiles silos, command centers, and communications systems. Both sides have upgraded their respective air defenses and deployed so-phisticated early warning systems against cruise missiles, ballistic missiles and space weapons. Finally, both sides are actively pursuing research and development programs for ballistic missile and anti-satellite defenses.[4]

Consistent with the previous discussion, comparisons of the numbers of nuclear weapon systems deployed by the United States and the Soviet Union provide only a partial explanation of the nuclear capabilities of these two nations. However, in the context of the following discussion, the numbers provide some insight into the current U.S.-Soviet strategic nuclear balance.

The Strategic Nuclear Forces
of the United States and the Soviet Union

The approximate current ICBM balance between the United States and the Soviet Union is summarized in Table 2.1.

New generation U.S. and Soviet ICBMs have highly accurate warheads, many of which have the capability of striking within 500 yards of a target over 7,000 miles away. Thus, both the United States and the Soviet Union have the capability to destroy a large number of relatively 'hard' targets, including a significant portion of the ICBM silos on the other side. To enhance this hard target capability, both nations continue to improve the accuracy of ICBMs equipped with Multiple Independently-targeted Re-entry Vehicles (MIRVs).[5]

Partly in response to the increasing Soviet threat to its land-based ICBM silos, the United States has continued to upgrade its force of Sea-Launched Ballistic Missiles (SLBMs). The Soviets have also made substantial improvements in this area. Table 2.2 summarizes the current SLBM balance between the United States and the Soviet Union.

Table 2.1:   U.S. and Soviet ICBMs (1988)

U.S. ICBMs	Number of Missiles	Number of Warheads
Minuteman II	450	450
Minuteman III	490	1470
MX	50	500
SICBM	0	0
U.S. Totals	990	2420

Soviet ICBMs	Number of Missiles	Number of Warheads
SS-11	440	1280
SS-13	60	60
SS-17	150	600
SS-18	308	3080
SS-19	360	2160
SS-25	100	100
SS-X-24	0	0
Soviet Totals	1418	7280

Notes:
1.   The U.S. road-mobile Small ICBM (SICBM) and the Soviet SS-X-24 are currently undergoing research and development. Barring treaty restrictions, these missiles will probably be deployed in the early 1990's.

2.   The Soviet SS-11 includes 420 missiles with three warheads each, and 20 older versions with one warhead each, for a total of 1280 warheads. The number of warheads listed for these missiles assumes that the Soviets have deployed the maximum number of Multiple Independently-targeted Re-entry Vehicles (MIRVs) for the newest version of the SS-11 missile.

Sources: The following sources for the above data are readily available to the general public: Campbell, C., *Nuclear Facts: A Guide to Nuclear Weapon Systems and Strategy*, Hamlyn Publishing Group Limited, New York, 1984;   Clauson, P., Krass, A. and Zirkle, R., *In Search of Stability: An Assessment of New U.S. Nuclear Forces*, Union of Concerned Scientists, Cambridge, MA, 1986; Weinberger, Caspar W., *Soviet Military Power 1987*, U.S. Government Printing Office, Washington, D.C., March 1987, and Weinberger, Caspar W., *Department of Defense Annual Report to Congress Fiscal Year 1987*, U.S. Government Printing Office, Washington, D.C., February 1986. The data obtained from the above sources were updated from other unclassified sources to approximate 1987-88 numbers.

The United States and the Soviet Union also continue to improve their manned bomber fleets. Table 2.3 summarizes the current balance between the U.S. and the Soviets with regard to intercontinental bombers.

In addition, the U.S. Strategic Air Command currently operates 56 FB-111A medium-range strategic bombers that can carry up to six Short Range Attack Missiles (SRAMs), six nuclear free-fall bombs, or combinations of the two. However, these aircraft cannot reach the Soviet Union from their U.S. bases without refueling. The FB-111As are in addition to the 170

Table 2.2: U.S. and Soviet SLBMs (1988)

U.S. SLBM Submarines	No. of Subs	Type Missile	Number Per Sub	Number of Missiles	Number of Warheads
Lafayette	18	Poseidon/C-3	16	288	2880
Ben Franklin	12	Trident/C-4	16	192	1536
Ohio	5	Trident/C-4	24	120	960
James Madison	1	Trident/D-5	24	24	192
Totals	36			624	5568

U.S. SLBM Submarines	No. of Subs	Type Missile	Number Per Sub	Number of Missiles	Number of Warheads
Yankee I	6	SS-N-6	16	96	192
Yankee II	12	SS-N-17	12	144	144
Delta I	12	SS-N-8	12	144	144
Delta II	9	SS-N-8	16	144	144
Delta III	14	SS-N-18	16	224	1336
Delta IV	4	SS-N-23	16	64	640
Typhoon	5	SS-N-20	20	100	600
Totals	62			916	3200

Notes:
1.   The numbers of Trident/D-5s, SS-N-18s, and SS-N-20s are approximate.

2.   The SS-N-18 carries from 3-7 warheads.

3.   The SS-N-20 carries from 6-9 warheads.

Sources: The following sources for the above data are readily available to the general public: Campbell, C., *Nuclear Facts: A Guide to Nuclear Weapon Systems and Strategy*, Hamlyn Publishing Group Limited, New York, 1984; Chant, C. and Hogg, I., *Nuclear War in the 1980s?*, Harper and Row Publishers, New York, 1983; Weinberger, Caspar W., *Soviet Military Power 1987*, U.S. Government Printing Office, Washington, D.C., March 1987, and Weinberger, Caspar W., *Department of Defense Annual Report to Congress Fiscal Year 1987*, U.S. Government Printing Office, Washington, D.C., February 1986. The data obtained from the above sources were updated from other unclassified documents to approximate 1987-88 numbers.

nuclear-armed FB-111 fighter-bombers based in the United Kingdom, which fall under the command of U.S. Air Forces Europe.[6]

Fifty-four other B-52Gs are equipped with non-nuclear Harpoon anti-ship missiles. However, it is possible to convert these aging aircraft back to service as nuclear weapons carriers, probably equipped with ALCMs and/or SRAMs.[7]

The U.S. is also developing the Advanced Cruise Missile (ACM) and the SRAM II. Both have longer ranges than the current ALCM and SRAM I, and will replace the earlier versions in the 1990s. Research and development also continues on the so-called 'Stealth' bomber, which might be deployed in the late 1990s.[8]

Table 2.3: U.S. and Soviet Intercontinental Bombers (1988)

Type of U.S. Bomber	Number of Bombers	Type of Nuclear Weapon	Number of Weapons/Bomber	Number of Warheads
B-52G	90	ALCM	12	--
		SRAM	20	--
		Free-Fall Bombs	60,000 lbs.	--
B-52H	90	ALCM	20	--
		SRAM I	20	--
		Free-Fall Bombs	60,000 lbs.	--
B-1B	60	ALCM	22	--
		SRAM II	38	--
		Free-Fall Bombs	125,000 lbs.	--
Total	240			2570

Type of U.S. Bomber	Number of Bombers	Type of Nuclear Weapon	Number of Weapons/Bomber	Number of Warheads
TU-95 Bear	100	AS-15	--	--
		AS-3 ASM	--	--
		AS-4 ASM	--	--
		Free-Fall Bombs	25,000 lbs.	--
Mya-4 Bison	45	Free-Fall Bombs	10,000 lbs.	--
Total	145			300

Notes:
1.   The AS-15 is an Air Launched Cruise Missile (ALCM) with a range of about 1860 miles. The current U.S. ALCM has a range of about 1550 miles.
2.   SRAMs are Short Range Attack Missiles designed to be carried by manned bombers. SRAMs have a range of about 100 miles and were originally designed as weapons for attacking enemy air defenses as a bomber penetrated enemy air space on its way to targets that would be attacked with gravity bombs.
3.   The AS-3 and AS-4 are short-range Air to Surface Missiles (ASM).
4.   The number of warheads given for both sides are approximate, since new warheads are constantly being added and old warheads are often eliminated.
5.   The numbers of weapons of each type are not available for publication. However, the approximate total numbers of warheads for both U.S. and Soviet bombers are readily available in the open literature.

Sources: The following sources for the above data are readily available to the general public: Arkin, W.M. and Fieldhouse, R.W., *Nuclear Battlefields: Global Links in the Arms Race*, Ballinger Publishing Company, Cambridge, MA, 1985; Campbell, C., *Nuclear Facts: A Guide to Nuclear Weapon Systems and Strategy*, Hamlyn Publishing Group Limited, New York, 1984; Clauson, P., Krass, A. and Zirkle, R., *In Search of Stability: An Assessment of New U.S. Nuclear Forces*, Union of Concerned Scientists, Cambridge, MA, 1986; Weinberger, Caspar W., *Department of Defense Annual Report to Congress Fiscal Year 1987*, U.S. Government Printing Office, Washington, D.C., February 1986, and Weinberger, Caspar W., *Soviet Military Power 1987*, U.S. Government Printing Office, Washington, D.C., March 1987. The data obtained from the above sources were updated from other unclassified documents to approximate 1987-88 numbers.

The Soviets have deployed about 160 TU-26/22M 'Backfire' medium-range bombers, which have a combat range of about 4,000 miles and can carry about 20,800 lbs. of weapons, including the AS-3, the AS-4, the AS-15, free-fall bombs, or a combination of these weapons. About 130 of these aircraft are allocated to Soviet Naval Aviation and the remaining 30 are assigned to strike roles in Europe. However, with refueling, the Backfire has the potential for striking the United States and returning to the Soviet Union. The Soviets are currently producing about 30 of these aircraft per year (1988).[9]

The Soviets are also developing the 'Blackjack' intercontinental bomber. This aircraft is slightly larger and faster than the U.S. B-1B, but has about the same combat range. This new bomber will have the capability to carry the AS-3, the AS-4, the AS-15, free-fall bombs, or a combination of these weapons.[10]

Additional insight into the U.S.-Soviet strategic balance can be gained by comparing the nuclear explosive power that can be delivered by U.S. and Soviet strategic delivery systems. This explosive power is usually measured in megatons. Table 2.4 provides such a comparison.

The Balance of Forces

Despite the large amount of information available on the composition of U.S. and Soviet nuclear arsenals, there is no broad consensus as to which nation would 'win' in a general nuclear war. In part, this debate arises because numbers alone do not provide conclusive answers. Different assessments of the strategic balance can be derived as a result of how numbers are combined, which elements of the forces are emphasized, and what assumptions are made about various operational factors and conflict scenarios. Asymmetries in force structures for opposing nations and alliances also complicate assessments. Finally, the U.S. and the Soviet Union have different doctrines concerning the purposes of nuclear weapons.

Thus, the number of missiles, bombers, and warheads provide only part of the picture. Additional factors include warhead accuracy, the explosive yield of warheads, the 'hardness' of targets, and the reliability of delivery and warhead systems. For example, the destructive potential of a warhead is a combination of both yield and accuracy. If targets have been hardened against nuclear blast (command and control centers, ICBM silos, etc.), accuracy is the more important determinant of destructive potential. If targets are 'soft' or unhardened, such as population centers or bomber and submarine bases, the relative advantages of accuracy compared to yield are not very great. Still, if optimally targeted, a small number of low-yield, accurate warheads can produce as much, or more, destruction against

Table 2.4:   Estimated Deliverable Megatons of Strategic Nuclear Warheads

U.S. Delivery System	Number of Systems	Number of Warheads	Deliverable Megatons
ICBM	990	2420	1197
SLBM	720	5568	413
Manned Bombers	240	2570	1745
Total	1950	10558	3355

USSR Delivery System	Number of Systems	Number of Warheads	Deliverable Megatons
ICBM	1418	7280	4402
SLBM	916	3200	1395
Manned Bombers	145	300	300
Total	2479	10780	6097

Notes:
1.   The energy yield of a nuclear weapon is expressed as the equivalent weight of TNT that would have to be exploded in one place to produce the same blast effect. However, a one megaton (one million tons of TNT) warhead does not have a blast effect a thousand times greater than that produced by a single kiloton warhead (1,000 tons of TNT).   The area of blast destruction increases by the cube root of the yield; thus, many smaller weapons spread their effects over a wider area compared to a single very large weapon.

2.   Nuclear weapons have a variety of radiation, electro-magnetic pulse, and fallout effects that do not exist with conventional explosives such as TNT. Also, the nature and extent of these nuclear effects depend on the type of warhead, the altitude of the blast, weather, and other environmental conditions.

Sources: The following sources for the above data are readily available to the general public: Arkin, W.M. and Fieldhouse, R.W., *Nuclear Battlefields: Global Links in the Arms Race*, Ballinger Publishing Company, Cambridge, MA, 1985; Campbell, C., *Nuclear Facts: A Guide to Nuclear Weapons Systems and Strategy*, Hamlyn Publishing Group Limited, New York, 1984; Clauson, P., Krass, A. and Zirkle, R., *In Search of Stability: An Assessment of New U.S. Nuclear Forces*, Union of Concerned Scientists, Cambridge, MA, 1986; The International Institute for Strategic Studies, "The Military Balance 1985/86", *Air Force Magazine*, Volume 69, Number 2, February 1986, The Air Force Association, Arlington, VA, 1986; Weinberger, Caspar W., *Department of Defense Annual Report to Congress Fiscal Year 1987*, U.S. Government Printing Office, Washington, D.C., February 1986, and Weinberger, Caspar W., *Soviet Military Power 1987*, U.S. Government Printing Office, Washington, D.C., March 1987.

dispersed, unhardened targets such as cities compared to a single warhead with a much larger yield, but less accuracy.[11]

In 1988, most analysts concede that U.S. ICBM and SLBM warheads are more accurate than their Soviet counterparts. Consistent with this, the U.S. has chosen to use lower yield warheads to obtain comparable destructive capability. However, as the Soviet Union increases its capability to produce smaller, more accurate warheads, it too appears to be moving towards warheads of smaller yield.

The reliability of delivery systems and warheads is also a significant factor in the strategic balance. There are two aspects to reliability. The first is peacetime reliability, which can be measured by the percentage of time that various delivery systems or warheads are available and not inactive due to repair or maintenance. In this sense, the reliability of U.S. systems appears to be greater than that of the Soviet Union. For example, the U.S. Minuteman, Trident, and Poseidon missiles are all solid-fuel rockets, while most of the Soviet ICBMs and SLBMs use highly corrosive and volatile liquid fuel. In addition to other problems, the extensive use of the less reliable liquid-fueled rockets causes more Soviet missiles to be down for repair or maintenance at any given time compared to their American counterparts. The Soviets clearly recognize this, and they are gradually developing new solid-fuel rocket systems.[12]

On the other hand, operational reliability refers to how well the delivery system and its warheads would function from the time of launch until the warheads explode on or above their intended targets. Most experts believe that the operational reliability of U.S. and Soviet missiles are about equal; the systems of both countries have a operational reliability of between 80 and 95 percent. However, the manned bombers of the U.S. are considered somewhat more reliable than their Soviet counterparts. This assessment is based, in part, on continued Soviet problems with the Bison and Backfire bombers, and by comparison, the proven combat record of U.S. B-52s and FB-111s.

In the past, a major factor in assessing the capabilities of a bomber was its ability to penetrate the opponent's air defenses to reach intended targets. This factor has become less important in recent years due to the development and deployment of Air-Launched Cruise Missiles (ALCMs), which give manned bombers the capability to launch warheads from outside the defended air space.

The deployment of ALCMs substantially multiplies bomber capabilities. The current U.S. ALCM is a small, subsonic, nuclear-tipped missile with a range of about 1550 miles and an accuracy to within 50 feet of its target. This accuracy allows it to be used against hardened targets such as command bunkers, ICBM silos, etc. Its terrain-following capability enables it to fly beneath most Soviet radar screens, which greatly increases its capability to penetrate Soviet airspace. More importantly, ALCM-equipped aircraft are now able to strike many targets without having to risk being shot down over heavily defended enemy territory. About 90 U.S. B-52s have been fitted with ALCMs; all B-52s that retain a strategic nuclear role may eventually be equipped with ALCMs. Most U.S. B-1Bs will also carry ALCMs.[13]

The Soviets are also developing and deploying ALCMs, especially on their Bear-H bombers. Most experts believe that at the present time Soviet ALCMs are inferior to their U.S. counterparts in terrain-following and guidance capabilities. However, based on past experience with other systems, this U.S. technical advantage cannot be expected to continue beyond the 1990s.

The Soviet Union has also deployed an extensive air defense system against U.S. manned bombers, and has frequently improved its capability. Nevertheless, the widely publicized delays in finding and intercepting what turned out to be a South Korean airliner in 1983 and the total inability of the system to detect a small private West German aircraft en route to a landing in Moscow's Red Square in 1986 point to continued deficiencies.

On the other side, the United States has allowed its air defenses to degrade considerably since the early 1960s, although there have been recent improvements in aircraft detection and warning systems, including new systems (over-the-horizon radar) to detect and track ALCMs that could be launched by Soviet bombers outside U.S. airspace. There have also been substantial recent upgrades in battle management systems, improvements in atmospheric surveillance radars, and the replacement of aging fighter-interceptors (F-106s and F-4Es) with newer, more capable aircraft (F-15s and F-16s).

In comparing the overall U.S. and Soviet strategic nuclear capabilities, it is worthwhile to analyze the perceived threat of a first strike. A first strike would involve a massive launch of warheads by one side against the other. The primary objective would be to destroy the strategic forces of the other side before they could be launched in retaliation.

Most analysts agree that a surprise Soviet first strike attempt against the United States would probably eliminate a substantial portion of the U.S. land-based ICBM force and a substantial portion of the U.S. bomber force. However, some ICBMs and bombers would survive, and so would most of the SLBM-carrying submarines at sea. The percentage of ICBMs, bombers and submarines that would survive depends upon the events leading up to a Soviet first strike attempt.

A successful U.S. retaliatory launch would depend upon the ability of the United States to detect, identify, and characterize a Soviet first strike attempt, to quickly make retaliatory launch decisions, and to exercise the command and control network to launch retaliatory forces. In a 'bolt out of the blue' scenario, the first Soviet warhead (SLBMs and possibly sea-launched cruise missiles) would likely be detected when they were about 20 minutes from inland U.S. targets (for example, U.S. ICBM silos), leaving very little time for decision making and transmission of orders to launch retaliatory forces. In a non-crisis environment, the nuclear forces of the United States operate at a level of alert or readiness, known as day-to-day alert. Currently, this means that 30 percent of the bombers are kept on ground alert, ready to launch within 15 minutes of an order to go, and more than 50 percent of the submarine force is always at sea. The ICBM force could also be launched within 15 minutes of an order to do so.

On the other side, the Soviets also fear a first strike by the United States. However, they currently do not keep any bombers on ground alert, and only 15 percent of their submarine fleet is at sea at any given time. Most analysts believe this lower alert rate is more a function of cost, reliability and operational capabilities than a measure of their level of concern.

However, few analysts believe that a first strike attempt by either side would occur as 'a bolt out of the blue' in a non-crisis situation, with neither provocation nor warning. A nuclear attack preceded by a period of extreme tension between the two superpowers seems more likely, and such a period might also include a conventional conflict, perhaps in Europe.

During a period of crisis or conventional conflict, both nations would probably increase their alert rates. More bombers would be placed on ground alert, some would be placed on airborne alert, and bomber forces would be dispersed to reduce their vulnerability to attack before they are airborne. The percentage of submarines at sea would also be increased, and command and control functions would be exercised to respond quickly to orders from national command authorities. Such moves would substantially increase the capability of either side to inflict a devastating retaliatory attack against any first strike attempt by its opponent. In this scenario, the likelihood of a successful first strike by either side is quite small, and the essential balance of power is preserved.

The Strategic Balance Between NATO and the Warsaw Pact

European nations have enormous industrial capabilities, large, highly educated populations, and historically demonstrated capabilities for world dominance. The geographic position of Eastern Europe adjacent to the Soviet Union adds to its current strategic importance. Further, there are strong political, cultural, and economic ties between Western Europe, Canada, and the United States.

Thus, in the event of a conflict between the superpowers, Europe would be a primary strategic concern for both sides, whether or not the sources of the conflict originated there. If a conventional conflict began in Europe, it would have a high risk of escalation into a general nuclear war between the Warsaw Pact, led by the Soviet Union, and the North Atlantic Treaty Organization (NATO), led by the United States.

From the Soviet point of view, the nuclear weapons and conventional forces, either deployed in Europe or rapidly deployable to Europe by the United States, represent a serious threat to Soviet dominance in Eastern

Europe and to the Soviet homeland. Also, the proximity of capitalist-oriented nations with higher standards of living compared to Soviet-dominated Eastern European nations is a source of unrest among European populations under communist rule.

In the West, NATO serves the common defense interests of the United States and its allies. For the U.S. and Canada, NATO provides a deterrent against Soviet interference with U.S. and Canadian economic and political interests in Western Europe and a first line of defense against potential Soviet aggression against North America. Also, the U.S. strategic nuclear capability complements NATO forces because it has a perceived deterrence value against the possibility of Soviet domination in Western Europe. Finally, the U.S. military commitment to protect Western Europe has allowed these nations to avoid a substantial portion of the cost of developing their own defenses to the point where they could, by themselves, deter the Soviets. For NATO, the current situation calls for immense trust between the U.S. and its European allies. The U.S. must trust its NATO partners to be willing to combat Soviet aggression, should it occur. On the other hand, the United States expects the Europeans to believe that the U.S. would be willing to risk its own homeland, through the threat of total nuclear war, as part of the defense of Western Europe. The current deployment of over 300,000 U.S. military personnel in Western Europe is an expression of European cooperation and the U.S. commitment to deter the perceived Soviet threat.

The overall strategic balance in Europe is reflected in the relative demographic, economic and military strengths of NATO and Warsaw Pact nations. Table 2.5 compares some demographic and economic data for these two opposing alliances.

NATO has always been a nuclear-armed alliance. The first nuclear presence was a force of 32 U.S. B-29 bombers that was stationed in Great Britain in 1949.[14] Because NATO's conventional force levels, in terms of manpower, combat aircraft, tanks and artillery, have always been less than that of the Soviet Union and other Warsaw Pact nations, nuclear weapons have always been NATO's 'deterrent' against a conventional Warsaw Pact attack. There have been several shifts of nuclear defense doctrine, from massive retaliation (via a European 'trip wire'), to the current doctrine of flexible response, but the first use of nuclear weapons in reply to an overwhelming conventional attack was NATO policy in the beginning and remains so today (1988). Both NATO and the Warsaw Pact have large numbers of nuclear weapons in Europe for battlefield use. Table 2.6 outlines the current numbers of warheads of both sides.

Nuclear weapons in Europe fall into three broad categories: short-range (artillery shells, nuclear air defense weapons, mines, ground attack aircraft equipped with bombs, missiles with ranges of less than 200 kilometers, etc.); medium-range (interdiction aircraft equipped with bombs and missiles

Table 2.5: NATO and Warsaw Pact 1984 Demographic and Economic Data

NATO Country	GNP in Millions of U.S.$	Population	Armed Forces	Annual Def Exp. (Millions of U.S.$)	Defense as a Percent of GNP
Belgium	78,101	9,890,000	91,570	2,553	3.3
Canada	331,310	25,150,000	83,000	7,027	2.1
Denmark	54,883	5,150,000	29,600	1,208	2.2
France	492,270	55,170,000	476,560	20,113	4.1
W. Germany	613,163	61,200,000	478,000	20,430	3.3
Greece	32,900	10,300,000	201,500	2,204	6.7
Iceland	3,354	239,000	0	0	0
Italy	348,385	57,150,000	385,100	9,929	2.9
Luxembourg	3,324	367,000	720	40	1.2
Netherlands	122,511	14,500,000	105,975	3,976	3.3
Norway	54,723	4,150,000	37,000	1,555	2.8
Portugal	19,446	10,280,000	73,040	629	3.2
Spain	161,327	39,500,000	320,000	3,862	2.4
Turkey	48,531	49,500,000	630,000	2,190	4.5
U.K.	400,038	56,020,000	327,100	21,995	5.5
U.S.	3,619,200	239,600,000	2,151,600	250,000	6.9
Total	6,383,466	638,166,000	5,390,665	347,711	5.5

Warsaw Pact Country	GNP in Millions of U.S.$	Population	Armed Forces	Annual Def Exp. (Millions of U.S.$)	Defense as a Percent of GNP
Bulgaria	37,100	8,970,000	148,500	1,491	4.0
Czech.	155,000	15,600,000	203,300	5,052	3.3
E. Germany	180,000	16,800,000	174,000	7,710	4.3
Hungary	67,200	10,800,000	106,000	2,136	3.2
Poland	181,000	37,500,000	319,000	5,911	3.3
Romania	119,000	23,500,000	189,500	1,345	1.1
USSR	1,920,000	276,500,000	5,300,000	288,000	15.0
Total	2,659,300	389,670,000	6,440,300	311,645	11.7

Notes:

1.   Different sources provide a range of U.S. dollar estimates for GNP and annual defense expenditures for Warsaw Pact countries. The primary reason for this is that different analysts have selected alternative methods of evaluating the value of goods, services and resources in Soviet-style communist countries. Analysts cannot just convert prices measured in communist nation currencies to U.S. dollars at official exchange rates, because prices serve a different purpose under a Soviet-style communist system compared to a Western-style capitalist system.

2.   Different sources also provide a range of estimates for the total number of persons in the armed forces of the Soviet Union. For 1984, estimates range from 3,850,000 (Union of Concerned Scientists) to 5,850,000 (Institute for Strategic Studies). The reason for this appears to be that the lower estimate does not include some 615,000 Soviet railroad and construction troops and about 705,000 command and general support troops. The 5,850,000 estimate did include these troops, but it did not include some 600,000 KGB and MVD troops.

3.   We have chosen to use the 5,850,000 estimate in Table 2.5, since active-duty support troops are included in the numbers for the active duty armed forces of NATO countries. We did not include the KGB and MVD troops in the table, since these internal security forces do not serve in an external combat or direct combat role.

Sources: For an explanation of the different methods for evaluating Warsaw Pact GNP and military expenditures, see "The Military Balance 1985-86", by the Institute for Strategic Studies, London, published in Air Force Magazine, February 1986. For an alternative point of view, see World Military and Social Expenditures 1987-88, by R.L. Sivard, written under the auspices of the Union of Concerned Scientists, World Priorities, Inc., Cambridge, MA, 1987. Other sources include: Chant, C. and Hogg, I., Nuclear War in the 1980s?, Harper and Row Publishers, New York, 1983; Weinberger, Caspar W., Department of Defense Annual Report to Congress Fiscal Year 1987, U.S. Government Printing Office, Washington, D.C., February 1986, and Weinberger, Caspar W., Soviet Military Power 1987, U.S. Government Printing Office, Washington, D.C., March 1987.

Table 2.6:   Nuclear Warheads in Europe (1988)

NATO Nuclear Warhead Type	U.S. Use	Number of Warheads Allied Use	Total
U.S. Free Fall Bombs	1,416	324	1,740
U.S. Depth Bombs	129	63	192
U.S. Pershing I	120	100	220
U.S. Pershing II	108	0	108
U.S. GLCM	464	0	464
U.S. Lance	324	368	692
U.S. Honest John	0	198	198
U.S. 8-Inch Artillery	506	432	938
U.S. 155 mm Artillery	594	138	732
U.S. Nike-Hercules	296	390	696
U.S. Nuclear Demolition	372	unk.	372
U.K. Free-Fall Bombs	0	376	376
U.K. SLBM	0	160	160
U.K. Depth Bombs	0	150	150
French Free-Fall Bombs	0	200	200
French ICBM	0	18	18
French SLBM	0	176	176
French SRBM	0	120	20
NATO Total	4,329	3,213	7,542

Warsaw Pact Nuclear Warhead Type	Soviet Use	Number of Warheads Pact Use	Total
Free-Fall Bombs	3,316	0	3,316
SS-20 IRBM	1,323	0	1,323
SS-4 IRBM	112	0	112
SS-12 SRBM	120	0	120
SS-22 SRBM	100	0	100
SCUD-B SRM	500	0	500
SS-23 SRM	48	0	48
Frog/SS-21 SRM	500	0	500
Scaleboard SRM	60	0	60
Artillery	900	0	900
Pact Total	6,979	0	6,979

Notes: Includes U.S. Pershing and GLCM, and Soviet SS-20, SS-12, SS-22 and SS-23 weapons that will be destroyed when the U.S.-Soviet INF agreement is ratified.

Sources: The following sources for the above data are readily available to the general public: Arkin, W.M. and Fieldhouse, R.W., *Nuclear Battlefields: Global Links in the Arms Race*, Ballinger Publishing Company, Cambridge, MA, 1985;   The International Institute for Strategic Studies, "The Military Balance 1985/86", *Air Force Magazine*, Volume 69, Number 2, February 1986, The Air Force Association, Arlington, VA, 1986, and Weinberger, Caspar W., *Soviet Military Power 1987*, U.S. Government Printing Office, Washington, D.C., March 1987.   The above data were updated from other unclassified documents to approximate 1987-88 numbers.

with ranges of from 200–1,000 kilometers); and long-range (aircraft and missiles with a range of 1,000 kilometers or more). The long-range weapons are often referred to as Long-Range Tactical Nuclear Forces (LRTNF) or 'Eurostrategic' nuclear weapons.[15]

Of the U.S. nuclear weapons in Europe, about one half are for the use of U.S. forces. The others are assigned to other NATO countries under 'dual key' control. This means that the warheads are controlled by the U.S., but the delivery systems are under European host nation control. The U.S. has bilateral agreements for dual key control with Greece, Italy, the United Kingdom, West Germany and the Netherlands.

Because any action that employed the first nuclear weapon would be critical to the survival of all countries in the alliance, NATO has evolved a complex structure of command and control and consultative procedures with host nations. However, in virtually all European war scenarios, the first nuclear weapons to be detonated will almost certainly be tactical, that is, used on the battlefield.

In theory, the governments of the 15 NATO nations would be consulted before a first use of nuclear weapons by NATO forces. In practice, matters would probably turn out differently. For example, suppose a U.S. division headquarters in central Germany, with custody of nuclear artillery shells, came under a massive Soviet conventional attack and was in danger of being overrun. The division commander would probably request permission to use nuclear artillery to stop the Soviet advance. In theory, the request would go up the chain of command: to army corps, to Central Army Group, to Allied Forces Central Europe, to the Supreme Headquarters Allied Powers Europe, and then to the Supreme Allied Commander Europe (SACEUR). From SACEUR, the request would go to the U.S. National Command Authority, where the President would consider the decision while trying to consult with the German Chancellor and other NATO heads of state. Exercises have shown that this whole process would take at least 24 hours, and the tactical moment for nuclear weapon use would have long since passed. Thus, in practice, it is highly unlikely that these cumbersome procedures would be used, and preplanned authorizations would be given to appropriate command levels.

All Warsaw Pact nuclear warheads and delivery systems remain under exclusive Soviet custody and control primarily because the Soviets simply do not trust their allies with weapons that could be used against Soviet forces. However, the fact that Soviet commanders have exclusive custody and control greatly simplifies and shortens the first use decision process, since first use need only be approved by Soviet national command authorities.

NATO's past and current dependence on nuclear weapons is a result of the perceived superiority of Warsaw Pact conventional forces. Since NATO's beginning in 1949, Western military analysts have been nearly unanimous in concluding that Warsaw Pact conventional ground forces are superior to their NATO counterparts in terms of manpower and in terms of the numbers of major weapon systems. Historically, this conclusion has been the primary justification for NATO reliance on nuclear weapons. This reliance serves both the 'trip wire' strategy that would trigger the use of American strategic nuclear forces in defense of Western Europe, and the use of battlefield nuclear weapons to slow or halt a massive Warsaw Pact ground attack. Also, NATO expects that its technical superiority with regard to weapon performance and troop and training would, to some degree, balance the superior numbers of the Warsaw Pact. Chapter 3 explores in detail how this dependence developed, and the appendix to this chapter contains tables that display the relative strength and likely uses of conventional aircraft, ground forces and maritime forces in the NATO-Warsaw Pact region.

Nuclear Weapons in Other Regions of U.S.-Soviet Confrontation

The United States, the Soviet Union, and other nations have deployed tactical nuclear weapons in the Pacific and other regions of the world. For example, the U.S., the Soviets and China have some 3,000 nuclear warheads in the Pacific. The Soviets and Chinese probably aim most of their nuclear-tipped missiles at predetermined targets on the Asian land mass, for use if a conflict should occur between these two countries. But the remainder of their tactical and naval nuclear warheads, as well as most U.S. nuclear weapons in the Pacific, are intended for battlefield or naval use.[16]

The U.S. and Soviet navies routinely carry nuclear weapons in the region, but the U.S. is the only nation that deploys warheads on foreign territory. About 150 U.S. nuclear warheads are in South Korea for use against North Korea. Since returning Okinawa to Japan in the early 1970s, the United States has no nuclear weapons on Japanese soil, and there is no evidence that the United States permanently stations warheads in the Philippines. Guam, a U.S. territory, contains the main stockpile for U.S. nuclear operations in the Pacific.[17]

China is the primary Asian concern of Soviet military planners. About 90 percent of Soviet ground forces in the Far East are directed against China and the growing Chinese nuclear capability. As a result, more than half of the combatant ships in the Soviet Pacific fleet are stationed at two naval bases (Vladivostok and Petropavlovsk) that have restricted access to the open ocean through narrow straits and have, therefore, become the focus for strategic plans of the U.S. Navy. The Sea of Okhotsk and ports in the Bering Sea are further restricted by heavy winter ice. The Tsushima Strait is the widest of the four passages that connect the Sea of Japan with the Pacific Ocean, and would become the focus of anti-submarine warfare against Soviet submarines by South Korean, Japanese and U.S. naval forces, supported by U.S. nuclear weapons.

The Soviet Pacific coast is more accessible than its other coasts, and its proximity to Alaska gives it a special status. Defending Alaska is therefore a high U.S. priority, and the U.S. has strategic war plans to deploy large forces to the Western Aleutian Islands (Adak, Shemya, etc.) where the use of tactical nuclear weapons would be likely. In general, Soviet forces in the Pacific must be prepared to face any or all of the forces of the United States, Japan, South Korea, and China.

Four of the five nuclear powers (except China) have allocated nuclear weapons—possibly as many as 3,000—for use outside of Europe and North Asia. Naval weapons are the most numerous, and include land and carrier based aircraft, and substantial numbers of anti-ship and anti-submarine weapons. The aircraft carrier is the preeminent means of projecting power along the coastal regions of Africa, Southeast Asia, the Indian Ocean, and other areas of the so-called 'Third World.' However, the role of battlefield nuclear weapons for use by ground forces is not significant in other than Europe, Korea, and areas such as the Middle East adjacent to Europe.

In sum, the major concentrations of tactical (non-strategic) nuclear weapons are in Europe (NATO versus the Warsaw Pact) and to a lesser degree the Pacific region. Not surprisingly, these regions are also the most likely areas of confrontation between the United States and the Soviet Union.

Prospects for the Future

The evidence indicates that the nuclear forces of the United States and the Soviet Union are in the process of a comprehensive transformation. The results of the strategic modernization programs of the Reagan Administration in the U.S. and the ongoing modernization programs in the Soviet Union are readily visible in the deployment of new strategic systems, including new generations of ICBMs, bombers, and ballistic missile submarines. On both sides, research continues on ballistic missile defense systems, air defenses, anti-satellite weapons, and more sophisticated battle management systems.

The pervasive theme of both U.S. and Soviet offensive strategic modernization is the conversion of offensive nuclear forces to a hard-target counterforce role. This conversion, if current programs go forward as planned, will increase the vulnerability of opposing strategic nuclear forces and command and control systems to a first strike attack. From the U.S. point of view, this new arms race has created a situation where the United States has the advantage of superior technology. As a result, the U.S. may, within a few years, be able to place at risk the current generation of Soviet land-based ICBMs with accurate warheads delivered from U.S. ICBMs, bombers, and submarines.

While some analysts view this as a positive development for the United States, the ultimate result may be a serious reduction in crisis stability. Soviet tendencies toward massive preemptive action may increase as a result of a belief that there is an increased U.S. threat to Soviet strategic systems. If such a perception is held by the Soviets the result could pose great risks to the security of the United States and its allies.

On the other hand, an alternative Soviet response may be to pursue expanded arms reduction treaties with the United States. For example, the Gorbachev initiatives with regard to INF in Europe may be a sign that future negotiations may result in substantial reductions in various types of nuclear weapons. However, reductions in the number or capabilities of nuclear weapons will also present a risk for the United States and particularly for Western Europe, because Warsaw Pact nations are perceived to have superior numbers of conventional forces. Without sufficient numbers of highly accurate nuclear weapons, NATO may, in turn, feel vulnerable to potential Soviet conventional attack or political coercion. This concern could be addressed by conventional arms limitation treaties (again, the 1989 Gorbachev proposal is an example) that might reduce the threat to NATO.

As the 1980s draw to a close, there are great hopes among NATO nations that fundamental changes are taking place in the Soviet Union. For example, since 1986, General Secretary Gorbachev has made special efforts to reduce West European fears with regard to Soviet military power. However, history provides NATO with ample reason for caution. Previous Soviet leaders have made similar statements, which at the time, were taken as an indication by some that the Soviet Union was evolving into less of a threat to the political and economic interests of the West. Events in Hungary (1956), Berlin (1949 and 1961), Cuba (1962), Czechoslovakia (1968), and Afghanistan (1979) tended to shock Western policy makers back to a more cautious stance.

One could also argue that in spite of historic evidence, there are both economic and political reasons that the Soviets under Gorbachev will make a genuine efforts to ease East-West tensions. Certainly, both sides would benefit by a reduction in military expenditures because the resources that are currently being devoted to 'defense' could be used for non-defense purposes.

In closing this chapter, it is worthwhile to point out that at least since the late 1970s, an essential parity, or equality, has existed between the strategic nuclear capabilities of the United States and the Soviet Union. Although the balance will likely evolve over time, both sides recognize the dangers of significant deviations from this balance. Thus, the underlying situation of parity, perhaps at reduced levels of nuclear weapons, will probably not change substantially in the foreseeable future.

Notes

1. Dean, Jonathan, *Watershed in Europe,* published under the auspices of the Union of Concerned Scientists, Lexington Books, Lexington, MA, 1987, 18–28; "New Service, NATO Arms Dispute Left Unresolved," *Gazette Telegraph,* March 4, 1988; Weinberger, C., *Annual Report to the Congress Fiscal Year 1988,* U.S. Government Printing Office, Washington, D.C., January 7, 1987, 61–63, 226–228; Weinberger, C., *Soviet Military Power 1987,* U.S. Government Printing Office, Washington, D.C., March 1987.

2. Weinberger, C., *Annual Report to the Congress Fiscal Year 1988,* U.S. Government Printing Office, Washington, D.C., January 7, 1987, 16–20; Sivard, R.L., *World Military and Social Expenditures 1987–88,* published under the auspices of the Union of Concerned Scientists, World Priorities, Inc., Washington, D.C., 1987, 41–53; Air Force Association, "The Military Balance 1985/86," *Air Force Magazine,* February 1986, 60–124; Office of Management and Budget, *Budget of the United States Government Fiscal Year 1988,* U.S. Government Printing Office, January 5, 1987.

3. Weinberger, *Soviet Military Power 1987,* 23–28.

4. Weinberger, *Soviet Military Power 1987,* 23–61; Weinberger, *Annual Report to the Congress Fiscal Year 1988,* 213–217; Aviation Week Staff, "Strategic Defense Initiative Blueprint for a Layered Defense," *Aviation Week Magazine,* New York, November 23, 1987; Union of Concerned Scientists, "Antisatellite Weapons," *Briefing Paper,* 1985; New York Times News Service, "Star Wars Laser Testing Underway," *Gazette Telegraph,* January 3, 1988.

5. Campbell, C., *Nuclear Facts,* Hamlyn Publishing Group Limited, London, 1984, 83–127.

6. Weinberger, *Annual Report to the Congress Fiscal Year 1988,* 218; Air Force Association, The Military Balance 1985/86, *Air Force Magazine,* 62, 323; Campbell, *Nuclear Facts,* 69–70.

7. Weinberger, *Annual Report to the Congress Fiscal Year 1988;* Arkin and Fieldhouse, *Nuclear Battlefields,* Ballinger Publishing Company, Cambridge, MA, 1985.

8. Weinberger, *Annual Report to the Congress Fiscal Year 1988;* Campbell, *Nuclear Facts.*

9. Weinberger, *Soviet Military Power 1987;* Campbell, *Nuclear Facts.*

10. Weinberger, *Soviet Military Power 1987.*

11. Campbell, *Nuclear Facts.*

12. Ibid.

13. Ibid.

14. Schwartz, D., *NATO's Nuclear Dilemmas,* The Brookings Institution, Washington, D.C., 1983.

15. Campbell, *Nuclear Facts;* Arkin and Fieldhouse, *Nuclear Battlefields.*

16. Arkin and Fieldhouse, *Nuclear Battlefields.*

17. Ibid.

Appendix: NATO and Warsaw Pact
Conventional Force Comparisons

Estimating Defense Expenditures

Estimating Soviet defense spending has always been difficult. For either NATO or the Warsaw Pact, military expenditures are not a measure of security, they are a measure of military force potential. However, Soviet defense expenditures have a major impact on Allied defense spending because force comparisons between NATO and the Warsaw Pact start with the size of the forces that NATO opposes, and that size depends most directly on the amount of Soviet defense spending. Alexander, Becker and Hoehn claimed in 1979 that the dollar value of Soviet military activities, net of pensions, exceeded the U.S. by 45 percent. With all personnel costs removed, the excess was 25 percent. Valued in rubles, the Soviet margin was also 25 percent.[1] While many analysts agree that the Soviets spend more for defense than the U.S., estimates of Soviet spending trends have been viewed with increasing skepticism in the last few years because assigning a monetary value to Soviet military equipment is almost impossible.

The cost of a weapon is related to its expected military performance, but expressing that cost in dollars, francs or pounds puts a western perception of benefits into the valuation process. For example, to arrive at a value for Soviet arms, the CIA estimates the U.S. cost of replicating a piece of Soviet equipment and then maintaining and operating the equipment using Soviet practices. This methodology ensures that no key performance characteristics are ignored, but it has the additional effect, when Soviet and U.S. costs are compared, of not providing an accurate measure of relative military performance.[2] Instead, this method results in a dollar cost of Soviet expenditures that is an upper bound on what it would cost to achieve the level of military performance represented by each piece of equipment.[3] In other words, although most of the major NATO allies could build a Soviet fighter the way the Soviets do, the allies could build one cheaper using their own technology, and the military performance would be the same. When each of these upper bound values is summed to arrive at the Soviet military budget, the result is a consistent over-estimation of the total amount of Soviet spending. Similarly, if comparison costing is done by valuing western military equipment in rubles, based on the cost of the Soviets replicating our designs, then the military performance represented by western expenditure would be overstated. Because there is no middle ground, every comparison of military equipment costs is biased. The CIA choice of dollar-costing Soviet equipment simply means that the bias always puts Soviet defense spending on the high side.

Non-Numerical Force Comparisons

Conventional force comparisons do not provide an accurate measure of relative military performance.[4] Thus, the tendency of NATO to concentrate on hardware often means that insufficient weight is given to Soviet/Warsaw Pact defense policy, and it adds to the feeling that the allies are only engaged in a technological arms race. The Soviets and the Warsaw Pact have three specific military principles that would be employed against NATO's conventional forces:[5]

- The 'law of negation of the negation'. Any new NATO weapons that appear to threaten or 'negate' a Soviet weapon must themselves be negated. One interesting corollary to this law (in light of the SDI) is that if two opponents have weapons of equal destructiveness, the advantage goes to the one that develops a defense first.
- The principle of coordination of mutually-supporting forces in combat. Each Soviet weapon is developed in relation to the capabilities of all other Soviet weapon types. Therefore, when the Warsaw Pact is faced with a threatening new NATO weapon, it can be expected to use two or more weapons to counter it.
- The principle of launching attacks with overwhelming forces at the outset of hostilities. The hardest blows should be unleashed at the very beginning of the battle.

It is how NATO's forces cope with these principles that will be important in combat, not force numbers derived from inflated spending estimates. In the near term, NATO's ability to function in combat against the Warsaw Pact will depend on how it responds to two difficult problems concerning conventional arms. The first problem involves determining the true nature of the conventional balance. The bulk of statistics indicate that the Warsaw Pact leads NATO. in most conventional weapons. It is not clear, however, that this lead is always significant because it is difficult to translate numbers of weapons into combat capabilities without knowing how the weapons will be used, both in terms of the tactical theory employed and with respect to the quality of the operators. For example, a 1988 study by the European Study Group on Alternative Security Policy claims that the NATO tanks, which outweigh Soviet Models by 11 metric tons, are more maneuverable and have better horsepower/weight ratios. In addition, the NATO tank force is far more modern than that of the Warsaw Pact where 70 percent of the tanks are older models that the West regards as obsolete. Also, twice the proportion of Western artillery is self propelled—another distinct advantage in a conventional war.[6] For these reasons, the Study Group believes that NATO conventional forces compare well to those of the Warsaw Pact, but this study falls into the same trap of hardware comparisons that has just been discussed. The real issue is how the obsolete tanks of the Warsaw Pact would be used to implement Soviet strategy.

In another example, an August, 1988 study for the Senate Armed Services Committee found that "NATO has considerable strengths on which to draw and is by no means a basket case in terms of conventional military power vs. the Warsaw Pact." Senator Carl Levin noted that if one just concentrates on simple quantitative balances one could overlook Warsaw Pact weaknesses that can be exploited "or lead NATO to squander its resources on efforts to redress numerical imbalances, when our most serious deficiencies may lie elsewhere."[7] Both studies raise serious questions about the true strength of NATO conventional forces. These questions must be answered before the levels of NATO's conventional forces can either be intelligently adjusted or negotiated.

The second controversy will arise after adequate measures of the conventional balance are developed. This controversy concerns whether NATO is prepared to redress imbalances in conventional forces or whether it will continue to buy defense on the cheap by relying on large numbers of nuclear weapons as inexpensive supplements to insufficient conventional forces. NATO members are generally not prepared to increase defense budgets and thus, additional spending for conventional forces, if it comes at all, will be at the expense of other programs. Candidates for funding reduction under such a scenario are likely to be non-U.S. strategic nuclear programs; for example, the British Trident.[8] Only after these two problems are addressed and at least partially solved can the Alliance either negotiate meaningful conventional force reductions or maintain appropriate and efficient levels of conventional forces. It is therefore worthwhile to look at NATO-Warsaw Pact conventional forces in some detail. These forces include large numbers of aircraft, tanks, artillery, other major conventional weapons, and of course, troops. We begin with aircraft, as shown in Table A2.1.

Probable Missions of Tactical Aircraft

For both sides, one of the most important wartime duties of tactical air forces in Europe would be to gain and maintain control of the skies, thereby allowing friendly ground, naval, and air forces to operate with minimal interference from enemy air attack. Tactical air forces would also be used to attack ground targets inside hostile territory as well as to support friendly forces in close combat with the enemy. These missions, together with tactical airlift of ground combat forces and supplies, largely determine the structure of both NATO and Warsaw Pact air forces.

The outcome of any air battle between NATO and Warsaw Pact tactical air forces would be decided by a whole host of factors, including the capabilities of some highly sophisticated aircraft that are produced by European NATO members. Other factors include air crew proficiency, command and control support, intelligence gathering and dissemination, air base survivability, logistics support, spare parts availability, and munitions sustainability. In all of these areas, the Soviets and other Warsaw Pact nations are perceived to have serious shortcomings compared to NATO air forces. Table A2.2 shows the latest (1988) estimates of NATO and Warsaw Pact ground forces available for immediate use in Europe.

Not including near-term reinforcements, NATO estimates conclude that the Warsaw Pact has a total strength of about 133 division equivalents compared to 90 for NATO; about 32,000 main battle tanks compared to 19,600 for NATO; about 18,000 anti-tank guided weapon launchers compared to 13,370 for NATO, and 23,000 artillery units (including mortars and multiple rocket launchers) compared to 14,200 for NATO. The Warsaw Pact is also believed to have substantial superiority in armored personnel carriers, although NATO holds the edge in attack helicopters.

However, there is controversy over these numbers. Even the numbers for NATO forces are controversial, because for political reasons, French and Spanish forces

Table A2.1: NATO-Warsaw Pact Combat Aircraft (1988)

NATO Aircraft	In-Place In Europe	Available For Reinforcement	Total
Fighter-Bombers	2,100	1,350	3,450
Fight-Interceptors	900	270	1,170
Reconnaissance	260	170	430
Bombers	0	75	75
NATO Totals	3,260	1,865	5,125
Warsaw Pact Aircraft	In-Place In Europe	Available For Reinforcement	Total
Fighter-Bombers	2,550	50	2,600
Fighter-Interceptors	2,700	100	2,800
Reconnaissance	650	40	690
Bombers	410	50	460
Warsaw Pact Totals	6,310	240	6,550

Notes:
1.   NATO numbers do not include France and Spain. France has approximately 136 long-range fighter bombers (Mirage IVA and IVP) and 75 shorter-range fighter-bombers (Jaguar and Mirage IIIE). All 211 of these aircraft are capable of carrying nuclear bombs. France also has 11 squadrons of fighter-interceptors, with a total of about 220 combat aircraft (Mirage IIIC, Mirage F-1C, and Mirage 2000C/B). Spain has 6 squadrons of fighter-interceptors, with a total of about 100 combat aircraft (F-4C, Mirage IIE, and Mirage F-C/E).

2.   Warsaw Pact numbers do not include Soviet strategic interceptors that are deployed to counter the U.S. long-range strategic bomber force.

3.   NATO and Warsaw Pact training aircraft are not included in the above numbers.

Sources: The following sources are readily available to the general public: Arkin, W.M. and Fieldhouse, R.W., *Nuclear Battlefields: Global Links in the Arms Race*, Ballinger Publishing Company, Cambridge, MA, 1985; Chant, C. and Hogg, I., *Nuclear War in the 1980s?*, Harper and Row Publishers, New York, 1983; Campbell, C., *Nuclear Facts: A Guide to Nuclear Weapon Systems and Strategy*, Hamlyn Publishing Group Limited, New York, 1984, and Weinberger, Caspar W., *Soviet Military Power 1987*, U.S. Government Printing Office, Washington, D.C., March 1987. The above data were updated from other unclassified documents to approximate 1987-88 numbers.

are not assigned to NATO's integrated command structure. Consequently, these forces are not usually counted in NATO figures. Clearly, the Soviet Union must take French and Spanish forces into account in planning their own defensive and offensive strategies. The Soviets have also been understandably adamant that these 'non-NATO' forces should be counted in force reduction negotiations concerning Europe.

In recent years, the Soviet Union has departed from its traditional secrecy and published its own force comparison figures. Not unexpectedly, NATO figures concerning Warsaw Pact forces do not match with those presented by the Soviet Union. For example, Soviet figures for 1987 show a NATO superiority in division equivalents and a rough equality in the number of tanks.[9]

Table A2.2:   NATO-Warsaw Pact Ground Forces

NATO Ground Force Unit	In-Place In Europe	Available For Reinforcement	Total
Army Division Equiv.	90	31	121
Main Battle Tanks	19,600	4,650	24,250
Anti-Tank GWL	13,370	9,210	22,580
Artillery/Mortar/MRL	14,200	4,150	18,350
Armored Pers. Carriers	32,850	8,650	41,500
Attack Helicopters	650	600	1,250

Warsaw Pact Ground Force Unit	In-Place In Europe	Available For Reinforcement	Total
Army Division Equiv.	133	97	230
Main Battle Tanks	32,000	20,000	52,000
Anti-Tank GWL	18,000	10,000	28,000
Artillery/Mortar/MRL	23,000	19,000	42,000
Armored Pers. Carriers	38,000	16,000	54,000
Attack Helicopters	960	10	970

Comparison of Totals

Ground Force Unit	NATO Total	Warsaw Pact Total	Difference
Army Division Equiv.	121	230	-109
Main Battle Tanks	24,250	52,000	-27,750
Anti-Tank GWL	22,580	28,000	-5,420
Artillery/Mortar/MRL	18,350	42,000	-23,650
Armored Pers. Carriers	41,500	54,000	-12,500
Attack Helicopters	1,250	970	+280

Notes:
1.   NATO numbers do not include France and Spain. France has approximately 12 division equivalents, 1,260 main battle tanks, 1,558 anti-tank GWL, 699 artillery/mortar/MRL, 4,646 armored personnel carriers, and 673 attack helicopters. Spain has approximately 4 division equivalents, 779 main battle tanks, 130 anti-tank GWL, 1,179 artillery/mortar/MRL, 890 armored personnel carriers, and 162 attack helicopters.
2. The number of division equivalents include active duty troops only.
3. Multiple Rocket Launcher (MRL), Guided Weapon Launcher

Sources: The following sources are readily available to the general public: Campbell, C., *Nuclear Facts: A Guide to Nuclear Weapon Systems and Strategy*, Hamlyn Publishing Group Limited, New York, 1984; Chant, C. and Hogg, I., *Nuclear War in the 1980s?*, Harper and Row Publishers, New York, 1983; The International Institute for Strategic Studies, "The Military Balance 1985/86", *Air Force Magazine*, Volume 69, Number 2, February 1986, The Air Force Association, Arlington, VA 1986; Sivard, R.L., in association with the Union of Concerned Scientists, *World Military and Social Expenditures 1987-88*, World Priorities, Washington, D.C. 1987, and Weinberger, Caspar W., *Soviet Military Power 1987*, U.S. Government Printing Office, Washington, D.C., March 1987.

Likely Missions of Ground Forces

U.S. Defense Guidance for 1984–88 states that: "in recognition of the weaker in-place [land] defense on the northern and southern regions [the United States should] place more emphasis and provide more visibility to NATO offensive exercises in the northern and southern regions." This document goes on to state that: "emphasis will be given to offensive moves against Warsaw Pact flanks," and "that this role should include both nuclear and conventional weapons."[10]

Table A2.3: Comparison of NATO-Warsaw Pact Maritime Forces (North
Atlantic and Seas Adjacent to Europe, 1986)

Maritime Force Unit	NATO Total	Warsaw Pact Total	Difference
Aircraft Carriers	17	4	+ 13
Cruisers	16	22	- 6
Destroyers, Frigates, and Corvettes	310	201	+109
Coastal Escorts, Patrol Boats	267	586	-319
Amphibious Assault Ships	128	212	- 84
Mine Warfare Craft	270	330	- 60
Attack Submarines	171	214	- 43
SLBM Submarines	35	44	- 9
Sea-Based Aircraft (including Helicopters)	832	205	+627
Land-Based Naval Aircraft (including Helicopters)	389	527	-138
Anti-Submarine Aircraft (including Helicopters)	462	209	+253

Notes: NATO numbers do not include France and Spain. France has 3
aircraft carriers with about 36 nuclear-capable fighter-bombers (Super
Etendards), 2 cruisers, 44 destroyers and frigates, 10 coastal escorts
and patrol boats, 6 amphibious assault craft, 23 mine warfare craft, 18
attack submarines, 6 SLBM submarines, and 127 naval aircraft (including
helicopters). Spain has 1 aircraft carrier, 15 destroyers and
corvettes, 101 coastal escorts and patrol boats, 30 amphibious assault
craft, 12 mine warfare craft, and 7 attack submarines.

Sources: The following sources are readily available to the general
public: The International Institute for Strategic Studies, "The
Military Balance 1985/86", *Air Force Magazine*, Volume 69, Number 2,
February 1986, The Air Force Association, Arlington, VA, 1986 and
Weinberger, Caspar W., *Soviet Military Power 1987*, U.S. Government
Printing Office, Washington, D.C., March 1987.

This strategy is known as 'horizontal escalation,' and would tend to diffuse enemy
strength in Central Europe. Also, it would tend to shift the battlefield from allied to
enemy territory via offensives based in Northern Europe and through the Mediterranean
Sea. In practice, this means that NATO would rely heavily on sea power to mount
and support flanking operations against Warsaw Pact territory. Thus, the strategic
balance in naval forces shown in Table A2.3 is also of great concern to NATO
planners for wartime operations against Warsaw Pact forces.

A counterattack along the northern flank would involve the use of bases in Britain,
Norway, Denmark, and Iceland, and substantial naval forces in the North Atlantic.
Such a counterattack would strike into the Baltic region and into the northern
reaches of the Soviet Union. Also, NATO dominance of northern European airspace
and coastal regions would be crucial to the safety of sea lanes between the United
States, Canada, and Western Europe.

A counterattack along the southern flank would involve land bases in Italy and
in other Mediterranean countries, and again, the use of substantial naval forces.
Such a counterattack from the Mediterranean region would be aimed at Warsaw
Pact nations from northern Italy, through the Balkans, into the southern reaches of
the Soviet Union.

Probable Missions of Maritime Forces

On the northern flank, the implementation of current NATO strategy would force a diversion of Warsaw Pact resources from the central front in Europe. It would also result in control of the North Atlantic sea lanes between the United States, Canada, and Western Europe. The success of this strategy would depend on the ability of NATO forces to intercept and destroy Soviet forces and to carry the war to Northern Soviet homeland bases. NATO naval forces, with the assistance of land-based air forces, would therefore mount attacks on northern Soviet bases and destroy Soviet naval and air forces deployed from these bases.

NATO neutralization of Soviet naval forces in the North Atlantic would depend, in part, on the U.S. Navy's nuclear-armed aircraft carrier battle groups and attack submarines that operate from bases around the North Atlantic rim. The U.S. currently has four aircraft carrier battle groups in the North Atlantic, complemented by strong British, Dutch, Norwegian, and French forces. NATO land-based aircraft that are assigned to air-sea warfare missions are stationed in Norway, Denmark, Britain, Iceland, and other locations. Although the Soviet naval presence is growing, the current balance of air and surface naval power in the North Atlantic is clearly in favor of the NATO alliance.

In the Mediterranean, the Soviet naval presence consists of about 45 to 50 ships at any given time: ten to twelve surface warships, seven to eight attack submarines, and two cruise missile submarines. However, the Soviets have no permanent naval bases in Mediterranean countries. Its ships spend most of their time at sea anchorages near the Spanish island of Alboran, near the Greek island of Kithira, in the Gulf of Sollum, and in the Gulf of Hamamet between Tunisia and Sicily. The Strait of Gibraltar (controlled by the British) at the the entrance to the Mediterranean severely restricts Soviet access to the Atlantic. Also, Turkey controls the straits from the Black Sea into the Mediterranean under the terms of the Montreux Convention.[11]

NATO naval forces clearly dominate the Mediterranean area. As the Mediterranean naval hub, Italy hosts the NATO bases that provide command and control for anti-submarine warfare and other naval operations. The U.S. Sixth Fleet in the Mediterranean has two carrier battle groups with over ninety aircraft each, about fourteen other warships, about four attack submarines, one Marine amphibious group, and twelve auxiliary ships, augmented by landbased air surveillance and anti-submarine warfare forces. Ballistic missile submarines also patrol the Mediterranean Sea from time to time, committed to NATO nuclear war plans.[12]

Even without the U.S. Navy, other NATO and French naval forces outnumber Soviet forces in the Mediterranean. One or two French aircraft carriers (with Super Etendard nuclear strike aircraft) have home ports in Toulon. The British also assign one or two frigates or destroyers with Lynx or Wasp nuclear-capable anti-submarine helicopters to its base at Gibraltar. Italy and Spain also have substantial forces in the Mediterranean region. Again, the balance of naval power is clearly in favor of the NATO alliance.

Notes to Appendix

1. Alexander, Arthur J., Becker, Abraham S., and Hoehn, William, *The Significance of Divergent U.S./USSR Military Expenditures,* RAND, N-1000-AF, February, 1979, v–53.

2. Hildebrandt, Gregory, *Capital Valuation of Military Equipment,* RAND, R-3212, January, 1985, 28–29.

3. Ibid., 29–30.

4. Ibid., 28–29.

5. Hansen, James H., "Countering NATO's New Weapons—Soviet concepts for War In Europe," *International Defense Review,* Volume 17, no. 11/1984, 1617–1624.

6. Chalmers, Malcolm, and Unterseher, Lutz, *International Security,* Summer, 1988.

7. Adams, Peter, "Congress at Odds with DoD on Military Balance," *Defense News,* September 5, 1988, 4.

8. Adams, Peter, "Allies Face Tough Choices if Nuclear Umbrella Shuts," *Defense News,* June 8, 1987, 1, 56.

9. Weinberger, C., *Soviet Military Power 1987,* U.S. Government Printing Office, Washington, D.C., March 1987; Campbell, C., *Nuclear Facts,* Hamlyn Publishing Group Limited, London, 1984, 83–127; Air Force Association, "The Military Balance 1985/86," *Air Force Magazine,* February 1986, 60–124; Dean, Jonathan, *Watershed in Europe,* published under the auspices of the Union of Concerned Scientists, Lexington Books, Lexington, MS, 1987, 38.

10. Dean, Jonathan, *Watershed in Europe,* 38.

11. Arkin, W., and Fieldhouse, R., *Nuclear Battlefields,* Ballinger Publishing Company, Cambridge, MA, 1985; Weinberger, C., *Soviet Military Power 1987,* Air Force Association, "Soviet Theater Estimates," October 1987, *Air Force Magazine,* March 1988, 68–69.

12. Arkin and Fieldhouse, *Nuclear Battlefields;* Air Force Association, "Soviet Theater Estimates."

3

NATO's Nuclear Addiction

NATO and Nuclear Weapons

Within a few years after it was established in 1949, NATO committed itself to a strategy that relied primarily upon the threat of using nuclear weapons to deter Soviet expansion in Europe. This commitment set the framework for the way the nations of NATO have allocated resources to the development, deployment, and maintenance of military forces.

Current concerns over the credibility of the U.S. nuclear guarantee to NATO and the alternatives available for future U.S.-Soviet disarmament negotiations are better understood when one appreciates the reasons behind NATO's nuclear addiction. This chapter therefore examines the rationale and the incentives behind U.S. and NATO policies with regard to nuclear weapons at different times; shows how various constraints developed that limit the flexibility of current policy decisions, and reveals some mistakes that should be avoided and successes that might be emulated in the future.[1]

The Balance of Power After the War

The balance of world power shifted radically as a result of World War II. The pre-war world was dominated by the European colonial powers, particularly Great Britain and France. After the war, the world was dominated by the military, political, and economic power of the United States and the Soviet Union. However, the implications of this new state of affairs were not immediately recognized by the victorious Allied Powers (the United States, Great Britain, France, the Soviet Union, and China). For example, Soviet military occupation of Eastern Europe was widely believed in the West to be temporary, and the Soviets were expected to be amenable to diplomatic pressure that would bring a resolution consistent with the wartime political hopes of East European populations and the long term political and economic goals of the Western capitalist nations.

Nor was it immediately apparent just how much the European imperial powers had been weakened by the war. In 1945, the British and French empires still extended over most of the globe. Nationalism and the decline of imperialism were not yet established facts of the postwar world. As Europeans faced the intensified problems of colonial administration over restive nationalities, the economic and political problems of postwar recovery, and the growing impatience of the U.S. government, which was committed to the dissolution of all overseas empires; they were forced to reconsider the benefits and costs of maintaining their great power status by retaining their colonies. Increasingly, the Europeans were forced to realize that they no longer had the military and economic muscle to be the prime movers in international politics, that they had depended on the economic and military power of the United States for their security for longer than they cared to admit, and that they would be increasingly overshadowed by the United States and the Soviet Union in world affairs.

U.S.-Soviet comradeship, forged on the battlefields of Europe, might have laid the foundation for peace in a better world. On April 25, 1945, the U.S. and Soviet armies met at Torgau after their respective drives across Europe, culminating a common wartime effort against the European Axis powers. "This is a great day, the meeting of two great nations; we hope this will be the basis for peace in this world to come," said a Soviet major, without oratorical affectation, as he shook the hand of an American soldier.[2] And yet, within a few years after the hot war had ended, the so-called cold war between the United States and the Soviet Union had begun.

A review of selected postwar events helps to explain how these two wartime allies turned into adversaries shortly after they attained military victory. For example, in September of that year, a Soviet writer, Leonid Sobolev, warned Soviet soldiers in a Pravda editorial not to be deceived by the tinsel of the West. The glitter should deceive no one, he cautioned, for only Soviet culture was genuine and healthy. The warning was motivated by fear that a large number of Soviet soldiers abroad might become contaminated with bourgeois ideas. This article, in retrospect, foreshadowed the approach of Soviet purges that soon took place in art and science, and of the intensified Soviet campaign against Western culture.[3]

Under Stalin, the postwar Soviet government coupled the attack on Western culture with a glorification of Soviet armies. The victory over the Axis Powers was presented as an exclusive triumph of the Soviet Union, and the contributions of the armies of the other allies were often cited as negligible. For example, Stalin called the African campaign of Field Marshal Montgomery a side show. According to Pravda, the second front in Europe was opened only when it had become evident that the Soviet Union was capable, without the help of the other allies, of defeating Fascist Germany. It was ironic that Stalin explained that the surrender of Japan was due to the timely intervention of Soviet armies, while the U.S. campaign in the

Pacific and the atomic bombing of Hiroshima and Nagasaki were regarded as minor episodes.[4]

From the point of view of the Soviet government, the United States represented both a military threat and a challenge to the doctrines of communism. The Soviets had not forgotten the U.S. military intervention during the revolution of 1917–21, the U.S. post-World War I attempts to isolate and weaken the fledgling Soviet communist regime, and the anti-Soviet U.S. press that continued to warn about the dangers of Soviet expansion in Eastern Europe. Finally, the Soviets were well aware that the United States had the atomic bomb and the means for delivering it to virtually any city in the Soviet Union.

While these rumblings of Soviet discontent with the culture, the wartime contributions, the foreign policies and the perceived military threat of the West were going on, the United States was unwilling to maintain a strong global military presence. The U.S. shift to a broadly internationalist military and political stance after the Japanese attack on Pearl Harbor proved fragile. Even during the war, it was under stress from traditional isolationist elements in the U.S. foreign policy establishment and in the U.S. Congress.[5] Within ten months after the war ended, President Truman compromised with the isolationists by curtailing U.S. global military commitments. In 1946, U.S. military troop strength was cut by almost 50 percent, and most of those that remained in service were stationed in the United States.[6] U.S. military cutbacks gradually eroded the relative power balance in the world for several years, and reinforced West European anxiety about the long-term commitment of the United States to European security and economic reconstruction.

U.S. retrenchment in world affairs was due in part to deeply rooted isolationist tendencies, simple war fatigue, the knowledge that the U.S. was the only nation with nuclear bombs and delivery systems, and faith in the ability of the United Nations to settle major international disputes. As it turned out, the United States and the Soviet Union were patently unable to resolve their differences within the United Nations.

By 1947, the differences between the two superpowers began to crystalize. Backed by the presence of Soviet troops, the Soviet government increased its political pressure on East European governments. This pressure resulted in Soviet annexation of several former Baltic nations and the institution of communist governments in Bulgaria, Poland, Romania, and Hungary. East Germany remained in the grip of the Soviet army of occupation. By 1948, Soviet postwar efforts had resulted in the triumph of a communist regime in Czechoslovakia and the neutralization of Finland and Austria. However, Yugoslavia under Tito had developed a somewhat anti-Soviet brand of communism, and continued to provide trouble for the otherwise communist monolith that developed behind what Winston Churchill called an 'iron curtain' across Eastern Europe.[7]

In 1948, the United States, under President Truman, formulated a foreign policy that offered support to any government that faced Soviet pressure and communist insurgency. This 'Truman Doctrine' was a historic turn away from isolationism in American foreign policy. The Marshall Plan accompanied the Truman Doctrine, and provided substantial economic and social aid to the war-torn nations of Western Europe. Although a Committee of European Economic Cooperation was set up as part of the Marshall Plan and the Soviet Union was invited to join, the Soviet government considered this committee to be merely window-dressing for U.S. anti-Soviet aggression and declined to participate.[8]

The Truman Doctrine, the Marshall Plan, the Tito heresy, and the not-so-subtle threat of U.S. nuclear weapons were all responses to Soviet foreign policy in the immediate post World War II era. In addition, Soviet military, political, and economic maneuvers in Eastern Europe were instrumental in causing the development of the Atlantic Alliance that began to take shape in 1948.

The formation of the Alliance culminated on April 4, 1949, with the signing of the North Atlantic Treaty by twelve nations.[9] This date serves as a milestone for the halt of the previously unchecked Soviet postwar expansion in Eastern Europe. However, the formation of NATO and the U.S. monopoly of nuclear weapons did not eliminate American problems in dealing with the Soviet Union. While the U.S. held the monopoly, the Soviet Union embarked on many cold war exploits, including the support of communist revolts in Greece and Turkey. In general, the U.S. government found it difficult to translate its monopoly of air-delivered strategic nuclear weapons (bombs) into a decisive political advantage in its dealings with an expansionist but non-nuclear Soviet government. However, the advocates of air power were able to influence the growing dependence of the United States on air-delivered strategic nuclear bombs as a tool of foreign policy.

Air Power Doctrine

The development of air power doctrine prior to and during World War II ensured that aerial bombing would play a dominant role in postwar U.S. military strategy. The Allied air campaign during the war included indiscriminate attacks on civilian centers with conventional incendiary bombs (Dresden, Cologne, Berlin, Tokyo, etc.) and of course, the attacks on Hiroshima and Nagasaki with the first nuclear bombs.

At no time was the debate on air power doctrine concerned with whether or not to bomb. Initially, it centered around the issue of daylight precision bombing versus nighttime blanket bombing. In order to cut bomber crew losses, daylight precision bombing was eventually abandoned in favor of daylight bombing of large civilian centers. To air power advocates, the results of the air campaign spoke eloquently for the future capabilities of strategic air power. The advent of a super (nuclear) bomb, almost custom-made for strategic use, gave air power advocates a decisive argument to persuade the U.S. military establishment that nuclear bombs were the most effective and efficient means for breaking the will of an enemy to wage war.

Although the final assessment of the effectiveness of the air campaign in Europe was not clear-cut, both the United States and Britain went ahead with postwar military policies that emphasized the strategic bombing. Soon after the war, the allocation of resources to the U.S. air forces jumped dramatically, and in a short time, the U.S. Army Air Forces became a fully independent service. In Britain, the Royal Air Force (RAF) Bomber Command also grew in size and prestige.[10] In this environment, it was natural for attention to focus on nuclear bombs, the most powerful and destructive ordnance for airborne delivery.

These factors interacted with perceptions of the Soviet threat. By 1947, it was perceived that Soviet postwar demobilization had been much less than expected. U.S. estimates of the military threat to Western Europe consistently put total Soviet military strength at 175 divisions. However, intelligence during this period was not accurate enough to assess the actual strength of these divisions. Much later, it became clear that Soviet divisions were smaller than their Western counterparts and not all were equally well stocked, equipped, or trained.[11]

The U.S. and the West Europeans could not hope to match 175 divisions with a comparable ground force. There were doubts that the manpower for so many divisions existed in the West, and even if it did exist, none of the West European nations, struggling during this period to recover economically, socially, and politically from the ravages of the war, were willing to place such a burden on their societies. Thus, from the late 1940s through the early 1960s, the pre-eminence of air power advocates, U.S. and NATO assessments of the Soviet threat, and the cost-effectiveness of nuclear weapons compared to ground forces provided the principal arguments for the primary reliance on nuclear weapons for European security.

The NATO Buildup

Even with this background, NATO's nuclear addiction was not inevitable. It took almost four years (1945–49) before a consensus was reached on the perceived need for a formal security arrangement to protect Western Europe. Communist-inspired revolts in Greece and Turkey and the communist coup in Czechoslovakia finally pushed the U.S. and the West Europeans to action. Even then, U.S. officials were reluctant to involve the United States directly in Western European security arrangements. During the negotiations between Britain and France that resulted in the Dunkirk Treaty (1947), and between these two countries and Benelux nations (Belgium, the Netherlands, and Luxemburg) to form the Western European Union in 1948, the United States assumed a friendly but distant attitude. In the negotiations leading to the formation of NATO, the U.S. displayed caution about making any concrete military commitments. As one observer noted, neither the Americans nor the Europeans were clear, even after the North Atlantic Treaty was signed, whether NATO would evolve into a military organization or remain basically a political guarantee of American assistance in the event of a war in Europe.[12]

The U.S. government was finally galvanized into more decisive action by increased Soviet belligerence after the North Atlantic Treaty was signed and by the outbreak of the Korean conflict in 1950. In April 1950, the U.S. government adopted NSC 68, a major policy document that defined U.S. objectives in the developing 'cold war' with the Soviet Union. By September of that same year, the North Atlantic Treaty signatories had decided that their alliance would indeed become a military organization.

Both military and political officials of the Truman administration advocated increases in air, naval, and ground forces to counter the Soviets. Increases in conventional air and ground forces as well as strategic nuclear forces (bombers) were considered essential to the NATO military program. To demonstrate U.S. resolve and strategic capabilities, nuclear-armed B-36 bombers were deployed to RAF Lakenheath, Great Britain, in January, 1951. In the early 1950s, specially lightened reconnaissance versions of this enormous aircraft could and did roam virtually at will over the Soviet Union at extremely high altitudes.

Arguments were also made for increases in army ground forces and tactical air power. For example, in 1951, U.S. Army Chief of Staff General J. L. Collins argued before a Senate hearing that: "Without adequate army forces on the ground, backed up by tactical air forces, it would be impossible to prevent the overrunning of Europe by the tremendous land forces of the police states, no matter what [strategic] air and sea power we could bring against them . . . it takes army troops on the ground to repel an invasion on the ground." General Omar Bradley, Chairman of the Joint Chiefs of Staff, made a similar point at these same hearings. He agreed that the deterrent provided by nuclear bombs was an essential part of American strategy, but he also stated: "As time goes on, if we can build up the complete defense of Europe to a point where it would not be easy to overrun it, there would be very grave doubt as to whether or not [the Soviets] could; in my opinion, when you reach that stage, the chance of war is reduced very, very materially."[13]

After these hearings, President Truman prevailed over domestic critics and won approval to station U.S. troops in Europe as part of the growing U.S. commitment to NATO. He did so with the understanding that the United States would provide only six divisions, and the West Europeans would provide the majority of the ground forces to offset the perceived Soviet conventional force superiority.[14]

From the start, nuclear weapons were included in NATO planning for ground forces in Europe. While strategic nuclear bombs provided the primary deterrent, technologies were being developed that would result, for the first time, in nuclear weapons that could be used for tactical purposes on the battlefield. In part, the desire on the part of the army for tactical nuclear weapons was a result of the Korean conflict. In Korea, U.S. army commanders became increasingly frustrated with their inability to fight a decisive ground campaign against large numbers of Chinese and North Korean troops. Interest turned to the potential of tactical nuclear weapons to generate decisive outcomes.

Even before the Korean War, the Joint Chiefs of Staff, stimulated by the interest of key army officers and civilian scientists, had begun to study the feasibility of and the potential uses for tactical nuclear weapons. For example, one study, called Project Vista, conducted at the California Institute of Technology and sponsored by the Department of Defense, examined the technical feasibility of 'bringing the battle back to the battlefield.' It concluded that tactical nuclear weapons were feasible, and Project Vista became the rallying point for advocates of the new concept of tactical nuclear weapons.[15]

Project Vista set off a lengthy debate within the national security community over the direction of the U.S. nuclear weapons program. The choice was seen as being between a tactical nuclear capability based on fission technology and a strategic thermonuclear capability based on fusion. The proponents of the latter choice, including the U.S. Strategic Air Command (SAC), pointed to the successful test of the first fusion device (1952). They charged that efforts to 'bring the battle back to the battlefield' were unnecessary, and because of the relative scarcity of fissionable material, the development of large numbers of tactical nuclear weapons posed a potential threat to the hydrogen (thermonuclear) bomb project. Supporters of Project Vista, on the other hand, were skeptical of the universal applicability of strategic air power and saw the development of tactical nuclear weapons as an opportunity for the army to get into the nuclear weapons business, from which the circumstances of policy and technology had previously excluded it.

Although the advocates of tactical nuclear weapons never considered conventional forces to be as peripheral as strategic air power enthusiasts did, they still thought that a pure conventional defense of Western Europe would be overwhelmed by the superior Soviet conventional forces. They also pointed out that tactical nuclear weapons had distinct advantages over conventional battlefield weapons. For example, tactical nuclear weapons would make enemy offensive troop concentrations much more risky, since troop concentrations would be attractive targets for nuclear weapons. Furthermore, tactical nuclear weapons would dramatically increase the firepower of self-contained army maneuver units (battalions), thus reducing the manpower and costs for units of a given firepower capability.

The 'New Look' Under Eisenhower

The Republican presidential campaign of 1952 placed a heavy emphasis on a balanced federal budget, with Eisenhower himself suggesting that cuts could be made in the U.S. defense budget. It was not surprising, therefore, that President Eisenhower should attempt to prune down the Federal budget of $79 billion that Truman had submitted to Congress just before he left office.

With the assistance of his Director of the Budget, Joseph M. Dodge, the new President proposed to make substantial reductions in the budget across all departments. However, his suggestions stepped on almost as many Republican as Democratic toes, and he created instant opponents concerning the budget in both parties.

Since a large portion of the budget went for national defense and nuclear weapons research (over 50 percent in 1953), it seemed clear to Eisenhower that, despite the Korean War and the cold war with the Soviet Union, the armed forces would have to do with less money. To the surprise of all concerned, the President proposed, with the support of the Secretary of Defense, to make most of the cuts in the defense budget at the expense of the air force, which stood to lose $5.2 billion. He also suggested that the air force lower its proposed strength from 143 wings to 120 wings. This, the President insisted, would be adequate for the national defense.

However, there were many influential persons, even in his own party, who thought otherwise. His decision represented a return to the 'balanced forces' principle, which called for relatively equal appropriations for army, navy and air force, and an abandonment of the idea, which the Truman administration had supported, that the air force, with its strategic nuclear weapons, was of paramount importance. A year later, however, the President reversed himself, and while lowering the total defense budget still further, he suggested that more money be put on the air force than on either the army or navy.[16]

It was in this environment that the Eisenhower administration decided to use relatively cheap nuclear weapons to justify dramatic cutbacks in relatively costly conventional forces. After almost six months of study within the Department of Defense and other agencies, the Eisenhower administration produced the basic planning document for the New Look, NSC 162/2, which was approved by the President on October 30, 1953. NSC 162/2 defined a dual national security problem: 1) the U.S. must meet the perceived Soviet threat, and 2) in doing so, the U.S. economy, institutions, and fundamental values must not be undermined. Within these constraints, NSC

162/2 analyzed the security implications of the world political situation for U.S. policy planning.[17]

NSC 162/2 contains subtleties notably absent from many of the public pronouncements that it generated. For example, the document argued that the Soviet Union was not likely to attack the United States or NATO deliberately, because such actions "would be almost certain to bring on a general war in view of U.S. commitments and intentions." It also predicted that at some point in time, both the United States and the Soviet Union would each have a nuclear retaliatory force large enough to make a first strike by either side unlikely. Finally, it pointed out that as general (nuclear) war becomes more devastating for both sides, the threat to resort to it becomes less credible as a deterrent against limited aggression. As a result, NSC 162/2 foresaw limitations on the very doctrine that it proposed—the doctrine of massive retaliation.

In the meantime, the Soviets had made significant progress in its own nuclear weapons program. The Soviet Union exploded its first atomic device in September of 1949, and progressed to its first thermonuclear explosion in August 1953. The Soviets had also developed aircraft for use as delivery systems: the Tupolev TU-4 (Bull) bomber (1948), which was essentially a copy of the U.S. B-29, and the TU-95 (Bear) bomber (1952), which in updated form, would remain in service through the 1980s and probably for the remainder of the century.

Given the fiscal constraints imposed by the Eisenhower Administration, the authors of NSC 162/2 considered the development of Soviet nuclear weapons as relevant only in the long term. For the short term, it was considered essential to cut back on conventional ground forces deployed throughout the world, leaving to allies the task of building up conventional forces for local defense.

However, NSC 162/2 contained some contradictions, including the following:

since U.S. Military Assistance must eventually be reduced, it is essential that the Western European states, including West Germany, build and maintain maximum feasible defensive strength. The major deterrent to aggression against Western Europe is the manifest determination of the United States to use its atomic capability and massive retaliatory striking power if the area is attacked.[18]

While the first statement calls for increases in Western European military capabilities, the second statement undercuts the incentives for the Europeans to do so. Further, the authors of NSC 162/2 failed to provide other incentives or to change Western European perceptions that they could avoid a massive military buildup by relying on the U.S. nuclear 'umbrella.'

In spite of problems, NSC 162/2 and the public statements of the Eisenhower Administration did create the impression, clearly intentional, that the United States was placing greater emphasis on nuclear weapons to replace the costly burdens of conventional defense efforts. This new policy was not merely declaratory; Eisenhower substantially reduced total military manpower during the first three years of his first term from about 3.45 million to 2.84 million, much of which reflected the demobilization after the Korean War. However, at the same time, the U.S. Air Force grew by over 20,000 men, the only service to gain in manpower during this period. The air force budget also grew by some $800 million in 1955, while at the same time, army and navy budgets were cut.[19]

However, Eisenhower was unable to sustain public support for the New Look policies during his second term. In 1956, the Administration proposed to make cuts in army and navy manpower by another 800,000 and to withdraw U.S. troops in Europe. The reaction from Congress and the West Europeans was overwhelmingly against such actions. The Eisenhower Administration had reached the limit of politically feasible military cutbacks.

Meanwhile, Great Britain and France also began to integrate nuclear weapons into their respective defense plans. The development of British and French nuclear forces during the 1950s would have significant consequences with regard to the development of NATO's nuclear addiction during the last decades of the twentieth century.

British Nuclear Weapon Programs (1939–88)

The British conceived of a program to develop nuclear bombs before the Americans were fully aware of the possibilities. Refugee German scientists had brought the implications of nuclear fission research to the attention of British scientists and government officials as early as 1939. By 1940, the British government had concluded that a fission bomb was probably feasible and certainly desirable.[20]

On this basis, the British government authorized research with the objective of producing a fission technology nuclear bomb. In 1940, although not formally in the war, the United States asked to participate in the British nuclear weapon program, with the hope of taking advantage of the substantial British lead in research. On the other hand, the British government wanted to retain independence in this new area of national security research and development, and rejected the American request, agreeing only to exchanges of technical information.

By 1943, the situation was reversed. The British program had slowed considerably due to insufficient resources during the peak of British expenditure for the war. The British government now turned to the United States with an offer to combine forces in a joint program. However, by this time, the U.S. needed no help, and key policy makers in the Roosevelt Administration had doubts about the reliability of British security arrangements and resented the British for their initial rebuff in 1940. As a result, the United States rejected the British offer.[21]

Without adequate resources to complete their nuclear weapon program during the war years, the British, through Prime Minister Churchill, continued to petition for collaboration on the U.S. Manhattan Project. By the time of the Quebec Conference of 1943, Churchill had won permission to collaborate with the U.S., but nuclear bombs would be built in the United States, not in Britain. This development had a negative impact on the postwar capabilities of Britain's nuclear weapon production industry. Even after the conference, the British contribution and the development of British nuclear weapons production facilities were substantially less than Churchill had hoped. At the end of the war, the United States emerged with technical expertise, nuclear weapon production facilities, and nuclear bombs. On the other side, the British had no production capability and no bombs.[22]

Immediately after the war, the British still hoped to develop nuclear weapons in collaboration with the U.S., but the U.S. Congress passed the McMahon Act (1946), which prohibited collaboration with any foreign powers on nuclear weapons. This ended the British hope of producing a nuclear bomb with U.S. help. The McMahon Act was a heavy blow to the British government now under the leadership of Prime Minister Attlee. It was not until 1958, when the McMahon Act was amended, that substantial collaboration resumed between the U.S. and the British on nuclear weapons development.

In late 1946, Attlee decided to proceed with the independent development and production of a British nuclear bomb. Slowly the British program progressed, and when Churchill regained office in 1952, he inherited from his predecessor a fission weapon that was nearly complete. A few months later, Britain detonated its first nuclear device, some three years after the Soviet Union. In 1954, after the U.S. detonated a fusion weapon, Churchill decided to follow suit. By 1957, shortly after the Suez fiasco, Britain had a thermonuclear device. About the same time, Britain developed an operational nuclear delivery system (the V-bomber force) that could strike the Soviet Union. It was hoped, on a political level, that the possession of nuclear weapons would arrest Britain's decline as a world power, or at least allow NATO policy to be developed to better serve British interests.

However, this did not mean complete nuclear independence from the United States. In spite of its capabilities to develop and manufacture nuclear warheads, Britain was dependent on the U.S. for key technologies associated with delivery systems. The V-bomber force, developed in Britain in the mid-1950s, had a nuclear capability, but this force faced the ever-tightening net of Soviet air defenses. Even Britain's own Blue Streak ballistic missile, capable of reaching Moscow from planned silos hewn out of Scottish granite, depended on U.S. designs for its motors and guidance systems. Blue Streak was cancelled in 1960 when its vulnerability to Soviet counterattack in its fixed silos became apparent. Meanwhile, the United States was laying out a plan for a 'triad' of bombers armed with SRAMs, land-based ICBMs, and SLBMs based on nuclear-powered submarines. The first and last of these weapon systems appeared to suit the perceived needs of British strategic forces.

In return, Britain had a major bargaining chip—its proximity to the Soviet Union at a time when certain U.S. strategic systems such as B-47 bombers, medium-range Thor missiles, and ballistic missile submarines needed forward operating bases. The U.S. Strategic Air Command had operational bases in Britain as early as 1951. In 1958, the British and the U.S. also agreed to deploy Thor missiles in Britain under dual-key control. In 1960, the U.S. Navy reached an agreement with Britain to use Holy Loch in Scotland as a fleet base for SLBM submarines. As part of these agreements, the British expected to receive the United States' most advanced strategic delivery system, the Skybolt air launched missile. The Skybolt would have allowed the V-bomber force to remain a viable offensive nuclear force throughout the 1960s.

However, faced with technical doubts about Skybolt's ability to work at all and aware of the vulnerability of U.S. bomber bases in the U.S. and abroad, the Kennedy Administration unilaterally cancelled Skybolt in 1962, without consulting the British. As a result, Prime Minister Harold Macmillan and President Kennedy met in late 1962 in Nassau to work out a new deal. The British got the Polaris SLBM, under an arrangement where the U.S. would provide the missiles and fire control systems, and the British would provide the submarines and the nuclear warheads.[23]

Thus, the development of an independent British strategic nuclear deterrent was, from the beginning, heavily dependent upon U.S. technology. These conditions remain essentially the same today (1988). Currently, Britain is a forward operating base for U.S. GLCMs, and once again has bargained to acquire the Trident II, the newest generation U.S. SLBM.

Throughout the post-World War II era, Britain faced the extremely difficult problem of cost. In spite of limited resources during a period of economic decline (late 1970s and early 80s), Britain actually achieved what few other NATO governments were able to do, it met the commitment agreed by the alliance in 1977 to increase defense spending in real terms by three percent annually. However, beginning in 1981, the problems of scarce resources and many defense commitments caused a continuing reappraisal of British defense commitments.

As indicated in Chapter 2, the British currently have four strategic nuclear-powered ballistic missile submarines, each carrying sixteen Polaris missiles. Thus, British submarines have the capability to deliver 64 nuclear warheads on Soviet targets. In the mid-1990s, the British are expected to deploy new submarines to replace its aging Polaris force. The new submarines will be armed with U.S. Trident II missiles, but with British nuclear warheads. Thus, a force of four or five new British submarines will carry some 512 to 640 multiple independently targetable reentry vehicle (MIRV) nuclear warheads.

The British also have a fighter-bomber force capable of striking targets in the Soviet Union. As indicated in Chapter 2, about 300 British-made nuclear warheads are carried on about 200 nuclear capable aircraft of three types: Jaguar, Buccaneer, and Tornado. These aircraft are stationed at four air bases in Britain and two in West Germany. Beginning in 1988, the Buccaneers and Jaguars are being replaced by a force of about 220 new Tornados. In addition, the British have nuclear-armed Sea Harriers on three aircraft carriers. This force is capable of delivering about 30 nuclear warheads on targets within a range of about 450 miles.

The British are committed to four key defense roles: the defense of NATO's central sector (the British Army of the Rhine and the Royal Air Force Germany); the air defense of the United Kingdom; the maritime defense of the Eastern Atlantic, and the independent nuclear deterrent. As early as 1981, the British decided that something might have to give, and this was before the expensive Falklands crisis. Although the debate continues today, the Trident II has not yet become the centerpiece of the British strategic nuclear force. If it does, the expense will probably mean cutbacks in the development and production of conventional surface warships and other forces, holding defense spending relatively constant at between five and six percent of British GNP.[24]

French Nuclear Forces (1930–88)

The events that led up to France's decision in 1957 to develop its own nuclear weapons and delivery systems began in the early 1930s, with the development of a sophisticated French nuclear scientific community. Its leader, Joliot-Curie, pioneered French fission research, and when World War II broke out, he offered to aid the British and American atomic weapons research programs. The United States showed no eagerness to accept Joliot-Curie's aid, primarily because of his association with the French Communist Party. This association foreclosed any U.S. cooperation with France on nuclear weapons development, both during and immediately after the war.[25]

Soon after the war, Joliot-Curie was placed in charge of the new Commissariat à l'Energie Atomique (1945–50), created by de Gaulle to direct French postwar nuclear research and development. Throughout the 1945–54 period, this effort consisted almost entirely of basic research and plans for commercial nuclear power development. Though certain influential French military officers expressed a strong interest in a nuclear weapons capability during this period, political leaders were, at least initially, more concerned with the postwar reconstruction of French economic and political infrastructures.

However, by 1954, the production of nuclear weapons and delivery systems was beginning to appear politically feasible. France's economy had recovered sufficiently to make the cost of such a program appear relatively attractive, given other budget priorities.

France's external relations also played a role in supporting the development of nuclear weapons. The British had already joined the United States and the Soviet Union in the nuclear club, and as a result, French officials were becoming increasingly sensitive to what they considered France's secondary status within NATO, particularly with respect to the British.

Also, France was involved in a costly and ultimately unsuccessful military effort to retain control of Indochina (1950–54). When France requested U.S. aid during the siege of Dien Bien Phu, the U.S. first considered using nuclear weapons to help break the siege, and then refused to provide any direct support at all. Finally, the U.S. decision to rearm West Germany and to bring it into NATO brought into sharp focus all of France's old fears of its traditional enemy.[26]

The debates in France over the production of nuclear weapons included inputs from influential French military officers. Among the many articles concerning nuclear weapons to appear at this time, the writings of General Pierre Gallois were the most influential. Gallois argued that once a nation that possessed nuclear weapons became vulnerable to nuclear attack from a potential enemy, its ability to extend a nuclear deterrent to cover its allies was eliminated. In other words, a nation that promised to defend its allies by risking a nuclear attack on itself was an unreliable ally; no political leader of such a country could be counted on to follow through on such a promise.

Gallois also argued that since nuclear offensive forces were likely to become increasingly invulnerable and hence unattractive targets for strategic retaliation, future nuclear deterrence would rest primarily on the countercity potential of a nation's nuclear arsenal. However, since the early 1980s, effective targeting of missile silos, air bases, and other non-mobile strategic forces has become a reality. Gallois' argument supporting a countercity strategy is therefore less persuasive today than it was during the 1950s. However, in the 1950s, Gallois' argument was remarkably consistent with the strategy that France eventually adopted for the potential use of its independent strategic nuclear arsenal.[27]

Gallois and other military officers were supported by political constituencies that favored French nuclear independence for other reasons. Such reasons included the following:

• Nuclear weapons were a symbol of national prestige.

- Nuclear weapons would provide France with greater leverage and input into NATO strategy, and would reverse the trend toward Anglo-American domination.
- Possession of nuclear weapons would provide France with greater international political leverage.
- Nuclear weapons would boost the morale of French military officers, which had been devastated by the experience of Dien Bien Phu.
- Nuclear weapons would give France a greater voice in international arms-control discussions between the East and the West.[28]

French opponents of nuclear weapons had their own set of arguments, which included the following:

- Nuclear weapons were immoral because of their indiscriminate destructiveness.
- The French economy was too weak to provide the resources necessary for a serious nuclear weapons program; it would therefore be more fruitful to develop a full-scale program for the peaceful uses of nuclear energy.
- France could afford only a primitive nuclear arsenal. Its delivery systems would not be capable of fulfilling either political or strategic objectives.
- The development of French nuclear forces would cause even greater political differences between France and the rest of NATO.[29]

In addition to military supporters, a substantial momentum had developed within French government bureaucracies to produce nuclear weapons, a momentum that could be overcome neither by public debate nor by the weak and politically indecisive governments of the Fourth Republic.

The nuclear debate in France was also influenced by France's perceived position within NATO. In the aftermath of World War II, French political and military planners saw two future threats to French security: the Soviet Union and West Germany. Throughout the late 1940s, France insisted on plans that took both potential threats into account. The Dunkirk Treaty of 1947 was directed against both the Soviet Union and Germany, and only because of American and Belgian intervention did the Brussels Pact of 1948, which established the Western European Union, avoid including anti-German language in its text.

Given its World War II experience, France was understandably sensitive about bringing West Germany into NATO. When the French government initiated discussions of a European Defense Community that would include West Germany, it suffered a severe political defeat at the hands of its own National Assembly. Its acquiescence to German entry into NATO in 1955 and to its subsequent rearmament was a grudging acceptance of several unpleasant realities: Anglo-American dominance of the NATO alliance; the military requirements of the defense of West Germany against Soviet expansion in Eastern Europe; and the growing Western acceptance of West Germany back into the family of democratic nations. However, France did exact a price for its acquiescence—the Bonn Government made a public commitment never to produce nuclear weapons on its own soil.

Capitulating to powerful military officers and bureaucrats and to other advocates of a French nuclear weapons program, the government of Guy Mollet (1956) made a secret formal commitment to proceed with a nuclear weapons program and established a committee within the Commissariat à l'Energie Atomique to implement this decision.[30]

Although the public arguments of Gallois and other military men may have appeared to be the main justification for the development of French nuclear forces, internal bureaucratic forces within the government and the perceived role of France within NATO were also important. In any event, the political leadership was so ineffectual during the last years of the Fourth Republic that elaborate political and strategic justifications were not needed to ensure the December 1956 decision. Strong personalities in the military and in the bureaucracies who supported the development of nuclear weapons were simply able to have their way, no matter what position was espoused by the leadership. How France would proceed with its nuclear weapons program was left for the Fifth Republic under de Gaulle (1958), who had a clear and compelling vision of the role of France in the world, and the strength to chart a new course consistent with this vision.[31]

Since 1958, France has developed nuclear weapons and delivery systems almost entirely within its own technological competence, and has evolved independent strategies for their use. The commitment to build up a triad of bombers and land and sea based ballistic missiles began with de Gaulle (1958) and continued unbroken through the Socialist administration of Francois Mitterrand, which took office in 1981. In fact, in the 1983 defense budget, the army was scaled down by seven percent to pay for France's very ambitious nuclear weapon and delivery systems programs.

The French Force Nucleaire Strategique (FNS) currently includes the Soutien Terre FNS (land-based missiles), the Force Aerienne Strategique FAS (longrange bomber force), and the Force Oceanique Stategique (missile submarine fleet). It also includes elements of the Gendarmerie FNS and Developements et Experimentations, which provide internal security and research and development, respectively.

The Soutien Terre FNS consists of two squadrons of missiles with nine missiles each, deployed in silos embedded in the rock of the Plateau d'Albion, with 140-ton concrete carapaces over each silo. These silos are designed to withstand the over-pressure of a one-megaton nuclear explosion less than a kilometer away. A mobile missile (SX) is under development.

As indicated in Chapter 2, the FAS has four squadrons of about 34 Mirage IVA bombers in its Strategic Air Force. These bombers are backed up by 11 KC-135 tankers. The bombers are armed with about 75 nuclear bombs, and are deployed at four main and five dispersal bases located in France. The Mirage IVAs will be replaced by new Mirage IVPs by the mid-1990s. These Mirages will be armed with air launched nuclear missiles. The French strategic bomber force is supplemented with 75 shorter-range Jaguar and Mirage IIIE fighter-bombers, armed with about 85 nuclear bombs, and 36 Super Etendards deployed on aircraft carriers with about 40 nuclear bombs.

The Force Oceanique Strategique is based on the Ile Longue Naval Base in Brest Bay, and includes five SSBNs, each with 16 M-20 missiles, each armed with a one-megaton warhead. A sixth submarine became operational in 1985 with a new missile, the M4, which carries six warheads. By 1992, the French will load the M4 into four of their six existing submarines. The M4 program will expand the French submarine force from today's 80 warheads to 496 warheads. France is also developing a fully MIRVed M5 missile and plans to build a seventh submarine, of a new design, to join the fleet in the mid 1990s. France also has the Armie Nucleaire Tactique, which includes five regiments equipped with six Pluton missiles with a range of 120 kilometers. These will be replaced in the early 1990s by a new battlefield missile called HADEs. By the mid-1990s, France will be able to strike over 500 targets in the Soviet Union with nuclear warheads.[32]

Prospects for the Future

Almost from its inception, NATO has largely relied on U.S. strategic nuclear forces, bolstered by U.S. tactical nuclear weapons based in Europe, to deter Soviet nuclear forces in Europe and the conventional capabilities of the Warsaw Pact nations. Yet European NATO nations have variously feared that the U.S. might not make good on its nuclear guarantee, or on the other hand, might do so and plunge Europe into a final nuclear catastrophe.

In December 1979, after months of negotiations, NATO agreed that five NATO nations would deploy U.S. Pershing II and GLCMs on their territory. These nations were Belgium, Italy, the Netherlands, West Germany, and the United Kingdom. This decision was touted as historic by U.S. policy makers, and was seen as a strengthening of the ties between the U.S. and its European allies. By 1986, 108 Pershing II and over 224 GLCM warheads were actually deployed.

Coincident with this deployment, the Soviet Union demonstrated a renewed interest in arms control negotiations. From the point of view of the United States, the Soviets have sought, through negotiations, to eliminate U.S. and other NATO nuclear forces that undermine Soviet offensive and defensive capabilities in Europe, while improving prospects for strategic trends that would be favorable to long-term Soviet objectives.

Despite speculation in the press, many analysts, particularly in the U.S. Department of Defense, believe that the Soviets have not changed their basic strategy toward NATO under Gorbachev (1988). This strategy remains the transformation of the political status quo in Western Europe to favor the Soviet Union. To achieve this, the Soviets will probably seek to:

• Preserve their considerable advantage in conventional forces in Europe;
• Weaken U.S. political and military ties to Western Europe;
• Encourage neutralist elements in West European nations, with special emphasis on anti-nuclear labor organizations, socialist political parties, and various peace groups; and
• Expand Soviet access to Western European credits, technology, and trade.

The U.S. Department of Defense and other analysts perceive that changes under Gorbachev are changes in short-term tactics rather than changes in long-term strategy. Such tactics have included attempts to forge links with West European nations based on geography (according to Gorbachev, "Europe is our common home"), the revival of prospects for a new detente with the United States, and an ambitious diplomatic campaign that includes a wide range of disarmament initiatives. These initiatives will continue to include efforts to decouple Western Europe from its alliance with the United States and to generate opposition to U.S. strategic programs that tend to nullify certain elements of Soviet conventional forces in Europe.[33]

After the INF treaty is fully implemented, the remaining nuclear forces in Europe will still show a decided NATO advantage in warheads. However, future reductions could create a Soviet advantage because Soviet conventional forces would no longer be offset by superior U.S., British, and French tactical nuclear forces dedicated to NATO.

The future demand for independent West European nuclear forces will depend, to a large extent, on the results of U.S.-Soviet disarmament negotiations. If the West Europeans perceive that U.S.-Soviet treaties will result in a decreased U.S. commitment to use nuclear forces to defend Western Europe, one alternative would be for the West Europeans to continue their current plans for strategic nuclear forces and to increase their conventional forces to match the Warsaw Pact. However, with the exception of the British, European NATO nations have been reluctant to increase their defense budgets to levels necessary to finance a massive buildup of conventional forces. Thus, as an alternative response to U.S.-Soviet nuclear disarmament, the West Europeans could increase the number of tactical nuclear weapons in their independent nuclear arsenals as a more cost-effective method of countering the Soviet conventional threat. Such a buildup would surely involve both British and French nuclear forces, and could also result in greater bilateral cooperation between the British, the French and West Germans in terms of military strategy and possibly, cooperation with regard to tactical nuclear weapon deployment. Of course, the West Europeans have a third alternative, and that is to accept Soviet military superiority and possibly the eventual Soviet domination of all of Europe.

Notes

1. There are a number of references that provide details. For example, see Schwartz, D. N., *NATO's Nuclear Dilemmas*, Brookings Institution, Washington, DC, 1983, 13–15. Also see Dean, J., *Watershed in Europe*, Lexington Books, Lexington, MA, 1987, 5–11.

2. Mazour, A. G., *Russia: Tsarist and Communist*, Van Nostrand Company, Inc., Princeton, NJ, 1962, 835.

3. Ibid., 835–836.

4. Ibid., 836.

5. Schwartz, *NATO's Nuclear Dilemmas*, 14.

6. Huntington, S., *The Common Defence: Strategic Programs in National Politics*, Columbia University Press, New York, 1961, 35–36; also see Schwartz, *NATO's Nuclear Dilemmas*, 14.

7. Mazour, *Russia: Tsarist and Communist*, 849; also see Churchill, W., *Triumph and Tragedy*, Houghton Mifflin Press, Boston, MA, 1953.

8. Mazour, *Russia: Tsarist and Communist*, 849.

9. Ibid.

10. Gowing, M., *Britain and Atomic Energy, 1939–1945*, MacMillian, London, 1964. Also see Pierre, A. J., *Nuclear Politics: the British Experience with an Independent Strategic Force, 1939–70*, Oxford University Press, London, 1972.

11. Quester, G., *Nuclear Diplomacy: The First Twenty-Five Years*, Dunellen, New York, 1970, 26–29; also see Schwartz, *NATO's Nuclear Dilemmas*, 17.

12. Osgood, R.E., *NATO: The Entangling Alliance*, University of Chicago Press, Chicago, IL, 1962; also see Schwartz, *NATO's Nuclear Dilemmas*, 18.

13. Department of State, *Foreign Relations of the United States 1950*, vol. 1: National Security Affairs; also see "Assignment of Ground Forces of the United States to Duty in the European Area," *Senate Hearings, 82 Congress, 2 Session*, U.S. Government Printing Office, Washington, DC, 1951, and Schwartz, *NATO's Nuclear Dilemmas*, 19.

14. Schwartz, *NATO's Nuclear Dilemmas*, 20.

15. According to Schwartz, several volumes of Project Vista have been declassified, and provide valuable insight on early U.S. nuclear planning.

16. Schwartz, *NATO's Nuclear Dilemmas*, 22–26.

17. See "Report to the National Security Council on Basic National Security Policy," *NSC 162/2*, referenced by Schwartz, *NATO's Nuclear Dilemmas*.

18. Ibid., 24.

19. See several U.S. Department of Defense Annual Reports to Congress, 1976–1989; also see Schwartz, *NATO's Nuclear Dilemmas,* 25–26.

20. Gowing, *Britain and Atomic Energy,* 1939–1945, 33–42; also see Schwartz, *NATO's Nuclear Dilemmas,* 26.

21. Gowing, *Britain and Atomic Energy,* 1939–1945, 147–177.

22. Schwartz, *NATO's Nuclear Dilemmas,* 27.

23. Campbell, C., *Nuclear Facts,* Hamlyn Publishing Group, Limited, London, 1984, 162–167.

24. Ibid., 162–167.

25. Scheinman, L., *Atomic Energy Policy in France Under the Fourth Republic,* Princeton University Press, Princeton, NJ, 1965; also see Kohl, W., *French Nuclear Diplomacy,* Princeton University, Press, Princeton, NJ, 1971, and finally, see Schwartz, *NATO's Nuclear Dilemmas,* 36–41.

26. Osgood, R., *The Case for the MLF: A Critical Evaluation,* Washington Center of Foreign Policy, Washington, DC, 1964; also see Schwartz, *NATO's Nuclear Dilemmas,* 36–41.

27. See Schwartz, *NATO's Nuclear Dilemmas,* 37, and footnote 5.

28. Kelly, G., "The Political Background of the French A-Bomb," *Orbis,* vol. 4, (Fall 1960); also see Schwartz, *NATO's Nuclear Dilemmas,* 36–41.

29. Ibid.

30. Scheinman, *Atomic Energy Policy in France Under the Fourth Republic;* Kohl, *French Nuclear Diplomacy;* and Schwartz, *NATO's Nuclear Dilemmas,* 39.

31. Schwartz, *NATO's Nuclear Dilemmas,* 40–41.

32. See Chapter 2 for details.

33. See Carlucci, F., *Soviet Military Power: An Assessment of the Threat 1988,* U.S. Government Printing Office, Washington, DC, April 1988.

4

Nuclear Proliferation

The Nuclear Weapon Club

The United States, the Soviet Union, the United Kingdom, France, and China are not the only nations that have the capability to produce nuclear weapons. Several other NATO nations, plus Sweden and Japan, could quickly develop and produce nuclear weapons if they chose to do so. This capability is not restricted to Europe and Japan. For example, India exploded a nuclear device in 1974 that used reprocessed plutonium from one of its nuclear reactors. This reactor was ostensibly designed for the peaceful generation of electrical energy. Although India has stated that it does not intend to develop nuclear weapons, it clearly has the capability to do so.

This chapter explores the evolving problem of nuclear weapons proliferation. This topic is of vital importance because the possession of nuclear weapons by nations that have a recent history of conflict adds to the risk of at least a regional nuclear war. The discussion includes an overview of the political and military incentives of nations that have a high potential for developing nuclear weapons. It also includes a brief analysis of the implications of proliferation for the nations that are currently members of the nuclear weapons club.

Nuclear Weapon Proliferation

It is widely accepted by military analysts that several nations are on the threshold of developing nuclear weapons. Some are suspected of having clandestinely developed small stockpiles of fission-based nuclear bombs deliverable by aircraft. Aside from India, Pakistan, Israel and South Africa are suspected of having already developed a nuclear weapon capability. Several other non-European nations have the sophisticated technology necessary to build nuclear weapons within a relatively short period of time. Nations in this category include Iraq, Brazil, Argentina, Taiwan, South Korea, and perhaps others.[1]

Some nations with incipient capabilities to produce nuclear weapons are in regions of endemic political instability: India and Pakistan in Southern Asia, Israel and Iraq in the Middle East, and white-ruled South Africa. In each region, there are clearly identifiable and persistent sources of inter-nation conflict and domestic unrest. For example, India's nuclear capability has caused a great deal of consternation on the part of Pakistan, India's traditional opponent in several border wars over the past 40 years. On the other side, Pakistan has indicated that it has the capability to quickly assemble nuclear warheads for use against India. While these two nations are not likely to directly threaten the United States, the Soviet Union, Europe, or Japan, any conflict involving nuclear weapons could have worldwide political repercussions that could cause superpower confrontation.

The problems of nuclear proliferation are related to national security, international diplomacy, and domestic politics. Incentives to acquire nuclear weapons include: the desire to provide a 'deterrent' against attack by a regional opponent, the desire to maintain national sovereignty by defeating an enemy in the event of war, and the desire to enhance both foreign and domestic political prestige and negotiating power.

There are international agreements that limit access to nuclear weapons by nations that are not members of the nuclear weapons club. The primary agreement is the 1968 Non-Proliferation Treaty (NPT). Largely the work of the United States, the Soviet Union, and the United Kingdom, the treaty divides the world into nuclear weapon states (the United States, the Soviet Union, the United Kingdom, France, and China) and non-nuclear weapon states (all other nations). The NPT promises full access to peaceful nuclear technology, subject to international safeguards, to all nations that promise not to build nuclear weapons. Article I bars parties to the treaty from helping non-nuclear nations to obtain nuclear weapon materials. Article II prohibits nonnuclear member nations from building or acquiring nuclear weapons. Article III requires parties to the treaty to accept safeguards on fissionable material suitable for use in nuclear weapons. Article III also makes the International Atomic Energy Agency (IAEA) responsible for managing the safeguard system. Article IV guarantees the right of all parties to the treaty to develop facilities for the peaceful use of nuclear energy, and obligates all parties to facilitate the exchange of nuclear equipment, materials and scientific information for peaceful uses. Article V goes even further and extends the right to use nuclear energy—even nuclear explosives—for peaceful purposes, including mineral extraction or large-scale engineering projects such as canal construction. However, all member nations must employ peaceful nuclear explosives only through an 'appropriate international body,' i.e., the IAEA. Article VI pledges all parties to the treaty to negotiate in good faith on measures to cease the nuclear arms race and to reduce and eventually eliminate all nuclear weapons. By 1988, 137 nations had ratified the treaty.

Notable exceptions include France, China, Israel, India, South Africa, Argentina, Brazil, and Cuba.[2]

Safeguards administered by the IAEA have several objectives: to account for nuclear materials; to make sure that they are not used for military purposes, and to detect any diversion of nuclear materials to military or unknown purposes. These safeguards include a system of regulations and procedures that check and cross-check the records and physical plants of nuclear facilities. IAEA reports cover all nuclear material production and all significant changes in the location of nuclear materials.

Safeguards are applied to a wide range of materials and facilities. Most materials under safeguards would have to be further processed in other facilities before they could be diverted for use in weapons. Where fissionable materials are contained in discrete items such as reactor fuel rods, accountability is relatively straightforward. Where materials are in undifferentiated bulk form such as a liquid solution or a gas, the problems of measurement can be very complex. Measurement and verification are accomplished by surveillance of key locations with monitoring cameras and other instrumentation; physical inspections; sampling and observation; and the use of seals and other techniques to ensure that no unreported movement of materials has occurred.

Until the mid-1970s, the physical security of both military and civilian nuclear facilities was considered the exclusive responsibility of the nations that owned the facilities. However, the rise in international terrorism during the 1970s raised questions about the adequacy of existing security procedures and the international consequences of failure. Following a declaration on the urgency of the security problem at the 1975 NPT review conference, the IAEA published recommendations on the levels of physical protection for both nuclear materials and facilities. The IAEA also published guidelines for physical protection of nuclear exports. The United States and other nations took steps to bring their regulatory requirements into line with these recommendations.

More recently, the IAEA negotiated the Convention for the Physical Protection of Nuclear Materials (1980). This convention now stands as the principal international instrument for dealing with the threat of subnational (terrorist) proliferation. The convention seeks to ensure adequate physical protection of nuclear materials during international transport, provides for international cooperation in protecting threatened nuclear materials, and ensures the recovery and return of materials that may be seized or stolen. Finally, the convention obligates its parties to enact criminal penalties for such activities as the theft of nuclear materials; unauthorized possession, use, transfer, alteration or disposal of such materials; or the threat to use nuclear materials for purposes of blackmail. This convention was opened for signature in 1980, and has been signed by 37 nations, including the United States and the Soviet Union.

However, the NPT and IAEA have little control over non-member nations that seek to develop their own nuclear weapons. Advocates for such development programs (India in particular) have argued that the NPT is inherently discriminatory because it preserves the right of nations that already have nuclear weapons to retain their nuclear arsenals, but denies the right of nations without nuclear weapons to acquire them. Also, the NPT specifies that members with nuclear weapons have agreed to substantially reduce their nuclear forces—an action they have thus far failed to honor. Thus, nations that profess the discrimination argument may decide in favor of or against obtaining nuclear weapons on the basis of whether the current nuclear powers decide to increase or to reduce their nuclear stockpiles.

Nations with incipient capabilities to produce nuclear weapons might find such weapons useful as a response to a potential nuclear rival. For example, Pakistan has clearly been influenced by India's nuclear program, and Iraq has been influenced both by the likely nuclear weapon capability of Israel and by the conventional military capabilities of Iran.

On the other hand, there are powerful disincentives to acquiring nuclear weapons. These include cost (tens of billions of dollars for research, testing, development, and deployment of weapons and delivery systems); the demanding technical requirements of weapon design and production; the operational problems of deploying effective and survivable nuclear forces; and in some countries the problem of overcoming intense and vocal domestic opposition to nuclear weapons. One or more of these reasons have so far dissuaded the nations of Europe (except Britain and France) and Japan from joining the nuclear weapons club.

In spite of the costs, India, Pakistan, Israel, and South Africa have demonstrated the technological capability and political willingness to develop nuclear weapons, and are therefore the most likely additions to the nuclear weapons club in the 1990s. Indeed, there is evidence that three of the four may already have small stockpiles of nuclear bombs suitable for delivery by aircraft, and all four have aircraft that are capable of delivering such weapons on targets in adjacent countries.[3]

The incipient nuclear weapon capabilities of the above four nations are of growing political concern to the United States and to the other major nuclear powers because the existence of such weapons in the politically volatile regions of Southern Asia, the Middle East, and Southern Africa adds to inherent regional instability. Further, these regions are of prime strategic concern to the United States and to the Soviet Union: Southern Asia because of its enormous population and India's capability for regional military dominance; the Middle East because of the military capabilities of Israel, Iraq and other nations, the periodic Arab-Israeli conflicts, and the fact that many Arab nations are a major source of oil; and Southern Africa because of its explosive racial problems, its strategic location adjacent to major sea lanes, and its value as the primary Western source of key minerals.

Proliferation in Southern Asia

India's relations with the United States have been cool since the mid-1950s, when Prime Minister Jawaharlal Nehru began to steer the recently independent India on a relatively neutral course between the superpower alliances. The U.S. did not help relations when U.S. Secretary of State John Foster Dulles developed an alliance with Pakistan, India's traditional enemy, as a member of an anti-communist alliance in Southern Asia. Also, India's persistent rivalry with China, which erupted in war in 1962 and persists in terms of periodic border clashes, drew India closer to the Soviet Union, particularly after the Sino-Soviet rift that began in the early 1960s. Thus, current Indian foreign policy includes confrontation with Pakistan and China, relative harmony in her relations with the Soviet Union, and friction in her relations with the United States.[4]

The friction with the United States intensified in 1971 when the U.S. openly favored Pakistan in the India-Pakistan war. A U.S. naval task force, headed by the aircraft carrier Enterprise, was sent into the Bay of Bengal, primarily to deter India from finishing off the military forces of West Pakistan after India had wrested East Pakistan from the control of the government in Islamabad. (East Pakistan soon became Bangladesh, a client state closely associated with India.) This U.S. interference left an indelible mark on Indian attitudes towards the United States.[5]

Motivated primarily by its perennial conflicts with Pakistan and China and its reaction to U.S. interference in regional affairs, India developed and detonated a nuclear device in 1974.[6] Since the detonation, other sources of U.S.-Indian friction have included the issue of U.S. nuclear fuel supplies for the Indian reactor at Tarapur, India's peacekeeping role in the civil war in Sri Lanka (Ceylon), and most importantly, U.S. connivance with Pakistan in support of the Afghan rebel forces that are battling the Soviet-supported government in Kabul.

Although relations between the United States and India have remained cool and occasionally acrimonious, they have not been adversarial. The Indian capability to produce nuclear weapons and the prospects for a full-fledged Indian nuclear force have yet to seriously damage cultural, economic, or nonnuclear scientific ties with the United States. Further, both India and Pakistan retain strong political, economic, and scientific ties with Great Britain, which granted independence to both nations in 1947. These ties have helped to maintain cordial relationships between the relatively new nations of the Indian subcontinent and the West Europeans, and they also provide diplomatic channels for the resolution of periodic disputes.

Perhaps the primary result of India's nuclear detonation in 1974 was the possible development of a nuclear weapon capability by the Pakistani government in Islamabad. Indeed, statements by President Zia in 1987 and 1988 indicated that Pakistan may already have a small stockpile of nuclear bombs in the form of easily assembled components.[7] According to Zia, such weapons, if they exist, provide a deterrent against India. Although it is not certain what course recently elected President Bhutto (November 1988) will follow with regard to nuclear weapons, any serious threat against the sovereignty of Pakistan, such as the threat that occurred in the 1971 war that resulted in the loss of East Pakistan, would provide strong incentives for the use of nuclear weapons against military targets in India. Of course, any use of such weapons by Pakistan would probably result in nuclear retaliation by India. Such a regional nuclear conflict would have global political repercussions, including potential superpower confrontation.

Whether Pakistan will deploy nuclear weapons is uncertain. It already has the capability to develop and produce nuclear weapons, including a stockpile of plutonium or weapons-grade enriched uranium, and it will certainly continue research on the design and fabrication of nuclear weapons. Indeed, Pakistan may have already covertly fabricated and stockpiled nuclear weapon components, stopping just short of final assembly, and it is possible that Pakistan has a small stockpile of assembled nuclear weapons.

The covert acquisition of untested or unassembled nuclear weapons just short of full-fledged deployment might satisfy most of Pakistan's incentives for joining the nuclear weapons club. Rumored possession of untested nuclear weapons may be sufficient to establish a deterrent relationship with India, assuage the demand by military leaders for a nuclear weapons capability, and establish Pakistan as a major player in the Moslem world.

Nevertheless, Pakistan's military leaders may persuade the government to push ahead with nuclear tests, and they may also demand a full-fledged deployment of nuclear weapons. In the 1990s, much will depend upon Pakistan's perceptions of how the acquisition and deployment of nuclear weapons would affect its political, economic and security relationships with the United States. Thus, the U.S. is likely to have substantial influence with regard to Pakistan's potential nuclear weapons activities.

It is interesting to note that India's nuclear test in 1974 was not followed by a decision to produce nuclear weapons. By 1977, the Indian government of Prime Minister Desai had stopped India's nuclear weapons program. The initial response of both the Desai government and that of Indira Gandhi (who returned to power in 1980) to Pakistan's efforts to acquire nuclear weapons included 'watchful waiting,' and warnings of readiness to carry out 'without hesitation' further nuclear explosions if national interest so demanded.[8] The limited threat posed by Pakistan's technical capabilities, and the potential international political and economic costs of resuming India's nuclear weapons program all contributed to continued restraint.

By 1981, pressures for India to restart its nuclear weapons program began to increase. Indian government warnings of a readiness to resume testing became more frequent, while there were reports of renewed activity at India's Pokharan nuclear test site. Even so, Indian responses to perceived Pakistani provocations have been restrained under the leadership of Prime Minister Rajiv Gandhi (1984–present). However, if Pakistan detonates a nuclear explosive device or there is unmistakable evidence that Pakistan has a stockpile of nuclear weapons, India would probably resume its program with the avowed purpose of developing a full-fledged nuclear force. It is also quite possible that India would follow the Israeli example with Iraq, and employ surgical air strikes against Pakistan's nuclear research and development facilities.

In addition to Pakistan, India will continue to be strongly influenced by China's growing nuclear weapons capabilities and conventional force modernization programs. India may decide to deploy a 'deterrent' nuclear force to oppose China's conventional forces that are deployed in critical areas along India's northern border. All of the components needed for an Indian nuclear weapons program are in place: ready access to significant quantities of indigenous nuclear explosive materials, medium range bombers and missiles developed from India's space program, sophisticated electronics production capabilities, trained manpower, and organizational skills. If India decides to resume its nuclear weapons program, it will place nearly irresistible pressure on Pakistan to produce and deploy nuclear weapons. Disincentives to doing so are likely to be outweighed by the perceived risks of doing nothing.

The Middle East: Nuclear Weapons in a Tinderbox

Prior to the 1967 Arab-Israeli war, France and other West European nations were the primary suppliers of arms to Israel. However, the Middle East policies of West European nations, particularly France, shifted dramatically after the war, due primarily to the overwhelming dependence of Western Europe on Arab oil supplies. Since 1967, the United States has been Israel's primary supplier of arms and economic assistance.

U.S.-Israeli relations since 1967 have been extremely complex. The U.S. has tried to influence Israeli behavior to promote U.S. strategic interests in the Middle East, including the limitation of Soviet influence, the maintenance of suitable relations with Arab oil-producing nations, and the preservation of Israel as an independent state. On the other hand, Israel has tried to manipulate U.S. military, political and economic support to promote Israel's perceived security interests, including its long term conflicts with the Palestine Liberation Organization and with Arab oil-producing nations.

Rumors of Israeli nuclear weapons have been widespread since the 1967 war, and are usually associated with weapon-grade fission material that may have been produced at the Dimona nuclear research facility in the Negev desert. While U.S. leaders have long been aware of the Israeli nuclear research program, this knowledge apparently did not directly influence U.S. policy toward Israel until after the October 1973 war. After 1973, U.S. willingness to resupply Israel with vast amounts of conventional arms was tied directly to the fear that Israel, seeing itself on the verge of defeat in some future conflict, would resort to the use of nuclear weapons.[9]

More likely than not, Israel has already produced a small number of assembled or nearly assembled nuclear bombs. As early as 1974, the U.S. Central Intelligence Agency concluded that Israel had nuclear weapons. The circumstantial evidence to support this conclusion includes Israel's reported clandestine acquisition of weapons-grade uranium, its refusal to allow IAEA inspection of the Dimona research facility, Israeli intelligence leaks about the assembling of nuclear bombs during the first days of the October 1973 war, its tough-minded readiness to take all steps necessary for its defense, its production of missiles designed to accommodate nuclear warheads, Israeli air force exercises of tactics for dropping nuclear bombs, and possible Israeli access to data from France's nuclear weapons tests. Also, in June 1981, former Israeli Defense and Foreign Minister Moshe Dayan acknowledged that Israel had the capability to build nuclear bombs.[10]

There are compelling incentives for Israel to covertly acquire nuclear weapons. These include the desire to hedge against unexpected military reverses or shifts in the Israeli-Arab balance of power, the deterrent effect of Israeli possession of nuclear weapons upon Arab leaders, and a belief in the value of last-resort nuclear weapons, either to deter direct Soviet military intervention or to induce U.S. military assistance lest nuclear weapons be used in the Middle East. Continuing U.S. sales of high-performance aircraft and other advanced military equipment to Egypt and Saudi Arabia are seen by Israeli leaders as lessening Israel's present conventional military superiority with regard to its neighbors. This has increased the pressure for Israel to demonstrate an overt nuclear capability. However, the greatest incentive for such a demonstration is the fact that by the mid-1990s, one or more Arab nations may have the capability to produce nuclear weapons.

To forestall such developments in Iraq, the Israelis attacked and destroyed Iraq's nuclear research reactor at Osirak on June 7, 1981.[11] This raid disrupted what both Israeli and U.S. officials increasingly believed was an attempt by Iraq—using its leverage as an oil supplier—to acquire the necessary components and materials for a nuclear weapons program under the cover of building up peaceful nuclear research facilities.

This raid, carried out by squadrons of Israeli F-15 and F-16 fighter aircraft supplied by the United States, was the first direct military action any nation had ever taken to prevent another nation from developing nuclear weapons. It unleashed a storm of controversy about the integrity of the NPT and the IAEA safeguard system. The IAEA treated the raid as a direct assault on the integrity of the agency. Less than a week after the raid, the IAEA board of directors voted that Israel should be considered for suspension from the agency. Later in the year, IAEA members voted narrowly to deny Israel's credentials to attend the next agency meeting. This move provoked the United States to temporarily suspend funding for the IAEA, and this was taken by agency officials as a threat to the survival of the safeguard system. Since then, U.S. funding has been restored, and so have Israel's credentials.

Israel's raid delayed but probably did not end Iraq's apparent quest for nuclear weapons. Even if the nuclear reactor at Osirak is not rebuilt, Iraq may pursue a secret project to build a plutonium production reactor by making use of its nuclear ties to France and Italy, and by buying 'gray market' nuclear components, materials, or expertise.[12]

It is likely that the Iraqi government believes that the acquisition of nuclear weapons is an appropriate response to Israel's possession of nuclear weapons. Possession of even untested nuclear weapons might deter nuclear blackmail by Israel, and could be viewed as a useful diplomatic tool in Middle East affairs.

Other Middle East nations have also been suspected of activities related to the development of nuclear weapons. Although Iran's extremely ambitious civilian nuclear program under the late Shah was suspended by the Khomeini government, there were reports in 1982–85 that Iran engaged in negotiations with West European nations for the completion of one or more nuclear reactors begun under the Shah.[13] However, the likely response of Iraq, Israel, and other Gulf nations to an overt Iranian nuclear weapons program will probably continue to keep any such activity under wraps. Also, the present Iranian government under the Moslem fundamentalist mullahs has strong religious doctrines that may continue to inhibit the development of the sophisticated technologies required for a nuclear weapons program.

Although Libya is a party to the NPT, there have been indications that Libya too has sought nuclear weapons. Using its leverage as an oil supplier, Libya tried unsuccessfully throughout the late 1970s and early 1980s to pressure India into providing sensitive technology and expertise for a nuclear weapons program. There have also been persistent reports (of uncertain credibility) that Libya funded Pakistan's enrichment program. These activities, coupled with Libya's open support for terrorist organizations, justify greater concern about Libya's intentions with regard to nuclear weapons than would otherwise be indicated by its immediate technical capabilities to produce such weapons.[14] A Libyan nuclear weapons program would substantially increase the pressure on Israel to intervene as it did with Iraq. Such a program might also increase the pressure on Egypt to cooperate with Israel to stop the Libyans from acquiring a nuclear weapons capability.

Although Egypt has a nuclear research reactor and could conceivably develop a nuclear explosive device in the 1990s, it is unlikely to do so. Any such development would almost certainly provoke a strong military reaction by Israel, and would immediately end the Egyptian-Israeli rapprochement that began with the Camp David agreements (1978). Also, the United States has become Egypt's major supplier of economic and military aid since the late 1970s, and would have substantial leverage to convince Egypt not to develop nuclear weapons. Finally, the Egyptian government signed the NPT, although the treaty was not ratified.[15]

South Africa and the Bomb

In August 1977, photographs taken by both Soviet and U.S. intelligence satellites revealed an apparent nuclear weapons test site in the Kalahari Desert. These photographs spurred widespread fears of an imminent South African nuclear weapons test that would use enriched weapons-grade uranium produced in South Africa's enrichment facility. A combined U.S., British, French, West German, and Soviet diplomatic effort was mounted to head off the apparent planned test. In response to this effort, the South African government indicated that it did not intend to develop nuclear explosive devices either for peaceful uses or as weapons. However, shortly thereafter, South African Prime Minister Vorster denied having provided such assurances, saying that ". . . as far as South Africa is concerned, we are only interested in peaceful development of nuclear facilities."[16]

On September 22, 1979, a U.S. VELA satellite, designed to monitor compliance with the 1963 ban on atmospheric testing of nuclear weapons, detected two bright pulses of light in the South Atlantic. The sequence and timing of these pulses closely resembled the signature of a nuclear weapon detonation. But in spite of an intense search by the United States and several other nations, no other unambiguous physical evidence of a nuclear test—such as radioactive debris, passage of a shock wave, electromagnetic radiation, individual eyewitness reports, or radiation in the upper atmosphere—was discovered.[17]

Nevertheless, it is possible that a nuclear test did occur without such confirming evidence. An expert panel set up by President Carter to resolve the·matter described a chain of highly improbable natural circumstances that could explain the double flash, but the panel also admitted that its explanation was not fully credible. The Central Intelligence Agency, the Defense Intelligence Agency, certain scientists at U.S. nuclear weapons laboratories, and the Navy's Oceanographic Laboratory disputed the panel's findings. To date, the initial presumption that a nuclear explosive test occurred remains neither proved or disproved.[18]

Rumored possession of tested nuclear weapons is a useful bargaining tool for the South African government. Western opposition to the demands of black-ruled African nations for the diplomatic and economic isolation of white-ruled South Africa derives, in part, from concern that one consequence of such isolation would be South Africa's overt testing and deployment of nuclear weapons. Also, such rumors signal the Soviet Union and black-ruled African nations that the risks and costs of military action against South Africa may be high. South African deployment of a small nuclear force capable of striking neighboring nations would visibly demonstrate its readiness to resist with all means the demands for black majority rule in South Africa.

Thus, the present state of uncertainty about South Africa's nuclear intentions serves the South African government well in the short term. Its opponents cannot be certain that if the destruction of white-rule appears imminent, South Africa's leaders might take desperate actions. This uncertainty has a tendency to forestall direct military action by the Soviet Union, Cuban troops in Africa, and adjacent black-ruled nations.

The deployment and potential use of South African nuclear weapons have associated risks. Such a deployment would probably cause a complete breakdown of South Africa's long standing efforts to develop closer security ties with Western nations. South African use of nuclear weapons against Cuban or Soviet forces would probably result in devastating retaliation by the Soviet Union.

For the foreseeable future, South Africa will probably keep its potential regional nuclear monopoly. Any effort by black-ruled African nations to obtain and deploy nuclear weapons will be hindered by their limited technical, scientific, industrial, and military infrastructures.

In the long term, the emerging 'Fortress South Africa' defense strategy of the white South African government—the tightening of the laager to meet both external and internal threats—also involves risks. These include increased diplomatic and economic isolation, increased legitimacy for Soviet or Soviet sponsored military intervention, and continued internal unrest. As part of this strategy. nuclear weapons cannot solve South Africa's problems associated with white minority dominance over a disenfranchised black majority population.

Latin America: The First Nuclear Free Zone

The Treaty for the Prohibition of Nuclear Weapons in Latin America, generally known as the Treaty of Tlatelolco, provides the foundation for the world's first nuclear free zone. The treaty was adopted in Mexico City in 1967, following several years of negotiations.[19]

Parties to the Treaty of Tlatelolco, like parties to the NPT, agreed to use nuclear energy exclusively for peaceful purposes. Also like the NPT, the Treaty of Tlatelolco calls for verification of non-proliferation pledges by the IAEA. However, the treaty also relies on a special organization, the Agency for the Prohibition of Nuclear Weapons in Latin America (OPANAL), which has the authority to conduct inspections in member nations if a charge is made that a party may be violating its commitments under the treaty.

Twenty-five Latin American nations have signed and ratified the Treaty of Tlatelolco (1988). One conspicuous exception is Cuba. All five nations with arsenals of nuclear weapons have ratified the treaty's Protocol II, in which they promise not to use or threaten to use nuclear weapons against full parties of the treaty. The United States, the United Kingdom, and the Netherlands have also ratified Protocol I, which bars them from introducing nuclear weapons on the soil of their Latin American possessions or in areas of territorial control. France, the only other outside nation with territorial interest in Latin America, has signed but not ratified Protocol I.[20]

Until 1986, Argentina and Brazil, Latin America's two largest countries, consistently refused to sign the Treaty of Tlatelolco. For many years, Argentine governments worked to develop a nuclear fuel cycle based on reactors fueled by natural rather then enriched uranium. According to many experts, the natural uranium fuel cycle is the most efficient and economical route to a nuclear weapons capability. In the mid-1970s, Brazil made a deal with West Germany to purchase eight nuclear power plants, a reprocessing facility, and enrichment technology, despite its enormous potential for producing electricity with hydroelectric facilities. Since the mid-1980s, both Argentina and Brazil have reduced their nuclear ambitions due to preoccupation with domestic matters, including political unrest and enormous public and private debt burdens, primarily to foreign banks.

Both Brazil and Argentina signed the Treaty of Tlatelolco in 1986. However, their respective ambitions with regard to nuclear capabilities have not been renounced, and may have only been deferred. It is entirely conceivable that both countries could actively pursue nuclear weapons programs in the 1990s, and both could have small stockpiles of nuclear weapons by the end of the decade.[21]

For the foreseeable future, technological constraints will continue to inhibit Cuba from developing meaningful programs to produce nuclear weapons. Although Cuba could conceivably obtain technology, facilities or actual nuclear weapons from the Soviet Union, such an occurrence seems highly unlikely. The Soviets have always been extremely careful about restricting nuclear weapons to their own military forces, and have always excluded Warsaw Pact and other allied nations from nuclear weapons technology in any form. Besides, any such activity with regard to Cuba would undoubtedly provoke a strong reaction from the United States. Given current Soviet policies with regard to the INF treaty and arms limitation talks, provoking the United States by nuclear activities in Cuba would be counter-productive.

Other Nations with Potential
Nuclear Weapon Capabilities

While the present pattern of events indicate that India, Pakistan, Israel and South Africa are the most likely nations to join the nuclear weapons club in the immediate future, Taiwan and South Korea also have strong incentives to develop nuclear weapons. In 1975, Taiwan's President Chiang Chin-Kuo acknowledged that studies and preparations for a nuclear weapons program were begun by his nation in the late 1950s and that by 1974, Taiwan had acquired the technical capability to manufacture nuclear weapons.[22] South Korea's initial efforts to acquire a nuclear weapons capability were apparently triggered in 1970, when the United States announced that one division of U.S. ground troops would be withdrawn from South Korea. The Korean Weapons Exploitation Committee was formed, and it voted to go ahead with the development of nuclear weapons.[23]

Taiwan's nuclear weapons program began as a response to China's nuclear capability, but increasingly it became a hedge against erosion of security ties with the United States. However, under economic and political pressure from the U.S., and fearful of provoking further erosion, Taiwan terminated its nuclear weapons program in 1977. It agreed to close and seal an experimental plutonium reprocessing facility that reportedly had secretly reprocessed small quantities of spent fuel. Taiwan also agreed not to engage in future activities related to reprocessing, and accepted restrictions on the use of its 40 megawatt nuclear research reactor—a type that had produced the nuclear explosive material for India's 1974 nuclear test. Apparently, the residual U.S. security guarantee and concerns about jeopardizing economic and political ties with the U.S. have sufficed to keep Taiwan from further nuclear weapons development activities.[24]

South Korea's initial attempt to develop nuclear weapons was primarily intended as a bargaining chip to stave off future U.S. troop withdrawals, and as a hedge in case such withdrawals continued. In late 1975, the United States, with Canadian support, successfully brought strong pressure on South Korea to terminate its nuclear weapons activities.[25]

Renewed interest by South Korea in developing nuclear weapons is one possible outcome of the current political unrest in South Korea. Political opposition groups have demanded a lessening of security ties with the United States and the withdrawal of U.S. troops. Although these groups apparently do not have strong support among most South Koreans, they may be able, over the next few years, to bring enough pressure to bear to cause the government to ask the U.S. to reduce its presence in South Korea, including the present arrangement where South Korean military forces are in effect under the command of the senior U.S. commander in South Korea. If the South Korean military should become more independent and gain more responsibilities for defense against North Korea, the pressure for South Korea to re-establish its nuclear weapons program would be intense.

Even if Taiwan or South Korea resume their nuclear weapons programs, this would not necessarily cause similar action by others in the region. Because of North Korea's more modest nuclear, industrial and technical base, it would not be able to match South Korea's nuclear weapons program in the foreseeable future, and it is unlikely that the Soviet Union or China would support a North Korean nuclear weapons program. Also, despite some speculation, a South Korean decision to develop nuclear weapons would probably not overcome Japan's strong inhibitions about starting its own nuclear weapons effort.

The Terrorist Threat

The trend of terrorist activity over the past 15 years (1973–88) has been unmistakably upward. As the number of incidents has increased, terrorism has also become more severe. Terrorists have acquired new capabilities and have demonstrated a greater willingness to kill. Perhaps even more disturbing, certain governments have become their accomplices. This is especially true with regard to the current (1988) governments of Libya and Iran.[26]

As indicated in Chapter 1, a nuclear explosive device could be obtained by a terrorist raid on one of the thousands of warhead stockpiles throughout the world, by hijacking a ship or an aircraft that carries nuclear weapons, or by obtaining fissionable materials and actually building a nuclear device. Terrorists could also sabotage nuclear power plants, causing widespread radioactivity, or hijack radioactive waste on its way to a disposal site and use it to contaminate water supplies or other elements of the environment.

In the past, terrorists often staged unexpected and dramatic incidents, and as a result, repeatedly caught governments, especially in the West, with their defensive guards down. The limited ability of governments to prevail during terrorist incidents in the past is cause for concern with regard to possible incidents involving nuclear materials. Although the possibility of U.S.-Soviet nuclear confrontation and the problem of nuclear proliferation among nations overshadow the potential problem of nuclear terrorism, it is possible for a terrorist related nuclear incident to cause substantial devastation and loss of life. Further, a nuclear incident involving terrorists could conceivably cause a confrontation between nuclear powers, especially in the Middle East, where several nuclear powers have substantial political and economic interests. That a nuclear terrorist incident has not yet happened may be more a result of the fact that no known concerted effort has been

Table 4.1: Major Terrorist Groups in the United States

Ethnic-Emigre'	Left-Wing	Right-Wing
Islamic Fundamentalists	Weather Underground	Aryan Nations
Puerto Rican Separatists	Black Liberation Army	The Order
Jewish Extremists	May 19th Communist Organization	Covenant, Sword & Arm of the Lord

Source: Hoffman, B., *Terrorism in the United States and the Potential Threat to Nuclear Facilities*, Rand Corporation, R-3351-DOE, January 1986.

mounted by a terrorist group, rather than the result of sufficient defenses against such an occurrence.

Although U.S. facilities and citizens are frequently targeted by terrorist groups abroad, terrorist incidents in the U.S. itself are far fewer than in Europe, the Middle East, South America, or Africa.[27] Nevertheless, three categories of terrorist organizations are active in the United States: ethnic separatist and emigré groups; left-wing radical organizations; and right-wing racist, anti-authority, survivalist groups. Some of these groups have expressed interest in using nuclear devices or sabotage to attain their political objectives.[28] The major elements within each category are listed in Table 4.1.

No terrorist group in the United States has yet attacked or attempted to sabotage a nuclear facility, and only a handful of publicly known threats have been made to do so.[29] However, the threat posed by domestic terrorist groups is not negligible. Based on past incidents and motivation, the U.S. based groups most likely to attack a nuclear weapons storage site or other facility appear to be Islamic fanatics and certain right-wing groups. Domestic left-wing groups appear to be the least likely to attack such a facility.[30]

Since the early 1980s, U.S. government officials have expressed concern over the presence of Islamic terrorist groups in the United States. This concern has lead to unprecedented physical security measures at U.S. government offices and military installations. Although attacks against U.S. government facilities have not materialized as once feared, the threat of Islamic terrorist violence is very real.

Further, Iranian and Libyan government officials have openly pledged support for Islamic terrorist activities against the U.S. government. For example, following a conference of Iranian clergymen in Teheran in 1982, the Khomeini regime reportedly established a special program to train Muslims from many nations as 'messengers of true Islam.' After receiving instruction in Iran, these 'messengers' were to return to their home nations to foment unrest and create a climate that would favor the adoption of fundamentalist Islamic precepts. Whether or not messengers were sent to Western nations is not publicly known.[31]

Terrorism in Western Europe, the Middle East, and Southern Africa, raises a number of issues of international concern that are apparently beyond the effective control of individual nations. For example, there is increasing international contact and cooperation among terrorist groups, including the flow of arms and the occurrence of joint operations. Methods of international communications and travel have proved both useful to and vulnerable to terrorists.

To date, no terrorist group has acquired a nuclear explosive device, although there have been several incidents related to possible theft attempts directed at American nuclear weapons storage sites in Europe. In the future, the possibility of a successful attempt cannot be overlooked. A nuclear device could be obtained by a raid on one of the thousands of warhead stockpiles throughout the world (particularly in Western Europe), by hijacking a ship or aircraft that carries nuclear weapons, or by obtaining fissionable materials and building a nuclear explosive device. However, this latter possibility is unlikely unless a terrorist group obtained active support from a national government with sufficient motivation and resources. Terrorists could also sabotage nuclear power plants or hijack radioactive waste on its way to a disposal site and use it to contaminate water supplies or other elements of the environment.

The prime responsibility for the apprehension and punishment of terrorists lies with individual nations and their respective law enforcement authorities. These authorities have often proved to be relatively ineffective with regard to prevention of terrorist acts. Thus, the ability of governments to prevail during terrorist incidents in the past has often proven to be severely limited.

Thus, the possibility of a nuclear terrorist incident poses a significant potential threat to the United States and other nations. Nuclear terrorism has been avoided primarily by the nature of the goals and motivations of terrorist groups rather than by the adequacy of defenses against terrorist incidents. Whether or not the terrorist threat will evolve into a terrorist demand for nuclear devices depends to a large extent on how governments react to terrorist incidents and whether or not they successfully address the underlying causes of terrorist activity.

The Future of Proliferation

Except for the Soviet Union, the acquisition of nuclear weapons by various nations has not fundamentally changed their respective political relationships with the United States. The prime evidence for this is the fact that since World War II, U.S. interest in bilateral arms control has been confined, for the most part, to negotiations with the Soviet Union. In only one instance has a conventional conflict involving an ally (Israel, 1973) prompted the United States to intervene in ways that were related to a policy of forestalling the possible use of nuclear weapons. In 1981, the U.S. also supported Israel, at least diplomatically, in its bombing raid on the Iraqi nuclear facility at Osirak.

If present trends continue, the proliferation of nuclear weapons will cause only minor perturbations in U.S. defense programs, and for the foreseeable future, U.S. strategic nuclear forces and defenses will be oriented almost exclusively toward the Soviet Union. The likelihood that any other nation will use nuclear weapons against the United States will remain low. However, two emerging trends suggest that the future may not resemble the past. The first is that relatively low-cost nuclear-capable delivery systems are becoming available, and the second is that the character of regional security is evolving in ways that pose serious problems for the regional alliances of the United States and the Soviet Union.

Technological advances in delivery systems have led members of the nuclear weapons club to develop and deploy highly accurate systems that can carry out selective strikes with limited secondary damage. For example, highly accurate cruise missiles, armed with conventional and nuclear warheads, are already significant elements in the arsenals of the United States, the Soviet Union, Great Britain, and France. In time, other nations will probably obtain these and other sophisticated delivery systems. Cruise missiles, launched from aircraft, surface ships, submarines, or from ground mobile launchers could easily become attractive nuclear warhead delivery vehicles for new nuclear nations, especially in view of the relatively low cost of such vehicles compared to ballistic missiles and manned penetrating aircraft.

Doctrines for use of low-cost delivery systems may also stimulate nuclear proliferation. Some U.S. and Soviet systems under consideration for deployment might obtain additional justification on the grounds that they could strike the nuclear forces and production facilities in new nuclear nations.

U.S. and Soviet deployment of new, highly accurate systems might give credibility to arguments in non-nuclear nations that such weapons would be useful additions to their own arsenals, both as a defense force and as a tool of diplomacy. Proponents would have additional evidence to support their contention that the superpowers are hypocritical about nuclear arms control and pose a menace not only to each other but also to nations that currently do not have nuclear weapons. Such arguments have precedence: both the British and the French used them to justify their development of independent nuclear forces during the 1950s and 60s.

Either a failure to follow the INF treaty with additional meaningful arms control agreements or the possible unraveling of existing bilateral agreements would cripple the prospects for additional multilateral non-proliferation agreements. The NPT, the Treaty of Tlatelolco, and the 1985 efforts for non-proliferation in the South Pacific would all be weakened by such outcomes. In turn, the political barriers for threshold nations to acquire nuclear weapons would be reduced. It is interesting to note that the Soviet Union would have the most to lose in a world of many nuclear powers, because the majority of these nations would probably be hostile to them. Although this aspect of nuclear proliferation might at first appear useful to the United States, the risks of regional nuclear wars that could cause superpower confrontation would seem to outweigh any possible diplomatic benefits. Thus, both the Soviet Union and the United States have incentives to cooperate on nuclear non-proliferation initiatives, regardless of the current nature of other aspects of U.S. Soviet relations. Indeed, joint efforts to limit the proliferation of nuclear weapons might be one of the more fruitful areas for U.S.-Soviet cooperation in the 1990s.

Unfortunately, the pace of nuclear weapons proliferation might not be as leisurely in the future as it has been in the past. If proliferation chains develop (a proliferation chain is defined as a rapid sequence of acquisition of nuclear weapons by nations that have a recent history of conflict), they will certainly have an impact on U.S. foreign and defense policies. Such chains could produce more groups of adjacent nuclear rivals: India, China and Pakistan; Israel and its neighbors Egypt, Iraq, Iran, and Libya, etc. The development of such chains would increase incentives for preemptive strikes (illustrated by Israel's strike against Osirak in 1981) and the likelihood of nuclear weapon use in the escalation of a conventional war. Proximity has always been a useful indicator of the likelihood of conflict in international relations; there is no reason to suppose that it will not be an important determinant for possible nuclear conflicts in the future.

The Impact of Proliferation

One way to look at the impact of proliferation on U.S. foreign and defense policies is by listing new nuclear nations according to the following four categories: major ally, regional ally, neither ally nor adversary, and finally, adversary of regional ally.[32]

For example, suppose that a major U.S. ally (West Germany, Japan, Canada, etc.) decided to acquire nuclear weapons because of dramatic changes in either its domestic affairs or in international conditions. It seems likely that the U.S. would make every effort to retain strong and friendly relations because the loss of such a military, economic, and political ally would be a decisive setback to the U.S. international position. U.S. failure to maintain friendly relations would also have profound consequences for U.S. military forces. Aside from the loss of military bases, an adversarial relationship would surely stimulate growth in U.S. offensive nuclear forces and strategic defenses. It should be noted that there is no inherent reason why the acquisition of nuclear weapons by a major ally would adversely affect its relations with the U.S. For example, the U.S. has maintained good relations with Great Britain and France even though both have acquired independent nuclear forces.

Clearly, it is in the interests of the United States not to permit relations with a regional ally to deteriorate to the point where the U.S. would not be able to dissuade it from acquiring nuclear weapons in the first place. However, while the acquisition of nuclear weapons by a regional ally such as Pakistan, Israel, or South Korea would affect U.S. foreign policy, it would not significantly affect U.S. strategic defenses. For example, an Indian-Pakistani nuclear standoff would probably result in a U.S. diplomatic effort to reduce tensions in the region, to limit Soviet influence over events, and of course, to forestall the use of nuclear weapons in case of war between the two nations. An overt Israeli nuclear force would strain the U.S-Israeli relationship, but would probably not cause an irreparable break. If past events are any guide, the U.S. would probably provide massive conventional military aid and diplomatic support to bolster Israeli security so that Israel would not have an incentive to use nuclear weapons in some future Arab-Israeli conflict. A South Korean nuclear force could be the cause or the result of a rupture in its current security arrangement with the United States. In either case, the possibility of a chain reaction of proliferation in the region might be resolved by cooperative diplomatic efforts by the United States, China, and the Soviet Union.

If a nation in the third category (neither ally nor adversary) overtly acquired nuclear weapons, U.S. foreign policy would be affected, but the impact on defense policy would probably be minimal. Bilateral relations would probably worsen in the short term. For example, the U.S. might impose economic or political sanctions. However, U.S. leverage in most of these countries is already quite limited (for example, South Africa). U.S. diplomatic efforts would probably be coordinated with those of major allies and perhaps even with the Soviet Union. These efforts would be directed toward reducing the incentives for the use of nuclear weapons as a last resort in any conventional conflict.

Nuclear proliferation in nations in the fourth category (adversary of regional ally) would cause serious problems for U.S. policy makers. This would be especially true in the Middle East. The use of nuclear weapons might appear to be great, and the national survival of a regional ally might be in jeopardy. For example, suppose that Iraq or Libya acquired nuclear weapons. The survival of Israel and possibly Egypt might be in jeopardy, the Arab-Israeli conflict might re-ignite, and the Middle East oil fields would be vulnerable to destruction or disruption. The United States would have strong incentives to become directly involved in the region in ways it never has before: by stationing permanent troops, formulating explicit security guarantees, and even contemplating preemptive strikes against nuclear forces, stockpiles or production facilities, either directly or by proxy. Nuclear activities by terrorist groups could become a reality. Such actions by the United States would also raise the likelihood of a U.S.-Soviet confrontation. Clearly, especially in the Middle East, the acquisition of nuclear weapons by an adversary of a regional ally is the most dangerous situation for the U.S. with regard to nuclear proliferation.

In the 1990s, the members of the nuclear weapons club may be forced to choose one or a combination of options to adapt to a world of more than five nations with the potential to deploy nuclear weapons. One option is that of neglect. The five nuclear powers could permit nuclear proliferation to proceed without attempting to influence events. Under this option, they would passively witness the proliferation of nuclear weapons, concentrate on the continued development of massive offensive arsenals for deterrence, and build elaborate arrays of air and ballistic missile defenses to protect themselves (to the extent possible) from nuclear attacks.

A second option would be to promote a realignment of alliances. This would involve a conscious effort by the five nuclear powers to modify regional security arrangements in favor of creating a ruling elite composed of the nations that now admit to having nuclear weapons. The aim of this realignment would be to formalize what is an implicit fact in world affairs: nuclear weapons are politically significant and automatically elevate the status of nations that possess them. By underscoring the distinction between nations that have and those that do not have nuclear weapons, the nuclear powers could promote the idea that nations with nuclear weapons will continue to dominate world politics.

A third option, consistent with option two, might be to adopt a policy of confrontation. The nuclear powers, acting alone or in concert, could impose or threaten to impose severe sanctions, including preemptive military action, against any other nation that appears intent on acquiring nuclear weapons.

A fourth option might involve a combination of disarmament efforts and the promotion of economic and political development in third world countries. According to proponents of this approach, reductions in superpower arsenals and the alleviation of the the gap between rich and poor nations might reduce the incentives for poor nations to acquire nuclear weapons.

A fifth option might be to incrementally adapt, as circumstances develop, to a world of more than five nations with nuclear weapons. Under this option, the U.S. and the other nuclear powers would use a mix of strategies tailored to specific aspects of nuclear proliferation as it evolves over time.

Attempts to control the spread of nuclear weapons under options four and five could employ any of the following political-military strategies:

- Continuation of superpower disarmament negotiations: The 1988 INF Treaty has set a positive precedent for future negotiations. Future efforts could include a continuation of the Strategic Arms Reduction Talks (START), and a follow-up on the June 1988 Gorbachev proposals to reduce conventional forces in Europe. This Gorbachev initiative appears particularly attractive, since the superiority of Warsaw Pact conventional forces compared to NATO counterparts is one of the primary reasons for NATO reliance on nuclear weapons.

- Strengthen the non-proliferation treaty: The NPT is the primary international agreement for limiting nuclear proliferation. Unless or until the NPT's legitimacy collapses due to the large number of nations that are either violating it or withdrawing from it, the United States could try to strengthen the treaty and improve its safeguard system. This strategy could include agreements among suppliers to strengthen regulations that limit the transfer of technologies that could be used to develop nuclear weapons.
- Promote pledges of non-use of nuclear weapons against nations that do not have such weapons: This approach has precedence in the protocols to Treaty of Tlatelolco. However, the U.S., in particular, would exercise caution in this area because such pledges could create serious doubts about the credibility of U.S. security guarantees to its allies in Europe and Asia.
- Promote the establishment of nuclear free zones: Precedents for this include the Treaty of Tlatelolco and the South Pacific Nuclear Free Zone Treaty. However, such agreements will be extremely difficult to negotiate in the regions of the world most likely to experience a nuclear conflict: Southern Asia, the Middle East, and Southern Africa.
- Maintain and enhance security guarantees: A major stimulus to nuclear proliferation will continue to be threats to the security of non-nuclear nations by regional adversaries. By maintaining and enhancing security guarantees, the United States and the other nuclear powers could both constrain the options of non-nuclear nations and provide assurances to them that would diminish their incentives to develop independent nuclear weapon capabilities. This strategy implies cooperation between the United States, the Soviet Union, Great Britain, France, and China to defuse regional crises, and to limit the actions of their respective regional allies, at least with regard to conflicts that could result in the use of nuclear weapons. Such cooperation occurred to some degree in the Gulf in the period 1981–88, although with limited results. Also, in cases where the establishment of security guarantees might be possible, the conditions demanded by non-nuclear nations might not be acceptable to the nuclear powers. Nonetheless, as the potential for nuclear weapon capabilities continues to spread, the maintenance and enhancement of security guarantees appears to be a logical course.

- Impose sanctions against nations that acquire nuclear weapons. Such sanctions could include economic and political actions as well as the use of military force. However, in the past, economic and political sanctions have not been particularly effective in deterring nations from doing what they had already planned to do. Economic sanctions are especially vulnerable to countermeasures. The use of military force in a manner similar to the Israeli raid on Osirak might be effective in certain situations; however, such actions pose obvious risks of further conflict, and clearly could not be used against nations with sizable military capabilities such as India, Japan, or a major European nation.

Both options four and five are consistent with current superpower disarmament negotiations, with efforts to strengthen international nonproliferation agreements, and with continued multilateral efforts to alleviate causes of conflict in Southern Asia, the Middle East, and Southern Africa. In any case, the choice of one or a combination of the above or other strategies must surely occur soon, because the problems of proliferation will only worsen if they are ignored.

Notes

1. Chant, C., and Hogg, I., *Nuclear War in the 1980s,* Harper and Row, Publishers, New York, 1983, 56–57.

2. The Nuclear Non-Proliferation Treaty (1968, 137 members) bans the transfer of nuclear weapons and technologies to nations that do not have nuclear weapons. It also requires those nations that have nuclear weapons to provide safeguards with regard to research and weapon production facilities and to negotiate, reduce and eventually eliminate nuclear arsenals. Other international agreements that pertain to non-proliferation include: The Treaty for the Prohibition of Nuclear Weapons in Latin America (Treaty of Tlatelolco, 1967, 25 nations), the Antarctic Treaty (1959, 35 nations), the Outer Space Treaty (1967, 95 nations), the Seabed Treaty (1971, 82 nations), and more recently, the South Pacific Nuclear Free Zone Treaty (1985, 9 nations). See National Academy of Sciences, *Nuclear Arms Control: Background and Issues,* National Academy Press, Washington DC, 1985, 243–246; Sivard, R., *World Military and Social Expenditures, 1987–88,* World Priorities, Inc., Washington DC, 1987, 32; Degenhardt, H., and Day, A.J., ed., *Treaties and Alliances of the World,* 4th ed., Gale Research Company, Detroit, 1986.

3. Chant and Hogg, *Nuclear War in the 1980s;* also see Nacht, M., *The Age of Vulnerability: Threats to the Nuclear Stalemate,* The Brookings Institution, Washington, DC, 1985, 177–180; and Marwah, O., "India's Nuclear and Space Programs: Intent and Policy," *International Security,* vol. 2 (Fall 1977), 96–121. Israel may also have warheads suitable for delivery by short range missiles. For Israel, see Quandt, W., *Decade of Decisions: American Policy Toward the Arab-Israeli Conflict 1967–76,* University of California Press, 1977.

4. Nacht, *The Age of Vulnerability.*

5. Ibid.

6. Ibid., also see Marwah, "India's Nuclear and Space Programs: Intent and Policy."

7. Congressional Quarterly, Inc., *The Nuclear Age: Power, Proliferation and the Arms Race,* Washington DC, 1984, 138–139; also see recent public statements in the press by President Zia, 1987–88.

8. Dunn, L., *Controlling the Bomb: Nuclear Proliferation in the 1980s,* Yale University Press, New Haven, CT, 1982, 48–49. Also see Congressional Quarterly, Inc., *The Nuclear Age: Power, Proliferation and the Arms Race,* 141.

9. Congressional Quarterly Inc., *The Nuclear Age: Power, Proliferation and the Arms Race,* 141–155.

10. Numerous sources have reached this conclusion. For example, see the National Academy of Sciences, *Nuclear Arms Control: Background and Issues,* 267. Also see Dunn, *Controlling the Bomb: Nuclear Proliferation in the 1980s,* 48–49.

11. Dunn, *Controlling the Bomb: Nuclear Proliferation in the 1980s,* 50.

12. Ibid., 50–52; also see Congressional Quarterly Inc., *The Nuclear Age: Power, Proliferation and the Arms Race,* 141–155.

13. Dunn, *Controlling the Bomb: Nuclear Proliferation in the 1980s,* 50–52; also see Congressional Quarterly Inc., *The Nuclear Age: Power, Proliferation and the Arms Race,* 141–155, and Nacht, *The Age of Vulnerability: Threats to the Nuclear Stalemate,* 184.

14. Dunn, L., *Controlling the Bomb: Nuclear Proliferation in the 1980s;* also see Chant and Hogg, *Nuclear War in the 1980s.*

15. Degenhardt and Day, *Treaties and Alliances of the World,* 77–82.

16. Dunn, *Controlling the Bomb: Nuclear Proliferation in the 1980s,* 53–55.

17. Ibid.; also see Chant and Hogg, *Nuclear War in the 1980s.*

18. Ibid.

19. Degenhardt and Day, eds., *Treaties and Alliances of the World,* 71; also see Banks, A., *Political Handbook of the World,* CSA Publications, Bighamton, NY, 1986, 768–769.

20. Degenhardt and Day, eds., *Treaties and Alliances of the World,* 77–82; also see Sivard, *World Military and Social Expenditures, 1987–88,* 32.

21. Degenhardt and Day, eds., *Treaties and Alliances of the World,* 77–82.

22. Dunn, *Controlling the Bomb: Nuclear Proliferation in the 1980s,* 56–57; also see Chant and Hogg, *Nuclear War in the 1980s.*

23. Ibid.

24. Ibid.

25. Ibid.

26. According to the United Nations (UN), not every act of violent insurgency is an act of terrorism. The UN has consistently exempted acts that derive from "the inalienable right to self-determination and independence of all peoples under colonial and racist regimes . . ." from its definition of terrorism. Thus, one analyst's terrorist may be another's freedom fighter, depending on the analyst's political persuasion. In December 1985, the UN General Assembly unanimously adopted a resolution condemning all acts of terrorism as 'criminal.' Yet the issue of which acts constitute terrorism remains unresolved, except for acts that were criminalized by previous

conventions, such as hijacking and hostage-taking of internationally protected persons. See UN General Assembly official records, December 1985, the Tokyo Convention 1963, the Hague Convention 1970, the Montreal Convention 1971, the International Convention Against the Taking of Hostages 1979, the Helsinki Final Act 1975, etc.

27. See the *Rand Chronology of International Terrorism* between 1968 and 1987. The United States was the country most targeted by terrorists abroad. However, according to FBI statistics, there was an average of 33 incidents per year within the United States during the period 1980–85. By comparison, France averaged 84 per year, and Italy averaged 56. However, West Germany averaged only 23 during the same period. Depending on the definition of terrorism, the numbers of incidents were generally much higher in Western Europe, the Middle East, Latin America, and Southern Africa compared to North America.

28. This is an updated version of a similar table presented in Hoffman, B., *Terrorism in the United States and the Potential Threat to Nuclear Facilities,* Rand Corporation, R-3351-DOE, January 1986. Much of the information in this section on terrorism in the United States was derived from seminal work done by Rand Corporation for the U.S. Federal Government. Data from Rand documents were supplemented by excerpts from major newspapers and from other sources as cited throughout this section.

29. The literature on nuclear terrorism tends to be speculative. It deals with the potential for nuclear blackmail, and the vulnerability of nuclear facilities, weapons, and materials. A large part of the literature covers various security methods designed to protect nuclear installations from potentially hostile elements. By the mid-1980s, there appeared to be a concensus that while there is a potential for nuclear terrorism, the utility of such acts is low, therefore the probability of nuclear terrorism is also low. However, state-sponsored terrorism, particularly by Libya and Iran, has a higher probability due to motivation and the greater resources that state support could bring to bear upon the achievement of a nuclear terrorist act. See Lakos, A., *Interational Terrorism: A Bibliography,* Westview Press, Boulder, Colorado, 1986, Section IX, for a comprehensive bibliography on terrorism.

30. Hoffman, *Terrorism in the United States and the Potential Threat to Nuclear Facilities,* 23–24, 34–36, 51–52.

31. Ibid., 20.

32. This paradigm was used by Nacht in *The Age of Vulnerability: Threats to the Nuclear Stalemate,* 183.

PART TWO

The Design of Nuclear Defense

5

Levels of Capability

Deterrence and Strategic Defense

Deterrence need not be totally dependent on inventories of offensive weapons. A given level of deterrence (national security) could be achieved by different combinations of offensive and defensive systems. Thus, offensive systems might be given up and replaced by defensive systems, holding the level of deterrence constant. Incentives that could foster such a trade include political benefits, military utility, and relative costs. Trading offense for defense could result in fewer nuclear weapons.

To understand the continuing evolution of deterrence, one must understand the current state of defenses against perceived nuclear threats. This and the following chapter therefore outline current and expected future nuclear defensive systems. The discussion includes general capabilities, current and future technologies, and the nature of the assets that could be protected in the event of a nuclear conflict. Defenses against lesser nuclear threats are also briefly explored. Finally, this and the following chapter includes references to the economic incentives that may eventually result in the substitution of defenses for offensive nuclear forces.

The Emphasis on Defensive Systems

For nearly forty years, the United States has based its strategic defense on the deterrence value of its offensive nuclear weapons and its ability to defend against aircraft that carry nuclear bombs. In the absence of arms control agreements, air, sea, and ground launched cruise and ballistic missiles will continue to present the major nuclear threat to the United States well into the twenty-first century. U.S. defenses against cruise missiles are rudimentary at best. Except for attack warning and attack assessment, the U.S. has no defense against nuclear warheads launched by ballistic missiles or from space.

U.S. military planners have expressed grave concern that rudimentary cruise missile defenses and lack of ballistic missile and space defenses leaves the United States vulnerable not only to a Soviet first strike, but also to an accidental launch, a launch by an insane Soviet subordinate commander, nuclear blackmail, coercion, or devastation by other potential adversaries that currently have or may obtain nuclear weapons in the near future.

To alleviate these perceived threats, the Reagan Administration embarked on the Strategic Defense Initiative (SDI, 1983) and the Air Defense Initiative (ADI, 1985) to upgrade U.S. defenses against ballistic missile, space, and atmospheric nuclear threats.

On the other side, the strategic defenses of the Soviet Union are oriented principally to counter manned bomber and ballistic missile threats from the United States, Britain, France, and China. Because it is virtually surrounded by potential enemies that have nuclear weapons and sophisticated delivery systems, the Soviet Union faces a much more complex strategic defense problem compared to the United States.

In November 1987, General Secretary Gorbachev acknowledged that the Soviet Union is also engaged in strategic defense research. He stated, "The Soviet Union is doing all that the United States is doing, and I guess we are engaged in research, basic research, which relates to [those] aspects which are covered by the SDI of the United States."[1]

In addition to its version of the SDI, the Soviet Union has continued to upgrade its current ballistic missile defenses. For example, the Soviets began a construction program in the early 1980s that will result in an expanded and upgraded ballistic missile defense system for the Moscow area. By 1990, this system will include a two-layer defense with 100 Anti-Ballistic Missile (ABM) launchers. These launchers have two types of interceptor missiles: a long-range modified GALOSH missile that is intended to engage ballistic missile reentry vehicles outside the atmosphere; and the GAZELLE, a shorter range, high-acceleration missile that is designed to engage reentry vehicles after they have reentered the atmosphere. The Soviets are also building a new phased array radar at Pushkino that will provide support for the Moscow ABM system.[2]

In the aggregate, the Soviet Union appears to be preparing a basis for an ABM defense of large portions of its national territory. The actions that suggest this include the construction of nine large phased array radars, including the controversial radar at Krasnoyarsk, upgrades and testing of new surface-to-air missiles, development and testing of ABM rapid reload and mobile ABMs, and the possible deployment of ABM components.[3]

The Soviet Union is also engaged in research on anti-satellite weapons at the Tyuratam and Sary Shagan test sites and other locations. For example, Soviet programs include the development and testing of interceptor missiles (Tyuratam) and high energy lasers (Sary Shagan) that may have the capability to damage or destroy U.S. satellites in low-Earth orbit.[4]

Since the early 1950s, the Soviet Union has continually upgraded its air defense radar system.[5] The Soviets also have large numbers of fighter interceptors and Surface-to-Air Missile (SAM) sites around the periphery of the Soviet Union and in other Warsaw Pact nations. However, there are deficiencies in the command and control network and in low-altitude radar coverage, as highlighted by the incident that involved a low-flying West German private aircraft that penetrated Soviet airspace and landed in Moscow's Red Square in 1986. Finally, like the United States, the Soviet Union has only rudimentary defenses against cruise missiles.

In sum, the United States and the Soviet Union have both made enormous investments in research, development, and deployment of strategic defenses. These expenditures will continue to some degree no matter which political party captures the U.S. White House in the 1992 and 1996 elections, and no matter how much progress is made in the current Soviet efforts at 'glasnost' and Gorbachev's efforts to emphasize consumer wants rather than perceived military needs.

U.S. Nuclear Defense Concepts

Over the past three decades, the defense of the North American continent against Soviet strategic nuclear forces has been the responsibility of the North American Aerospace Defense Command (NORAD). This command includes both U.S. and Canadian forces. If a nuclear conflict should occur, NORAD would provide little more than warning that a ballistic missile attack was on the way and would alert National Command Authorities in time to launch U.S. retaliatory forces. However, NORAD does have the capability to mount an effective defense against manned aircraft.

NORAD's primary attack warning, attack assessment, and command and control center is the Cheyenne Mountain Complex (CMC), which is buried deep under a mountain near Colorado Springs, Colorado. The CMC processes centers for data from sensors that can detect Soviet ballistic missiles and from other sensors that can detect manned bombers, and to a certain extent, cruise missiles. NORAD also has sensors that detect, categorize, and track space vehicles.

Command and control communications networks connect the CMC with seven Regional Operations Control Centers (ROCCs) and selected sensors, including certain space-based sensors, 20 terrestrial space threat warning sensors, 11 ballistic missile warning sites, and up to eight E-3 Airborne Warning and Control System (AWACS) aircraft. In turn, the ROCCs communicate with Over-the-Horizon Backscatter (OTH-B) radar sites, 139 microwave radar sites, 15 U.S. fighter-interceptor squadrons, and one Canadian fighter-interceptor squadron. By the mid-1990s, there will be 12 OTH-B radars that will provide full perimeter and skip-zone radar coverage out to approximately 1800 miles from the U.S. coasts, and from zero to over 100,000 feet in elevation. With the exception of a small number of Canadian ground-to-air anti-aircraft missiles, fighter-interceptor squadrons provide the only current active defense against Soviet nuclear weapons.[6]

Pressures for a ballistic missile defense would not have caused an official resurgence of interest were it not for the fact that recent advances in certain technologies indicate that it may be technically possible to develop effective defenses against incoming ballistic missiles and warheads. Thus, in 1983, President Reagan directed an intensive study to describe a research program that would develop technically feasible defenses against ballistic missiles and to assess the implications of such a program for the prevention of nuclear war, deterrence of conventional aggression, and the enhancement of prospects for successful arms control negotiations. The subsequent study concluded that advanced defensive technologies might offer the potential to significantly reduce the military utility of a Soviet first strike against the United States and its allies. Further, the study outlined a research program that could clarify future technical options for a ballistic missile defense program.

To implement such a research program, now known as the SDI, President Reagan established the SDI Office (SDIO) directly under the Secretary of Defense. The primary purpose of this office is to direct the research and development program whose specific objectives include the elimination of the threat of ballistic missile attacks on the United States and to counter the possibility of the Soviet development of additional ballistic missiles defenses.

Another program, similar in intent to the SDI, was set in motion in 1985 to upgrade U.S. air defenses (the ADI). This program is directed by elements of the Air Force Systems Command, including the Electronics Systems Division at Hanscom Air Force Base in Massachusetts and various laboratories located at the Rome Air Development Center (RADC) in upstate New York.

In the 1970s and early 1980s, the U.S. also initiated programs to upgrade the protection systems for its nuclear weapon production and storage sites. These programs were designed to defend the sites against espionage and terrorist attacks, and include hardening storage facilities against the effects of conventional explosives, improved lighting, and more stringent standards for reaction forces.

In sum, the United States and Canada have deployed a number of systems to provide attack warning, attack assessment, command and control, and active defenses (primarily fighter-interceptor aircraft). Research and development programs (SDI and ADI) have been started that will result in new systems in the 1990s and beyond. Beginning with air defense, key current and planned systems are outlined in more detail in the following sections.

The U.S. Air Defense System

Among its several functions, the NORAD Cheyenne Mountain Complex (CMC) is the primary attack warning and attack assessment center for atmospheric threats against North America. CMC air defense components include: the Air Defense Operations Center (ADOC), the Aerospace Defense Intelligence Center (ADIC), and most important, the NORAD Command Post (NCP). The ADOC obtains attack warning, track, and other atmospheric event data from the seven NORAD Region Operations Control Centers (ROCCs), certain sensor sites, and certain Greenland, Iceland, and United Kingdom (GIUK) sites. The ADIC receives information from a variety of sources, and provides intelligence reports and summaries to both the ADOC and the NCP. The NCP provides the focal point for command and control of NORAD air defense forces. It also provides attack warning and attack assessments to the National Command Authorities (NCA), the National Military Command System (NMCS), the U.S. Strategic Air Command (SAC), the Canadian Government and the governments of certain other U.S. allies.[7]

The Systems Control Operations Center (SCOC) and the Weather Support Unit (WSU) support the air defense function of the NCP. The SCOC provides real time management of CMC computer resources, communications, and power production. The WSU provides weather information, including weather reports on conditions at U.S., Canadian and Soviet airfields. Additional command elements associated with the NCP include the Back-Up Facility (BUF), located at Peterson Air Force Base, Colorado, and the Rapid Emergency Reconstitution (RAPIER) mobile command unit.

If the CMC and the BUF are destroyed, RAPIER would provide NORAD command and control functions and would organize surviving forces during and after a nuclear attack. NORAD command and control functions could also be provided by specially equipped aircraft, including E-3 AWACs.[8]

The CMC is totally dependent on external sources for atmospheric event data. The communications networks that provide these data utilize military and commercial satellites, terrestrial microwave routes, buried cables, and various other communications media. These networks feed data from and through the ROCCs into the CMC.

In 1983, seven new ROCCs replaced the aging NORAD Semi-Automatic Ground Environment (SAGE) and Back-Up Interceptor Control (BUIC) facilities, and the manual system in Alaska. The new ROCCs are located at Tyndall Air Force Base, Florida; Griffiss Air Force Base, New York; McChord Air Force Base, Washington; and March Air Force Base, California. One ROCC is also located at Elemendorf Air Force Base in Alaska and two more are collocated at North Bay, Ontario. These seven ROCCs are the primary command and control centers for NORAD air defense. The ROCCs communicate with OTH-B radars, the North Warning System, 85 microwave radars (47 in the contiguous U.S., 14 in Alaska, and 24 in Canada), E-3 AWACS aircraft, five U.S. active duty and 10 Air National Guard fighter-interceptor squadrons, and one Canadian squadron.[9] A ROCCs ability to fulfill its mission is heavily dependent on communications with external systems and agencies. Inputs to each ROCC are provided by the radars located in its area of responsibility. Additional inputs are provided by the CMC, the FAA, and several agencies external to the air defense system.

The United States is currently building a system of 12 OTH-B radars. These new radars will dramatically extend the distance at which hostile aircraft can be detected. The OTH-Bs high frequency signals reflect off the ionosphere to travel well beyond the horizon to a distance of about 1,800 nautical miles.[10] OTH-B radars overcome a major drawback of conventional line-of-sight ground-based microwave radars, whose ranges are limited by the curvature of the Earth, and are generally effective out only to about 200 nautical miles. Another advantage is that OTH-Bs can detect objects flying at any altitude, from the ionosphere to just above the Earth's surface. Thus, low-flying penetrating bombers and surface-skimming cruise missiles cannot escape being detected, as they would be by flying under the beam of a conventional microwave radar. The OTH-B radars will be able to detect advanced penetrating bombers, such as the Soviet supersonic Backfire and Blackjack, and possibly, recently developed Soviet nuclear-armed cruise and air-to-surface missiles. When completed, OTH-B radar coverage for the detection of atmospheric vehicles will provide a complete coverage perimeter around the United States and Canada, except for the polar region, which will be covered by the North Warning System.[11]

Although the OTH-Bs represent a major improvement in North American air defense radar coverage, they cannot be used to cover the over-the-North Pole route, where OTH-B capabilities are extremely limited by the aurora borealis, which involves substantial ionospheric disturbances. Thus, the polar route will be covered by the North Warning System. This new system will consist of updated microwave radars.

When completed, the new North Warning System will consist of 13 long-range radars and 39 shorter-range 'gap filler' radars.[12] These radars will form a line beginning on the Northwest coast of Alaska, extending across Northern Canada, and down the East coast of Labrador. The North Warning System radar coverage will overlap with the coverage of the OTH-B radars on the East and West coasts of the United States. The locations of North Warning System sites follow the same pattern as the old DEW Line. GIUK radars will probably be upgraded and will remain in service through the 1990s.

The 13 North Warning System long-range radar sites will correlate information from their respective radars with additional information from the adjacent gap filler radars. This correlated information will be passed on to appropriate ROCCs via digital and voice communications circuits. The appropriate ROCCs will display the data, determine the nature of the tracks, and pass hostile, unknown, and special tracks to the CMC.

Certain ROCCs will have the capability to communicate through the North Warning System sites to fighter-interceptor and E-3 AWACS aircraft that may operate in the North Warning System area of radar coverage. These ROCCs may use these communications links to direct intercepts, to direct the engagement of enemy aircraft, and to direct the performance of airborne attack assessment functions.

In addition to early warning, microwave radars provide aircraft control and surveillance features that cannot be provided by the OTH-Bs. The microwave radars in the air defense network are grouped according to four systems: in addition to the North Warning System, NORAD employs the Seek Igloo System, the Pine Tree Line and the Joint Surveillance System in the contiguous United States. The aging Distant Early Warning (DEW) Line is being largely replaced by the North Warning System.

Thirteen new Seek Igloo minimally attended radars are deployed from Cold Bay and King Salmon on the Alaskan Peninsula north along the Alaskan coast to Cape Lisburne, and along a line stretching from Sparrevohn north to Indian Mountain, and then east to Murphy Dome and Fort Yukon in Alaska. Seek Igloo radars provide aircraft detection, tracking and interceptor control for the Alaskan NORAD Region, which has its headquarters at Elemendorf Air Force Base near Anchorage, Alaska. In conjunction with the North Warning System, the OTHB radars in Alaska, and the FAA radar at Kenai Airport, the Seek Igloo radars provide contiguous radar coverage around the perimeter of Alaska and coverage over most of the interior of the state.

Each Seek Igloo radar site has a Ground-to-Air Transmit-Receive (GATR) radio facility that provides two-way communications links between the site and fighter-interceptor and E-3 AWACS aircraft that may be operating in the area. The Alaskan NORAD ROCC can communicate directly with such aircraft via two-way voice and digital communications links that connect the Alaskan ROCC to the GATRs, and thus to the aircraft.

The old Pine Tree Line consisted of twenty-four Canadian Air Defense sites, each with an aircraft control and warning radar and a collocated height finder radar. These sites were deployed in a line from Holberg, British Columbia, on the West coast to Gander, Newfoundland, on the East coast. Each site had communications links to its respective ROCC, and each site had a GATR facility that could be accessed by the site or its respective ROCC for direct, two-way communications to fighter-interceptor and E-3 AWACS aircraft. Beginning in 1986, the Canadians began to deactivate 17 of the 24 sites. The remaining sites are on the East and West Coasts, and will receive updated radars and communications systems. Canada has also invested substantially in the North Warning System and participates with the United States in the deployment and operation of certain OTH-B radar sites.[13]

The Joint Surveillance System (JSS) includes 47 microwave radars deployed around the perimeter of the contiguous 48 states. JSS radars contribute to the NORAD air defense mission by detecting and tracking aircraft and by providing ground-air-ground radio communication for ROCC command and control of fighter-interceptors. The current network consists of nine military radar sites and 38 joint use military-FAA radar sites. All but seven have collocated height finders. JSS coverage extends about 200 nautical miles beyond the U.S. coastline, however, gaps in coverage may exist along some parts of the U.S. border.[14]

Also, like all line-of-sight radars, JSS radars cannot detect aircraft and cruise missiles that fly under their radar beams. Thus, the JSS system is considered a supplement to the OTH-B system with regard to attack warning. However, JSS radars have the capability to accurately track aircraft, and they provide control and surveillance features that cannot be performed by OTH-B radars.

The U.S. Ballistic Missile Warning System

NORAD operates a missile warning system that can detect and characterize ballistic missile launches from the Soviet landmass and from key locations in the oceans adjacent to the North American continent. Sensors include the satellite early warning system, the Ballistic Missile Warning (BMEWS) radars at Clear, Alaska; Thule, Greenland; and Fylingdales Moor, United Kingdom. Other sensors include the Perimeter Acquisition Radar Attack Characterization System (PARCS), Pave Paws radars, the Cobra Dane Radar, and certain other radars designed to detect sea-launched ballistic missiles (SLBM).

All of these sensors communicate directly with the missile warning center in the NORAD CMC.[15] Because of the potentially severe consequences of reacting to a false report, NORAD employs more than one technology to detect missile launches. While a naturally occurring phenomenon might produce a false alarm from one type of sensor, only ballistic missile launches can trigger all of the sensor technologies. Thus, all reports of launches are cross-checked with reports from alternative types of sensors to alleviate the possibility of false alarms.

According to reports published in the open literature (defense journals, etc.), the U.S. satellite-based early warning system consists of three satellites: one over the Eastern Hemisphere and two over the Western Hemisphere.[16] The purpose of this system is to detect launches from SLBM, ICBM, and fractional orbital bombardment systems. These satellites are launched either from the space shuttle orbiter or by a Titan 34D booster into a 22,300 mile high geosynchronous orbit about the earth. The primary sensor for each satellite is a 12-foot infrared telescope with its line of sight offset 7.5 degrees from the cylindrical axis of the spacecraft, which points toward the earth. As the satellite slowly spins on its axis, the sensor's field of view scans a wide circle. Infrared energy is gathered by a Schmidt-type optical system and focused on an array of 2,000 lead sulphide detectors, each of which 'sees' a terrestrial area less than two miles square; this allows both detection of a missile's heat plume and determination of its launch site. These data are relayed through satellite and ground communication links to ground processing stations and then to the CMC, where the information is further processed and correlated with information from other sensors.[17]

If a ballistic missile attack should occur, the first warning would probably come from the satellite early warning system. However, simply detecting a rocket plume does not mean that an attack is under way; this satellite system sees dozens of Soviet space launches and ballistic missile tests every year. Thus, NORAD procedures require the receipt of attack indications from more than one source before issuing an attack warning. For ICBMs, the vital second source confirmation would come from the BMEWS radars.

The BMEWS radars at Clear, Thule, and Fylingdales have been operational since the early 1960s. The Clear and Thule sites are equipped with pulse-Doppler detection radars. Originally, these 400-by-165 foot parabolic-torus reflectors scanned the horizon for incoming missiles by using a series of feeds located at the focal points of the torus and switching transmitter power from one feed to another. However, recent upgrades include more modern phased-array technologies.[18]

At all three BMEWS sites, targets detected by the large fixed array radars can be tracked by a tracking radar. The main element of this radar is a hydraulically driven 84-foot parabolic dish that scans at 10 degrees per second (azimuth). It is capable of several search modes as well as target acquisition and tracking. It is protected by a spherical radome 140 feet in diameter. The tracking system has an approximate range of about 3,000 miles.[19]

Other recent improvements to the BMEWS include modifications to the tactical operations room, replacement of the original computers, and improvements to radar resolution by changing the radar band width and improving the pulse shape. These changes allow the system to discriminate objects that are closely spaced, thus increasing its ability to detect and discriminate MIRVed warheads.[20]

The current BMEWS upgrades at Clear, Thule, and Fylingdales provide substantial U.S. radar coverage for Soviet ICBM launches from the landmass of the Soviet Union. However, the apparent size of the radar coverage area is deceptive because at the limit of its 3,000 mile range, a BMEWS radar beam is about 1,000 miles in elevation above the earth.[21] Thus, most Soviet ICBM launches would not enter BMEWS radar beams until they have already reached relatively high altitudes.

While the BMEWS system is primarily concerned with ICBMs, warning of an SLBM attack is the primary mission of the Pave Paws system. This system consists of four phased-array radars, located at Cape Cod Air Force Station in Massachusetts, Beale Air Force Base in California, Goodfellow Air Force Base in Texas, and the fourth at Robins Air Force Base in Georgia.

The Pave Paws radars are operated by the Strategic Air Command. Although they are most frequently used for tracking objects in space, they maintain a constant watch for SLBMs, and report directly to the NORAD CMC with regard to their SLBM detection mission. Each unit uses two 102 foot arrays with provision for 5,400 elements. These arrays are mounted on adjacent sides of a building and inclined from the vertical to provide a total of 240 degrees of coverage in azimuth and 85 degrees in elevation. The system is estimated to have an effective SLBM detection range of about 3,000 miles.[22]

Until recently (1987), SLBM detection to the south was provided by a phased array radar (AN/FPS-85) at Eglin Air Force Base in Florida and an obsolescent parabolic dish radar (AN/FSS-7) at MacDill Air Force Base, also in Florida. However, these radars are scheduled for deactivation as their missions are gradually taken over by the Pave Paws radar at Robins.

SLBM launches from the lower Arctic Ocean behind BMEWS can be tracked by the PARCS radar located in Concrete, North Dakota. The PARCS is a single faced phased array radar left over after the Army's Safeguard anti-ballistic missile system was deactivated in the early 1970s.

U.S. Space Defense

Over the past two decades, communications and intelligence gathering satellites and various space-based sensors have become essential elements for command, control, and direction of military forces for both the United States and the Soviet Union. For example, both sides have space-based sensors to detect ballistic missile launches, and both depend upon communications satellites for global communications and navigation.

Both nations have also demonstrated a keen interest in developing anti-satellite capabilities that could destroy or incapacitate the satellites of the other side.[23] Attack warning, attack assessment, and defense against potential anti-satellite threats have therefore become serious concerns of both the United States and the Soviet Union. Neither nation currently has much capability for active space defense, except for some satellites that can maneuver in orbit. However, both have some capability to provide warning of certain anti-satellite threats by detecting and identifying objects in space.

For the United States, NORAD has established the Space Detection and Tracking System (SPADATS) to detect, identify, and catalog objects in earth orbit and deep space. SPADATS receives its primary inputs from the Air Force Spacetrack System, the Naval Space Surveillance System (NAVSPA-SUR), and from certain Canadian operated sensors. Inputs from Air Force Systems Command radars and from NASA are also used. Data from sensors are sent to the Space Surveillance Center in the CMC where they are identified and cataloged. Key parameters for each object are stored in CMC computers. At present, the CMC data base contains about 5,700 items, of which only 10 percent are operational satellites. The rest are essentially space junk: burnt-out rocket stages, pieces of debris from spacecraft of various sorts, etc. NORAD uses sensor updates and the data base for three purposes: space surveillance, warning and attack assessment of possible Soviet anti-satellite attacks, and the possible future task of identifying and tracking Soviet satellites for 'negation,' the official term for U.S. anti-satellite operations.[24]

Space surveillance involves identifying all items in near-earth space and keeping track of what they do. For example, the Soviet Union uses earth satellites for support of their operational military forces, which makes information about Soviet satellites and other space vehicles very valuable to the United States. To keep track of Soviet and other space activities, SPADATS uses a worldwide array of sensors.

On the remote island of Shemya in the Aleutians, the huge phased-array Cobra Dane radar provides a backup for the BMEWS system and forms a major part of SPADATS. Specifically designed for the detection and tracking of ICBMs, SLBMs, and satellites, the Cobra Dane radar is 98 feet in diameter and is composed of 35,000 elements, 15,000 of which are active at any one time. The system has a range of 25,000 miles in its space tracking mode. Its location just 500 miles from the Soviet Union allows it to cover a 120-degree, 2,000 mile swath of the Soviet ICBM test range. When used to collect data on Soviet missile tests, its electronically-steered beam can track up to 100 objects simultaneously while providing precise data on up to 20 targets. In an early warning role, Cobra Dane can provide information on 200 target tracks to NORAD, and in a surveillance mode, it is said to have a 99 percent probability of detecting a baseball-sized object at a range of 2,000 nautical miles. The Cobra Dane system has been in operation since 1977.[25]

Augmenting Cobra Dane in its surveillance role is the shipboard Cobra Judy, which is a single-faced phased-array radar installed aboard the U.S.S. Observation Island. Cobra Judy was developed in response to an Army Ballistic Missile Defense Command requirement to track Soviet MIRVs during testing, and was built in 1979. An additional higher frequency radar was added in the mid-1980s to increase the system's target resolution.[26]

The U.S. Navy contribution to space surveillance is NAVSPASUR, which detects orbital objects as they pass through an electronic 'fence' over the continental United States. NAVSPASUR is a multistatic continuous-wave radar deployed along a great circle from Fort Stewart, Georgia, to San Diego, California. Three transmitting stations and six receiving stations are interspersed along this line; the transmitters have large linear arrays that project stationary vertical planar fan beams, and the receivers use multiple-array interferometers to measure the angle of arrival of signals. Data are forwarded to the system's operations center in Dahlgren, Virginia, where satellite position is determined and sent on to NORAD. NAVSPASUR has been in operation since 1960, and was upgraded during the mid-1980s to double its range from 7,500 to 15,000 nautical miles.[27]

The BMEWS and Pave Paws radars also perform space surveillance functions, and together with Cobra Dane, Cobra Judy, NAVASPASUR, and the FPS-85 radar at Eglin Air Force Base in Florida, they form the radar backbone of the U.S. space track system. Other radars that provide data for the system include the Air Force Systems Command missile test range radars at Vandenberg Air Force Base, California, Antigua, and Ascension Island; the U.S. Army's Altair radar at the Kwajalein missile range; Air Force Space Command radars at San Miguel in the Philippines and at Pirinclik, Turkey; and the Haystack and Millstone Hill deep space radars that are operated by the Massachusets Institute of Technology's Lincoln Laboratory. A new radar on Saipan is expected to join the system by 1990.[28]

To augment U.S. deep space radars, NORAD relies on two optical systems: Baker-Nunn telescopes and Ground-based Electro-Optical Deep Space Surveillance (GEODSS) sensors. Both systems use electronically-controlled telescopes that scan specific areas of space; objects traversing that area can by identified by correlation with the known star background.

Two aging Baker-Nunn telescopes are still in use; one is operated by Canadian personnel at St. Margarets on Canada's eastern coast, and the other by the Air Force Space Command at San Vito, Italy. Baker-Nunn telescopes can track objects as small as a football out to about 50,000 miles. However, the system has two serious drawbacks for space defense use. First, the sky segment that the target object will traverse must be known in advance, and second, the system requires development of photographic plates, which takes about 90 minutes, far too slow to react to an event like a Soviet anti-satellite attack.[29]

The GEODSS system was developed to circumvent the drawbacks of the Baker-Nunn system. GEODSS uses a telescope that is electronically synchronized with the earth's rotation; but instead of photographic plates, a low-light video camera provides electronic imaging for computer processing and display. The system has two telescopes that each have an 86-inch focal length and a moving target indicator system. Each unit is capable of precision tracking of objects beyond geosynchronous Earth orbit (about 22,300 miles). GOEDSS sites are operational at Socorro, New Mexico; Taegu, Korea; and on Mount Haleakala, Hawaii. Two other sites are being built: one on Diego Garcia in the Indian Ocean and another at an unspecified location in Portugal.[30]

For the 1990s, NORAD is intent on modernizing and improving the current system. Many NORAD officials also want to develop new space-based surveillance systems, which might use infrared or radar sensors, or a combination of the two. But sensor coverage from space is an expensive proposition, and the technologies for space-based radar and advanced infrared sensors are just beginning to be developed. However, these new systems could eventually have the capability to identify and track Soviet satellites for U.S. anti-satellite operations.[31] Much of NORAD's future direction will depend on the outcome of new technology experiments like the Teal Ruby infrared sensor experiment, which is being developed to explore the possibilities of tracking aircraft from space, and on the attitudes of succeeding administrations toward SDI, ADI, and anti-satellite research and development.[32]

U.S. Nuclear Defense Command
and Control Communications

Over the past two decades, the immediate concern of U.S. command and control communications planners has centered on the reliability and survivability of the communications networks that would be used to orchestrate retaliatory nuclear strikes on the Soviet Union. Such systems include communications satellites, airborne and ground-mobile command posts and communications systems, and fixed ground facilities that are hardened against nuclear effects. Less attention has been paid to the reliability and survivability of the command and control communications necessary to orchestrate effective attack warning, attack assessment, and prolonged defense against a nuclear attack.

With the exception of the NORAD Cheyenne Mountain Complex (CMC), certain satellite systems, a few ground-mobile units, and E-3 AWACS aircraft, none of the components of NORAD's command and control system are considered to be capable of surviving an major nuclear strike by the Soviet Union. For example, the ROCCs were built as a peacetime air sovereignty system and are in 'soft' facilities. Part of the rationale for this is that neither the ground-based radars nor the communications supporting the ROCCs are considered very survivable during a nuclear attack.

Current NORAD defense communications networks includes leased commercial landlines (telephone lines), microwave systems, satellite-based systems, and ground-air-ground radio systems. These systems interconnect attack warning and attack assessment sensors (satellite warning sensors, phased-array radars, BMEWS, microwave radars, ground-based space detection systems, etc.) with the ROCCs. ROCCs also communicate with interceptor air bases for alerts and scrambles and with the CMC. Few of the commercial leased systems are encrypted, and none are hardened against nuclear effects (blast, electromagnetic pulse, etc.). Communication between ROCCs, radar sites, E-3 AWACS, and interceptor aircraft is accomplished by a combination of ground-air-ground radio links and satellite links. With the possible exception of certain satellite-to-aircraft links, all of these links are highly vulnerable to disruption by nuclear effects.

A first strike by the Soviet Union would almost certainly include warheads designed to destroy or disrupt U.S. fixed nuclear defense installations (ROCCs, radars, air bases, etc.) and would also include warheads designed to severely degrade or destroy communications networks (lines severed, antennae destroyed, electromagnetic pulse damage, ionospheric disturbance, etc.). A plausible scenario for a Soviet first strike would include an attack by Soviet air and sea launched cruise missiles and SLBMs that would precede an attack by ICBMs. Such a 'precursor attack' would be aimed at destroying U.S. command and control communications systems that are designed to orchestrate retaliatory strikes and to mount an effective prolonged defense of the U.S. homeland.

However, even with a surprise Soviet first strike, some nuclear defense assets, including parts of communications networks, could be expected to survive (missed targets, inactive radars, overlooked sites, ground-mobile and airborne elements, hardened or protected facilities, portions of the civilian telephone network, space-based systems, etc.). Since the 1950s, NORAD and other defense agencies have had ongoing programs to facilitate the reconstitution of surviving communications elements. The ability to systematically reconstitute surviving assets would be critical to a prolonged defense and post-war recovery.

Soviet Strategic Defense Concepts

The Soviet military structure is quite different than the military structure in the United States. The Soviet Armed Forces are organized in five separate services: Strategic Rocket Forces, Ground Forces, Troops of Air Defense, Air Forces, and Navy. For example, functions performed by the U.S. Air Force are spread across three of the Soviet services. In addition to five services, the Soviet Union has Troops of Civil Defense, Troops of the Tyl (rear services), Construction Troops, and other support organizations, all of which are under the Ministry of Defense. In addition, the Soviet Armed Forces includes the Border Guards, subordinate to the KGB, and the Internal Troops, subordinate to the Ministry of Internal Affairs (MVD). When speaking of the Army of the Soviet Union, Soviet officials usually refer to the Strategic Rocket Forces, Ground Forces, Troops of Air Defense, and Air Forces.[33]

The Strategic Rocket Forces (SRF), established in 1959, operate all land-based ballistic missiles with ranges greater than 1,000 kilometers. Little is known about SRF organization and internal functions outside the Soviet Union, but it is first among the services, with its commander taking precedence over those of the other services, regardless of his military rank. The Ground Forces are numerically the largest of the five services, with about 1,990,000 personnel. Ground Forces are divided into motorized rifle and tank troops, airborne troops, rocket troops (tactical) and artillery, and troops of air defense. All 210 divisions are trained and equipped for chemical, biological, and/or nuclear warfare.

The Troops of Air Defense (Voyska PVO) was formed in 1948 as PVO-Strany. In the early 1980s, air defense aircraft in border regions of the Soviet Union were merged with tactical air units of the Soviet Air Forces. There were also changes in air defense districts. Assets of air defense units of the Ground Forces were transferred to the Troops of Air Defense. Changes in the organization of Troops of Air Defense may have taken place in early 1988, but the extent of the changes are not known. For example, between October 1985 and September 1986, the First Deputy Commander of Troops of PVO was reassigned as Commander, Troops of Air Defense of the Ground Forces. This suggests a return to the structure that existed through the late 1970s. The three major components of Troops of Air Defense have approximately 2,250 fighter-intercepters, some 9,000 surface-to-air missile launchers, and a huge radar network. Two other components, anti-rocket defense (PRO) and anti-space defense (PKO), continue to grow in importance.

The Soviet Air Forces reorganization that started several years ago has continued through 1988. In border regions, aircraft and helicopters designated as 'frontal aviation' are designed to maintain air superiority and to strike targets in the 'operational depth' of an opponent. 'Army aviation' aircraft are designed primarily to attack mobile targets at 'tactical depth,' and to provide direct support to Ground Forces in combat. Both frontal and army aviation are in the Air Forces of the Military District, which are subordinate to the commanders of the Theaters of Military Operation (TVD).[34] Strategic bombers and strike aircraft are combined into five air armies. These include about 165 Bison and Bear bombers, 565 medium-range Blinder, Badger, and Backfire bombers, 450 Fencer strike aircraft, more than 300 tanker, reconnaissance, and electronic countermeasures aircraft, plus fighter escort aircraft. Most strategic combat aircraft are equipped to carry either nuclear or conventional weapons.[35] Transport Aviation includes some 600 fixed-wing aircraft. The transports of Aeroflot, the Soviet airline, with 1,600 medium and long range transports, are considered a full time ready reserve for military airlift functions.[36] Finally, the Soviet Navy is considered by most observers to be the second largest navy in the world, next to the United States. In addition to surface ships and ballistic missile and attack submarines, the Soviet Navy has aircraft carriers of the Kiev class, and a mix of carrier-based helicopters and fixed-wing aircraft. Naval Aviation has land-based fighters and reconnaissance aircraft, and a limited number of surveillance aircraft, transports, and bombers. The total Naval Aviation force currently exceeds 1,600 aircraft.[37]

Soviet military doctrine advocates close coordination between strategic offensive and defensive forces. On the offensive side, Soviet SRF missiles are designed to attack enemy nuclear forces, including silos, missile sites, airfields, naval bases, weapons depots, and nuclear command and control facilities. They would also attack other elements of enemy military forces, including transportation links and industrial facilities. Soviet SLBMs and bombers could serve either as part of a preemptive attack force or as a reserve during a prolonged nuclear conflict.

In the event that the Soviets fail to execute their preemptive option, they would depend on their early warning networks to provide them with sufficient warning time to launch their strategic offensive nuclear forces. This network includes ballistic missile launch detection satellites, phased array radars, over-the-horizon radars, and microwave radars that can determine the general direction of ballistic missile and air attacks and provide up to 30 minutes warning.[38]

If the SRF does not launch some or most of its missiles before an enemy attack, the Soviets have made provisions for the survival of SRF forces and command systems. For example, their missile silos, launch control systems, and their command, control, and communications facilities have been hardened against the effects of nuclear detonations. The Soviets also have highly survivable rail and road-mobile missiles in their newest generation of ICBMs. These 'defensive' techniques are designed to give SRF units and the command structure the capability to survive and operate during a prolonged period of nuclear conflict.

As indicated earlier, the Soviet Union is currently modernizing its ballistic missile defense system around Moscow by replacing old, reloadable above-ground GALOSH launchers with a two-layer defense composed of silo-based long-range, modified GALOSH missiles and silo-based GAZELLE high-acceleration missiles. In addition, the Soviets are continually modernizing their air defenses and attack warning and attack assessment systems.

In sum, Soviet military doctrine advocates close coordination between offensive and defensive forces to support strategies designed to fight and win a general nuclear war. For strategic defense, the Soviets have deployed a number of systems to provide attack warning, attack assessment, command and control, and active defenses (ballistic missile defenses, surface-to-air missiles, and fighter-interceptor aircraft) to complement their strategic offensive forces. Research and development programs similar to the U.S. SDI program have been started that will result in new systems in the 1990s and beyond.

Less information is available concerning the capabilities of Soviet strategic defense systems compared to the information available on U.S. systems. However, enough is known from the open literature to assess Soviet defensive capabilities and to compare these capabilities to those of the United States.

Beginning with air defense, key current and planned Soviet systems are outlined in the following sections.

The Soviet Air Defense System

The Soviet Union has continuing programs to modernize their air defense forces. As a result, Soviet air defenses are better able today (1988) to counter air strikes into Warsaw Pact territory by U.S. and NATO air forces. Substantial progress has also been made to counter U.S. and NATO cruise missiles. In contrast to the air defense weapons of the 1970s, the new Soviet Surface-to-Air (SAM) missiles and supporting radars possess increased mobility, making them more survivable. In addition, a greater number of Soviet interceptor aircraft are able to engage low-altitude targets and can fly longer missions, thereby permitting Soviet projection of air defenses well beyond the borders of Warsaw Pact nations.[39]

In 1980, both strategic and tactical border air defenses were subordinate to the local Military District (MD) commanders. Since 1986, the trend has been back to centralization under the strategic homeland Air Defense Forces. All strategic SAMs, radars, and interceptor aircraft are now under the direct control of air defense headquarters in Moscow. Conversely, tactical SAMs and radars have been subordinated to the Soviet Ground Forces for defense of Soviet ground forces in combat.[40]

While the number of Soviet aircraft committed to strategic air defense has remained at about 2,250 for the past five years or so, the interceptor force has been improved substantially. For example, many vintage 1950s and 1960s aircraft such as the YAK-28P (Firebar), TU-128 (Fiddler), and Su-15 (Flagon) have been replaced with over 160 MiG-31 (Foxhound) and 100 Su-27 (Flanker) aircraft. These new fighters have look-down-shoot-down systems, which gives them the capability to detect and destroy targets flying at low altitudes. Also, the Soviets are expected to produce two new fighters in the mid-1990s: an offensive counter-air fighter for air superiority and a defensive counterair fighter, both with greater capabilities than the Flanker B models currently in service.[41]

The Soviets are also deploying increasing numbers of Ilyushin Il-76 (Mainstay) Airborne Early Warning and Control (AEW&C) aircraft. The Il-76 has both an airborne radar for detecting targets flying at low-altitude and the capability to direct Soviet air defense interceptors to targets beyond the range of ground-based systems. The combination of Il-26 and longer range interceptors like the MiG-31 gives the Soviets their first capability to project strategic air defenses beyond the periphery of Warsaw Pact nations.[42]

Like the United States', successful Soviet air defense operations depend in part on air defense radars and command and control communications between radar sites, command centers, interceptor aircraft, and SAM batteries. In addition to phased-array radars for the latest SAMs, major advances include early warning radars with three-dimensional (azimuth, height, and range) capabilities and improved detection capabilities against low-flying targets. The Soviets also have over-the-horizon radars, including a new system deployed east of Vladivostok on the Eastern coast of the Soviet Union. Command and control communications systems have also been upgraded to improve the chances for survivability and continued operation during a nuclear attack.[43]

Unlike the United States, which has no Surface-to-Air Missiles for strategic air defense, the Soviet Union has a massive force of radar-guided SAMs. The major strategic SAM activity of recent years was the deployment of the SA-10, which reached an initial operational capability in 1980. Since then, it has entered the Soviet inventory as a replacement for three older strategic SAM systems: the SA-1, 2, and 3. The introduction of the SA-10 has enhanced the Soviet SAM force capability to track and engage multiple targets simultaneously. It also provides low-altitude detection and intercept capabilities that have been historically lacking in Soviet SAM forces. Supported by new phased-array acquisition and guidance radars, the SA-10 represents the first credible Soviet capability against targets with a small radar cross section, including a limited capability against cruise missiles. Since 1981, about 150 SA-10 launch units have ben deployed in defense of major military and industrial centers. About 50 of these units are deployed around Moscow. The Soviet plan to deploy the even more capable SA-X-12B SAM system in the early 1990s.[44]

The Soviets have also continued to adjust their SAM deployment to maintain a multi-layered air defense of the Soviet homeland. A recent example was the deployment of long-range, high-altitude SA-5 systems to Eastern Europe, where they now provide overlapping coverage over the Baltic Sea and the East-West German border. By exporting this system to their Warsaw Pact allies, the Soviets have not only enhanced the air defense of those countries, but have extended the air defense buffer zone for the Soviet homeland. SA-5s in East Germany pose a significant threat to key NATO reconnaissance and U.S. E-3 AWACS aircraft, even when they operate in West German air space.[45]

Soviet Ballistic Missile Defense

The Soviet Union has the world's only operational Anti-Ballistic Missile (ABM) system. The system is deployed in the Moscow area and is currently being upgraded to include a two-layer defense with 100 modernized missile launchers. When fully operational in 1990, the system will defend selected command centers and other facilities in the Moscow area.

By 1990, the Moscow ABM system will include two new types of interceptor missiles: a long-range missile (GALOSH) that is designed to engage ballistic missile reentry vehicles (RVs) outside the Earth's atmosphere; and a shorter range, high-acceleration missile (GAZELLE) that, like the now deactivated U.S. SPRINT ABM missile, is designed to engage RVs after they have reentered the Earth's atmosphere. New, hardened silos have been constructed for the new interceptor missiles. The Soviets are also completing the construction of a large phased-array radar at Pushkino. This radar, which provides 360-degree coverage, will support the Moscow ABM system by performing acquisition and tracking functions.[46]

Like the U.S., the Soviet Union began building a phased-array radar network in the 1970s. Currently, there are nine radars in this network, forming nearly a complete ring of ballistic missile detection coverage for the Soviet homeland. These new radars duplicate and augment the ballistic missile attack warning and attack assessment coverage provided by the older HEN HOUSE ballistic missile early warning radars, but they also provide the detailed tracking data which would be required for a nationwide ABM system. Since these radars take a long time to construct, this new network probably will not be fully operational until the mid-1990s.

From the point of view of the United States, the Soviet phased-array radar at Krasnoyarsk may constitute a violation of the U.S.-Soviet ABM Treaty. Evidence suggests that this radar is primarily designed for ballistic missile detection and tracking, not for space-tracking as the Soviets have claimed. The Krasnoyarsk radar also closes a major gap in the coverage of the Soviet ballistic missile attack warning and attack assessment system. All nine Soviet phased array radars in this network have the capability to provide warning of a ballistic missile attack in time to activate Soviet strategic offensive and defensive forces and to perform ABM battle management functions during an attack.[47]

Soviet Space Defenses

The Soviet Union has developed and deployed a number of space systems designed to support military operations on Earth. Like the United States, the Soviets have a satellite network that provides warning of ICBM launches. They also operate several types of space-based reconnaissance systems, including the RORSAT and EORSAT, which can be used to locate naval forces.[48]

In addition, their satellite reconnaissance capability has been refined, and their space-based electronic intelligence gathering systems are currently being upgraded. The Soviets are also working on a space-based surveillance system to detect the launch of U.S. SLBMs as well as a system to detect European and Chinese ballistic missiles. The Soviets will probably have the technical capability to deploy such systems during the 1990s. The Soviets have also continued to develop and deploy radar-mapping satellites. These are designed for mapping ice formations, and will greatly enhance the Soviet Navy's ability to operate in polar regions. Like the United States, the Soviets have satellite communications networks and navigation systems.[49]

However, the Soviet ground-based satellite tracking system is far less capable than the world-wide network deployed by the United States. Nearly all Soviet satellite tracking stations are located on the landmass of the Soviet Union, and are primarily located down-range from the test facilities at Tyuratam, Kapustin Yar, and Sary Shagan. Major tracking facilities are also located on the Kamchatka Peninsula adjacent to the Bering Sea.

On the other hand, the Soviets are developing and may deploy anti-satellite weapons that could pose a serious threat to U.S. satellites in low-Earth orbit. The current Soviet operational anti-satellite weapon is a ground-based interceptor missile. It uses a radar sensor and a pellet-type warhead, and can reach low-altitude satellites that come within the slant range of the launch site. The interceptor launch site is located at the Tyuratam test facility in the south-central Soviet Union, and consists of two launch pads, storage space for interceptors, radars, and other support systems. The nuclear-armed GALOSH ABM also has an inherent anti-satellite capability, and the Soviets are also developing ground-based lasers that may pose a serious threat to U.S. satellites by the late 1990s.[50]

Soviet Nuclear Defense Command and Control Communications

Even more than the United States, the Soviet Union has invested heavily in survivable command and control communications networks. These networks are designed to orchestrate nuclear strikes against the U.S., Western Europe, and China and to facilitate a prolonged defense of the Soviet homeland. Like the United States, such systems include communications satellites, airborne and ground-mobile command posts and communications systems, and fixed ground facilities that are hardened against nuclear effects. However, the Soviets have placed greater emphasis on hardened facilities and landlines, whereas the United States has concentrated more on satellite and airborne systems.

Like U.S. systems, Soviet radars, air bases, and other 'soft' facilities are highly vulnerable to blast and other nuclear effects. Soviet communications networks connect attack warning and attack assessment sensors (satellite warning systems, phased-array radars, microwave radars, ground-based space detection systems, etc.) with regional defense command centers. In turn, these centers communicate with interceptor air bases for alerts and scrambles and with Soviet national command centers that are buried deep underground in the Moscow area. However, most of the sensors and some of the communications networks are not hardened against nuclear effects (blast, electromagnetic pulse, etc.).

A retaliatory nuclear strike by the United States would almost certainly include warheads designed to destroy or disrupt Soviet fixed nuclear defense installations (radars, air bases, etc.) and would also include warheads designed to severely degrade or destroy communications networks (lines severed, antennae destroyed, electromagnetic pulse damage, ionospheric disturbance, etc.). Further, the United States has highly accurate warheads that are specially designed to 'dig out' hardened underground Soviet command centers.

Soviet Passive Defenses

Unlike the United States, the Soviet Union has a massive civil defense program. This program includes deep underground bunkers, tunnels, special subway lines, and other facilities beneath Moscow, other major Soviet cities, and the sites of major military commands. Much of the underground system is designed to protect and support the Soviet leadership during a nuclear battle. Other facilities and procedures are intended to protect key elements of the Soviet population, including the scientific and technical elite.

The Soviet civil defense system provides a substantial capability for the Soviet leadership to survive a nuclear attack, to function during an extended nuclear war, and to reconstitute key elements of the Soviet population that would be necessary to support their industrial base after a nuclear war has ended. For example, the deep underground facilities beneath Moscow provide the leaders of the various ministries of government the opportunity to move from their peacetime offices through concealed passages down to protective quarters below the city. Once there, the Politburo, the Central Committee of the Communist Party, the Ministry of Defense, the KGB, and key elements of other state ministries could remain sheltered while they orchestrate the conversion of the nation to a wartime posture. A highly redundant communications system, consisting of both on-site and remote elements, supports these underground complexes and permits the leadership to send orders and receive reports. These underground facilities also have sophisticated life support systems capable of protecting their occupants against nuclear effects as well as chemical and biological weapons.[51]

European Perspectives on Nuclear Defense

Over 2,700 NATO and 3,500 Soviet nuclear delivery vehicles and about 9,000 nuclear warheads are deployed in Europe or facing Europe. Additional nuclear weapons in the United States and the Soviet Union are readily available to reinforce any operations in the European theater. In the surrounding seas, naval forces have still more warheads, bringing the region's total to about 17,000, which is about one-third of the world's nuclear arsenals. With the highest density of nuclear weapons in the world, any conflict in Europe has a grave potential of quickly escalating to a nuclear conflict.

Europeans have responded by constructing elaborate attack warning and attack assessment sensor systems oriented toward Warsaw Pact nuclear armed aircraft. They also have substantial active anti-aircraft defenses, including large numbers of anti-aircraft missiles and fighter-interceptor aircraft. Passive defenses include massive underground bunkers, hardened communications networks, and comprehensive civil defense programs.

However, European nations on both sides of the iron curtain have no warning sensors that are capable of detecting ballistic missiles, and no active ballistic missile defenses. Like the United States and the Soviet Union, sensors and defenses against cruise missiles are rudimentary at best.

Since 1985, the United States has persistently sought West European participation in the SDI program, with limited results. West Europeans appear to be attracted by the technology and the economic benefits of SDI research and development, but they have serious reservations about U.S. and Soviet deployment of such systems.

For example, the West European public tends to view ballistic missile defenses as a dangerous escalation of the nuclear arms race. Many believe that such defenses would provide an incentive for a superpower to mount a pre-emptive first strike on its opponent, and such a conflict would inevitably involve Europe. Also, an effective U.S. ballistic missile defense would tend to reduce the credibility of the U.S. pledge to respond to the defense of Western Europe because the U.S. homeland would not be at risk in any European conflict. In addition, the governments of the United Kingdom and France have expressed concern that an effective Soviet ballistic missile defense would reduce the deterrence value of their independent nuclear forces.

As a result, West Europeans have been, at best, lukewarm to the prospects of effective U.S. and Soviet ballistic missile defenses that encompass large areas of superpower homelands. They are also reluctant to develop their own such defenses because of the enormous potential costs and the low utility of such defenses against the Soviet conventional threat to Western Europe. Also, they have expressed the concern that the Soviets could overwhelm any Western European ballistic missile defense by simply deploying more missiles, which would be an expensive escalation of the arms race.

However, Western European military establishments have expressed a greater interest in the military technologies that would result from SDI research. European defense industries are attracted by the prospect of economic benefits and in some cases, have actively sought U.S. SDI contracts. Advanced sensor systems, battle management computers, weapons for the defense of small areas (missile silos, command centers, etc.), and applications to conventional forces are of particular interest. These potential applications are also of great interest to the U.S. and Soviet military establishments and defense contractors, and they are understandably reluctant to share these technologies with other nations. Only time will show how the issues of SDI technology transfer will be handled in the NATO alliance.

The Status of Nuclear Defenses

Since the beginning of the nuclear era, U.S. strategic planners have stressed the concept of deterring nuclear war by threatening retaliation in kind should an adversary use nuclear weapons. At the same time, U.S. defense policy has continued to rely on U.S. nuclear weapons to help deter conventional attack, primarily because larger conventional forces are far more expensive than nuclear forces, and neither the U.S. nor its allies, apparently, are willing to spend larger sums on defense.

Defenses against nuclear weapons can alter deterrence in at least two ways. First, they can protect the offensive nuclear forces of the defended country. Second, defenses can reduce the number of enemy warheads that reach military and civilian targets in defended areas. Both could alter the demand for nuclear warheads in the defended country. From a planner's point of view, a dollar or ruble spent on defense could replace a dollar or ruble spent on offense, since both contribute to deterrence. As long as the amount of deterrence gained per dollar or ruble spent on defense exceeds the amount deterrence gained per dollar or ruble spent on offense, the incentive will be to substitute defense for offense, holding the level of deterrence constant.

Despite continued budget cuts in Fiscal Years 1988–89, the U.S. SDI program has made significant progress toward its stated goal of supporting an informed decision in the early 1990s on deploying a ballistic missile defense. Since the beginning of the SDI, a series of technology developments and experiments have demonstrated the potential for using advanced technology to construct an effective strategic defense against incoming nuclear missiles. For example, the U.S. has successfully demonstrated the ability to intercept targets both within the atmosphere and in space. Advances have also been made in the development of directed energy weapons (lasers, particle beams, etc.) and in new sensor technologies. Computers have been used to simulate weapons and nuclear battles, and to demonstrate conceptual battle management systems. Based on these and other developments, the U.S. Defense Acquisition Board recommended in 1987 that certain SDI technologies enter the demonstration and validation phase of the defense acquisition process. Thus, the stage has been set for the deployment of a large scale prototype system to test concepts 'in the field' that have been successfully demonstrated in the laboratory and in tests of component systems.

The U.S. is also modernizing its air defense forces to correct deficiencies in sensors (cruise missile detection, replacement of the aging DEW line, etc.), command and control communications (improve survivability with regard to nuclear effects, etc.), and intercept capability (replacement of F-106 and F-4 aircraft with F-15s and F-16s). For the longer term, research and development under the ADI will be directed toward countering Soviet development of 'stealth' aircraft and cruise missiles.

On the other side, the Soviets have pursued wide-ranging programs to blunt the effects of a nuclear attack on the Soviet Union. These programs reflect Soviet military doctrine, that calls for equal attention to defensive as well as offensive capabilities. Soviet defense planners clearly recognize the importance of space and ballistic missile defense systems. According to the Soviets, the primary purpose of a space defense system is to destroy enemy military space systems in orbit. The Soviets are testing several anti-satellite systems, including systems that employ special aircraft, ground launched missiles, and ground based lasers. For ballistic missiles, the Soviet Union has the world's only operational anti-ballistic missile defense system, which is currently being upgraded with new GALOSH and GAZELLE interceptor missiles.

In addition, the Soviet Union has an operational air defense system that dwarfs the air defense system of the United States. The Soviet system employs a large number of interceptor aircraft, anti-aircraft missiles and artillery, command centers, radars, and communications networks to protect territory, military forces, and other key assets throughout the Soviet Union. This system is continually being upgraded; recent additions include over-the-horizon radars, new interceptor aircraft, and new anti-aircraft missiles.

Finally, the Soviets have developed passive defenses that include massive underground bunkers to protect political, economic, and military leaders, and hardening of communications networks against nuclear effects.

Soviet writings on the nature of war suggest that strategic defenses will be expanded to include defenses against cruise missiles and precision-guided conventional munitions. Also, as indicated recently by General Secretary Gorbachev, the Soviet Union has its own version of the SDI program.

Thus, there is every reason to expect that the development of nuclear defenses by both superpowers will continue, at least at the level of research and development. Whether or not there will be an eventual substitution of defenses for offensive forces remains to be seen. At this point, it that can be said that if the amount of perceived deterrence gained per dollar spent on defense exceeds the amount gained per dollar spent on offense, the economic incentive for substitution will be present.

The next major decision point for the U.S. will occur in the early 1990s, when the President and Congress must decide whether or not to deploy some sort of ballistic missile defense system. From the Soviet point of view, such a deployment would increase their current strong emphasis for developing new and modernizing current strategic defenses.

Notes

1. Carlucci, F., *Soviet Military Power,* U.S. Government Printing Office, Washington, DC, April 1988, 55.

2. Carlucci, *Soviet Military Power,* 55–58; also see Arkin, W., and Fieldhouse, R., *Nuclear Battlefields: Global Links in the Arms Race,* Ballinger Publishing Company, Cambridge, MA, 1985, 73–78.

3. Carlucci, F., *Soviet Military Power,* 56.

4. Campbell, C., *Nuclear Facts,* Hamlyn Publishing Group, London, 1984, 182, and Weinberger, C., *Soviet Military Power,* U.S. Government Printing Office, Washington DC, March 1987, 50–51, and Carlucci, *Soviet Military Power,* 64–65.

5. Carlucci, *Soviet Military Power;* Weinberger, C., *Annual Report to the Congress, FY 1988,* U.S. Government Printing Office, Washinton, DC, pp. 26–27. As anecdotal evidence, one of us (Gertcher) was involved in an analysis of the Soviet air defense radar network in the mid-1960s. As part of this work, an attempt was made to locate and identify all Soviet radars by sticking colored pins in a map of the Soviet Union and Eastern Europe (scale: 1:3,000,000). The radars were so densely populated in certain areas, especially around Moscow and Leningrad, that all of the pins would not fit in their proper locations on the map. Current research (1988) indicates that the density of Soviet radars has grown rather than decreased in recent years.

6. DCS Comptroller, NORAD, *Pocket Information Handbook,* October 1984. Also see Arkin and Fieldhouse, *Nuclear Battlefields: Global Links in the Arms Race;* and "NORAD Profile," *Defense Electronics Magazine,* August 1985, Volume 17, Number 8, pp. 105–108. It is also worth noting that the organizational structure of the U.S. Air Force Space Command is interlocked with the structure of NORAD. Its commander is also the commander-in-chief of NORAD and the commander of the Aerospace Defense Command, NORAD's U.S. Air Force Component. The relationship between Space Command and NORAD is primarily operational; Space Command manages most of the assets that NORAD uses for its ballistic missile and space warning missions. NORAD's deputy commander-in-chief is always a Canadian officer.

7. For an excellent overview of the U.S. command and control structure that would operate during pre, trans, and post nuclear attack, see Blair, B., *Strategic Command and Control: Redefining the Nuclear Threat,* Brookings Institution, Washington, DC, 1985, 212–280. Also see "NORAD Profile," *Defense Electronics Magazine;* and "The Military Balance, 1985/86," *Air Force Magazine,* Air Force Association, February 1986, 62–63.

8. Blair, *Strategic Command and Control,* 273–274.

9. "The Military Balance," *Air Force Magazine,* 62–63.

10. Boutacoff, D., "Backscatter Radar Extends Early Warning Times," *Defense Electronics Magazine*, Volume 17, Number 5, May 1985, 71–83.

11. "Focus: Air Force to Test OTH-B Against Small Targets," *Defense Electronics Magazine*, Volume 19, Number 9, September 1987, 26.

12. Gumble, B., "Air Force Upgrading Defenses at NORAD," *Defense Electronics Magazine*, Volume 17, Number 8, August 1985, 105.

13. Carlucci, F., *Annual Report to the Congress, Fiscal Year 1989*, U.S. Government Printing Office, Washington DC, February 11, 1988, 239–240.

14. Gumble, "Air Force Upgrading Defenses at NORAD," 98.

15. Blair, *Strategic Command and Control*, 212–280; also Gumble, "Air Force Upgrading Defenses at NORAD," 86–88; and "The Military Balance," 62.

16. Gumble, "Air Force Upgrading Defenses at NORAD," 98.

17. Ibid.

18. Blair, *Strategic Command and Control*, 212–280; also see Gumble, "Air Force Upgrading Defenses at NORAD," 98–99.

19. Gumble, "Air Force Upgrading Defenses at NORAD," 98–99.

20. Ibid.

21. Ibid.

22. Raytheon Advertisement, *Defense Electronics Magazine*, Volume 19, Number 9, September 1987; also see Gumble, "Air Force Upgrading Defenses at NORAD," 98–99.

23. Campbell, C., *Nuclear Facts*, 182–183. The United States had a limited anti-satellite capability from 1963 to 1975, using nuclear-tipped Army Nike-Zeus missiles from Kwajalein Atoll and U.S. Air Force Thor missiles from Johnson Island. The use of nuclear warheads in space was prohibited by the Outer Space Treaty of 1967. The Soviet Union began tests of a co-orbital 'hunter-killer' satellite in 1968, using the SS-9 Scarp booster. Soviet tests continued intermittently during the 1970s, and were discontinued during the abortive U.S.-Soviet Anti-Satellite limitation talks of 1978–79. Tests were resumed in the early 1980s. Rumors have long persisted of Soviet operational capability to destroy U.S. satellites in low earth orbit with a direct-ascent missile or with ground-based lasers. Unsubstantiated claims have also been made of orbiting Soviet battle stations equipped with infrared homing interceptors, capable of destroying U.S. spacecraft. Meanwhile, the U.S. has regained a limited anti-satellite capability with the F-15 aircraft and a Vought anti-satellite missile.

24. Gumble, "Air Force Upgrading Defenses at NORAD," 103.

25. Ibid.

26. Ibid.

27. Ibid.

28. Ibid.; also see "The Military Balance," 62–63.

29. Gumble, "Air Force Upgrading Defenses at NORAD," 103–104.

30. Ibid.

31. Ibid.

32. "Space Based Surveillance," *Defense Electronics Magazine*, Volume 19, Number 9, September 1987, 48.

33. "Organization of the Soviet Armed Forces," *Air Force Magazine*, Air Force Association, March 1988, pp. 61–62; also see Carlucci, *Soviet Military Power*, 13–16, and "The Military Balance," 79–85.

34. "Organization of the Soviet Armed Forces."
35. See Chapter 2.
36. "The Military Balance."
37. See Chapter 2. Also see Carlucci, *Soviet Military Power.*
38. Carlucci, *Soviet Military Power.*
39. Ibid., also "The Military Balance."
40. "Organization of the Soviet Armed Forces."
41. Carlucci, *Soviet Military Power.*
42. Ibid.
43. Ibid.
44. Ibid.
45. Ibid.
46. Ibid.
47. Ibid.
48. Ibid.
49. Ibid.; also Weinberger, C., *Soviet Military Power.*
50. Ibid.; also see note 23.
51. Carlucci, *Soviet Military Power;* also Weinberger, *Soviet Military Power.*

6

Evolving Technologies

Let me share with you a vision of the future which offers hope. It is that we embark on a program to counter the awesome Soviet missile threat with measures that are defensive. Let us turn to the very strengths in technology that spawned our great industrial base and that have given us the quality of life we have today.
—President Reagan

Strategic Defense Initiatives

President Reagan's March 23, 1983 speech was the beginning of an effort to explore technologies that may contribute to a U.S. ballistic missile defense. This effort, called the 'Strategic Defense Initiative' (SDI), may generate new and unique defense concepts, and systems. By the late 1990s, the United States may have the capability to deploy some elements of a ballistic missile defense for key areas, such as U.S. ICBM complexes.

For over a decade, the Soviet Union has had its own version of a strategic defense initiative. It also has an operational ground-based ballistic missile defense system for the Moscow area. Further, the Soviets have a massive program to update existing strategic defenses as well as to develop new technologies for more sophisticated ballistic missile defenses.

This chapter outlines the elements of ballistic missile defense and provides an overview of both U.S. and Soviet ballistic missile defense programs. It also discusses certain political and economic issues associated with strategic defense budgets, and outlines possible Soviet responses to U.S. efforts to develop and deploy sophisticated ballistic missile defenses. Finally, this chapter explores the implications of U.S. and Soviet SDI programs for crisis and arms race stability.

Deterrence Based on Defense

If ballistic missile defenses are deployed on a large scale by the United States and the Soviet Union, they may significantly alter superpower warfighting capabilities. Such defenses, coupled with effective space and air defenses, have the potential to foster an evolution away from a dependence on offensive nuclear weapons for deterrence. As stated in the previous chapter, this shift is more likely if the amount of deterrence gained per dollar spent on defense is greater than the amount of deterrence gained per dollar spend on offense, although such an economic relationship has yet to be proved.

However, there are also military reasons for ballistic missile defenses. Incentives include concern over the vulnerability of ICBM silos to increasingly accurate enemy missiles and the perennial concern over the vulnerability of manned bomber bases, communications facilities, and other 'soft' military targets. Ballistic missile defenses offer a way to defend such targets.

If ballistic missile defenses are not built, there are strong political and military incentives to build more units of offensive strategic forces (ICBMs, bombers, etc.), harden infrastructures such as command and control communications, and increase the number of nuclear warheads. The purpose of such enhancements would be to insure that sufficient forces would survive a first strike by an enemy, and then be able to destroy the warmaking capabilities of the attacker. Thus, if a potential enemy realizes that such a capability exists, a first strike will not take place and deterrence is preserved.

If ballistic missile defenses are perceived to be effective and relatively cheaper than ballistic missiles, the prospects for successful U.S.-Soviet negotiations and reductions in the number of strategic weapons may be enhanced. This result would be consistent with President Reagan's vision of deterrence based on defensive systems and reduced numbers of nuclear missiles.

On the other hand, some analysts have argued that a unilateral deployment of a ballistic missile defense by the United States could destabilize the balance of power between the United States and the Soviet Union. According to this argument, the Soviets may perceive that the U.S. intends to use ballistic missile defenses to make U.S. strategic nuclear forces (ICBM complexes, etc.) invulnerable to Soviet attack, just as the U.S. might believe that the Soviets had similar intentions if they continue to expand their existing ballistic missile defenses. From the Soviet point of view, a pre-emptive attack might be desirable to eliminate an enhanced U.S. capability to fight and win a prolonged nuclear war.[1]

In any case, a comprehensive ballistic missile defense has the potential to be much more expensive than any other strategic defense system ever developed. There are at least three reasons for this: 1) Many elements of a ballistic missile defense system would be deployed in space, 2) The development of a ballistic missile defense pushes the state of the art of many technologies more than ever before, and 3) In the near term, such a system would be an addition to the existing defense structure.[2]

According to the U.S. Department of Defense, a 'Phase I' deployment of a ballistic missile defense would provide a 'layered' defense of key areas such as ICBM complexes and other elements of U.S. strategic nuclear forces. The defense would be layered because it would attempt to intercept attacking missiles and warheads that are in the boost, post-boost, mid-course, and terminal phases of flight. Phase I would include both ground-based and space-based weapons. Some weapons would have interceptor missiles with conventional warheads. Other platforms could have directed energy weapons such as high energy lasers. In early September 1988, Lieutenant General Abrahamson, head of the Strategic Defense Initiative Office (SDIO), briefed Congressional leaders on the Phase I portion of a three phase plan for deployment. In September, 1988, Phase I was reviewed and approved by the Defense Acquisition Board at the Pentagon. A decision on whether or not to deploy Phase I of a ballistic missile defense is still planned for the mid-1990s. Phases II and III have yet to be defined, presumably they would include extending the defense to include more areas and would include more sophisticated weapons and battle management systems.[3]

The U.S. debate over whether to proceed with a ballistic missile defense leads to consideration of both economic and deterrence problems. In brief, the economic problem is as follows: Given the resource allocations that currently exist for defense, what will happen if, in addition, the United states develops and deploys a totally new system—a system that will compete vigorously with existing defense and nondefense programs for resources. The deterrence problem involves Soviet perceptions and likely responses to the U.S. development and potential deployment of ballistic missile defenses.

According to General Abrahamson, the September 1988 plan for Phase I had a price tag of $69 billion. This was a reduction from a June 1988 estimate of $115 billion. The General attributed the estimated cost reduction to 'optimizing technology', and the substitution of ground-based interceptors for about half of the planned space-based interceptors.[4]

Both the U.S. and the Soviets recognize that an effective ballistic missile defense could contribute to deterrence by reducing the perceived benefits to an attacker of launching a nuclear strike. Since the United States began its SDI effort in 1983, the Soviets have demonstrated that they have no intention of being left behind. As a result, the U.S.-Soviet arms competition has shifted to a new and, according to proponents, a less dangerous phase, since both sides may be evolving toward an emphasis on the development of strategic defenses rather than offensive nuclear weapons. Thus, the demand for nuclear weapons could, in the long run, be reduced as resources are shifted from offense to defense in both nations.

In 1988, the Soviet Union probably spent between four and five billion dollars on strategic defense procurement. By contrast, the United States spent less than one billion. On the other hand, the United States and the

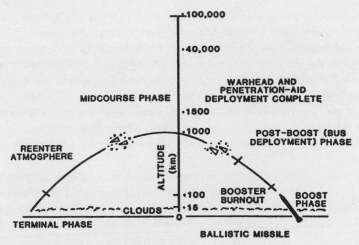

Figure 6.1: Phases of a Ballistic Missile Flight
Source: Caspar Weinberger, *Annual Report to Congress, Fiscal Year 1987,*
U.S. Government Printing Office, Washington, D.C., 1986.

Soviet Union both spent about $17 billion on total strategic forces in 1988. Soviet expenditures on SDI-type research and development are not publicly known; however, according to the U.S. Department of Defense, the Soviet SDI effort is comparable in scope to that of the United States.[5]

The Elements of Ballistic Missile Defense

Ballistic missiles are launched from the earth's surface, rise through the atmosphere into space along a suborbital trajectory, and reenter the atmosphere about a hundred miles from their targets. Ballistic missile defense involves the detection, tracking, engagement, and destruction of ballistic missiles at some point in their trajectory prior to the detonation of their warheads.[6] Trajectory phases are shown in Figure 6.1. In the boost phase, a ballistic missile accelerates up through the atmosphere and into space. For a short time the missile moves relatively slowly and, expends a very large amount of propulsive energy. The infrared radiation associated with the exhaust plume from the burning rocket fuel is easily observable and can be used to detect and track the missile launch.

Following the boost phase, a postboost vehicle (essentially a third or fourth stage of the missile—also known as a 'MIRV bus') separates from the burnt-out booster and may deploy multiple warheads (multiple individually targeted reentry vehicles, or MIRVs) and penetration aids. The latter include reentry vehicle (RV) decoys, chaff, aerosols, electronic jammers, and balloons, all designed to confuse the detection and tracking systems of the defender.

The postboost phase is significant because the process of deploying multiple objects in space from a single missile may increase the number of space objects associated with a single launch by a factor of 100 or more. This complicates the defender's problems in identifying, tracking, and discriminating real warheads from decoys and penetration aids. The problem is particularly important if the defender's system has limited fuel, such as would occur for space-based chemical lasers that would be expected to operate for extended periods during a nuclear exchange. Consequently, 'birth-to-death' tracking, and track-file maintenance, and other efficiency measures are critical.

Once the postboost phase is completed, the 'MIRVed' warheads and decoys follow a ballistic trajectory in space. This portion of the flight, known as the midcourse phase, can last up to twenty minutes. This phase provides a relatively long time span for discrimination of real warheads from decoys and for possible warhead intercept and destruction.

Reentry into the atmosphere marks the end of the midcourse phase and the beginning of the terminal phase. Reentry heating usually destroys decoys, which must be made from relatively lightweight materials to avoid taking up valuable space, adding weight, and reducing warhead payload aboard the MIRV bus. Heating also destroys other penetration aids such as chaff and balloons. This process is known technically as 'atmospheric strip-out.' Atmospheric strip-out eliminates much of the discrimination problem faced by terminal defenses. However, the terminal phase is characterized by extremely compressed decision and engagement 'windows,' for very little time remains before the warheads reach their targets. Also, certain decoy designs could survive to very low altitudes in order to force a firing and intercept commitment by terminal defenses.

Finally, although defensive sensors can readily detect and track the extremely hot and energetic reentry vehicles, the defensive weapons allocated to each warhead must have very high velocities to reach the warhead before it detonates above or on its intended target. The geometry and time scale of terminal defense dictate that defensive weapons must be located near the defended target. Consequently, terminal defense concepts have traditionally focused on defense of relatively localized high-value targets, such as ICBM silo complexes, certain military bases, or selected population centers. Technically, this is referred to as a 'point defense,' as opposed to a broader 'area defense.'

The technical requirements and phenomenologies associated with terminal ballistic missile defense have been thoroughly worked out over the past 25 years. Some specialists also believe that boost phase intercept, particularly with satellite-launched, kinetic-kill missiles, is also relatively well defined. They point to the resurgence of interest by the SDIO in such weapons as a potential option for a near-term Phase I deployment by the United States.

Table 6.1: Strategic Defense Initiative Budget Requests (Planned as of Calendar Year 1985)

Program Category	Fiscal Year (Millions of Dollars)					
	1984	1985	1986	1987	1988	1989
Surveillance, Acq., Tracking and Kill Assessment	366.5	545.9	1386.3	1874.9	2538.0	3065.0
Directed Energy Weapons	311.3	376.4	965.4	1195.6	1435.0	1677.0
Kinetic Energy Weapons	196.8	256.0	859.7	1238.6	1480.0	1675.0
Systems Analysis and Battle Mgt.	10.0	99.0	243.3	272.5	303.0	358.0
SDI Support	106.3	112.0	258.2	316.7	400.0	514.0
Sub Total	990.9	1389.3	3712.9	4898.3	6156.0	7289.0
SDI Program Mgt.	0.5	8.0	9.2	10.0	10.0	10.0
Total	991.4	1397.3	3722.2	4908.3	6166.0	7299.0

Sources: Bosma and Whelan, *Guide to the Strategic Defense Initiative*, Pasha Publications, Arlington, VA 1985. Also see Department of Defense, *Report to Congress on the Strategic Defense Initiative*, 1985, and *IEEE Spectrum*, September, 1985, p. 61.

The U.S. SDI Program

One year after President Reagan's March 23, 1983 'Star Wars' speech, the Strategic Defense Initiative was moving ahead at a billion-dollar annual funding level. This was a remarkable achievement in a defense environment that normally includes several years of studies before any major new program can be passed in Congress. The ability to move the program so quickly to that funding level resulted from the fact that much of the technology needed for SDI was already under development. For example, the Army already had substantial ballistic missile defense programs in surveillance and tracking, interceptor missiles, and terminal defense battle management. The Air Force and the Defense Advanced Research Projects Agency (DARPA) had several programs under way in directed energy weapons and space surveillance. At least 25 separate Department of Defense programs were aggregated and restructured to form the SDI. Table 6.1 provides a summary of the SDIO request for funds for Fiscal Years 1984 through 1989.

The surveillance, acquisition, tracking and kill assessment category includes research and development programs for detecting, acquiring and tracking ballistic missiles and discriminating reentry vehicles and decoys over all phases of the ballistic missile trajectory. Directed energy weapons programs include research and development of high energy lasers and particle beam weapons. Kinetic energy weapons programs include the development of hypervelocity missiles and electromagnetic launch weapons. Systems analysis and battle management programs involve the development of technologies for battle management and command, control and communications. Finally, SDI support programs include the development of technologies in four key areas: survivability of elements of the defense system; lethality of candidate weapons and vulnerability of hardened targets; the development of space power systems; and the development of space logistic support.

There are also certain related programs which are not listed in the SDI budget shown above. These include improvements for strategic surveillance and warning systems, upgrades for the NORAD Cheyenne Mountain Complex, the development of an air-launched miniature homing vehicle, and the upgrading of orbital support and tracking facilities worldwide.

The five program categories shown in Table 6.1 account for all planned SDI funding. As such, the table can be considered a 'wish list.' Based on estimates made in 1985, the SDIO hoped to spend about $33.13 billion on research and development through Fiscal Year 1990. However, Congress cut the funding for Fiscal Years 1987, 1988 and 1989 by substantial amounts; authorizations for 1987 and 1988 were about $3.9 billion for each fiscal year. Only $4.1 billion was authorized for 1989, and the 1990 budget will probably be reduced by about $1.1 billion.[7]

Support and Concern in Congress

The perennial problem faced by SDIO officials is to squeeze enough money out of Congress to meet near-term research and development goals. The SDIO wants as much as $11 billion more for its programs through 1990 than those programs were scheduled to receive from the Departments of Defense and Energy ($33.13 billion). In all, the SDIO has indicated that it expects to consume about 15 percent of the research funds allocated to the Department of Defense.[8]

SDI critics contend that Department of Defense projections may be misleading. The 15 percent figure cited by the SDIO relates to the total projected research, development, test and evaluation portion of the defense budget, which includes funds for upgrading defense systems already in place. As for 'seed corn' weapons research, the SDI may actually consume about one-third of the total available funds by 1990. If this is true, the SDI cuts deeply into the research on other new weapons concepts, especially for the Army and Navy.[9]

Although Congress did not approve all of the money requested by the Reagan Administration, they demonstrated reluctance to cut or restructure the program drastically. Supporters included Republicans who followed the President's lead, space and military enthusiasts, and Republicans and Democrats who simply saw economic benefits for their congressional districts or states. In this regard, the SDIO has helped its cause by issuing contracts to companies in congressional districts all across the country. It has also won some support from universities that have agreed to carry out contracts in such areas as optical computing, advanced materials and space-based power supplies. The same patterns of Congressional action and SDIO contracting can be expected for the next four years under the Bush Administration.

Another area of Congressional concern is the lack of estimates on the ultimate cost of deploying a ballistic missile defense system. Estimates vary, depending on the source, from several hundred billion dollars to over one trillion. Those in the best position to make educated guesses—the SDIO officials themselves—have been reluctant to do so. The official SDIO position is that because research is still preliminary and no system has been decided upon, any discussion of cost is premature. In addition, they have said that the cost of such a system would be spread out over many years. Recent estimates for a Phase I deployment have ranged from $115 billion (June 1988) to $69 billion (September 1988). Given the SDIO's own statements about cost uncertainties, the recent $69 billion estimate for Phase I cannot be considered credible without substantial supporting evidence.[10]

If completed, a ballistic missile defense system would be a permanent addition to the Department of Defense operations and maintenance budget and would require enormous annual expenditures just to keep it going. The American Federation of Scientists estimated that the additional cost to the taxpayers would be between $50 billion and $200 billion per fiscal year for a system that would protect substantial portions of the United States. However, it is unclear at this point whether the architecture of an actual system, if one is deployed, will follow the architecture used by the American Federation of Scientists in developing their cost estimate.[11]

In the past, research for weapons has spawned valuable non-military technologies. The development of warplanes during World War I helped create commercial aviation. The Manhattan Project gave birth to nuclear power. The construction of U.S. intercontinental ballistic missile systems speeded up the development of semiconductors and computers. Will the SDI, potentially the largest and most ambitious weapons program in history, follow this trend? Proponents say yes. They stress that the program should stand on its military merits; however, SDI research could generate a variety of non-military inventions, including lasers for atomic microscopy, lightweight materials for cars and planes, computers built of optical components, and relatively low-cost space transportation.

Critics have argued that the value of potential SDI spin-offs may be exaggerated. Further, SDI could inhibit rather than inspire commercialization of new technologies. At least in the short term, critics have stated that the

SDI siphons off scientific and engineering talent that otherwise would be working on civilian projects. As a result, civilian industries have to pay higher wages and salaries to attract the services of those scientists and engineers that remain in the civilian industry labor pool. Second, critics have argued that the SDI diverts vast amounts of money and manpower into largely classified defense projects, causing SDI technologies to be unavailable to companies that would use them for civilian applications.

Finally, the Reagan Administration lobbied hard to gain support for the SDI from U.S. allies, particularly in Europe. It argued that the SDI will enhance existing European defenses against an attack by the Soviet Union. Also, SDI would give participating allies the latest in U.S. high technology.

However, critics have argued that the SDI could expose rather than protect U.S. allies. Current U.S. policy postulates that the United States might use nuclear weapons to stop a conventional Soviet attack on any NATO nation. Europeans have expressed concern that if, as the United States has suggested, the U.S. and the Soviet Union both have effective ballistic missile defenses, Warsaw Pact troops could attack Western Europe without fear of retaliation by ballistic nuclear missiles. Also, if the Soviets have even a 'light' strategic defense, it could mean the death knell of the whole independent strategic nuclear force posture of France and Great Britain.

It is economic rather than strategic considerations that make the SDI most tempting to U.S. allies. Companies in Japan, Israel, West Germany and the Netherlands, among other nations, have expressed interest in obtaining contracts. In fact, even countries that have officially denounced SDI seem to welcome the potential benefits to their domestic economies. For example, the Danish Parliament passed a resolution saying that they oppose deployment and R&D for weapons in outer space. However, as the Danish Washington Embassy's First Secretary, Carsten Sondergaard, noted: "It's not a law, it's only a resolution. Companies can participate, and some are."[12]

The Soviet SDI Effort

The Soviet Union has a growing network of large, phased-array ballistic missile detection and tracking radars, of which the Krasnoyarsk radar is a part. Such radars are essential to terminal ballistic missile defenses. Since such radars take years to construct, their current existence might allow the Soviets to move rather quickly to construct a nationwide, ground based ballistic missile defense system. The U.S. Department of Defense has estimated that the Soviets could undertake a rapidly-paced anti-ballistic missile (ABM) system deployment that would strengthen the current defenses of Moscow and defend key targets in the Western Soviet Union and East of the Urals by the mid-1990s.[13]

In addition, the Soviets have probably conducted tests involving the use of surface-to-air missile (SAM) components in an ABM mode. The SA-10 and SA-X-12 SAM systems may have the potential to intercept some types of ballistic missiles. According to the U.S. Department of Defense, all of the Soviet Union's ABM and ABM-related activities suggest that they may be preparing an ABM defense of its national territory.[14]

The Soviet Union has also initiated a substantial research program into advanced ballistic missile defense technologies. The Soviet program, according to General Secretary Gorbachev, covers many of the same technologies that are being explored in the U.S. SDI effort. The Soviet program includes research and development of high energy lasers, particle beams, and kinetic energy weapons.[15]

Most of the Soviet high energy laser research takes place at the Sary Shagan Missile Test Center, where the Soviets also conduct traditional ABM research. According to the U.S. Department of Defense, the Sary Shagan research facility includes several air defense lasers, a laser that may have a low earth orbit anti-satellite capability, and a laser that could be used in tests for ballistic missile defense applications. The Soviets appear to be capable of supplying the prime power, energy storage, and auxiliary components needed for most laser and other directed-energy weapons. They have developed a rocket-driven magnetohydrodynamic generator that produces over 15 megawatts of electrical power. The Soviets may also have the capability to develop the optical systems necessary for laser weapons to track and attack targets high in the atmosphere and in space. According to the Department of Defense, the Soviet high energy laser program at Sary Shagan and other locations costs the equivalent of about one billion dollars per year.[16]

Although the Soviets have made substantial progress with high energy laser research and development, it is doubtful that they could deploy an operational system for ballistic missile defense until at least the late 1990s. However, the Soviets could probably use existing ground-based prototype lasers for anti-satellite operations within a very short time period.

Since the late 1960s, the Soviets have conducted research on space-based particle beam weapons. The U.S. Department of Defense estimates that the Soviets may be able to test a prototype space-based particle beam weapon intended to disrupt the electronics of low-earth orbit satellites in the mid-1990s. A space-based weapon designed to destroy satellites could follow later. A weapon capable of destroying missile boosters or warheads probably would not be ready until after the year 2000.[17]

The Soviets also have a variety of research programs on kinetic energy weapons that use the high-speed collision of a small mass with the target as the kill mechanism. In the 1960s, the Soviets developed an experimental weapon that could shoot streams of particles of a heavy metal such as tungsten or molybdenum at speeds of nearly 25 kilometers per second in air and over 60 kilometers per second in a vacuum. The Soviets could probably deploy a short-range, space-based system of this type that would be useful for anti-satellite applications, space station defense, or for close-in attack by a maneuvering satellite in the 1990s. However, long-range, space-based kinetic energy weapons for defense against ballistic missiles probably could not be developed until about the year 2000.[18]

Finally, the Soviet Union is, like the United States, engaged in research and development of advanced computer systems and sensors that would provide battle management support for ballistic missile defenses. However, the Soviets appear to be far behind the U.S. in these areas, and have, according to the U.S. Department of Defense, substantial programs to obtain Western computer and sensor technologies by exploitation of the open literature and by espionage.

In sum, the Soviets are involved in a substantial effort to develop sophisticated ballistic missile defenses and have their own version of the U.S. SDI program. Their funding levels for SDI research and development are, according to the U.S. Department of Defense, comparable to the funding levels of the United States.

However, except for their existing ballistic missile defenses around Moscow and their incipient anti-satellite capabilities, they appear to be significantly behind the United States in the development of high-technology space-based systems, sensors, and battle management computers. It would appear unlikely that the Soviet Union could deploy a space-based ballistic missile defense system much before the year 2000. However, they clearly have the capability to expand and improve the ground-based terminal defense system for the Moscow area, and to deploy similar systems for the defense of key targets in the Soviet Union west of the Urals in the mid-1990s.

The Future of the U.S. and Soviet SDI Efforts

The U.S. and Soviet SDI programs set the stage for a general overhaul of superpower nuclear warfighting capabilities. This assessment suggests a range of alternative futures.

First, the U.S. and Soviet SDI programs could result in an array of advanced strategic defense systems that could be folded into a joint U.S.-Soviet agreement to deploy defenses as part of a mutual renunciation of 'offensive dominance.' This outcome, which could include balanced reductions in nuclear warheads and a balanced build-up of strategic defenses on both sides, was the guiding rationale of the Reagan Administration at the 1985 Geneva arms talks. Such an outcome appears to be a possibility, given recent statements in 1988 by both Reagan and Gorbachev. An agreement along this line could result from Strategic Arms Reduction Talks (START) that could take place during the Bush Administration (1989–1992).

However, there are strong political and military incentives to continue to rely upon offensive strategic nuclear weapons, including ICBMs and SLBMs, for deterrence. These incentives are particularly strong for the Soviets because they will continue to find it difficult to compete with the United States in the development of high-technology ballistic missile defenses that require enormous amounts of resources. On the U.S. side, there are strong military incentives to use strategic defenses primarily to protect ICBM complexes and other military targets. This approach could increase apprehensions on the Soviet side with regard to U.S. intentions. Thus, a renunciation of offensive dominance and an acceptance of strategic defense for deterrence would require a substantial degree of statesmanship and trust by both sides.

The above scenario would result in a serious reduction in the utility of British and French independent ballistic missile forces (ICBMs and SLBMs), which could be effectively neutralized by Soviet ballistic missile defenses. How such a situation would be perceived by European NATO members is uncertain; one possible response would be a NATO build up of conventional forces to counter the Warsaw Pact conventional threat.

At the other end of the spectrum, the U.S. and Soviet SDI programs could continue as research and development programs only, with little or no deployment of advanced systems. The Soviets would keep their ground-based ballistic missile defense system for the Moscow area, and the U.S. would remain essentially defenseless against a ballistic missile attack. Under this scenario, the U.S. would probably continue to develop and deploy advanced surveillance and sensor systems, including some that would be based in space. However, the U.S. would probably cut back research in 'hard kill' weapons and related battle management and support systems.

The above scenario is clearly not the one sought by the Bush Administration, but could result from current Congressional attitudes. On the Soviet side, such an outcome would relieve the enormous pressures on resources that would occur under a program to deploy advanced ballistic missile defenses. Both sides would probably remain tied to a deterrence based on offensive strategic nuclear weapons. If there is any pattern that should be kept in mind when evaluating the future of the U.S. version of the SDI, it is that the U.S. has repeatedly embarked on advanced, politically driven research and development programs in defense, only to stop them abruptly before they were completed. This pattern could easily occur with SDI.

Advocates, Critics, Claims and Counterclaims

The ultimate goal of a comprehensive strategic defense is to eliminate the threat of nuclear weapons. It is widely agreed, however, that by itself, a strategic defense against ballistic missiles, atmospheric threats and space-based nuclear weapons cannot achieve such a goal because of technical limitations on defense and the potential enhancements that are available for offensive systems. What then, can a strategic defense do, short of the complete elimination of the threat of nuclear weapons?

Many claims have been made by advocates.[19] Some have said that a comprehensive strategic defense can:

1. Enhance deterrence by protecting retaliatory forces and populations and by denying the enemy the goals of aggression.
2. Provide stability by preventing destruction of national command authorities, battle management functions, command and control networks and the retaliatory systems of both sides.
3. Protect NATO allies by eliminating the U.S. self-deterrence problem with regard to the the defense of NATO; i.e., the nuclear threat to the U.S. homeland would be lessened in any NATO-Warsaw Pact confrontation.
4. Limit damage and provide the opportunity for termination of hostilities at a relatively low level, if deterrence fails.
5. Promote reductions in offensive forces by allowing defense to be traded for offense with no change in national security (deterrence).
6. Bolster arms control measures by reducing the potential advantage to be gained by cheating.
7. Render nuclear weapons obsolete by building defenses that make offensive counters uneconomical.
8. Prevent damage from third country nuclear powers, terrorists, accidental launches, and attacks by mad subordinate commanders.

This rather optimistic list is countered by critics who charge that strategic defense would create the following problems:[20]

1. Defenses that decrease self-deterrence would make war more likely. A future leader of either the United States or the Soviet Union may someday be convinced that nuclear war is winnable.
2. The Soviet response would include limited defenses which could undermine the current British and French nuclear threat to the Soviets.
3. A fortress America mentality could develop which would decouple U.S. concerns from those of our allies.
4. Imperfect defenses would foster a crisis unstable situation, since a first strike offense could overwhelm the strategic defense. Also, a ragged defense could provide incentives for a retaliatory second strike.

5. Strategic defense would create a new arms race as both sides attempt to overcome the defenses of the other side by building up offensive forces.

6. The SDI will scuttle the ABM Treaty, a treaty which some believe is a monument to superpower sensibility.

7. Strategic defense will extend the arms race to the heavens, and such travesty must be prevented.

8. The U.S. has more to lose in space than the Soviets. Thus, the extension of conflict to space favors the Soviet Union.

9. Imperfect defenses can protect Soviet high value assets (their command and control and warmaking systems. but not U.S. high value assets (its population). This asymmetry would give the Soviets coercion advantage in the event of symmetrically deployed defenses.

10. The Soviet Union is better prepared to renounce the ABM Treaty than the U.S. since they outspend the U.S. on research, they already have massive air and civil defenses, and they have the only operative ballistic missile defense system in the world (Moscow).

11. Population defense is technically not feasible and anything less is not a worthwhile goal.

12. Even if feasible, strategic defense would be expensive and would detract from other more immediate needs, both defense and non-defense.

These pros and cons for strategic defense form the background of the current international debate. However, a carefully managed transition from an offense-dominant deterrent to a defense-dominant deterrent, coupled with reductions in strategic nuclear weapons, might achieve many of the positives while mitigating some of the negatives. Such a transition is discussed in detail in Chapter 16.

Perspectives on Strategic Defense

In choosing a U.S. strategy that would result in a shift from offense to defense by both superpowers, it is important for the U.S. to anticipate Soviet responses to U.S. actions. Indeed, the Soviet initial response to the U.S. SDI effort is already fairly clear. Politically, they have decried the U.S. SDI as destabilizing and provocative. On the other hand, they have intensified their own SDI efforts. If the U.S. SDI effort continues, the following potential Soviet responses, either singly or in combination, could occur during the 1990s.[21]

1. Enhance their offense:

- The Soviets could significantly increase the size of their strategic nuclear forces at the expense of their conventional forces. Some would consider this an effective form of unilateral conventional force disarmament.
- Expand their strategic nuclear forces at the expense of domestic and other military programs. This decision would not only doom future offensive arms control agreements, but would trigger a new round in the arms race—something the Soviets have indicated that they would like to avoid.
- Shift the focus of their strategic nuclear force structure to SLBMs, cruise missiles and advanced-technology aircraft. Because of geography and force survivability, both the Reagan and Bush administrations have indicated that they consider these weapons more stable than ICBMs during a crisis.
- Sidestep U.S. defenses by use of coordinated sabotage involving nuclear, chemical or biological weapons. However, such a strategy is better suited for a blackmail attempt than for a disarming first strike.
- Shift their targeting priorities from defended U.S. ICBMs and other strategic systems to less defended U.S. assets, such as war-supporting industrial centers and conventional military installations. However, a Soviet attack on such U.S. assets would probably unleash a devastating U.S. response by protected strategic nuclear forces.
- Develop offensive countermeasures, such as reduced burn time boosters and advanced decoys to assist their ICBMs in penetrating U.S. defenses.

2. Enhance their own strategic defenses:

- This could involve both enhancing their current air defenses and building additional ballistic missile defenses to deal with the increased size of surviving (protected) U.S. strategic nuclear forces. U.S. policy makers have long maintained that Soviet spending on military defenses are preferable to Soviet spending on offensive forces. On the other hand, the implication for the U.S. might be to develop a capability to defeat new Soviet defenses so that U.S. offensive weapons may proceed to their targets unimpeded in the event of hostilities. Such a U.S. response would probably trigger new rounds in the arms race.

3. Attack U.S. Defenses:

- The Soviets could maintain that ballistic missile defense systems deployed in space are an intolerable violation of their national sovereignty and attack them (and them alone), either during or upon completion of a U.S. deployment. Thus, it becomes crucial to be able to defend space-based ballistic missile defense systems, or else the U.S. will get into the ironic position of being forced to threaten an attack against Soviet assets to deter them from attacking the U.S. defensive system. On the other hand, the U.S. could declare that its space based systems are extensions of U.S. sovereignty, similar to historical precedents concerning naval vessels on the high seas. Thus, the Soviet aversion to direct confrontation makes plausible the argument that the Soviets are unlikely to choose to attack U.S. defenses.

4. However, a more likely Soviet response to a U.S. ballistic missile defense deployment would be to:

- Undertake extensive diplomatic and treaty initiatives to slow U.S. strategic defense programs while continuing their own SDI program.
- Deploy defensive systems along with the U.S. in order to degrade U.S. the capabilities of strategic nuclear forces.
- Enhance offensive forces to penetrate U.S. defenses, something the U.S. is already doing.

In addition to the above Soviet responses, U.S. decision makers must consider the impact of a ballistic missile deployment on crisis stability and arms race stability between the super-powers. The essential question is whether a ballistic missile defense would alleviate or exacerbate near-term and long term stability. The answer to this is complex, since some types of defenses contribute to stability and some do not. Further, defenses that contribute to crisis stability may be arms race unstable. The following discussion illustrates the complexity of the debate.

Suppose that the United States deploys Phase I of a ballistic missile defense, and that this system protected U.S. strategic nuclear forces (ICBMs and bomber bases), national command authorities (the President, Secretary of Defense, etc.), and selected command, control, and communications systems. Such a defense would introduce doubt on the part of the Soviets that they could mount a successful first strike against key elements of U.S. strategic forces. However, such a defense would also add to U.S. capabilities to mount a first strike against the Soviet Union. For example, the Soviets might fear that the U.S. would launch its less survivable nuclear forces and save its protected forces in case the Soviets chose to retaliate (in any case, this is the U.S. argument against the Soviet deployment of rail-mobile and road mobile ICBMs). Conceivably, the deployment of such defenses could promote crisis stability by removing the Soviet incentive for a pre-emptive first strike and by demonstrating that the U.S. only intends to protect its capability to retaliate if it is attacked first.

The Soviet Union could counter the U.S. Phase I deployment by conducting a massive buildup of its strategic nuclear forces to overwhelm U.S. defenses. Thus, U.S. defense of its strategic nuclear forces could contribute to arms race instability with regard to nuclear forces. However, several factors could reduce the likelihood of such a Soviet buildup. First, if defensive systems were much cheaper than the offensive systems necessary to overcome them, then an offensive buildup would not be an economical response. This could drive the Soviets to the bargaining table, perhaps to trade offense for defense. Another possibility is that the Soviets may not perceive the defense of current U.S. strategic forces as a destabilizing threat, since such forces do not support a first strike. Thus, an alternative Soviet response would be to build defenses for their own strategic nuclear forces. From the U.S. point of view, this would be the most satisfying near term response, since it would promote crisis stability, and the arms race would be channeled into a buildup of defensive forces rather than offensive forces.

An alternative U.S. deployment of ballistic missile defenses could involve a defense of the U.S. population and its urban industrial base. Such a deployment, particularly without a defense of strategic offensive forces, could be viewed as crisis destabilizing, because it is a posture for a U.S. first strike against the Soviet Union. The Soviets, seeing U.S. cities protected, could conclude that in a crisis, the U.S. would launch its unprotected strategic nuclear forces before they could be destroyed on the ground. Further, the U.S. would have a good posture for weathering the Soviet retaliatory response, because U.S. cities would be protected. Thus, the incentive for the Soviets to launch a pre-emptive first strike would also be increased. Such a situation is inherently crisis unstable. Such a U.S. posture would also be arms race destabilizing if the Soviets chose to overcome U.S. city defenses by an offensive buildup. With 'soft' defended targets, the economics appear to favor the offense, at least with near-term technologies. Thus, an offensive buildup would probably be an economically viable response to a city defense.

Clearly, the stability issue is complex. The above discussion could be extended indefinitely by argument and counter argument. However, if the U.S. does deploy a ballistic missile defense for its strategic nuclear forces, such a defense would certainly improve the current U.S. ability to threaten the highest valued assets in the Soviet Union by increasing the probability that sufficient U.S. forces would survive a Soviet first strike and be capable of delivering a devastating retaliatory strike.

On the other hand, if the United States had sufficient defensive forces to protect its strategic nuclear forces, cities, and its conventional forces, it would have the ultimate in crisis stability because the Soviets would probably never use their strategic nuclear forces, or if they did, the U.S. would avoid serious damage. There are several reasons why the U.S. will probably never achieve such a dominant position. First, if strategic defense attained a clear superiority, there would be justified pressures in Congress to decrease funding for offensive forces, thereby impairing the U.S. ability to threaten Soviet high value assets. Further, the Soviets would probably attempt to achieve similar defenses, thereby making the offensive task very difficult for both sides. While a balanced buildup of both sides might be crisis stable in the short run, it would tend to be arms race unstable in the long run because both sides would be tempted to achieve dominance by building more strategic nuclear forces.

In sum, there is an interplay between offense and defense in achieving stability. The U.S. and the Soviet views of stability are asymmetric in that the U.S. would perceive that a position of U.S. dominance was very stable, whereas the Soviets would feel the opposite, and vice versa. The most crisis stable situation from the U.S. point of view is probably arms race unstable as the Soviets would find such a situation unacceptable. It would seem likely that a position between the two extremes of U.S. dominance or Soviet dominance would prove to be acceptable to both sides, and would at least improve crisis stability from a global point of view.

Arms Control and SDI

A major argument for SDI is that it could enhance the prospects for meaningful arms reduction talks between the United States and the Soviet Union. According to proponents, arms control and the SDI could be mutually reinforcing in the following ways:

1. Near-term systems could alleviate verification problems associated with reductions in strategic nuclear forces (better surveillance).
2. Defensive systems could take over the damage limiting requirement of deterrence. This requirement is currently met by strategic nuclear forces on both sides that are designed as counterforce weapons.
3. For a given level of deterrence, effective defenses could be substituted for offensive strategic nuclear forces.

As indicated earlier, U.S. and Soviet SDI programs could also lead to all out defense competition. According to proponents, this type of competition is preferable to competition with regard to building offensive strategic nuclear forces.

Arms control, on the other hand, can contribute to strategic defense by:

1. Limiting all out offensive competition, thereby making the defensive task easier for both sides.
2. Limiting MIRVs, decoys, and countermeasures, which would also make the defensive task easier for both sides.

3. It is possible that treaties could also limit all-out defense competition (See ABM Treaty).
4. An arms control agreement that allowed trade offs of some offensive forces for the right to protect others would allow both sides to assure retaliatory capability.

Although the SDI and arms control may be mutually reinforcing from the U.S. point of view, this does not insure Soviet acceptance of the same philosophy. Indeed, it is unlikely that the Soviets will ever agree to negotiated treaties unless they perceive such treaties to be in their own best interest. However, this might be the case for arms control if:

1. The Soviets conclude that U.S. strategic nuclear forces offer an intolerable challenge to their defenses and to their ability to execute effective counterforce attacks.
2. The Soviets are pessimistic over their ability to defeat predicted U.S. defenses even in a Soviet first strike.
3. The Soviets are optimistic over their prospective competitive performance in developing and deploying effective strategic defenses.

In any case, the U.S. can only take the position that the Soviets will do what is in their own interest with regard to arms control negotiations. It is clearly in the U.S. interest to foster Soviet incentives to come to the negotiating table to reduce strategic nuclear forces. To the extent that the development and deployment of selected strategic defenses foster such incentives, it is in the U.S. interest to proceed with ballistic missile defense development and deployment.

Prospects for the Future

Without question, the SDI will generate new and unique defense concepts, architectures and systems. If deployed, sophisticated ballistic missile defenses have the potential to substantially alter the warfighting capabilities of both superpowers. President Reagan's 1983 SDI speech gave the development of key strategic defense technologies a substantial political push. However, there are reasons to expect that SDI will receive less enthusiastic Presidential support under the Bush Administration.

The popular notion that a 'star wars' defense against ballistic missiles would negate the threat of assured nuclear destruction of cities and populations does not necessarily follow. According to several prominent scientists, the development of a 'leak proof' ballistic missile defense is not technically feasible, even with substantial improvements in key technologies. Further, strong arguments have been make against a leak proof defense from the crisis stability point of view.

The proper U.S. perspective with regard to strategic defenses must be formed by considering many scenarios and likely Soviet responses. For example, one possible Soviet response would be to attempt to overpower the U.S. defense by building more and better offensive systems. The hope against such a response is that U.S. defenses would be reliable and would be relatively inexpensive to develop, deploy, operate and maintain. If the Soviets perceive that overpowering U.S. defenses is relatively more expensive than building an effective strategic defense of their own, then perhaps a major purpose of the SDI will have been served. However, such a cost differential between offensive and defensive systems has yet to be proved.

Another possible U.S. approach would be to develop a ballistic missile defense that protects the national command authorities, strategic nuclear forces, and key command, control and communications systems. However, such an approach would not attempt to protect U.S. cities and population per se. Such a defense might improve the credibility of U.S. offensive forces and might enhance the U.S. ability to deter by threatening punishment by protected retaliatory forces in case of a Soviet first strike. Extending strategic defense to U.S. conventional forces and to selected urban areas would also deny Soviet objectives in the event of war by preventing a U.S. defeat and by enhancing the U.S. recovery process should a nuclear exchange occur. Thus, a limited strategic defense, as long as it is not perceived by the Soviets as a U.S. first strike posture, has deterrence merit.

Another perspective involves U.S. political realities. Any ballistic missile defense, whether it provides a limited or a leak proof defense, would be designed, developed and deployed over several decades. Several political administrations in Washington would necessarily be involved, and political philosophies often change with changing administrations.

If the U.S. SDI program is to result in deployed systems, proponents would be well served by an evolutionary design, development, and deployment schedule. Milestones should be set so that each administration can point to specific accomplishments and can change, enhance or redirect programs after particular milestones are achieved. This calls for a development and deployment strategy that remains flexible, involves parallel lines of development, and results in deployment of usable systems consistent with the four-year political cycle.

In conclusion, a strategic defense against ballistic missiles does offer some hope that the arsenals of the superpowers can evolve away from offensive nuclear missiles and toward a defensive posture that would result in a more crisis stable, less dangerous world. While alternative strategies, architectures and systems may be debated, the overall goal of deterrence and peace can be appreciated and supported by all sensible parties.

Notes

1. Bethe, H., Garwin, R., Gottfried, K., Kendall, H., "Space Based Ballistic Missile Defense," *Scientific American,* New York, October 1984; also see "Pros and Cons of Strategic Defense," separate articles by Edward Teller and Carl Sagan, *Discovery Magazine,* September 1985.

2. Weida, W., and Gertcher, F., *The Political Economy of National Defense,* Westview Press, Boulder, Colorado, 1987, 179.

3. McMillin, S., "Revised Missile Defense Plan is Unveiled Before Congress," *Gazette Telegraph,* October 7, 1988.

4. Ibid.; also see "Cuts in Component Size Shrink Cost Estimates for Star Wars," *Gazette Telegraph,* October, 24, 1988.

5. The President's Fiscal Year 1989 Budget requested $4.6 billion for SDI as part of the Department of Defense Budget. An additional $0.4 billion for SDI was included in the budget request for the Department of Energy. The Congress actually authorized about $4.1 billion for SDI. Office of Management and Budget, *Budget of the United States Government,* FY 1989, U.S. Government Printing Office, Washington DC, 1988.

6. Weida and Gertcher, *The Political Economy of National Defense,* 185–187. Also see Canan, James, *War in Space,* Harper and Row Publishers, New York, 1982; Carter A., and Schwartz, D., *Ballistic Missile Defense,* Brookings Institution, Washington, DC, 1984, and numerous Department of Defense publications.

7. "Cuts in Component Size Shrink Cost Estimates for Star Wars," *Gazette Telegraph,* October 24, 1988.

8. "Star Wars, SDI: The Grand Experiment," *IEEE Spectrum,* September 1985, p. 56.

9. Ibid.

10. "Cuts in Component Size Shrink Cost Estimates for Star Wars."

11. Weida and Gertcher, *The Political Economy of National Defense,* 190.

12. "Star Wars, SDI: The Grand Experiment," 61.

13. Weinberger, C., *Soviet Military Power,* U.S. Government Printing Office, Washington, DC, April 1987, 49.

14. Ibid., 50.

15. Carlucci, F., *Soviet Military Power,* U.S. Government Printing Office, Washington DC, April 1988, 55.

16. Ibid.

17. Ibid.

18. Weinberger, C., *Soviet Military Power.*

19. For a detailed discussion, see Washburn, D., and Gertcher, F., *The Strategic Defense Initiative: Background, Transition and Strategy Evolution,* RDA-TR-180072-007, for Air Force Space Command, December 1984.

20. Ibid.

21. Ibid.

PART THREE

The Economics
of Nuclear Weapons

7

Nuclear Weapon Infrastructure

The United States, the Soviet Union, and the other nuclear powers have enormous infrastructures that support the operation and production of nuclear weapons. In addition to certain components of the operational forces discussed in previous chapters, the infrastructure includes research and development laboratories and extensive production facilities. For example, each nuclear nation has specified government agencies that are responsible for producing nuclear warheads. These agencies control facilities for the manufacture of nuclear materials—mostly plutonium, enriched uranium, and tritium—from raw materials. These materials are then fabricated into warheads and mated to missiles, bombs, or other devices at other government facilities.

Nations with nuclear weapons also have extensive facilities for the production of delivery systems, which include: ICBMs, SLBMs, bombers, fighter-bombers, cruise missiles, artillery shells, land mines, and various nuclear weapons for naval forces. In the United States, France, and Great Britain, these delivery systems are produced, for the most part, by defense contractors in search of profits and organizational longevity. In the Soviet Union and China, delivery systems are produced in government-owned facilities that have, like most large bureaucratic organizations, a deep-rooted concern with regard to their continued existence and growth.

Therefore, this chapter defines the scope of the infrastructure that supports the development and production of nuclear weapons. It includes discussions of production facilities for nuclear warheads and a brief discussion of that portion of the defense industrial base that produces nuclear warhead delivery systems. As a consequence, this chapter also serves as a transition from the previous discussion of nuclear dilemmas and defenses to 'The Economics of Nuclear Weapons.'

The Infrastructure in the United States

In the United States, nuclear weapon operations employ between 115,000 and 120,000 persons. These figures reflect primarily military personnel that perform duties at about 50 U.S. main bases that support strategic bombers, missiles, and naval combat forces, and about 160 bases in Europe and the Pacific Basin that support theater nuclear forces.[1] The duties of these people include weapons operations, maintenance, security, custody, and related command and control communications. In Fiscal Year 1988, the U.S. Department of Defense (DOD) budget for strategic force nuclear operations and maintenance was about $40 to $45 billion. Funding for the operation of non-strategic nuclear forces is difficult to define, since one would have to make arbitrary allocations among the costs of dual-capable delivery systems such as fighter-bomber aircraft, naval forces, artillery, and short range missiles. However, nuclear-specific U.S. costs in NATO, based on manpower allocations, were about $12 billion in 1988.[2]

Department of Defense support for operational forces is provided by the Defense Nuclear Agency (DNA). This organization performs research on the effects of nuclear weapons to determine how to make U.S. military systems more survivable during a Soviet nuclear attack. Nuclear effects research also assists military planners in selecting targets for U.S. nuclear weapons. DNA also supports operational forces by ensuring the day-to-day control, safety, security, and logistics for U.S. nuclear weapons located in arsenals and on delivery systems around the world. In addition, DNA conducts accident exercises to train military and civilian personnel to respond effectively to accidents involving nuclear weapons or production facilities. Finally, DNA conducts underground nuclear tests at a Nevada test site, and maintains the Johnston Atoll nuclear testing facility, should atmospheric or underwater nuclear testing be resumed. About 90 percent of DNA's annual budget of about $420–$450 million (1988) is for the nuclear research, development, test, and evaluation (RDT&E) programs described above.

The U.S. Department of Energy (DOE) is responsible for research, development, testing, production and retirement of U.S. nuclear warheads. All DOE nuclear weapons-related facilities are government owned and contractor operated. Thus, fewer than 2,300 of the approximately 63,000 people working in these facilities are government employees.

DOE facilities include three national laboratories: Lawrence Livermore, Los Alamos, and Sandia. It also has an associated nuclear test site in Nevada. The three laboratories have a combined staff of approximately 20,000 personnel, and a combined 1988 annual operating budget of about $2 billion. Roughly half of this budget was devoted to nuclear weapons activities (other laboratory activities include fusion and power research, support for the Nuclear Regulatory Commission, etc.).[3]

The DOE also operates seven nuclear warhead production facilities and three nuclear materials processing facilities, each with different capabilities and responsibilities. The final assembly of most nuclear warheads takes place at the Pantex plant in Amarillo, Texas. The 1988 operating budget for the seven plants was about $2.5 billion, with a total staff of more than

25,000 people. Nuclear materials processing is accomplished at the Savannah River Plant in South Carolina, the Y-12 plant at Oakridge, Tennessee, and the plutonium processing plant at Hanford Reservation in Washington. The annual operating budget for these three plants was about $2 billion (1988), and the staff includes more than 18,000 people (1987).[4]

The forty-two year old, highly structured relationship between the DOD and the DOE (and its predecessors, the Atomic Energy Commission and the Energy Research and Development Agency) is a result of the Atomic Energy Act of 1946. This legislation resolved the issues of the postwar debate over civilian versus military control of atomic energy and weapons programs. A key requirement of the law is that the President retains control of all nuclear weapons and 'special nuclear materials.' These fundamental requirements exist today, in spite of many changes in nuclear weapons and their deployment. Today, most weapons are in the custody of military forces for readiness and operational reasons. Control of these weapons, however, remains in the hands of a civilian Secretary of Defense and of course, the President.[5]

In a broader sense, one could argue that the nuclear warhead production infrastructure also includes laboratories and research centers other than those owned by the DOD and DOE. For example, certain universities have grants for scientific research on aspects of nuclear warhead development. A number of defense contractors also do significant research outside of government facilities. The extent of such work is difficult to ascertain; however, the authors are personally aware of a number of research grants at several major universities and a rather large number of DOD and DNA contracts with defense research firms.

Nuclear weapon delivery systems include a variety of military aircraft, missiles, ships, submarines, and artillery units. The U.S. aerospace industry produces by far the largest number of delivery systems, accounting for both aircraft and missiles. The largest U.S. manufacturers of military aircraft include Boeing, Rockwell International, General Dynamics, Grumman, Lockheed, and McDonnell-Douglas. The major producers of missiles include Martin Marietta, General Dynamics (Convair Division), McDonnell-Douglas, and Ling-Temco-Vaught (LTV). Major manufacturers of missile engines include Aerojet Corporation, Rocketdyne (a division of Rockwell), Morton-Thiokol, and United Technologies. In 1987, military aircraft production cost the U.S. government about $1.55 billion. About one-third to one-half of this production was for nuclear-capable aircraft and components. Missile engines and parts accounted for an additional $40 million in 1987.[6]

After aircraft carriers and ballistic missile submarines, strategic nuclear bombers are the most expensive delivery systems. For example, the B-2 bomber, which may be produced by Lockheed, will cost between 42 and 70 billion 1988 dollars for a fleet of 132 aircraft. By contrast, a force of

100 silo-based MXs will cost about $22 billion, a force of 480 D-5 SLBMs will cost about $37 billion, and a force of 550 single-warhead Small ICBMs, including mobile launchers and support systems, is expected to cost about $40–50 billion. Clearly, these delivery systems involve major commitments by aerospace firms and require the employment of many thousands of people, often over a five to 10 year period. Some aircraft, like the venerable B-52 bomber (produced by Boeing), has lasted for decades and has resulted in extended production runs, and extensive maintenance and support contracts.[7]

Most aerospace firms depend heavily on DOD contracts. For example, in 1984, over 60 percent of Rockwell International's sales were to the U.S. government, primarily to the DOD. In the same year, about 90 percent of Martin-Marietta's sales were to the U.S. government. At the low end, about 30 percent of Boeing's sales were to the U.S. government. However, the return on investment for government aerospace contracts averaged between 10 and 15 percent, somewhat less than the average return on civilian contracts. Employment in the aerospace industry includes about 550,000 production workers, and a total work force of about 1,151,000, including management, research and development, and support staff.[8]

Over the past decade, U.S. government ship construction dominated the U.S. shipbuilding industry's workload. For example, in 1986, Navy and Coast Guard ship construction, conversion, and repair contracts accounted for approximately 90 percent of the work force within the active shipbuilding base. Despite this fact, the industry is experiencing a long-term decline in employment, caused mainly by growing competition from shipbuilding facilities in Japan, Korea, and other nations in the merchant marine construction market. In this market, the United States ranks 17th in gross tonnage of ships produced.[9]

Based on information available as of October, 1986, the employment level in the active shipbuilding base will continue to decline gradually through 1989, and then stabilize at about 93,000 production workers. Ship repair and second-tier shipyards (barges, tugboats, supply boats, etc.) may account for an additional 7,000 to 10,000 production workers. By 1989, total employment in the industry is expected to be about 125,000 to 130,000 workers (production, support, management, etc.). Thus, the industry is expected to be especially concerned about increasing its work for the Navy and Coast Guard, not only for new production, but in terms of long-term maintenance and repair contracts.[10]

The Infrastructure in the Soviet Union

In the Soviet Union, nuclear weapon operations employ about 420,000 persons. These figures reflect the total military personnel employed by the

Strategic Rocket Forces (300,000), Navy nuclear forces (20,000, primarily ballistic missile submarines), and Strategic Aviation (100,000). The duties of these people include weapon system operation, maintenance, security, custody, and command and control communications. The fraction of the Soviet military budget accounted for by the strategic nuclear forces is not known, however, it is believed to be comparable to that of the United States.[11]

The Soviet defense industry has a very different organization than that in the United States. While the U.S. depends overwhelmingly on private defense contractors, the Soviet government is the sole employer for all defense production. The Soviet government is also virtually the sole owner of all means of industrial production, down to and including ordinary hand tools.

The Soviet government operates its industrial economy through a system of hierarchically organized production ministries. The broad objectives of military and civilian goods production are set by the Politburo. These objectives are largely a result of long-range political goals set by the Communist Party. Military goods production objectives are implemented by the production ministries, in consultation with the military. At the plant level, specific production goals are set by centralized decision making, with some participation by lower units. For nuclear weapons, the decision process has a strong input by top commanders and scientists employed by the Strategic Rocket Forces, the Navy, and the Strategic Aviation Forces.

Soviet nuclear weapons are produced by plants under the control of the Medium Machine Building Ministry. Its size and level of technology is thought to be roughly equivalent to the U.S. production complex operated jointly by the DOD and the DOE, including all of their private sector contractors. The Arzamas Laboratory, south of Gorky, and facilities at Kyshtym, Moscow, Leningrad, and Semipalatinsk are reportedly responsible for Soviet nuclear weapons design. Uranium and plutonium are produced at more than ten major facilities, both military and civilian. Nuclear warheads are assembled and mated with their nuclear materials at plants in Sverdlovsk and Novosibirsk; final assembly takes place at Chelyabinsk. The Soviets have tested nuclear warheads at 20 sites, including East and West Kazakh, five sites in Siberia, Semipalatinsk, and two on the island of Novaya Zemlya. The Novaya Zemlya and Semipalatinsk sites are reportedly still active.[12]

Soviet production of nuclear warhead delivery systems, including ICBMs, SLBMs, aircraft, ships, and ballistic missile submarines, has shown consistent growth since the early 1980s. This growth is consistent with the U.S. build-up of strategic systems under the Reagan Administration.

The Soviet military effort consumes about 12–15 percent of the Soviet Gross National Product (GNP). Thus, the Soviets carry more than double the defense burden compared to the United States, where defense spending accounts for about six percent of GNP. The concentration of military spending is especially heavy in certain industries. For example, the burden is particularly heavy in the machine building branch of Soviet industry, where the defense industrial ministries absorb almost 60 percent of the output.

Applied research and development programs fall within the purview of the industrial ministries. Each ministry has scientific research institutes, design bureaus, and test facilities that support the development of their products. Nine defense industrial ministries conduct most of the applied research and development for new Soviet military capabilities. About 50 design bureaus are involved in developing major military systems that are in turn supported by almost 250 subsystem and component design bureaus. Each defense industrial ministry has its own test facilities to evaluate the performance of its products, and these facilities are complemented, and in some cases replicated, by test facilities of the Ministry of Defense.[13]

The Ministry of Aviation Industry (MAP) is in many ways typical of the defense industrial ministries. It designs and builds aircraft and aerodynamic missiles for all branches of the Ministry of Defense and Ministry of Civil Aviation. It supervises a large array of research organizations, including the Central Aerodynamics Institute and the Central Scientific Research Institute of Aviation Motor Building. MAP has eight active aircraft design bureaus and seven air-breathing-missile system design bureaus. These are supported by 16 component and accessory design bureaus and 10 bureaus that develop air-breathing engines. MAP's test facilities include flight and static test capabilities at Ramenskoye Air Base near Moscow. Reflecting the continuing high priority of its products (including the Blackjack bomber and several new fighter-bombers), MAP's facilities grew by about 25 percent from 1978 to 1988.[14]

The Soviet leadership is very pragmatic about technological deficiencies compared to production in the United States and other Western nations. Even their most optimistic predictions do not call for attaining technical ascendency over the West before the 21st century. They are, however, concerned about the qualitative edge in Western nuclear weapons and delivery systems. To reduce this edge, the Soviets invest heavily in basic research and development in key technologies, particularly with regard to guidance systems for ICBMs, advanced aircraft, and silent running technologies for ballistic missile and attack submarines.

The Soviet centralized management structure uses its control over resource allocation to ensure that the most modern technologies and the best scientists and engineers are devoted to military research, development and production. Of course, this means fewer resources are available for the research, development, and production of civilian goods. This situation has continued to cause unrest among Soviet consumers, which has caused significant pressures on the Soviet leadership for reform.

The Infrastructure of Other Nuclear Nations

In Great Britain, nuclear weapon operations employ about 6,000 persons. These figures reflect the total military personnel assigned to four Resolution class ballistic missile submarines (2,300 people in 1986), three squadrons of Sea-Harrier aircraft aboard aircraft carriers (about 700 people in 1986), and 11 squadrons of Tornado, Buccaneer, and Jaguar nuclear-capable aircraft (about 3,000 people in 1986). The duties of these military personnel include weapon system operation, maintenance, security, custody, and nuclear command and control communications.[15]

The British nuclear warhead production complex is managed by the Controller of Research and Development Establishments, Research and Nuclear Programmes (CERN) in the Ministry of Defence. It consists of three primary research and production facilities that employ some 8,000 people. The British also have one laboratory that designs nuclear warheads: the Atomic Weapons Research Establishment at Aldermaston. British nuclear materials are produced mainly at Calder Hall, Chapelcross, and Windscale. Final warheads are assembled in facilities at Cardiff and Burghfield.[16]

In France, nuclear weapon operations employ about 18,000 people. These figures reflect about 4,900 naval personnel assigned to five ballistic missile submarines and other naval nuclear forces, about 10,200 assigned to land-based strategic nuclear aircraft, about 2,800 assigned to Army strategic nuclear forces, and about 800 nuclear force-related persons in the Gendarmerie. The duties of these military personnel include weapon system operation, maintenance, security, custody, and nuclear command and control communications.[17]

French nuclear weapons production is managed by the Commissariat à l'Energie Atomique (CEA). French laboratories include the Saclay and Grenoble Centers for Nuclear Studies, and certain laboratories under the CEA's military applications branch. Ten French locations have been identified as nuclear warhead production sites, but little is publicly known about specific facilities for warhead fabrication. Nuclear materials are produced at Marcoule, Miramas, and Pierrelatte.[18]

Nuclear warhead production facilities in Great Britain and France employ substantial numbers of people and absorb significant percentages of defense research and development funds. However, with the possible exception of France, the economic incentives for continued production are relatively moderate compared to those within the U.S. warhead production industry. Pressure from the anti-nuclear movement in Europe probably has more influence on British politicians than any pressure from unions or industrial groups that want to continue or expand nuclear weapons production.

Both the British and the French have substantial defense industrial bases, and have demonstrated the capability to produce sophisticated nuclear warhead delivery systems. The British have developed and deployed a force of ballistic missile submarines that carry a total of between 512 and 640 nuclear warheads. Although the missiles were produced in the U.S., the submarines (and the warheads) were produced in Britain. The British also have a viable military aircraft industry that produces Tornado, Buccaneer, Sea-Harrier, and Jaguar fighter-bombers that can carry nuclear warheads. The French produce land-based ballistic missiles, ballistic missile submarines, and nuclear-capable aircraft, including Mirage IVA strategic bombers.

In both countries, nuclear weapons and delivery systems are symbols of national prestige and demonstrations of commitment to NATO. In addition to supporters in the military, there are influential supporters in both British and French government bureaucracies for the continuation of viable, independent defense industrial bases. Defense spending in Great Britain was about $35 billion in 1988, accounting for about three percent of GNP. In France, defense spending was about $25 billion in 1988, accounting for about six percent of GNP. Both nations also produce for the lucrative non-nuclear weapons export market, with Britain accounting for about five percent of the market and France accounting for about 11 percent (the Soviet Union and the United States together account for over 50 percent). Production of nuclear warhead delivery systems continue to account for significant portions of defense budgets in both nations (about one-quarter to one-third of total defense expenditures).[19]

In China, nuclear weapon operations are conducted by the Strategic Rocket Forces, naval units assigned to operate and maintain one ballistic missile submarine, and air force units assigned to about 80–90 aircraft that can carry nuclear weapons. The numbers of people assigned to strategic nuclear forces are not publicly known, however, the duties of these people include weapon system operation, maintenance, security, custody, and nuclear command and control communications.[20]

The Chinese ministry responsible for nuclear warhead production is not publicly known, however, some forty Chinese locations have been identified as uranium mining and enrichment facilities. Chinese nuclear materials are produced at Lanzhou, Yumen, Baotou, Hong Yuan, Jiuquan, and Urumaqui. Nuclear weapons production and assembly plants have been identified at Lanzhou, Baotou, and Haiyen.[21]

Not much is publicly known about the Chinese defense industrial base. However, it is known that China has the capability to produce short and medium range ballistic missiles, ballistic missile submarines, and nuclear capable aircraft. The Second Artillery of the People's Liberation Army, as the strategic rocket forces are known, is now believed to have about six ICBMs, each with a two-megaton warhead. The Chinese defense industry is probably producing SLBMs for the Navy's single diesel-powered ballistic missile submarine. Also, the Chinese Air Force has about 80–90 B-6 (Soviet

TU-16) bombers that were produced in China (with Soviet assistance in the early years) and a few other fighter bombers capable of carrying nuclear weapons (see Chapter 1 for details). Clearly, nuclear weapons and delivery systems are symbols of national prestige and a demonstration of Chinese power with regard to the Soviet Union and India, the only industrial nations that appear threatened by Chinese nuclear forces.

All of this implies some degree of sophistication in the Chinese defense industrial base, with growing capabilities. However, the production of nuclear warheads and delivery systems probably puts a significant strain on Chinese resources, particularly with regard to its extensive use of scarce scientific and technical personnel. These scarce resources would otherwise be working in the civilian goods sector, which has serious problems supporting the wants of the enormous Chinese population.

The Future of Nuclear Weapon Production

Arms reduction agreements between the United States, the Soviet Union, and the major East-West alliances (the Warsaw Pact and NATO) in the 1990s will probably reduce the number of nuclear weapons in existence and significantly cut back on the production of new weapons. However, there are constituencies in each nation that benefit from the continued production and deployment of nuclear warheads and delivery systems. These constituencies include military organizations that operate and maintain nuclear weapons, nuclear warhead development and production facilities and the vast defense industries that produce warheads and delivery systems.

Incentives for continued production include genuine concern over maintaining the strategic balance between the nuclear powers, international political prestige, and of course, economic incentives related to defense industry profits and employment. The influence that various groups will have in impeding cutbacks in nuclear weapons production is a major element of the discussion in the remaining chapters.

Notes

1. Carter, A., Steinbruner, J., and Zraket, C., *Managing Nuclear Operations,* The Brookings Institution, Washington, DC, 1987.

2. Gertcher, F., and Kroncke, G.T., *U.S. Aerospace Industry Space Launch Vehicle Production,* a Preliminary Report for the National Defense University by R&D Associates, RDA-TR-301200, Colorado Springs, Colorado, December 1985; also see Carter, A., Steinbruner, J., and Zraket, C., *Managing Nuclear Operations.*

3. Carter, Steinbruner and Zraket, *Managing Nuclear Operations.*

4. Ibid.

5. Ibid.

6. Gertcher and Kroncke, *U.S. Aerospace Industry Space Launch Vehicle Production.*

7. Carter, Steinbruner and Zraket, *Managing Nuclear Operations;* various other sources include the *Budget of the United States Government, FY 1988 and FY 1989,* U.S. Government Printing Office, Washington, DC, 1987–88.

8. Gertcher and Kroncke, *U.S. Aerospace Industry Space Launch Vehicle Production;* also U.S. Department of Commerce, *U.S. Industrial Outlook,* U.S. Government Printing Office, Washington, DC, January 1987.

9. Gertcher and Kroncke, *U.S. Aerospace Industry Space Launch Vehicle Production;* also U.S. Department of Commerce, *U.S. Industrial Outlook.*

10. U.S. Department of Commerce, *U.S. Industrial Outlook;* also Aerospace Industries Association of America, Inc., *Aerospace Facts and Figures 1984–85,* published by Aviation Week and Space Technology, Washington, DC, 1984.

11. "The Military Balance 1985–86;" also Carlucci, F., *Soviet Military Power,* U.S. Government Printing Office, Washington, DC, 1988.

12. Arkin, W., and Fieldhouse, R., *Nuclear Battlefields: Global Links in the Arms Race,* Ballinger Publishing Company, Cambridge, Massachusetts, 1985.

13. Ibid.; also Carlucci, F., *Soviet Military Power.*

14. Ibid.

15. "The Military Balance 1985–86;" also Arkin and Fieldhouse.

16. Ibid.

17. Ibid.; and Campbell, C., *Nuclear Facts: A Guide to Nuclear Weapon systems and Strategy,* The Hamlyn Publishing Group, Limited, New York, 1984.

18. "The Military Balance 1985–86;" also Arkin and Fieldhouse.

19. U.S. Arms Control and Disarmament Agency, *World Military Expenditures and Arms Transfers 1985,* ACDA Publication 123, Washington, DC, August 1985.

20. Arkin and Fieldhouse.

21. Ibid.

8

Nuclear Weapons and the Competition for National Resources

Competition for General Resources

Nuclear weapons allow both U.S. and western European defense spending to be lower than it might otherwise be by offering a relatively inexpensive alternative to the conventional forces that would provide equivalent amounts of military strength. As a result, nuclear weapons dominate what Boulding calls the international 'threat system':

> The international system is the major part of the total social system where threat predominates as a social organizer . . . [and] the principle product of the war industry is threat capability. . . . One of the real problems of the international system has been the absence of adequate theory. We have had a pretty good theory of the exchange system for a long time now. This is economics. The theory of the threat system, and especially the theory of the interaction between the threat system and the exchange system, is still in a rather primitive stage.[1]

Nowhere is this lack of theory more acute, or could its contribution be greater, than in the allocation of national resources. Competition for resources is often waged in the political arena, but the outcome of resource allocation decisions has both immediate and long term economic impacts.

In spite of the fact that they are often a major determinant of the future economic viability of large regions of this planet, international resource allocation decisions have a strong political element and often seem to defy rational economic analysis. Thus, this chapter considers only the implications of allocating and reallocating U.S. national resources, with the specific resources devoted to nuclear weapon production being of particular interest. The direct impact of these decisions on the economies of specific regions of the United States will be discussed in the chapters that follow.

Delivery vehicles and the associated command and control networks that make up nuclear forces are often constructed in facilities that also make conventional weapons and that compete for resources in the same way that conventional weapons do. However, nuclear warhead construction is narrowly focused on a unique industry and set of resources that must be analyzed as separate entities.

Future decisions to reduce the number of nuclear weapons may affect the allocation of U.S. resources if:

- The U.S. no longer built nuclear warheads, irrespective of what it elected to do with its current stockpile of nuclear warheads.
- The U.S. disposed of its stockpile of nuclear warheads or if it disposed of the delivery systems for those warheads.
- The U.S. converted the nuclear warhead industry and/or the delivery system industry to produce something else.

The resources allocated to nuclear weapon production are constrained primarily by military requirements and defense budget restrictions. This chapter investigates the various ramifications of this situation and then uses the results to evaluate the likely effects of the three reallocation decisions listed above.

To allocate resources efficiently, they must be distributed between competing interests in a manner that best satisfies U.S. national priorities. U.S. national priorities evolve as a result of interactions between the Executive and Legislative branches of each new political administration. These two branches often place unrealistic demands on scarce national resources in order to please various constituencies that have conflicting goals for resource allocation. Unrealistic as they are, the resulting national priorities provide the primary guidance for allocating federal money through a U.S. budget that has accounted for over 21 percent of the GNP in recent years.

In the 1989 U.S. Budget, the major categories for actual spending (budget outlays) are identified in Table 8.1. These categories encompass everything that the government does, but they provide no guidance for allocating resources. In fact, they even give conflicting views of the national priorities (based on order of appearance, size of budget, or increase in budget.)

Given a lack of clear priorities, and the fact that a new budget is generated each year, it is fair to ask how decisions about national spending are actually made. When adequate priorities do not exist, real national concerns may be altered as regional economic interests attempt to influence the budget. In addition, in the absence of clear priorities that the voters can understand and support, even national leaders may find that an appeal to regional economic interests is necessary to sell budget programs. For example, instead of stating the goals and objectives of our policy of nuclear deterrence in a compelling manner, President Reagan, when campaigning in Columbus, Ohio, made a point of stressing that the nuclear freeze movement could

Table 8.1: 1989 Budget Outlays

Budget Category	Sub-Category ($Billions)	Budget Outlay) ($Billions)	% Change 1988-1989
National defense of which:		294.0	3.0%
Atomic Energy Defense	7.9		4.1%
Other	6.0		11.2%
International discretionary programs		15.6	1.0%
Domestic discretionary programs		169.1	5.3%
Space and science	13.1		20.2%
of which:			
NASA related	10.6*		29.0%
Transportation and Public Works	28.3		0.0%
Economic Subsidies & Development	43.1		4.2%
Education and Social Services	31.3		3.6%
Health Research & Services	24.2		6.2%
Law enforcement & Govt Functions	29.3		7.5%
Entitlements & other mandatory programs		511.5	4.0%
Total		990.2	

*budget authority

Source: *FY1989 Budget of the United States*, Office of Management and the Budget, U.S. Government Printing Office, Washington, D.C., 1988, 2b--1 to 2b--19.

hurt Columbus's economy because it would mean the cancellation of the B-1 bomber that was partially made in the area.[2]

There is a major difference between these two approaches to selling defense programs. When defense programs are debated on their own merits and are compared based on their contributions to defense and their relationship to other national priorities, it is natural to consider the trade-offs that are involved if one program is adopted instead of another. However, when programs are sold by appealing to regional economic interests, the decision to adopt the program becomes fragmented and the trade-offs involved are difficult to discern. In other words, the opportunity costs of a national decision cannot be adequately considered within a regional framework.

In Appendix 1 a case is presented that illustrates this problem. The community of Colorado Springs initially tried to use defense spending to enhance its economic growth by attracting programs that were associated with important national priorities. However, when national priorities began to shift, the community changed its emphasis to one of *influencing* those priorities to try to ensure a continued flow of government spending in the region. This kind of regional response is a growing problem. Large defense projects require so much capital and such a long lead time that a region can easily become dependent on a defense program that is wedded to obsolete priorities. When the main concern is regional growth and not national priorities, the opportunity costs to the nation of pursuing the region's objectives are seldom considered.

Another major priority debate involves the general emphasis that the U.S. (and, as later Chapters will discuss, the European allies and the Soviet Union) should place on programs that address social and economic concerns instead of defense in a time of constrained budgets. Increasingly, arguments about this issue stress that social and economic programs are an either/ or proposition when compared to defense spending. In spite of the deficit situation in the United States, and in spite of the tight budgets that this and other countries have been forced to maintain, it is not clear that this 'trade-off' argument is correct.

According to the Organization for Economic Cooperation and Development (OECD), public expenditures, particularly for social programs, have increased much faster than economic output in all major industrialized nations.[3] During the period of this study, the U.S. also had two major military buildups, one in Vietnam, and one under the Reagan Administration. Based on national priorities and spending behavior during this period, it is difficult to say what would have happened if the U.S. had elected to make different choices. This is an important point to remember as we consider the resource allocation problems in the rest of this chapter. As Boulding puts it

We cannot simply assume that if something goes down when the military goes up that this was a cause-and-effect relationship. . . . If we were to bring the war industry down to the proportionate level of the thirties, assuming that we maintained full employment . . . it is not altogether easy to say what would expand. The evidence suggests that personal consumption would expand and so would civilian government, but in what proportions it is not easy to say, and indeed this may well depend on the particular policies and sentiments which happen to be in operation at the time.[4]

The Nuclear Forces Budget as Part of the National Budget

According to the Fiscal Year 1989 U.S. Government Budget, the Department of Defense absorbed about 27 percent of U.S. Federal expenditures and about 6.2 percent of GNP in 1989. Within the defense budget, budget authorizations for the creation of strategic deterrence, the development, purchase and maintenance of nuclear weapons, and the command and control system necessary to employ these weapons comprise all or part of

Table 8.2: Mission Categories of Defense Forces ($ billions)

Major Mission and Program	1987 Actual	1988 Estimate	1989 Estimate
Strategic Forces[1]	21.1	21.0	23.4
General Purpose Forces	114.9	110.7	114.1
Intelligence and Communications	27.7	28.0	28.1
Airlift and Sealift	7.1	5.6	5.9
Guard and Reserve	15.7	16.2	16.6
Research and Development[2]	27.5	32.5	32.6
Central Supply and Maintenance	22.7	24.1	24.1
Training, Medical and Personnel	35.5	35.9	36.6
Administration	6.6	5.8	6.0
Support of other nations	.7	.8	.8
Special Operations	------	2.6	2.6
Total Budget Authority	279.5	283.2	290.8

[1]Excludes Strategic Systems Included in R&D
[2]Excludes R&D in other program areas on systems approved for production

Source: FY1989 Budget of the U.S. Government

several of the force programs in Table 8.2 and all of the line items shown in Table 8.3.

If strategic forces only generated costs in the shared budget categories (Intelligence, Communications, R&D) in the same proportion that mission funds are split between strategic and conventional forces (17 percent to 83 percent), the budget authority related to strategic nuclear weapons would be at least 14 percent of the defense budget—a figure that generally agrees with DoD statements that 15 percent or less of the defense budget goes for nuclear forces. However, a paper by the Institute for Policy Studies claims that expenses for nuclear forces account for 30 percent of the R&D budget, 40 percent of intelligence and communications budget, and that it also accounts for 5 percent of the general purpose forces budget and 10 percent of the support forces budget—areas not generally associated with nuclear spending.[5] This agrees more closely with another estimate of the cost of nuclear forces, prepared by the Center for Defense Information (CDI) in 1985, that claims that the cost of preparing for nuclear war with the Soviet Union was $29.8 billion in 1980 and that it increased to $51.8 billion

Table 8.3: Atomic Energy Defense Activities ($ billions)

Major Mission and Program	1987 Actual	1988 Estimate	1989 Estimate
Weapon R&D, Test, Production	4.18	4.21	4.24
Weapon Materials, Prod. & Waste Management	2.53	2.70	2.97
Naval Reactor Development	.58	.61	.63
Other Research	.19	.23	.26
Total Budget Authority	7.48	7.75	8.10

Source: FY1989 Budget of the U.S. Government

in 1983 and to almost $90 billion by 1987.[6] These figures, which attempt to take into account training and operations costs that are not counted by the DoD, place the total amount of resources devoted to strategic weapons at about 22 percent of all funds spent on defense (including Department of Energy funds, FEMA, etc.) This amount is equal to about 6 percent of the entire Federal budget.

A 1984 study by the Congressional Budget Office lends some support to these higher figures. This study estimated that the U.S. could save $30 billion over a 15 year period simply by retiring more nuclear warheads than it replaced, and it claimed that planned spending for strategic nuclear forces would absorb over 17 percent of the defense budget in the following five years.[7] Classification problems and difficulties in assigning individual mission costs to systems that have both conventional and nuclear roles (as is the case in communications and intelligence) make a precise determination of the total costs of nuclear deterrence almost impossible. But even with the substantially higher costs cited by CDI, the tremendous offensive and deterrent power created by nuclear weapons is still a bargain when compared to the cost of conventional forces.

When viewed from the perspective of past military buildups, both the nuclear and conventional defense spending increases of the Reagan Administration were small enough that the initial Keynesian effects were roughly comparable to those experienced in recent nondefense programs. In a 1986 study, the National Academy of Engineering found that

> the [Reagan] defense program [was] by no means the largest or the quickest to develop. . . . The Korean War Buildup was so rapid and massive that the market could not adjust quickly. In the face of a rapid increase in defense outlays, the civilian economy's continued growth could not be sustained; resources had to be directed to defense work. . . . The rate of increase in defense expenditures during the Korean War (1950–1953) was seven times larger than the rate of the most recent increase (1980–1985); it was two times greater during the Vietnam buildup (1965–1968).[8]

This is further confirmed by a 1982 DRI study that found that the effects of defense spending on the U.S. economy were similar to those of nondefense spending.[9] However, a more important question involves the long term implications of allocating resources to non-defense or defense uses. This topic will be addressed throughout the remainder of this chapter.

Competition Between Defense Spending and Spending for Social Programs

The general position of the social activists has been that

> Recent increases in defense spending have come at the expense of more worthy welfare programs and . . . if continued, these increases in defense

expenditures will eventually undermine our commitment to the Great Society established under President Johnson. Having abandoned hope that tax increases or a more vigorous economy might increase governmental revenues which would then support expanding welfare programs, many observers are turning their attention to the possibility of transferring funds from the Department of Defense to the Department of Health, Education and Welfare as a solution to the fiscal stringency of our times.[10]

Citizens of the United States have been unwilling to support increased taxes to finance either defense or non-defense spending. As a result, increases in spending in both areas over the last several years have come by enlarging the federal deficit. As James Clayton noted, "as one of the two great superpowers in the world, it is ironic that the U.S. has both defense commitments and welfare efforts which are really quite modest by international comparisons."[11]

Outlays to social programs normally take the general form of transfer payments. In current year dollars, from 1965 to 1970 Federal transfers to personal income doubled, and from 1970 to 1976 they roughly tripled, rising from $55 billion to $154 billion.[12] From 1976 on, the rate of increase in these transfers slowed considerably, and although previous rates of increase were clearly not sustainable, this slowing also roughly coincided with the Carter Administration's increased emphasis on defense spending during the period 1978–1979.

In addition, the Carter administration proposed shrinking the overall size of the federal sector from 22.6 percent of GNP in 1978 to 21.0 percent in 1981.[13] This, when coupled with Carter's plans for increased defense spending, meant that unless economic growth was substantial, there might be a trade-off between defense and non-defense spending. The rate of increase in social spending slowed even more under the Reagan Administration and the feeling grew that there was a direct trade-off between defense spending and social spending. Since nuclear weapons were the most morally offensive weapons to most Americans, it was obvious that if increases in defense spending were going to be attacked, the attack ought to center around these weapons. Clayton goes on to claim "that it should be more widely understood that defense and welfare do not necessarily come at the expense of one another. Each has a life of its own; neither need rob the other in order to prosper. . . . Rather than robbing each other, defense and welfare advocates have banded together in a war to increase the federal deficit."[14]

However, there is a big difference in the strength of the constituencies for the two kinds of government spending. It is much harder to form a constituency for transfer payments because of the diverse impact of these expenditures. As Robert DeGrasse points out:

Unemployment benefits are paid to anyone who qualifies, no matter where they live. On the other hand, contracting for a tank or building a hydroelectric dam directly affects a specific area. The difference is politically important. Members of Congress can demonstrate their political effectiveness back home by steering federal purchases into their states. The responsibility that any one senator or representative can claim for additional transfer payments is usually less clear.[15]

Although good data do not exist on specific competitions for national resources between defense projects and social spending over the last ten years, the growth rates of the various federal budgeting categories seem to indicate that defense projects have generally had more success in getting funded. However, this does not imply that more social programs would have been funded if the defense programs had not existed.

Competition Between Defense Spending and Economic Goals

This issue has achieved prominence because of the apparent relative economic decline of the United States during a period that began with the Vietnam War and continued during the Carter and Reagan administrations. Books like Paul Kennedy's *The Rise and Fall of the Great Powers* postulate that the stress induced by the burden of military expenditures is so great that national decline is inevitable unless the U.S. gives up part of its military commitments and reduces the national resources it devotes to defense. In commenting on this theory, James Schlesinger notes that "What we see is a picture of relative decline, which was unavoidable given our unnatural and unsustainable position at the close of World War II. . . . It is scarcely logical to feel nostalgic about an era that we sought so hard to bring to a close."[16]

It is important to know if defense spending contributed to an economic decline in the United States because nuclear weapons are both cheap and ready substitutes for the expensive conventional forces that are necessitated by the world-wide commitments of the U.S. If defense spending can cause economic decline, and if nuclear forces were reduced (or eliminated and replaced with more expensive conventional military forces), a further and perhaps accelerated economic decline might be anticipated. This potentially destructive competition could occur in several areas: land and raw materials, capital, labor, and research and development.

One type of resource competition centers around potential users of the factors of production that our national resources represent. Of these factors, land and the raw materials derived from the land are usually not significant considerations. This may change if a critical material is required for defense use, and if the need for that material causes the United States to alter its foreign policy or its defense resources in order to guarantee its supply. While this scenario may apply to U.S. operations in the Gulf to ensure the flow of oil from the Middle East, it would be difficult to say whether the end result of that operation was an increased use or supply of natural resources. If scarcity of a raw material means that the defense uses of the material deprived civilian industry of required amounts of the substance, this could adversely affect the non-defense users of the material. However, aside from isolated examples, like the shortage of rubber during WWII, there are few relevant examples of this situation in the last thirty years.

The amount of private capital that defense companies raise in the open market is subject to the normal forces of that market. However, to the extent that defense industries receive government subsidies, profits in these industries may be inflated.[17] As a result, allocation of private capital to the defense sector may be significantly altered. The fact that many companies (General Dynamics, FMC, BMY, Singer, etc.) have left the nondefense market and now concentrate on defense business provides evidence that higher profits are available in defense contacting. And a study by the Department of Defense confirmed that higher profits were earned by defense contractors than by comparable durable goods industries in the period 1980 to 1983.[18] However, in the absence of a general shortage of capital, the effect on the non-defense industries of any misallocations would be minimal.

If 'crowding out' occurs as a result of government borrowing to finance deficits, a shortage of capital may result in rising interest rates. However, it is not correct to blame the cause of a deficit on a single type of government expenditure (in this case, defense) when all other parts of the federal budget also contribute to the deficit. Even though crowding out may raise the cost of capital in all industries, it is not possible to say how much of that effect is directly due to defense expenditures.

In recent years, concern about the military demand for engineering and scientific labor has grown as the issue of American competitiveness has evolved. Of the classic factors of production, labor has the most likelihood of being affected by any competition with defense for national resources, and because strategic nuclear delivery systems and warheads represent the highest levels of military technology, these weapon systems are most likely to compete for the best engineering and scientific labor.

DeGrasse[19], and other critics of defense spending, in a 1980 report to the House Armed Services Committee, claimed that because unemployment was low among skilled technical and professional workers at the start of the Reagan defense buildup, demand for engineers was so great that salaries rose dramatically.[20] Hence, the military spending that occurred during the first two years of the Reagan presidency may have caused inflation in high technology sectors while the rest of the economy remained depressed, and it may have taken a disproportionate number of engineers and scientists out of the civilian sector and placed them in military projects. The result was that engineering talent became more expensive for all firms, and competitiveness of non-defense firms that could not employ enough engineers and scientists was diminished.

Military projects compete for all kinds of labor, but if unemployment is not abnormally low, and if the supply of new workers is adequate, increased competition for labor between defense and non-defense sectors would not be important. A 1986 study by the National Academy of Engineering indicates that this was true for engineering and scientific labor, even during the period of rapid expansion that accompanied the Reagan defense buildup. The study found that defense spending increased less between 1980 and 1985 than in either the Korean or Vietnam war periods. However,

> research, development, testing and evaluation expenditures were $27 billion in 1985, an increase of 55 percent since 1980. Procurement (which includes the purchase of weapons and material), a $70 billion item in 1985, increased by 62 percent. . . . Growth in these expenditures, in addition to the increase in nondefense activities suggested by the 12 percent growth in real Gross National Product in the 5-year period, generated a substantial increase in the number of engineers employed—about 200,000, or 14 percent.[21]

Thus, even though increases in defense spending during the Reagan buildup were not as large as those in previous buildups, specific increases for R&D were substantial enough to cause problems if problems were likely to occur. However, the National Academy of Engineering could not identify any of the problems one might expect. For example, the study found that:

- The High Technology Recruitment Index maintained by Deutsch, Shea, and Evans, Inc. "suggests that in the mid-1980s, when defense production was rising sharply, the companies included in the Index did not find it difficult to fill scientific and technical positions."[22]
- Despite the increase in defense outlays in the 1980s, there is no evidence that the defense program seriously depleted the supply of Ph.D.-level engineers and scientists available for non-defense work. Of 'experienced' engineering bachelor's and master's degree-holders surveyed by the National Science Foundation (NSF) fewer were engaged in defense work in 1984 than in 1972 and 1974.[23]
- A related question is whether the defense program draws 'the best and the brightest' engineers away from civilian industries ". . . [but] there is no evidence at present that either the defense sector or the commercial sector is lacking in appropriate representation of the 'best' of our engineers."[24]

These statements, when coupled with the fact that "average salaries were almost identical for those entering commercial work as for those entering government contract work (mostly defense) in 1983–84"[25] indicate that the supply of engineers and scientists easily filled the needs of both the defense and nondefense sectors. Apparently, the destructive competition for engineering labor that has been the focus of so much defense criticism neither occurred nor was it responsible for the declining U.S. competitiveness in international markets.

Competition for Resources in Research and Development Programs

Military R&D is an important part of research in all major powers, and it is a critical element in maintaining strategic nuclear forces and in creating deterrence. In the U.S., military R&D is 70 percent of all federally funded R&D and 30 percent of total R&D, and in the Soviet Union it is estimated to be at least 50 percent of all R&D.[26]

Military research and development is used to create civilian and military technologies in both the developed countries and in many countries, such as Spain, whose economies are far less advanced.[27] In fact, the development of civilian technology 'spinoffs' is a major rationale used to justify the continued production of arms in most European countries. In the attempt to generate civilian technology through military spending, the United States has been no different than most of her allies and enemies over the last forty years. As the National Academy of Engineering reported, "a second effective policy [for increasing the number of engineers] after World War II was federal direct support for research grants and contracts—in such areas as military, nuclear, space, energy, environmental technology and medical research, as well as in basic scientific research."[28]

One line of thought is that research is research, and whether or not the competition for research money is won by defense projects, the outcome will be about the same. However, military R&D has three broad, generally unique characteristics that set it apart from other kinds of R&D:

- It diverts scientists and engineers from civilian pursuits.
- It is not driven by a profit motive so it can distort new technology by encouraging expensive applications with little marketability in the private sector.
- It may lead to governmental control of the scientific and technological information that is developed.[29]

These three items imply that the kind of research that is done when government R&D funds are spent on the military may not satisfy the requirements of commercial operations and other governmental sectors whose projects were not funded.

However, the Department of Defense's selection of R&D programs poses a more serious problem for potential non-military users of this research. Most military R&D is applied research for weapons and little goes toward basic research that would expand the technology base. Only 12 percent of the budget for U.S. military R&D is spent for technology base programs (excluding the SDI program).[30] And while total military research and development rose from $17.7 billion in 1981 to $30.7 billion in 1989 (in constant 1982 dollars), the amount spent on basic technology research actually fell from $2.79 billion to $2.59 billion over the same period.[31]

Critics of defense R&D contend that the decision to allocate federal R&D funds to military programs that generate little basic research will have serious long run implications. For example, in 1981 Simon Ramo claimed that "In the past thirty years, had the total dollars we spent on military R&D been expended instead in those areas of science and technology promising the most economic progress, we probably would be today where we are going to find ourselves arriving technologically in the year 2000."[32]

Proponents of military R&D respond that 'spinoffs' from military technology affect all sectors of our economy and that these spinoffs enable us to recoup the money that was spent on defense-related R&D. They cite spinoffs from early military spending that resulted in the concepts of mass production, interchangeable parts, and the use of semiautomatic and automatic milling machines. In addition, they note that military research and development created the ENIAC computer and it was responsible for most early microchip development.[33]

However, recent experience with spinoffs has not been good. A study by the House Task Force on Economic Policy and Growth found that despite the claims of defense advocates, recent military research and development hasn't generated many 'spinoff' benefits to the civilian economy.[34] Relying on spinoffs from military programs is generally regarded as a very inefficient way of getting civilian research done when compared to direct funding of civilian projects.[35]

Currently, spinoffs from military research appear to be claimed most frequently to justify and generate public support for military programs. For example, the Idaho National Engineering Laboratory announced a program to promote technology transfer to the Idaho region at the same time that the Special Isotope Separator (a facility that used laser technology to generate weapon grade plutonuim) was being sold to the Idaho public. And when proponents of the SDI were pushing for early deployment, it was announced that roughly 200 descriptions of SDI technology innovations in biomedical technology; electronics, command, control, communication and computers; power generation; power transmission and storage; and materials and industrial processes were available for public use by U.S. citizens and corporations "who meet eligibility standards."[36]

Research and Development is clearly the major area where the military, in general, and strategic systems, in particular, have won the competition for national resources. Thus, it can be anticipated that a substantial number of R&D resources might become available for non-military use if nuclear disarmament was achieved. Such a shift of resources, even without nuclear disarmament, is probably warranted. If the benefits of past government funded R&D had outweighed the costs, one would expect to find a growing technological superiority in the United States. However, this has not been the case. American firms have experienced their greatest losses to foreign industries in those areas like aircraft, electronics and machine tools where military R&D predominates. U.S. productivity has also declined—something one would not expect if the technology developed through defense contracts really enhanced products and production methods.[37] At a minimum, we have advanced no faster than our competitors who have used non-military research—and often, at a far greater cost.

Competition for Resources with Other Defense Applications

In a 1984 interview, George Keyworth, the Science Advisor to the President, discussed the historical rationale for the use of tactical nuclear weapons and the opportunities that may arise for their replacement:

> Tactical nuclear weapons have one primary advantage that made them attractive in the postwar years. And that is that they are . . . cheap means of achieving a significant military capability. But that is achieved through a truly brute-force approach . . . [now we] can develop a supersmart munition that can have an accuracy over great distances. . . . This is a better military weapon because it can be used without threat of escalation.[38]

The concept of the cheap, brute force weapon also applies to strategic nuclear weapons, and when mixed with the more esoteric idea of deterrence, it has led to a three-way competition for Department of Defense resources between the elements of the strategic triad (and now, the SDI), the users of tactical nuclear weapons, and the non-nuclear conventional forces. On the one hand, tactical nuclear weapons are cheap. They can replace a significant number of conventional forces in a major war as long as escalation is not an important consideration. On the other hand, neither tactical nor strategic nuclear weapons can perform the day to day military tasks usually required of conventional U.S. forces (fighting in small, limited engagements in poorly defined conflicts where escalation must be avoided). In addition, strategic forces are designed to be used only as a last resort, and often represent pure additions to the military budget (as is case with the SDI), replacing no older weapons, freeing up no other parts of the military budget, and rendering most other military weapons inconsequential if the strategic forces are used.

In his paper "Rethinking Our Conventional Forces," author Barry E. Carter notes that "with the advent of nuclear weapons, conventional military forces have generally become the stepchild of United States defense concerns. . . . This is unfortunate since about 70 percent of the U.S. defense budget goes for the purchase, maintenance, and operation of conventional forces."[39] It is also important, because these same conventional forces would become the sole heirs to the military budget if nuclear disarmament was achieved.

One attempt to solve the resource allocation problem these factors have created within the Department of Defense is represented by a new DoD budgeting concept called 'competitive strategies' that decides what weapons and tactics should be supported in the military budget by choosing those that will best exploit Soviet weaknesses. The reponse of the individual services to this program points up the fact that not only is resource competition within the Department of Defense greatly complicated by the constraints in the preceding paragraphs, but in the final analysis, it is primarily based on interservice rivalry. For example, a proposal derived from the competitive strategies approach to budgeting was opposed by the Navy because it concentrated on the NATO air and land battle.[40] In another case, an attempt to reallocate $3 billion to the Navy was opposed by the Army because the $3 billion would come from the FY1990 Army budget and would reduce troop strength by 10,000 people.[41]

It is not news that interservice competition for resources has stymied past attempts to develop an efficient, overall defense plan. However, this behavior probably provides the best picture of how priorities and resource allocations might be reoriented if a nuclear free environment was attained. First, it is logical to assume that some uniformed services would oppose those elements of nuclear disarmament that would remove or distinctly alter a major part of their mission. Included in this group would be the U.S. Air Force and, to a lesser degree, the U.S. Navy. The Army, and within the confines of the Navy establishment, the Marines, would probably both support most kinds of nuclear disarmament because a return to conventional warfare would expand their missions and funding.

Second, if complete disarmament became a reality, and if, as is very likely, the expense of converting to conventional forces meant that the DoD budget was severely constrained, the uniformed forces could be expected to fight fiercely to retain as much of the conventional mission as possible and to force resource tradeoffs that would generally be made at the expense of other services. These tradeoffs would inevitably involve long-standing

U.S. overseas commitments, many of which, if evaluated in the light of a conventional war scenario, would probably be prohibitively expensive. This would be particularly true of our commitments to the defense of the NATO region. As Richard Barnet has noted, "it is difficult, even impossible, to cut the military budget without cutting commitments. The first step is to bring the 'commitments' into the light of day. Most American taxpayers have not even heard of many of them. Few know why they were made in the first place, and even fewer know what difference thirty or forty years may have made with respect to these obligations."[42]

In short, with complete nuclear disarmament, the scene would be one of intense interservice squabbling for resources complicated by equally intense political and military squabbling over international commitments. Although the outcome of this process can only be guessed, the U.S. defense establishment is ill-equipped to deal with the resource reallocations it will entail.

The problems currently associated with resource allocations required by the Strategic Arms Reduction Talks (START) agreement and with the attempt to fund the SDI both provide excellent indications of the likely result of a situation that requires the military services to deal with a full or partial nuclear disarmament. Because the START agreement would result in the loss of about half of the U.S. nuclear warheads, a fight erupted between the Navy and the Air Force "in an interservice struggle over the warheads that would be left. . . . The key elements of the struggle are targets and deployment. The service that ultimately Is assigned responsibility for most Soviet targets gets the most warheads and the funding that goes with them."[43]

Another indication of the the likely outcome of any attempt to reallocate resources in the face of a reduction of nuclear weapons is provided by the Strategic Defense Initiative. As a pure addition to the defense budget, the SDI replaces nothing and contributes nothing until it is fully operational. This created few problems when SDI budgets were small, or when overall U.S. defense budgets grew quickly during the first part of the Reagan Administration, making competition for resources between the military services unnecessary. However, when the size of the U.S. deficit combined with declining public support for further defense spending to cause stagnation in the defense budget, cracks were quick to develop in the service's support for the SDI program.

In early 1988, a Congressional staff study found that the first deployment of a 'Star Wars' antimissile defense in space could not occur before 1998 at the earliest because of a lack of heavy-duty rockets to put weapons into orbit.[44] Then, in March of 1988, the SDI Organization raised the cost of the a Phase 1 missile defense deployment to between $75 and $150 billion— almost double what had been quoted to Congress one year earlier.[45] A House

Staff Report "Strategic Defense, Strategic Choices" that followed this rev-
elation estimated that the 10 year cost of the SDI could be between $249
and $452 billion, with annual costs in 1996 between $28 and $52 billion,
and between $41 and $81 billion in the year 2000.[46] Following this criticism,
the SDIO quickly lowered the cost of Phase I deployment to $69 billion,
but the credibility of the program's cost estimates was now gone.[47]

These factors damaged the support of the military services for the SDI,
not because of mission considerations, but because of the effect the SDI's
increased need for funds could have on the service's own budgets. As a
senior DoD official said "SDI is going down the tube [because] the military
services hate it. They're scared to death of SDI costs. The service chiefs
are doing a lot of ranting and raving in internal meetings about where SDI
is going."[48]

Conversions of Military Resources
from Nuclear to Conventional Uses

The increased expense of conventional forces, and the fact that the Soviet
Union is probably better prepared to wage conventional warfare in Europe
than is the West, have already forced military leaders to consider whether
some strategic weapon systems might be able to function in a conventional
role. For example, General John Chain, Commander of SAC, has proposed
that the G model of the B-52 bomber be retained for convention mission
use instead of buying newer planes and equipment. He argued that budget
constraints and possible future arms accords could make it difficult for
theater commanders to acquire all the new conventional assets they need.[49]
And in a 1984 paper written for the National Defense University, Thomas
A. Keaney proposed that the B-1B bomber could also undertake a number
of conventional missions.[50]

In addition, weapon systems that can deliver tactical nuclear warheads
are all well suited to the use of conventional warheads and could be easily
converted. However, many strategic systems are so firmly linked to the use
of nuclear warheads that it is unlikely that they would be allowed to exist
if either a reduction or elimination of nuclear weapons was accomplished.
For example, the Pershing II missile (or one of its derivatives) and the
Minuteman II ICBM, have both been suggested as members of a new class
of missiles that would be armed with conventional, high powered, highly
accurate munitions that would make appealing conventional systems. These
missiles would use shaped charges, hypervelocity projectiles, fragmentation
bombs and earth penetrating warheads.[51] However, there is little chance
that either missile would survive any agreement to reduce nuclear arms.

The slim chance of converting strategic systems, and the certain need
after a nuclear accord is reached for conventional weapons with increased

capabilities, have led Congress to fund two new initiatives to begin to redress shortfalls in conventional weapons. The Balanced Technology Initiative (BTI) is meant to develop new technologies for conventional warfare and is expected to have initial costs of about $700 million. The Conventional Defense Initiative (CDI) will buy new conventional weapons and encourage cooperation among the NATO allies in conventional warfare matters.[52]

The effect of a nuclear disarmament agreement on reallocating manpower resources within the Department of Defense is not clear. To the extent that the presence of nuclear weapons promotes the illusion that the chance of being in combat is minimal, nuclear weapons may also increase the attractiveness of the All Volunteer Force. Thus, a force that is formed around the principle of fighting large conventional conflicts and absorbing the losses that this kind of warfare entails may have trouble recruiting the additional soldiers that will be required.

Summary

In the competition for national resources, strategic weapon systems have probably only had a major direct effect on research and development. Their direct effects in all other areas have been marginal, at best. However, these systems, along with tactical nuclear systems, have been cheap compared to the conventional forces that they replaced. Thus, the indirect effect of nuclear disarmament is that while it might mean more federal R&D funds for civilian projects, it is also likely to mean a greater requirement for defense spending and an increased level of competition with civilian projects if a comparable level of conventional strength is to be maintained.

Within the military itself, several services are likely to oppose any nuclear disarmament agreements that reduce their missions (and budgets), and interservice rivalry and bickering will probably determine how conventional resources are allocated. In addition, each of the services will have every motivation to press for increased conventional capabilities unless international commitments are greatly reduced. Within the political arena, this chapter, in conjunction with Chapter 9, demonstrates that unless alternative ways are found to allocate federal 'pork barrel' money, many regions may initially oppose nuclear agreements and if such agreements are reached, these regions will press for increased conventional defense spending to make up for the lost strategic spending.

Thus, this appears to be a classic 'lose—lose' situation where disposing of nuclear weapons will be opposed by many special interest groups and, if nuclear reduction agreements are reached, these groups will also be in an excellent position to make a conventional rearmament as expensive as possible. All or part of the three scenarios in the following chapter are likely to come into play at that time.

Notes

1. Boulding, Kenneth E., "The Deadly Industry: War and the International System," in *Peace and the War Industry,* Kenneth E. Boulding, ed., Aldine Publishing Company, 1970, 10–11.

2. Denton, Herbert, "Reagan Cooly Received on Midwest Swing," *Washington Post,* October 5, 1982.

3. "The Rise in Public Expenditure—How Much Further Can It Go?" *The OECD Observer,* May, 1978, 8.

4. Boulding, 6–7.

5. Klare, Michael, "Defense budget hides as much as it reveals about true nuclear spending," *Oakland Tribune,* April 29, 1984, B7.

6. For a complete discussion of the assumptions and methodology employed by the CDI, see *The Defense Monitor,* Vol. XII, No. 7, Center for Defense Information, Washington, D.C., 1983, 1–16 and "Hard Military Choices," *New York Times,* May 28, 1985, 19.

7. Biddle, Wayne, "Study Says Plan to Reduce Nuclear Weapons May Save $30 Billion," *New York Times,* March 27, 1984, 1.

8. *The Impact of Defense Spending on Nondefense Engineering Labor Markets,* A Report to the National Academy of Engineering by the Panel on Engineering Labor Markets, Office of Scientific and Engineering Personnel, National Research Council, National Academy Press, Washington, D.C., 1986, iii, 3, 5.

9. Data Resources, Inc./McGraw Hill, "Defense Spending and Jobs," *Defense Economics Research Report,* Vol. II, No.11, November, 1982, 4.

10. Clayton, James L., *Does Defense Beggar Welfare?,* Agenda Paper No. 9, National Strategy Information Center, New York, 1979, 2.

11. Ibid., 55.

12. *Economic Report of the President,* Government Printing Office, Washington, D.C., 1978, 343.

13. Pechman, Joseph A., ed., *Setting National Priorities: The 1979 Budget,* The Brookings Institution, Washington, D.C., 1978, 88.

14. Clayton, 57, 58.

15. DeGrasse, 6.

16. Schlesinger, James R., "Debunking the Myth of Decline," *The New York Times Magazine,* June 19, 1988, 35–36.

17. For numerous examples of subsidies to the defense industry see Chapter 8 of Weida, William J., and Gertcher, Frank L., *The Political Economy of National Defense,* Westview Press, 1987.

18. *Defense Financial and Investment Review,* U.S. Deparment of Defense, Washington, D.C., June, 1985.

19. For example, see DeGrasse.

20. U.S Congress, House Committee on Armed Services, "The Ailing Defense Industrial Base: Unready for Crisis," a report of the Defense Industrial Base Panel, U.S. Government Printing Office, Washington, D.C., December 31, 1980, 13.

21. *The Impact of Defense Spending on Nondefense Engineering Labor Markets,* 5.

22. Ibid., 8.

23. Ibid., 10.

24. Ibid.

25. Ibid., 11.

26. Hollaway, David, *The Soviet Union and the Arms Race,* 2nd. ed., Yale University Press, New Haven, Conn., 1984, 134.

27. Molero, Joe, "Foreign Technology and Local Innovations: Some Lessons Learned from Spanish Defense Industry Experience," in *The Relations Between Defence and Civil Technologies,* Philip Gemmett and Judith Reppy, eds., Dordrecht: Kluwer, 1988.

28. *The Impact of Defense Spending on Nondefense Engineering Labor Markets,* 4.

29. DeGrasse, 12.

30. Reppy, Judith, "Conversion From Military R&D: Economic Aspects," 38th Pugwash Conference, Dagomys, USSR, 29 August-3 September, 1988, 2.

31. Thompson, Mark, "Research, development for defense takes beating," *Gazette Telegraph,* Colorado Springs, Colorado, April 3, 1988.

32. Ramo, Simon, *The Bulletin of the Atomic Scientists,* October, 1981, 20.

33. Thomas, Bill, "Military Spinoffs, Engines of Change," *Best of Business Quarterly,* Spring, 1988, 45.

34. Seib, Gerald, "Defense Buildup Threatens Long-Term Economic Growth, House Report Asserts," *Wall Street Journal,* April 24, 1984, 62.

35. For a description of these problems see: "Labs Struggle to Promote Spinoffs," *Science,* No. 240, May 13, 1988, 874–876.

36. Gilmartin, Trish, "SDI Organization Announces Availability of Technology for Private Applications," *Defense News,* November 2, 1987, 15.

37. DeGrasse, 13–14.

38. Keyworth, George A. II, in an interview with Roger Fontaine, *Washington Times,* October 19, 1984.

39. Carter, Barry E., "Strengthening Our Conventional Forces," in *Rethinking Defense and Conventional Forces,* Center for National Policy, Washington, D.C., 1983, 19.

40. Beyers, Dan, "New Priorities Plan May Cost Navy," *Defense News,* February 29, 1988, 3.

41. Carney, Larry, "Army Fears Loss of $3 Billion and 10,000 Troops in Huge Budget Shift to Shore Up Navy Firepower," *Defense News,* June 13, 1988.

42. Barnet, Richard J., "Rethinking National Strategy," *The New Yorker,* March 21, 1988, 104–114.

43. Adams, Peter, "Air Force, Navy Vie for Targets Under START Warhead Limits," *Defense News,* June 13, 1988, 51.

44. Cushman, John H. Jr., "Shortage To Hurt S.D.I., Study Says," *New York Times,* June 12, 1988.

45. Gilmartin, Trish, "Pentagon Doubles Price of Phase One Strategic Defense Scheme," *Defense News,* March 14, 1988, 1.

46. Gilmartin, Trish, "10-Year Cost of SDI Could Rise to $452 Billion," *Defense News,* June 6, 1988.

47. McMillan, Sue, "Revised Missile Defense Plan Is Unveiled Before Congress," *Gazette Telegraph,* Colorado Springs, Colorado, October 7, 1988.

48. "Pentagon sours on 'Star Wars'," *Gazette Telegraph,* Colorado Springs, Colorado, April 3, 1988, 1.

49. Beyers, Dan, "B-52 Could Get New Lease on Life as Alternative to Newer, More Costly Planes," *Defense News,* May 2, 1988, 28.

50. Keaney, Thomas A., *Strategic Bombers and Conventional Weapons,* Monograph 84-4, The National Defense University, Washington, D.C., 1984.

51. Adams, Peter, "U.N.S. Eyes Non-Nuclear Strategic Missile Class," *Defense News,* August 31, 1987, 1.

52. Polsky, Debra, "DoD Readies $700 Million Conventional Arms Effort," *Defense News,* December 21, 1987, 1,8.

9

The Impact of U.S. Regional Defense
Spending on the Inertia for Nuclear Weapons

It is often assumed that international political factors are the only significant impediments to discarding nuclear weapons; i.e., that nations are simply unable to cooperate to achieve nuclear disarmament. However, in the United States many special interest groups derive economic benefits from the production, deployment, operation, and maintenance of nuclear forces. Such groups may oppose the elements of nuclear disarmament that adversely affect these benefits.[1]

Since few examples of nuclear weapon production are available for study, and because the moral implications of the actions reviewed in this chapter usually prevent a frank discussion of the motives of the groups involved, the impact of the 'economic benefit factor' on the structure of U.S. forces has been largely ignored. However, in those cases of nuclear weapon production that are available, and in other cases similar enough to allow analogies, special interest groups and regional political forces have often sought to advance short-term economic interests even when those interests did not coincide with the good of the nation as a whole (and sometimes even when their own health and safety might be threatened).[2] This chapter identifies three reasons for this behavior: the special nature of contracts for strategic weapon systems, the unique nature of strategic weapon research, and regional economic dependence on defense spending. All of these create an 'inertia' for acquiring or continuing contracts for nuclear weapons or delivery systems. While this chapter concentrates on the United States, to some degree all three of these reasons for inertia undoubtedly apply to France and Great Britain, and it is our suspicion that elements of the first two reasons apply strongly to the Soviet Union and, to a lesser degree, to China.

Inertia and the Production of Nuclear Weapons

The use of federal funds to create regional economic benefits is as old as the United States itself. However, as the methods by which these funds are channeled to specific areas have evolved, so have the nature of the forces that attempt to secure continued or increased funding. Initially, the vehicle by which federal funds were allocated was the construction of infrastructure. Roads, bridges, canals and the like were chosen because they provided an easy way to target specific areas and because they were defensible projects for every congressional district. The infrastructure that was created allowed continuing economic development, and it increased the standard of living for the residents of the region where the funds were spent. Whether this was the original purpose of the spending or a by-product of an attempt at pork barrel politics did not matter.

After the Korean war, the focus of spending for pork barrel projects began to change. Defense projects increasingly became the vehicle of choice for politicians who wanted to use federal funds to stimulate the economy of a region, and with this change of spending came a coincident change in the focus of efforts required to secure or continue the spending. However, another difference also occurred. Now the projects that resulted from the spending did not leave behind any infrastructure or facilities that could provide a long term economic benefit to a region. This meant that only a continuous series of projects could give steady economic stimulation, and continually justifying a series of projects required an ever-increasing definition of military needs.

The use of weapons of deterrence as a vehicle for channeling federal funds into a region marks yet another step in the evolution of this process. Since deterrence is an illusive concept, clearly specifying military requirements is also difficult. As a result, such projects are easier to defend on a continuing basis. But these projects also represented, for the first time, the development of weapons that could pose an extreme threat to both the user and to the enemy. In other words, as the methods used to assign federal spending to a region have evolved from infrastructure projects to constructing the weapons and delivery systems of nuclear deterrence, the externalities that accompany these projects continued to increase. And because these projects do not create lasting economic benefits, the rise in externalities was accompanied by a coincident rise in efforts to either retain existing weapon production projects or to secure new ones.

This chapter provides one case study on the regional economic and political effects of nuclear weapon production and an appendix on the regional economic and political effects of a combination of defense spending for conventional forces and strategic defense is also included in this book. Both these studies document the sources of regional pressures for continued spending for strategic defense or for nuclear weapon production. They demonstrate how local economic concerns can easily outweigh national priorities, more efficient uses of taxpayer's dollars, and statements of national policy. They also illustrate that when major defense programs make a regional economy dependent on federal funding, the opportunity costs and the externalities levied on the nation or the region itself are irrelevant as the region seeks additional federal spending or tries to keep the spending it already has.

It is increasingly apparent that for many residents of the regions where these weapons are made, maintained or operated, economic concerns outweigh either the national requirement for the weapon or the negative externalities that may accompany its production. These factors are likely to result in opposition to rational attempts to either eliminate certain types of nuclear weapons and delivery systems or even define limits on the production of such systems.

The Special Nature of Contracts
for Strategic Weapon Systems

The Department of Defense buys millions of staples, and yet one hears no stories of problems with staple makers or of communities vying to become the staple supplier for the U.S. Government. From an economic point of view, what makes a contract for staples different from a contract for a nuclear warhead or for a nuclear delivery system like a MX or a B-1 bomber? Staple contracts are not contentious because many manufacturers can produce staples in many different locations. The award of a contract to produce staples does not rule out the award of similar contracts in other regions of the United States. However, the decision to place a contract for MX missiles is, by definition, a decision to award that contract to a single producer—Martin Marietta. And, because of the way defense plants operate, it is also a decision to spend a stated amount of Government money in one or more well-defined regions of the United States.

This makes contracts for major weapon systems ideal candidates for pork barrel legislation. It turns what could be a normal acquisition process into fierce competition where the winning firm not only experiences the corporate growth or stability that creates regional economic stimulation, it also establishes itself as a monopolist in the production of that particular system. In this case, the loser not only faces the kind of corporate decline that can lead to regional employment losses, but it is also permanently denied the chance to participate in the production of that weapon system, except as a subcontractor.

In the specific case of nuclear warhead production, the decision to purchase additional warheads even avoids the risk involved in the contract award process. Warheads are produced in a series of government facilities, most of which are managed by private companies modeled after the old arsenal system. Just as the decision to build rifles was, at one time, a decision to spend money in Springfield, Massachusets, now the decision to build nuclear warheads is a decision to spend money in places such as Broomfield, Colorado, (the Rocky Flats plant) and Aiken County, South Carolina (the Savannah River plant). From a regional standpoint, the effective result is the same: a monopoly producer has been created or is being perpetuated.

Large military contracts can significantly affect the economy of a specific region. In this respect, they are identical to any other legislative pork barrel project. They can be targeted precisely, and they require the support of a broad group of politicians, all of whom have their own favorite programs that can be passed as part of a package deal. But military contracts for nuclear weapons and delivery systems have characteristics that make them particularly ill-suited for use in a pork barrel context. These contracts are sold to voters based on their potential economic impact, not on their merits as elements of national defense. In the process, the economic factor may overwhelm a fundamental requirement that is normally imposed prior to any weapon system acquisition; namely that it have a specific number of units and/or certain operational characteristics that directly address well-defined military requirements.

Because military requirements for many strategic weapon systems are not precisely defined, regional economic impacts have been particularly critical in gaining Congressional approval of these weapons.[3] If, during this process, the specific requirements for the defense project are not clearly stated, the purpose of the contract becomes, in the eyes of the populace, one of regional economic stimulation. Thus, when a contract has been sold on its economic benefits, it is understandable that people will attempt to retain that contract in their community for the same reasons. And when people are not convinced of the purpose or operational necessity of the weapon produced by the contract, it is equally understandable that arguments about obsolescence and military missions carry little weight.

The Special Status of Nuclear Weapons

In his book *Strategy,* Edward Luttwak states that "armed forces are usually maintained to preserve institutional continuity for possible future war, for internal repression, or even for tradition's sake, and only rarely for any deliberate purpose of suasion."[4] However, Luttwak also notes that "now that overt purposes of deterrence have been made fashionable by Great Power discourse, they are much more likely to be invoked in rationalizing the upkeep of military forces."[5]

Military forces that contain nuclear weapons whose only mission is deterrence are very different in nature from other military forces. Nuclear forces are meant to create an attitude on the part of a potential enemy that will deter him from taking some action. For example, the forces that are usually referred to as the 'U.S. nuclear deterrent' are really offensive forces with nuclear weapons that have the capability to elicit responses from either allies or enemies that are favorable to U.S. interests.[6]

Since nuclear weapons are not actually used, they create problems when decisions to fund and construct them arise. In general, the more removed a weapon is from battlefield use, the less likely it is that the weapon will be used in a conflict that has elements in common with the past experiences of the armed forces. This means that the assumed scenario for the use of a nuclear weapon, and the tactics to be employed in that use, are both new and highly probabilistic. This contrasts, for example, with the likely scenarios and tactics for using an M-1 tank. Here, although the weapon is new, the experience of past use is transferrable with a high degree of certainty.

Nuclear weapons create an atmosphere of deterrence, a task that varies as intangible aspects of the mental state of an enemy or ally change. The tank, in comparison, is a specified part of a unit with a relatively fixed mission—and it is subject to use and use-like training. One result of this difference is that tanks, transport aircraft and fighters, to name just a few, are usually purchased with the idea of establishing a certain number of active units to perform certain missions. Because of past experience with these systems, one can calculate the number of tanks or fighters necessary to perform a wide range of missions. On the other hand, MX missiles or B-1 bombers are purchased in whatever quantity Congress or the Pentagon decides will create an appropriate (but unmeasurable) attitude on the part of those nations whose actions the U.S. wishes to modify. And if budget constraints intervene, it is not unusual to see a sudden decision that the desired attitude can be created just as well with fewer weapons.

Such 'fuzziness of purpose' and lack of measurement make weapons like the MX missile and B-1 bomber difficult to sell based on characteristics and mission. Such weapons are more likely to be sold based on their potential to stimulate a region's economy. However, selling weapons this way makes it much more difficult to either stop production or disband active units after the weapon's time or mission (however defined) has passed. This creates a strong tie between regional economic benefits and the production of the weapons involved in nuclear deterrence, and it has also created the *economic inertia* that makes it difficult to do away with the weapons of nuclear suasion, even if a political solution to the nuclear dilemma is obtained.

In an attempt to more accurately describe the forces that might oppose even a reasonable agreement on nuclear disarmament, the rest of this chapter discusses various forms of economic inertia that have evolved around the construction of nuclear weapons. This inertia has its beginning in the factors that have just been discussed, but it is the Congressional interest that comes from the use of weapon contracts for regional economic stimulation that creates a powerful force for continued weapon production. The following case illustrates how these factors were combined in the state of Idaho and how they may have led one member of the Idaho Congressional delegation to oppose the Intermediate Range Nuclear Force (INF) treaty between the United States and the Soviet Union.

The Case of Nuclear Weapon Production in Idaho

In the 1980's, the nuclear facility known as the Idaho National Engineering Laboratory (INEL) was rapidly running out of work. This huge facility had been built in the desert west of Idaho Falls, Idaho, in the 1950s, and had done much of the pioneering research in nuclear energy as well as developmental and training work in support of the Navy nuclear submarine program. But the 1980s were hard times for nuclear energy, and the INEL needed to develop replacement programs.

Troy Wade, who had been the manager of INEL and was departing to become head of DOE's nuclear weapon production, had stated that he believed that only defense-related projects would be available in the future for the facility.[7] So it was no surprise when the two candidate programs suggested for location in Idaho by the Department of Energy (DOE)—and heavily supported by administrators at the INEL and the political delegation from Idaho—were the New Production Reactor (NPR) and the Special Isotope Separator (SIS). The NPR would replace an aging plant at Hanford, Washington, and would produce tritium for hydrogen bombs. The SIS would produce plutonium for military uses.[8] Placing it at the INEL would result in the construction of a plutonium processing plant west of, and upwind from, Idaho Falls.

The Demand for Weapon-Grade Plutonium

The requirement for a plutonium processing plant of any kind was based on two assumptions: first, that there was a real demand for the product (plutonium) the plant would produce and second, that a possible 'breakout' of the Soviet Union might, for reasons that were not specified, require a surge in U.S. plutonium production.[9] Since no market mechanism was available to determine an accurate demand for weapon-grade plutonium, an assumed demand was derived from classified DoD requirements. Thus, as the Draft Environmental Impact Statement (DEIS) for the proposed plant noted, all requirements for plutonium can be traced to a single source: the Nuclear Weapons Stockpile Memorandum (NWSM).[10] This document, developed annually by the Departments of Defense and Energy, uses guidance from the Joint Chiefs of Staff to establish the plutonium production necessary to support all warhead production and retirement schedules, and other special nuclear material requirements. As such, it defines the demand for plutonium.[11]

The Nuclear Weapons Stockpile Memorandum has no Congressional input, although it is the result of the first step in a DoD budgeting exercise that usually inflates nuclear weapon requirements in anticipation of future Congressional cuts. For example, in the period 1981–1987, the NWSM consistently overstated the number of warheads that were eventually produced—sometimes by a factor of 2. However, unlike budget requests for strategic and tactical nuclear weapons, the plutonium production requirements in the NWSM are not reduced when the budget review process cuts military requests for warheads and delivery vehicles. Instead DOE's production of plutonium must, by law, respond to the inflated NWSM numbers. Thus, the NWSM did not try to anticipate likely Congressional budget reductions after 1987 that further reduced the number of warheads to be produced.[12]

Senator Mark Hatfield has said that the "annual stockpile documents may be useful in setting goals for warhead production . . . [but] they have little value as justification for specific future requirements."[13] In addition, even if the NWSM had been a good reflection of actual demand for plutonium, as a classified document, whatever rationale it established for producing more plutonium was not available to the residents of Idaho.[14]

The DEIS and other Idaho National Engineering Laboratory publications also cited the need for a weapon-grade plutonium production facility that could provide rapid increases in output.[15] This capability to surge was part of a response by the Department of Energy to a potential Soviet 'breakout' that might increase the need for nuclear weapons. However, the U.S. defense industrial base is incapable of surging to provide the delivery systems (i.e., missiles, aircraft, submarines, etc.) to carry warheads to the Soviet Union. Evidence of the inability of the U.S. to surge in delivery vehicle production is readily available in

- A 1980 House Armed Services Committee special panel report that stated that a surge was not possible due to deficiencies in the subcontractor level and severe shortages of skilled manpower.[16]
- A 1982 report from a bipartisan group of defense experts at the *Conference on Improving National Security by Strengthening the Defense Industrial Base* that found the ability of the Defense Industrial Base to surge was almost non-existent.[17]
- A 1985 Air Force study that found "the aerospace base cannot surge . . . [that] no surge plan exists, [and that the] subcontractor base is the critical element."[18] This study also found that even the lesser goal of mobilization was unobtainable.[19]

Because of this inability to produce additional delivery systems, any increased production of weapon-grade plutonium would have to be stored. In addition, a 1988 report prepared for the Air Force by RAND Corporation stated that the economic and technical constraints facing the Soviet Union made any breakout highly unlikely.[20] All of these factors made a U.S. surge in delivery vehicle production so unlikely that building a weapon-grade plutonium production facility to provide surge capabilities made no sense. The potential demand for plutonium was even further degraded by probable arms reductions where the extensive half-life of plutonium allowed warheads from discontinued weapons to be reused.

The combined effect of all these factors precipitated a statement from Secretary of Energy Herrington in February, 1988, on the occasion of the closing of the 'N' reactor at Hanford, that the DOE was "awash in plutonium."[21] This was echoed by Troy Wade during his testimony on the SIS plant in Idaho when he said "Our opponents argue that we do not need SIS to provide nuclear material in the near term. That is a fact and we do not dispute it. However, neither our opponents nor ourselves can accurately predict the nuclear materials requirements a decade from now."[22]

Selling the Special Isotope Separator to Idaho

Other than rudimentary information about the purposes of both plants, the NPR and SIS programs were neither presented nor sold to the people of Idaho based on their roles in fulfilling either national requirements or military missions. Instead, in most people's eyes these plants simply replaced employment that was being lost due to the decreased workload at the Idaho National Engineering Laboratory, and Senators James McClure and Steve Symms tried to make it abundantly clear that their political pull had been largely responsible in securing the plants for Idaho.[23] The reasons for building the plants were so poorly understood that the Idaho Falls Chamber of Commerce, in a message to DOE citing the support of Idaho for the two projects, could only say "this . . . [Chamber] has the sense that there are solid and valid reasons why the NPR . . . [and] the SIS, if they are to be built anywhere, should come to the INEL."[24]

Without 'solid and valid' reasons why the plants were needed and, if they were needed, why Idaho would be the preferred location for their construction, the site selection process was turned on its head, with Idaho actively lobbying to have the plants built based on the economic benefits that this would provide to the region. Employment and economic growth potential were continuously stressed by state and local politicians, civic leaders, and a booster group from the Idaho Falls Chamber of Commerce. And any comments or questions regarding public safety and health issues, or addressing the actual need for the facilities—aside from creating local employment—were treated by community leaders (and, in particular, the head of the local Republican Party) as both wrong-headed and 'anti-Idaho'.[25] One article was even written for the local paper claiming that it was possible to be a Republican in Idaho and still oppose the SIS plant.[26]

Federal law mandates that government projects like the SIS be subjected to a thorough review of their environmental impact. Also included in this law is a requirement to determine likely social and economic effects of the facility. This process results in an Environmental Impact Statement (EIS) that is first published in draft form, then debated in local hearings in the impacted region, and finally published as a document that theoretically acts as the foundation for the decision to build the project. In actuality, EIS's are prepared by various consulting agencies that depend on the government for their livelihood, and they normally tend to justify whatever decisions were originally made about the project.

However, public opinion still plays a major role in deciding the fate of any government project, and by the time hearings on the draft environmental impact statement for the SIS were scheduled early in 1988, it had become clear that public opinion was turning against the SIS. In Idaho, three groups became actively involved in reversing this trend:

1. A group composed of local businessmen and coordinated by the local Chamber of Commerce had a direct economic interest in having the SIS built in Idaho. Most members of this group lived in Idaho Falls, Idaho, the city closest to the Idaho National Engineering Laboratory and hence, most likely to gain from increased business activity (most employees of a new SIS were expected to live in Idaho Falls.) The business group stressed potential local economic impacts from construction of the plant and the possibility of the facility drawing new, high technology businesses into the region. Aside from this, the group concentrated on short-run economic benefits from the SIS and neither discussed nor appeared to recognize that long run externalities might also be involved. For example, they believed that Idaho had an excellent chance of attracting both the national Supercooled Superconducting Collider (SSC) project and the SIS to the INEL—apparently not realizing that the lifestyle concerns that were a major criteria in selecting the site for the SSC were not compatible with living next to a plutonium processing plant. This group also demonstrated neither knowledge nor concern about the national requirement for the SIS, preferring to argue instead that "as long as its going to be built somewhere, it may as well be built in Idaho." And finally, this group showed no understanding of the way that government funds are actually expended, and it treated the gross project budget figure as if it would all be spent in Idaho. This business group, along with the Unions, formed an umbrella group (Yes, Yes, SIS) to actively promote the SIS.

2. A group composed of unions whose members would benefit from employment gained by constructing the SIS. Most of this group were residents of Pocatello, Idaho, which is located about fifty miles south of Idaho Falls. Pocatello was the home of several heavy industries, and all were in decline. As a result, the community was in a severe recession and many union members had exhausted their unemployment benefits. This group regarded potential externalities from the SIS as irrelevant when compared to the actual economic hardships they faced. And although they tended to quote the published figures for peak SIS construction employment as if these were the number of permanent annual jobs the SIS would provide, their attitude was best summed up by one member who stated that as long as the SIS created a single job it was worth building—irrespective of any externalities that might arise. Although this group was not particularly concerned about whether there was a national requirement for the SIS, when the subject was addressed, it was usually in the sense that "if the government says we need it, who are we to question that decision."

3. The small Congressional delegation from Idaho also rallied to the defense of the project. This group numbered among its members Senators Steve Symms and James McClure, both of whom had been faithful Republican supporters of President Reagan's conservative agenda. In particular, both men had been advocates of the Reagan defense buildup, even though Idaho gained almost no direct benefits from those expenditures. In fact, Idaho's economy was very depressed, and aside from some legislation that had favorably affected the timber industry in the northern part of the state, it was unclear these men had been able to produce any significant pork barrel spending for their constituencies. For this reason, the SIS was widely regarded in both Washington, D.C., and Idaho as a political payoff—mostly to Senator McClure—for past support of the Reagan Administration. Whether or not this was true, Senator McClure was an active proponent of the SIS program, and while he continually stressed its regional economic benefits, he also attempted to enunciate the national need for the facility and for the additional plutonium it would produce. This was necessary because budget restrictions were growing, and continued approval of Congress was necessary to assure SIS funding. Senator McClure's arguments concerning the demand for plutonium and the possibility of a Soviet breakout have already been mentioned, but he also added a strong note that the classified information to which he was privy allowed him to understand the national security issues, and anyone who disagreed with the SIS plainly didn't.

This argument was hard to sustain in the face of statements by both the Secretary of Energy and the manager of the DOE nuclear weapons program that there was no need for the plutonium that the SIS would produce. In fact, when this was revealed in March, 1988, during the Idaho hearings on the Environmental Impact Study, Representative Albert Bustamante (D-Texas) immediately proposed legislation to stop all funding of the SIS (and transfer the money to a military project in his district.) This action, which further emphasized the political nature of the decision to build the SIS in Idaho, resulted in an open fight between the Texas and Idaho congressional delegations as each sought to secure the same federal funds for their districts. The House leadership ordered the two groups to settle their differences in conference, and the result was an agreement that Lawrence Livermore National Laboratory would have to demonstrate that the SIS process was feasible in a production mode before the end of March, 1989. Until such a demonstration was made, the House agreed to withhold construction funding for the SIS.[27]

In early 1988, the potential of achieving an Intermediate Range Nuclear Force (INF) Agreement presented another challenge to the SIS plant in general, and to the Idaho Congressional delegation in particular, because it decreased the need for new nuclear warheads while, at the same time, it increased the supply of older warheads that could be recycled. Both of these activities further reduced the demand for plutonium. Thus, it was not surprising when members of the Idaho Congressional delegation came out against the proposed treaty. Both Senators Symms and McClure joined only four other U.S. Senators in supporting an attempt by Senator Jesse Helms (R-S.C.) to kill the treaty, and Senator Symms also voted against the final treaty.[28] While their opposition was made in terms of the conservative political agenda, it was unusual for either Senator McClure or Senator Symms to oppose a program supported by the President. To observers in Idaho, the opposition of the Idaho delegation seemed to be primarily based on the economic losses to the state that a completed agreement might entail.[29] If this was the case, both Idaho senators, by opposing the INF treaty, had carried to the ultimate extreme the potential outcome of every process where a contract for nuclear weapon production is used primarily for regional economic stimulation.

Regional Employment from Plutonium Production in Idaho

Keeping employment at the INEL constant was a major concern for its managers and for local officials in Idaho. Total employment at the Idaho National Engineering Laboratory was 10,100 when the SIS was proposed. Employment was expected to remain flat over the following 10 years if the SIS was built, and to rise only slightly if the New Production Reactor (NPR) was constructed.[30] Potential nuclear programs were often discussed, not in the context of what they would produce, but instead, on the levels of employment they would provide. For example, the INEL's statement about the SIS implied that a major purpose of the new plant would be to keep employment levels at the National Engineering Laboratory at 'predicted' levels.[31]

The fact that Idaho's economy was based on a number of sectors (mining, agriculture and timber) that were depressed made the SIS's budgeted cost of almost $1 billion seem ideal for generating new jobs. Unfortunately, two misleading figures, the $1 billion budget figure and a second set of figures for construction cost ($550 million) and peak construction employment (440 jobs) that were often used by all parties discussing the issue quickly became the standard points of reference for the likely regional economic impact of the project and for selling the SIS to the citizens of Idaho.[32]

While no attempt was made by the Department of Energy to misinform people about the true economic impact of the SIS, neither was any attempt made to dispel the common impression that $1 billion was going to be spent in Idaho and that 440 people were going to be employed during the entire construction phase. The vacuum created by a lack of specific regional impact data allowed these figures to take on a life of their own,[33] and this proved useful in the political effort to sell the SIS to Idaho where it was the perception of economic benefits, not the benefits themselves that were important. As the following paragraphs indicate, the true regional economic impact from the SIS would be much lower than these figures implied.

The employment multiplier for the southeast Idaho region affected by the Idaho National Engineering Laboratory had been calculated to be 2.36.[34] Thus, each direct job created by the SIS would, in turn, create another 1.36 jobs in the region, adding a total of 2.36 jobs to the economic base. During its construction, the number of direct jobs created by the SIS would vary greatly depending on the length of the construction phase: each million dollars of reduced spending due to a slower construction pace would depress annual employment during SIS construction by approximately 38 jobs.[35] Similarly, according to the *Draft Environmental Impact Statement on the SIS,* the "hiring of operating personnel would commence with the construction of the SIS." Thus, levels of both construction and operating employment were linked to the construction schedule for the SIS. Flowing from these sources of employment were additional jobs in the local community and increases in the state and regional tax bases.

In addition, the DOE FY1989 OMB Budget Request shows that the SIS was a concurrent development project.[36] This means that the operating plant was to be planned and constructed at the same time that the processes necessary to make the plant function were being developed. Because concurrent development causes uncertain schedules and increased project cost, the economic impact of SIS construction could not be accurately determined without first estimating how long it would take to develop the plutonium AVLIS technology that was to be used in the plant.[37] If the SIS program experienced delays due to problems with AVLIS technology, annual employment during the construction phase of the project would be reduced.

The choice of AVLIS technology to process plutonium at the SIS clearly involved a high degree of expense and uncertainty. In hearings on the FY1985 DOE budget, DOE stated that "the SIS process has the highest cost (in total dollars and in dollars per gram of additional plutonium) of the various methods of increasing productivity. The SIS process also requires the most lead time and is the most technologically uncertain."[38]

The high degree of uncertainty was also documented in the Draft Environmental Impact Statement for the SIS project.[39] In fact, this was the first DEIS to carry a disclaimer which stated:

Neither the United States Government nor any agency thereof, nor any of their employees, makes any warranty, express or implied, or assumes any legal liability or responsibility for the accuracy, completeness, or usefulness of any information, apparatus, product or process disclosed . . . [40]

This uncertainty was important because the project to develop AVLIS technology for the SIS had been started in 1975 and was scheduled to be completed in FY 1990. However, models of this research effort showed that the development of AVLIS technology was about five years behind schedule in 1988, implying that there would be large delays in construction of the SIS and corresponding decreases in the amount of employment that the plant would provide.[41]

The number of direct jobs created in Idaho by the SIS would be further depressed to the extent that money allocated to the project was spent outside the state because of a lack of industry and research facilities in Idaho. For example, Jan Hager, a contractor for the SIS, stated that the "SIS will . . . require millions of dollars worth of high technology equipment, much of which will have to be purchased out of state."[42] And Lamar Trego, of Westinghouse Idaho Nuclear, felt that Idaho could only "provide as much as $20 million of the project's special equipment needs."[43] Further, much of the limited technical equipment provided by Idaho would come from areas of the state outside of the region directly associated with the INEL. These factors further reduced the direct employment associated with the construction of the SIS.

Data from the Department of Energy and Lawrence Livermore National Labs showed that even after technology was developed and construction on the plant was started, very little work on the SIS would actually be done in Idaho. Out of a construction budget that was estimated to be $527 million between 1988 and 1994, less than $36 million, or 6.7 percent was likely to be spent in Idaho.[44] In sum, most of the money spent on the SIS would purchase expensive, technologically advanced equipment that would be imported into Idaho and simply bolted to the floor of the SIS. The money would be spent, and the jobs created, elsewhere.

Many indirect jobs related to the SIS were also supposed to be created as technology was transferred from the SIS to businesses in the local region. The INEL even loaned an individual to the state of Idaho to "aid efforts to attract out-of-state high technology business."[45] But technology is portable, and there is little reason for any company to incur the costs associated with a move just to locate closer to the origin of the technology. In fact, while the Stevenson-Wydler Technological Innovations Act of 1980 mandates the transfer of technology from government to private companies, it does not permit constraints on the location in the United States where that technology is used. Because SIS technology was developed at Lawrence Livermore National Laboratory and then exported to the INEL, if location was a factor in the transfer of this particular technology, one would expect the interested company to locate in California.

Thus, both the Idaho congressional delegation and the DOE attempted to sell the SIS to Idaho based on inflated accounts of the economic benefits that would occur. And DOE Secretary Herrington, who had become directly involved in the campaign of the Republican candidate for Congress from the Idaho Falls area, added to the problem by intentionally distorting the role that had been played by the incumbent Congressman Richard Stallings (D-ID) in supporting the SIS. Secretary Herrington, who had sent a letter to Congressman Stallings expressing his gratitude when Stallings had played a major role in preventing Congressman Bustamante from killing the SIS, claimed that Stallings was hindering the efforts to secure the plant for Idaho and only by electing a Republican could the district secure "defense programs and more jobs."[46]

It was these perceptions that were important in a political approval process, not the military requirement for the facility or the actual economic benefits that would be derived, and there was no incentive for anyone to destroy these perceptions by questioning the military's need or the employment and budget figures that were thrown around. Everyone in the debate understood that the prime purpose of this project was to preserve the budget and the strength of the INEL and, in turn, the economic base of the region.

Externalities

Although the average resident of Idaho probably had not heard the term externalities—those side effects associated with a project that fall on persons other than those responsible for its operation—the debate over the SIS was one that attempted to balance positive public perceptions about employment with the negative aspects of potential externalities. Through 1987, the small groups on the political fringe that were trying to stop the SIS continued to gain popular support and to grow in strength. Apparently, supporters of the SIS had assumed that the twin issues of jobs and economic development would be sufficient to gain local approval for the project, but by the end of 1987 it was apparent that the arguments of the anti-SIS movement were beginning to convince an increasing number of local residents. It was at this point that the unions, local business interests and politicians joined forces to save the project. Their campaign, which stressed only the economic benefits of the SIS, gave no weight to the possible externalities and made no mention of any national requirements for the project. It concentrated, instead, solely on the issues of jobs and economic growth.

It is common practice for economists to consider among the costs and benefits of a project the externalities. In the case of the SIS, externalities are costs that could arise from radioactive pollution, crowding, ground water contamination, and other factors. For example, the Department of Energy stated that "during operation of the SIS facilities, accidents could occur that would result in atmospheric emissions of radioactivity."[47] Such externalities must be considered because only by calculating all costs can a resident of a region make an informed decision about a proposed project. However, because different regions have different priorities, only the citizens of the region itself can decide how important various externalities are.

As the citizens of Idaho debated the merits of the SIS, two externalities achieved the most attention. The first was the danger inherent in producing and handling plutonium. Plutonium is one of the most hazardous elements known. The Department of Energy had admitted that "during SIS operations, small quantities of radioactive material would be released to the atmosphere from the Plutonium Processing Building."[48] Emissions from the SIS, accidents that occurred while plutonium was being transported to or from the SIS, or accidents at SIS facilities were all likely to have adverse effects on the region around the plant. However, the SIS was relatively isolated and the INEL had a good safety record, so although a vocal minority continued to stress this issue, costs that might arise from accidents associated with plutonium were not considered a serious problem by most of the population.

This remained true even when, in the midst of the campaign to promote the NPR and SIS facilities, an externality that might entail very high costs appeared. Scientists found that radioactive waste had leaked into sediment beds 110 and 230 feet below a Radioactive Waste Management Complex that was located at the INEL. More than 2 million cubic feet of transuranic waste had been buried at the Complex in steel drums, wooden crates and cardboard boxes prior to 1970, and leaks of radioactive waste now threatened the Idaho aquifer.[49] The Department of Energy recognized that this crisis could create adverse publicity that would damage plans to build the NPR and SIS. It therefore accelerated testing and monitoring of the problem and, with much fanfare, established a $45 million, three year program that was supposed to lead to a cleanup of the nuclear waste.[50]

Even with DOE's announced cleanup program, one would assume that the discovery of radioactive waste problems during a campaign to establish new nuclear plants at the INEL would have some effect on the relative weight that local citizens—and more importantly, local community leaders—would give to potential costs of such plants. However, this was not the case. In fact, in the article disclosing the plan to study the leaks, the local paper noted that "the remedial program is expected to employ an additional 60 people at the RWMC [Radioactive Waste Management Center] in 1988 and another 120 to 130 in 1989"[51] as if the cleanup of nuclear spills was just one more potential job benefit to be gained from the INEL.

A second externality that was given a great deal of weight by many residents of Idaho was the military nature of the SIS project. The INEL had always had more non-weapon related projects than other DOE facilities, but it had also served in a major training and development role for the nuclear submarine program. However, the residents of Idaho continued to believe that most work at the INEL was dedicated to peaceful uses of atomic energy. With about 65 percent of current DOE budgets devoted to nuclear weapon research, development, and production[52], and with the SIS proposed to produce plutonium for nuclear weapons, it was now clear that defense programs would play a major role in the future of the INEL. This realization caused a surprising amount of discomfort among the residents of the region and it seemed to carry far more weight than other concerns about safety or economics.

However, even though these were concerns to residents living around the INEL, the average Idaho citizen had trouble grasping the abstract nature of externalities associated with plutonium production, particularly when these were compared with the perceived economic benefits of the SIS project. In the end, people readily accepted erroneous budget and employment figures, but they were unable to relate to the problems that might arise from accidents that only had a calculated probability of occurring.

The Elements of Economic Inertia

If a region can be convinced it has become so dependent on the jobs related to nuclear programs that its political and economic leaders will engage in the kinds of activities discussed in the case of Idaho, what will similar communities who face more adverse economic circumstances and who are dependent on jobs created by various elements of nuclear weapon or delivery system production do when their economies are threatened by an end to nuclear deterrence? The following sections discuss the various factors that may create regional dependence and contribute to the inertia to maintain nuclear weapon production for economic reasons. The careful reader will discover elements in almost all of these sections that played an important role in the proceeding case.

Economic Inertia and the Contract Proposal

One way to limit the impact of regional economic issues on the decision to buy and build nuclear weapons is to make certain that feasibility and usefulness of the weapon have been clearly established. This is often difficult to do because the only individuals with enough knowledge to evaluate a proposed weapon usually either work for the Department of Defense or for a contractor who will build the weapon. For obvious reasons, these people are likely to be committed to their particular project and restricted in their public statements by the classified nature of their work. In fact, in the defense sector there is a saying that 'the only reason that a project cannot be brought to completion is a lack of funding for development.'

In a recent case, the "military contractors that [will] profit the most from developing a space-based antimissile system [were] assigned the task of deciding its feasibility . . ."[53] This feasibility study designated the likely size and cost (and, by implication, the construction locations) of the weapons involved in the SDI. In the process, this group also initiated the growth of economic inertia associated with various SDI projects when specific organizations and regions began to discover the potential benefits each would gain from the SDI. In this case, the tendency to approve the project was heightened by the fact that four Republican members of key committees in the approval process represented constituencies that would receive the largest share of SDI work.[54]

In partial recognition of the problems inherent in having someone who builds part of a weapon either evaluate or manage the construction of the project, the Strategic Defense Initiative Office (SDIO) originally prohibited companies that built the hardware for SDI from becoming the overall system integrator (i.e., the system manager). However, when this rule excluded "some of the nation's strongest and most diverse industrial firms" from the bidding, SDIO allowed all companies to compete for the system integrator position.[55] The potential economic benefits to the successful bidder further increased the economic inertia emanating from those regions containing that company's plants.

Military Research as a Proxy
for U.S. Government–supported R&D

When government funds are limited, and when large amounts of government spending are devoted to military contracts, it is natural to try to use defense funds to subsidize non-defense interests. In the case of research and development, many people claim that the U.S. can only maintain a technological lead in civilian products through discoveries that result from government funding of advanced military projects, and by their very nature, many advanced defense projects are related to defensive or offensive nuclear weapons. In this respect, the funding of SDI is a classic case. In fact, one defense consultant claims that SDI is simply "a means of justifying a large budget in order to maintain our lead in the battle for the technological high ground."[56]

Most arguments that favor this kind of activity do not consider inefficiencies that may arise from using military funds to accomplish non-military goals. Instead, proponents claim that continued U.S. economic success is based on technological superiority, and that the only way to get the research funds to stay ahead is by having the government fund advanced weapon development. The unstated, but understood, second element of this argument is the assumption that the U.S. is unwilling to spend money on civilian research programs. Therefore, advanced military weapon research must be used as an alternative source of funds to generate new technologies. Statistics show that this second assumption is fairly accurate. In 1985, the Department of Defense (or the Department of Energy, which was working on defense nuclear projects) absorbed over 60 percent of all federal research dollars, and that percentage has steadily increased.[57] The Department of Defense has often used this fact in testimony before Congressional committees to claim that it enhances national competitiveness by developing advanced technologies.[58]

This has created an atmosphere in which the Department of Defense has become the major source of funds for research in many advanced technologies. For example, in 1987, Department of Defense cuts in Research and Development funds for microwave power tubes threatened the existence of an entire $500 million industry.[59] The main consumer of microwave tubes is the Department of Defense, but it is even less likely that industries with both military and civilian markets could persuade another government agency to assume DoD's funding role if Defense funding of their R&D is curtailed. The unknowns that would accompany a reduction in defense spending for research are sufficient to create a sizable inertia in the research community for continued defense participation. And such participation may be either curtailed or drastically altered if an important class of advanced weapons is discarded.

While it is generally believed that the academic community, a major provider of defense funded research, would gladly reject defense funds in favor of money from other sources, a more likely situation involves the loss of relatively certain defense R&D funding with only a probability of gaining other funds. Whether academic researchers would be willing to risk losing defense funds depends on how confident they felt of gaining another source.

Here again, the limited evidence points to the academic community as one more source of economic inertia—if not for nuclear weapons themselves, at least for the type of research that would lead to the possibility of improved versions of these weapons.

For example, Carnegie-Mellon University hired lobbyists from eight of Pittsburgh's major corporations, employed a consulting firm headed by a former Secretary of Defense, and had the Pennsylvania congressional delegation exercise its considerable political muscle to win a Department of Defense contract to establish a multi-million dollar software research center.[60] This kind of campaign by a university to win a defense contract implies a commitment to make every effort to retain that contract in the future, and when funds from a defense contract become an integral part of a school's budget, continuing the contract can even be an essential part of the institutions existence.

Employment and Inertia for Nuclear Weapons

The sheer size of the facilities required to produce, deploy, operate, and maintain nuclear weapons and delivery systems tends to dominate the economy and the employment market in any community in which such facilities are located. This domination is even more pronounced when the community is isolated, as is often the case when the development of nuclear materials is required. These factors, coupled with the massive amounts of money allocated to large defense projects, virtually guarantee that the location of a defense plant in any community other than a major city will make the economic health of that community dependent, to a major degree, on the continued existence of the plant.

As the Appendix on the case of Colorado Springs, Colorado, illustrates, even large cities and whole states can become dependent on defense contracting work. This is particularly true in the western part of the United States where most states face the common economic dilemma of having too much of the region's prosperity generated by outside forces—chiefly commodity users and federal government spending—and too little by internal economic development.[61] This has even occurred in more developed states like California, where $35 billion of defense-aerospace contracts in 1985 provided one third of the manufacturing jobs in the San Francisco and Los Angeles areas and two thirds of the jobs around Santa Clara and the Silicon Valley.[62] In the isolated Antelope Valley in southern California, a group of the largest defense contractors adds nearly a billion dollars a year to the local economy, and twenty percent of the valley's population of 155,000 works for aerospace defense firms.[63]

The Colorado Springs Case shows that the results of the dependency created by these conditions are twofold: first, a lack of internal development helps create a dependency on federal spending, and second, the presence of large amounts of federal dollars continues to stifle internal development while, at the same time, creating a tremendous inertia in the region aimed at ensuring continued federal spending. The cycle of dependency this creates on the part of metropolitan and rural areas alike has been noticed by a few Western civic leaders who have tried to limit further increases in defense spending in their regions. Although it also has definite political overtones, the vote of the Board of Supervisors of the city of San Francisco to prohibit the stationing of a battleship group in their harbor is an isolated example of this kind of action.[64]

However, the general attitude of politicians and community leaders toward regional defense spending tends to be just the reverse of the San Francisco case. In fact, in a statement that foreshadows the kind of struggle one can anticipate if large numbers of nuclear weapons and delivery systems are ever scrapped, the lieutenant governor of California urged the state to wage 'economic war' to force the federal government to continue to support California's shipyards and harbors. Noting that for the last 50 years the federal government had been a major partner in funding the ports, Lieutenant Governor Leo McCarthy said that "since FDR, the federal government [has] understood that it had to fund . . . as a way to stimulate businesses . . . and as a way for jobs to be created."[65]

Because contracts for nuclear weapons and delivery systems are so large and such a rich source of regional spending, even politicians whose political platforms make them leading Congressional doves find that they must support these weapons. Senator Alan Cranston of California made peace a central issue of his unsuccessful presidential campaign, but he has avidly supported the B-1 bomber built in his state by North American Rockwell. Senator Howard Metzenbaum of Ohio has been a leading critic of the Department of Defense, but he firmly supports the B-1 because major parts of the aircraft are made in Cincinnati and Columbus. This is the kind of response one would expect from major centers of B-1 construction, but in this case, the 5000 subcontracts for the bomber are spread over 48 states, greatly increasing the inertia in favor of this weapon.[66]

Politicians who choose to ignore local impacts do so at their peril. When Representative Nick Mavroules led the fight in the House against the MX, he did so even though Massachusetts would gain 7000 direct jobs from building the missiles. But potential contractors for the missile were quick to rally Mavroules' constituents against his vote. Workers in the AVCO plant in Wilmington, Mass. (maker of the MX re-entry vehicle) circulated petitions claiming that Rep. Mavroules was 'anti-Massachusetts'. And Sylvania Systems of Westboro (MX electronics) published statistics showing that a total of 23,000 direct and indirect jobs could be created in Massachusetts.[67] The message was clear: vote for the weapon because of its local economic impact—and don't worry about anything else.

Special Cases of Economic Inertia Arising from Employment Losses Due to Curtailed Projects

While the forces that attempt to secure new defense spending for a region are strong and numerous, those that are aroused when existing contracts are threatened are more powerful and more easily organized. As William Greider has noted, "everyone knows it's easier to vote against a weapon while it's still on the drawing board; once it's in production, only the brave or the foolish will vote to abolish jobs back home."[68] This is particularly true if the contract that is threatened represents a major input to the economy of a rural area, an isolated locale, or a small community.

For example, the Chernobyl nuclear accident of 1986 raised concerns about the safety of a similar 'N' Reactor on the Hanford Nuclear Reservation outside of Richland, Washington, that was used to produce plutonium for military weapons. The economy of the Richland area was already depressed due to problems accompanying the Washington Public Power System bond default and the consequent cessation of work on the last two of its five power generating reactors. A Battelle Memorial Institute study on closing the 'N' Reactor facilities—this closing occurred in 1988—discovered that this action would cost the state of Washington 13,800 jobs by the end of 1996. 6000 of those jobs would be lost at Hanford itself, at an annual cost of $481 million in personal income and $33 million in state revenues. The loss of 6000 jobs out of the 14,500 total jobs at Hanford would depress property values and would hurt local financial institutions, hospitals and social service agencies. The job loss was even expected to increase stress-related disorders, drug abuse, alcoholism and suicide.[69] Statistics like these are guaranteed to get the attention of every politician and community leader in an affected region and yet, this is a perfect example of the type of closure that would accompany a decision to discard nuclear weapons.

Another area of potential economic inertia that is associated with the employment generated by existing defense contracts may be particularly difficult to handle if defense contracts are curtailed under the scenarios just discussed. For the last thirty years there has been an effort to use the military forces of the United States to accomplish social goals that were either not related or remotely related to their missions. Parts of this effort resulted in the assimilation and equal treatment of women and minorities— a laudable and generally successful effort. But other programs involved subsidizing, through set-asides,[70] the economic development and well-being of minority-owned firms. In this respect military contracting has emerged as a key battleground in the efforts to provide more economic opportunity to minority owned businesses. Not only are there huge sums at stake . . . but minority businessmen and politicians say they want to use the military budget to set an example for supplier relationships in both the public and private sectors.[71]

Thus, while one may argue the merits of incurring costs in the defense budget to subsidize certain contractors in order to pursue various social goals, the important point is that, albeit unwittingly, another strong force for economic inertia has been created, and this potential tradeoff may involve social goals for minorities and the desire to reduce the number of nuclear weapons.

Notes

1. For evidence to support this contention see Weida, William, and Gertcher, Frank, *The Political Economy of Nation Defense,* Westview Press, Boulder, Colorado, 1987.

2. For example, on October 18, 1988, a representative of DOE speaking on the McNeil Lehrer Report on National Public Radio stated that DOE's operations had put production goals ahead of public safety.

3. This point will be explored in detail in the following section.

4. Luttwak, Edward N., *Strategy: The Logic of War and Peace,* The Belknap Press of Harvard University Press, Cambridge, Massachusets, 1987, 195.

5. Ibid., 270.

6. Ibid., 197–198. Luttwak notes that there is presently a "distorted, quasimechanical, view of 'deterrence' as an *action* of one's own, rather than an intended political response . . ."

7. "Weapons Production More Than Jobs, Payroll, Economy," *The Post Register,* Idaho Falls, Idaho, August 10, 1987, A–4.

8. Ibid.

9. A breakout refers to actions on the part of the Soviets to abrogate the 1972 anti-ballistic missile treaty and field a widespread anti-missile system. The U.S. response to such a breakout would be to build a large number of new missiles to overwhelm the Soviet system.

10. *Draft Environmental Impact Statement—Special Isotope Separation Project,* DOE/EIS-0136, Idaho National Engineering Laboratory, U.S. Department of Energy, Idaho Operations Office, Idaho Falls, Idaho, February, 1988, S–1.

11. Hatfield, Mark O., *The Plutonium Cushion—A Report On U.S. Defense Plutonium Needs And The Hanford N Reactor,* October, 1987, 4.

12. Ibid., 4, 5.

13. Ibid., 5.

14. In the context of federal government budgeting, it is not unusual that the NWSM—a document meant to justify budget requests—overstated requirements. However, in this case the inflated requirements are translated by law (the Atomic

Energy Act of 1954) into a demand for weapon-grade plutonium that DOE must meet.

15. *Draft Environmental Impact Statement—Special Isotope Separation Project, S-1,1-3 and SIS at INEL,* a publication of the INEL, 1987, Slide 2.

16. *Conference on Improving National Security by Strengthening the Defense Industrial Base,* Harvard University, May 10-12, 1982.

17. Ibid.

18. *Blueprint for Tomorrow (Executive Brochure),* U.S. Air Force, Aeronautical Systems Division, Wright-Patterson AFB, Ohio, 1985, 46.

19. Ibid., 48.

20. Lambeth, Benjamin, and Lewis, Kevin, *Likely Soviet Responses to the SDI,* RAND Corporation, 1988.

21. Barker, Rocky, "Texan Says SIS Should Be Scuttled," *The Post Register,* Idaho Falls, Idaho, March 28, 1988.

22. Barker, Rocky, "DOE Sets 2 More Hearings," *The Post Register,* Idaho Falls, Idaho, March 25, 1988.

23. Pratter, Mark, "'Winds of change' buffet senior senator," *The Post Register,* Idaho Falls, Idaho, July 31, 1988.

24. "Chamber Panel Sensitive to SIS Impacts," *The Post Register,* Idaho Falls, Idaho, August 16, 1987, A-5.

25. "Weapons Production More Than Jobs, Payroll, Economy," *The Post Register,* Idaho Falls, Idaho, August 10, 1987, A-4; and *Life Guard Idaho,* a publication of The Snake River Alliance, July, 1987.

26. Malloy, Chuck, "Not all 'good' GOPers for SIS," *The Post Register,* Idaho Falls, Idaho, May 22, 1988.

27. Malloy, Chuck, "Stallings Links SIS with START Talks," *The Post Register,* Idaho Falls, Idaho, April 17, 1988.

28. Adams, Peter, U.S. "Senate Endorses INF Treaty After Conservatives Give Up Fight," *Defense News,* May 30, 1988.

29. Malloy, "Not All Good GOPers for SIS."

30. Don Ofte, INEL manager in: Malloy, Chuck, "Ofte predicts INEL job rate to stay stable," *The Post Register,* Idaho Falls, Idaho, Jan 6, 1988.

31. "Completion of research programs such as the Loss of Fluid Test (LOFT) program and Power Burst Facility (PBF) requires new major projects such as SIS to maintain INEL employment at the predicted 10,500 average level through fiscal year 1990." *SIS at INEL,* 2.

32. At least one of these figures was cited in virtually every newspaper article on the SIS. For example, see Barker, Rocky, "State Asks For Oversight Panel," *The Post Register,* Idaho Falls, Idaho, March 27, 1988.

33. For discussions of how popular beliefs were shaped by this misunderstanding see "Economist: SIS job numbers misleading," *The Post Register,* Idaho Falls, Idaho, April 17, 1988 the Twin Falls, Idaho, *Times News,* April 16, 1988.

34. Hoffman, C.A., G.R. Wells, R.D. Balsley, and J.H. Davis, *Socioeconomic Impacts of the Idaho National Engineering Laboratory,* Idaho State University, Center for Business Research and Services, Pocatello, Idaho, 1986.

35. *Regional Multipliers—RIMS II,* U.S. Department of Commerce, Bureau of Economic Analysis, May, 1986, 84.

36. "Construction Project Data Sheets," *FY 1989 OMB Budget Request—Atomic Energy Defense Activities,* U.S. Department of Energy, Washington, D.C., May, 1987.

37. Both uranium and plutonium Atomic-Vapor Laser Isotope Separation (AVLIS) Projects are based on the use of copper-vapor lasers to generate light frequencies that will photoionize selected atoms of uranium or plutonium, thus allowing these isotopes to be extracted by an electric field. However, while the uranium AVLIS project had been subjected to extensive operational testing, the plutonium project had very important differences and difficulties associated with its development and operation. These differences required both the use and modification of the uranium AVLIS technology, and large amounts of new development, to make the plutonium process operational. Although there had been some co-mingling of funds between the two projects, the differences between the two were so significant that while the success of the uranium project was important to the plutonium project, full development of the uranium project in no way assured a similar outcome for the plutonium project. The status and rationale of both programs are explained at length in "Laser Isotope Separation of Uranium" and "Laser Isotope Separation of Plutonium," *Energy and Technology Review,* UCRL-52000-87-7, July, 1987, pp. 34–37. For a specific discussion of the effects of the decision to use concurrent development on the costs of the SIS, see Cite to My EIS Review.

38. Given these factors, the choice of the AVLIS technology was curious. However, it did hold the promise of providing highly purified plutonium, and this seemed to be an overwhelming concern of the DOE. House Appropriations Committee, FY1985 Hearings for the FY1985 Energy and Water Development Appropriations, Part 4, 431.

39. *Draft Environmental Impact Statement—Special Isotope Separation Project,* S–3, 1–1, 2–12, 2–15, 2–37.

40. Statement contained inside the front cover of the *Draft Environmental Impact Statement—Special Isotope Separation Project.*

41. Testimony of William J. Weida at the hearings on the Special Isotope Separation Project, Idaho Falls, Idaho, March 25, 1988.

42. Jan Hager, a contractor for the SIS speaking in: Brugger, Brad, "SIS Would Open New World For Technology Transfer," *Idaho State Journal,* Pocatello, Idaho, January 13, 1988.

43. Lamar Trego, Westinghouse Idaho Nuclear Co., in: Fields, Dave, "Proposed center could lure SIS spinoffs to area," *The Post Register,* Idaho Falls, Idaho, Dec 10, 1987.

44. Based on construction employment figures provided in *TMI-4/Rev. 0/2-17–88,* Lawrence Livermore National Laboratory and Westinghouse, Inc., February 17, 1988, and assuming an employment multiplier of 2.3 and a job creation rate of 16.5 per million dollars of construction (from the RIMS II Idaho Model).

45. DOE press release, December 4, 1987.

46. "DOE chief: Waste plant No. 1 priority," *The Idaho Statesman,* Boise, Idaho, July 20, 1988.

47. *Draft Environmental Impact Statement,* s–4.

48. *Draft Environmental Impact Statement,* 4–12.

49. *Life Guard Idaho;* Barker, Rocky, "Andrus Is Pleased With Cleanup Plan," *The Post Register,* Idaho Falls, Idaho, August 30, 1987, A–1.

50. Barker, Rocky, op. cit. It should be noted that this article also stated there is no practiced technology for removing so much radioactive waste and soil. INEL officials said that the cleanup could cost as much a $1 billion and would be hazardous for workers unless a new technology is developed.

51. Ibid.

52. "Report Urges that Pentagon Pay for Its Nuclear Warheads," *New York Times,* July 17, 1975, 17.

53. Biddle, Wayne, "Star Wars Conflict of Interest Seen," *New York Times,* April 30, 1985, D–17.

54. Ibid.

55. Gilmartin, Trish, "Firms Scrap for Key SDI Job as Defense Alters Bid Rules," *Defense News,* August 24, 1987, 1.

56. Ryan, Bill, "SDI: A Boost for the Technology Battle," *Defense News,* August 10, 1987, 20.

57. "No Reaganomics," *The Economist,* February 11, 1984, 77, 79.

58. Reich, Robert B., "High Tech, A Subsidiary of Pentagon Inc.," *New York Times,* May 29, 1985, 23.

59. Leopold, George, "Study Concludes Pentagon's R&D Cuts Threaten U.S. Microwave Industry," *Defense News,* August 24, 1987, 5.

60. Muscatine, Alison, "Computer Bid Fails," *Washington Post,* November 15, 1984, C1.

61. Carlson, Eugene, "Economists See Difficult Days Ahead For West and Midwest," *The Wall Street Journal,* September 30, 1986, 19.

62. "California's Second Look at its Defense Dollars," *U.S. News and World Report,* February 25, 1985, 62, 63.

63. Reese, Michael, and McAlevey, Peter, "'Aerospace Valley' Takes Off," *Newsweek,* July 15, 1985, 56–58.

64. "California's Second Look at its Defense Dollars."

65. Davies, John, "Calif. Urged to Wage 'Economic War'," *Journal of Commerce,* April 12, 1985, p. 14.

66. Greider, William, "Birds of a Feather: Hawks and Doves Flock Together for Defense Dollars," *Milwaukee Journal,* August 12, 1984, 1.

67. Ibid.

68. Ibid.

69. "Study Cites Cost of Closing Reactor," *The Post Register,* Idaho Falls, Idaho, September 2, 1987, B–3.

70. These are defense contracts on which bidding is restricted to special groups.

71. Stevenson, Richard W., "The Big Push for Pentagon Dollars," *New York Times,* July 5, 1987, 1.

10

Nuclear Weapons and Competition for the Allies' National Resources

This chapter deals with the economic factors that affect spending for strategic weapons by the major U.S. allies who are economically strong enough to be world class military powers—should they choose to be. As this chapter will show, the economic realities faced by all of these countries have had a major role in shaping their defense establishments and in determining the mix of conventional and strategic forces they have chosen to deploy.

The Allies: Implications of Current Force Structures

The fact that the U.S. built and deployed strategic nuclear weapons has meant that allies like the United Kingdom and France could have greatly reduced defense programs. Until the late 1970's, this resulted in a considerable reduction of their defense expenditures. In addition, because the U.S. chose to be a technological leader in military weapons after WWII, our allies did not have to. This saved the allies a good deal of money, but it also gave the U.S. advantages in technology and competitiveness that the allies could not afford to cede. As a result, certain European members of the NATO alliance have also attempted to maintain complete weapon industries and to wage technological competition in defense goods while, at the same time, constructing a well organized and efficient military alliance. The conflict between these goals, and the differences between the attitudes of the U.S. and the NATO allies toward spending for social programs, form the basis for much of the strain within the NATO alliance.

NATO forces have been structured to overcome numerical deficiencies through technological superiority and the use of tactical nuclear weapons. The use of nuclear weapons has also tied the United States to any potential European conflict, guaranteeing that the United States would not 'sit out' a war between Europe/NATO and the Warsaw Pact. Nuclear disarmament, or a situation in which one or more NATO members enjoyed protection from air and missile attack through enhanced defenses, would result in a need to redesign NATO forces to operate in a conventional warfare environment. Such changes would cost considerably more than the present NATO defense establishment and would cause increased competition for national resources in each of the NATO countries. The role of the United States in the redesigned NATO forces would also have to be redefined. Thus, the resulting changes would have political, budgetary, research, force structure, and defense industrial base implications.

The Allies: The Status of the European Defense Industrial Base

The European Defense Industrial Base was largely rebuilt after WWII. But as technology accelerated, European defense industries found themselves increasingly unable to compete with those in the U.S. There are several reasons for Europe's eroding competitive position in the defense arena. First, only the United States and the Soviet Union have large indigenous weapon markets that allow economical production runs. The Europeans must rely on exports or collaborative projects to create enough demand to yield efficient production runs, and export markets are often not appropriate places to absorb the high technology weapons that are the mainstay of the NATO forces.

Second, there has been an unwillingness on the part of European nations to spend funds for military uses instead of for other, competing social objectives. This has slowed the rate of growth and modernization of the European NATO defense establishment, and it further decreases the size of the European defense market. Third, these factors triggered a destructive cycle of uneconomical production runs that caused lower profits (or losses) on the weapons produced. This left less money for research and development of future projects, resulting in lagging weapon technology. This, in turn, caused lower sales, which again lowered production run size and, as the cycle repeated, further lowered profits.

For these reasons, the Europeans have increasingly resorted to joint production of major weapons, a decision that has often resulted in weapons that are too expensive to compete in international markets (for example, the Tornado fighter-bomber aircraft). The European Defense Industries have also relied on an extensive use of offsets[1] to increase export sales. While offsets have helped to sell arms, they have also decreased revenues from export weapon sales and reduced funds available for research and development of future systems. These factors have left European defense industries less able to respond to requirements for structural changes, such as the reorientation of the NATO defense establishment that would result from nuclear disarmament or from the introduction of enhanced air and ballistic missile defense systems.

European defense industries evolved in response to a NATO organization that required high technology weapons in combination with nuclear armaments to overcome its numerical inferiority to the Warsaw Pact. In the process, these industries also became an integral part of the system that generates new technologies for all European manufacturing and a structural change in NATO would have implications for each member of this relationship.

For example, one result of nuclear disarmament could be to stop research and production of whole classes of weapons and delivery systems such as ICBM's, ballistic missile submarines, strategic bombers or nuclear warheads. This would have limited consequences for various technologies that are also employed in non-defense industries in a few countries like France. Similar consequences would be noted in a wider range of countries if improved air and missile defenses were available. In these situations, a number of alternative European defense industry structures might serve the needs of European NATO forces. And apart from the changes that revised force requirements would cause, the removal or limitation of nuclear threats to the European defense industries would, in themselves, have an impact on the industry structure that evolved. Thus, the effect on the European defense industry of either nuclear disarmament or nuclear defense would be two-fold. First, a direct economic impact would arise from the need to adjust to different NATO force structure and weapon requirements. And second, an indirect economic impact would follow the recognition that the role of European defense industries, and their potential survivability, have both changed.

The Allies: The Ability of European Defense Industries
to Compete for Technologically Advanced Weapon Contracts

A 1988 Aerospace Industries Association report found that the complete dominance by the U.S. of the free world's aerospace markets had ended, and it called for increased research to keep the U.S. ahead. In the 1960's, the U.S. had a virtual monopoly in the aerospace market. By 1975, the U.S. share of the market had dropped to about 70 percent, with France, Britain and West Germany accounting for the remainder. However, the U.S. market share was still 70 percent in 1985, even though many new competitors had entered the market.[2] Thus, while the U.S. was holding its market share, the new competitors were taking part of the 30 percent market share that had been gained by the Europeans.

Since WWII, the Europeans have not had an easy time competing with the U.S, particularly in the high technology areas that typify strategic delivery systems. In spite of a concerted effort to trade for defense items with the European allies, the U.S. still awards 94.3 percent of its prime contracts

Table 10.1:   Top Ten Non-U.S. Defense Recipients of U.S. Defense
Contracts

Name	1986 Contract Amount ($Millions)
Defense Facilities Admin. (Japan)	$451.1
Federal Republic of Germany	$417.5
Canadian Commercial Corporation	$404.9
Motor Oil Hellas (Greece)	$380.6
Bahrain National Oil	$282.7
Rolls-Royce (U.K.)	$261.8
Scallop Petroleum (U.S. Subsidiary)	$211.3
Honeywell (U.S. Subsidiary)	$128.1
MIP Instandsetzungsbetric (FRG)	$122.4

Source: U.S. Department of Defense reported in Silverberg, David,
"Domestic Sources Reap Bulk of U.S. Prime Contracts," *Defense News*,
October 5, 1987, 15.

to domestic sources based on dollar value. This accounts for 92.7 percent of all contracts awarded.[3] Table 10.1 lists the top ten non-domestic defense contractors in 1986. Note that most of these contracts awarded to non-domestic sources are for oil and maintenance, not for defense products and certainly not for high technology items.

There are several reasons for the apparent inability of the Europeans to compete. One is a well-known U.S. hesitancy to have foreign sources for items that are essential defense goods. But just as important, the defense industries of Europe are both less efficient and often, less technologically advanced than comparable U.S. industries. As a result, they are simply not competitive. For example, out of almost 2000 Request For Proposals (RFPs) connected with the SDI that were circulated in Britain in 1985 in an attempt to get U.K. support for Star Wars, British industry was able to respond to less than 15.[4] In fact, the inability of Europe to compete with the U.S. on SDI-related technology caused the U.S. to start the European Architecture Study, whose main purpose was to shift some business to European Industry.

Other examples of the inability to compete are plentiful. In one, the NIMROD airborne warning and control aircraft was given every opportunity to succeed (including massive subsidies by the British government) and still couldn't successfully implement technologies that have been in operational use by the U.S. for over ten years. The project was finally cancelled and Boeing was awarded the contract (with a 130 percent offset).

Competition and Defense Trade

Another very important source and use of defense funds—the trade in weapons—has a direct impact on the defense burden carried by the U.S. and the Allies. If this trade is balanced between countries in an alliance, it does not alter the burden associated with other alliance-related expenditures.

But if this trade is one-sided (as is the case with the U.S. and NATO), the results are an economic gain for the nation with the larger sales, and an economic loss for the nation with smaller sales. In spite of a commitment by the United States to maintain a balanced 'Two Way Street' approach to defense purchases, several factors, the most important of which is U.S. insistence on having the capability for indigenous production of each item purchased, caused a large imbalance in defense trade.[5] In 1984, this imbalance meant that the U.S. sold $3.28 of weapons to Europe NATO for every $1 of weapons it purchased. The result of this imbalance has been to increase the U.S. GNP and U.S. tax receipts through the action of the GNP multiplier[6] and similarly, to increase the defense costs of the other NATO countries.

In 1986, the U.S. maintained a 1.62:1 ratio of defense trade with Europe in the critical aerospace sector. NATO countries purchased $3.24 billion worth of U.S. aerospace goods and the U.S. purchased $1.9 billion worth of European aerospace items.[7] This kind of defense trade imbalance is likely to persist because the larger U.S. industrial base gives the United States a competitive advantage over other NATO countries in those weapon systems that are the most complicated and most expensive. As a previous section demonstrated, Europe has generally been unable to compete successfully in this high tech arena, and this situation will not improve until the U.S. agrees to transfer technology to the other NATO members and then buys advanced weapons from those countries so that efficient production runs are possible.

Purchases of this kind are unlikely because to maintain its defense industrial base, the United States insists that it be able to produce every weapon it buys. As a result, foreign purchases, when they do occur, have limited benefits for the selling country. For example, in January, 1985, the U.S. decided to purchase an Italian-made Beretta pistol for its armed forces. This deal was worth about $56 million, but instead of the U.S. buying all the weapons from Italy, the purchase agreement was constructed to allow production of the pistol to be transferred to the U.S. no later than the third year of the contract.[8] Similar contracts were used in the purchase from the U.K. of the AV8-B Harrier 2 and the purchase from the French of the Mobile Army Communication System (that was built by GTE).

When industries are maintained, either out of national pride or a feeling of necessity, in spite of the fact that they cannot compete, the result is invariably higher costs. How such industries would respond to a reduction in nuclear forces that resulted in the need to rebuild conventional forces is problematical. On the one hand, the increased production that would come from a large conventional buildup might increase the efficiency of the European defense industries. On the other, efficiency may not be improved and costs may stay high if the problems are deeper than simple production run constraints. Efficiency and cost problems have been discussed by the

NATO allies for years, and the most commonly suggested solution has been to engage in cooperative arms production under the assumption that costs will be lowered by the larger production runs that result. This is discussed in the following section, but it should be noted that it assumes that costs are high because production is low, and not because of other reasons such as poor management or too much bureaucracy.

The Allies: NATO Arms Cooperation

Collaboration is the antithesis of competition. It is supposed to save money through agreements to eliminate duplication while competition is supposed to save money by encouraging duplicate efforts and choosing the cheapest alternative. Both can't be correct, and there is little doubt that competition is actually cheaper.[9]

Buying weapons from the U.S., as had been the general practice after WWII, cost Europe both jobs and pride. However, serious efforts to collaborate on the production of high performance, advanced technology military equipment only started in the 1960's when Europeans were cutting defense budgets and looking for cheaper ways to make weapons. One of the early deals from this era, the Puma-Gazelle helicopter (U.K.-France), was so successful that it eventually led to the NATO family of weapons concept In 1978. Later, in a program plagued by too many production lines and too much production assigned to monopoly producers, a number of European nations collaborated on the F-16 with the U.S. The Europeans then tried to collaborate to produce a fighter on their own, but the Toronado project got entirely out of hand. A supranational bureaucracy was added to the project, increasing costs by 30 percent to about $37 million per aircraft when the Allies could have purchased the superior F-14 for about $36 million.[10]

In the last ten years the U.S. has established so many obstacles to collaboration with the Allies that it has been almost precluded from participating in these agreements. There are three reasons this has occurred:

1. The U.S. generally prohibits sales of the weapon to third countries. Since U.S. producers don't have to export to survive, this restriction is normally unimportant. However, the Europeans do have to export, and if they can't do it with the U.S., they will make agreements with each other so they can sell the weapons they produce.
2. The U.S. is very concerned about technology transfer to communist countries. As a result, it has much tighter controls than the NATO countries and this further complicates the export question.
3. The SDI exacerbates the first two problems if it gives the U.S. even more of a technological and cost advantage. The U.S. already spends

twice as much on procurement and three times as much on R&D as all 10 European countries combined.[11]

Collaboration with the United States is still a very attractive proposition for the Allies because of the potential for technology transfer. The chance for technology transfer is present in every collaboration, but agreements with the United States often contain the chance to learn the newest technologies while, at the same time, they add unique problems because of the strict rules that prohibit the transfer of those technologies. For example, in 1988 the U.S. was trying to enter into a collaborative agreement with the NATO allies to develop the new advanced tactical fighter. If the allies shared the costs of developing this aircraft on a 50/50 basis, the U.S. had to determine how to protect its most sensitive technology from some of the NATO partners while still competing with other nations (such as France) that offer to make the same NATO members full partners (with access to all technology involved) in their development efforts.[12] The U.S. has been unsuccessful in dealing with these problems on several occasions in the past, and as a result:

- it has been unable to collaborate with its Allies.
- it has had to bear the entire cost of developing the project.
- the NATO alliance has wound up with two concurrent development efforts, with all the duplication that entails.

In spite of the obvious shortcomings and increased costs, European military people like collaborative efforts because they are hard to cancel and are almost immune from political meddling. More importantly, collaborative efforts require the allies to rely on one another in a way that strengthens the NATO alliance. The military knows that the money saved by doing things cheaper would not come back to them, but the cooperation that collaboration fosters is a major and lasting benefit. Thus, these agreements may be best viewed as ends unto themselves.[13]

Should a reduction of nuclear arms take place, it is difficult to forecast whether collaborative agreements would allow enough efficiency (and low enough costs) to complete a conventional buildup within the budgets of the European nations and whether U.S. restrictions on technology transfer would prohibit it from joining the allies in a meaningful way. However, the Europeans may have a chance to find out if successful collaboration is possible as they make the transition to the environment created by the Single European Act of 1993. This transition will play a major role in shaping the European Defense Industrial Base of the future and hence, in determining how the European Allies would respond to future requirements for additional defense production.

The Allies: The Single European Act of 1993

By 1986, all common market countries had signed the Single European Act that will become law on January 1, 1993. It will allow Europe to function much like the United States with free transit across borders and more economic unification. The act covers all NATO members except Iceland, Norway and Turkey, but many believe the NATO alliance may be left behind during the economic changes that will occur as the act creates expanded markets and increased competition for European defense industries in both Europe and the United States. Willy de Clercq, European Community Commissioner, has noted that "one cannot exclude the fact that the single market will help U.S. and Japanese firms penetrate the European Market."[14]

European defense ministries have resisted the changes embodied in the act because they are reluctant to give up political power. According to NATO officials, these changes will permanently alter the character of European defense production and will create long-run requirements for:[15]

1. A unified European research agency analogous to the Defense Advanced Research Projects Agency (DARPA) to avoid duplication and cut costs in European weapon research.
2. A European-wide procurement agency.
3. More multilateral European projects like the European Fighter Aircraft (EFA) as free borders make it possible to establish industries in a number of countries. Maj. Gen. Luis Esguevillas, staff group chairman of the Independent European Programme Group (IEPG) has noted that "Eventually defense firms in Europe will need production in a large enough scale to be competitive with the United States and Japan."[16] A stronger, unified Europe may be in a better position to promote this kind of production. For example, the European Fighter Aircraft consortia was able to lower prices by getting four countries to buy 750 aircraft.
4. Standardized Memoranda of Understanding (one of the normal contractual tools in the weapons trade) to simplify business.
5. Greater concentrations of defense industries into international consortia. These could be powerful competitors because they can generate more resources and larger production runs, again lowering the unit price.

None of this will be easy to accomplish because of the varied interests of the countries involved. Rupert Scholz, Defense Minister of the Federal Republic of Germany has said that Europeans must produce high-performance weapons at low cost "while observing national industrial policies. National interests must be respected. . . ." However, he then added "I believe that these specific interests will lose their importance in the coming years."[17]

This statement sums up the likely outcome of the Single European Act—national interests eventually giving way to forces that create a more unified and stronger European defense industrial base. If this effort succeeds, the Europeans should be in a better position to accommodate shifts in defense production arising from either a nuclear disarmament or from an operational defense against strategic nuclear weapons.

Selling Nuclear Defense to U.S. Allies

Europe's ability to generate the high technology required to participate in the construction of advanced nuclear defenses was highlighted in 1985 when the Reagan Administration attempted to cultivate European support for the SDI by getting the Europeans involved in research and development for the project. This was an effort to overcome initial Allied resistance to the Star Wars program that was based on fears that the U.S. was preparing to go it alone, that the Europeans could never imitate such an expensive plan, and that while SDI was too far-fetched to ever work, it could siphon funds from the effort to combat the more imminent Soviet threat.[18]

Some European opposition was softened when the U.S. began to demonstrate that a few elements of the Star Wars program were feasible and when it made an effort to show the Allies that parts of SDI could be used to defend their countries against medium range missiles.[19] However, European ambivalence toward the SDI continued, and the French proposed the Eureka research and development program as a parallel to the SDI. The reason for Eureka was two fold: first, the French assumed that the SDI would generate major commercial spinoffs, and second, they assumed that these spinoffs would be more accessible to the Americans than to the Europeans.[20]

The validity of these assumptions is open to question. For example, a 1985 report on the state of British R&D found that "if Britain is to break the vicious circle of decline, an important precondition must be a reduction in the relative size of the defence sector and level of military R&D. . . . Britain has got to reorient her technology away from the defence sector and towards the civilian market. . . . Most military R&D leads to *product* innovation. Much of the innovation on which civilian industry depends is, however, in improvement in the manufacturing *process*, not in new product development."[21]

These findings were contradicted by a 1978 study by the European Space Agency (ESA) that surveyed military and civilian space-related research (and not just defense R&D). The ESA report tried to measure the overall economic benefits from R&D in the space sector. Benefits were identified in four areas: commercial, technological, organization and methods, and the work factor. The overall benefit to cost ratio was 2.7.[22] The study used only partial measures and may be biased on the high side, however it does provide an economic rationale for space-related research (and for SDI and strategic delivery vehicle research).

Although Eureka was a parallel effort to Star Wars, its only purpose was to develop commercial technology; i.e., to do direct research instead of waiting for spinoffs to develop. But when 18 European nations launched the Eureka project on November 5, 1985, it already appeared to be foundering because of political squabbling, insufficient funding, and fuzzy planning. France wanted governments to subsidize R&D, Britain wanted private funding. Italy wanted a central agency to run the entire project; Germany, France and Britain didn't.[23] As doubts over both Eureka and the SDI persisted, the Reagan Administration developed plans to give large amounts of the SDI research to the Allies to enlist their political support for Star Wars. Estimates in 1986 were that between $300 and $400 million would be given to the Allies in FY1987, mostly for research on defending against intermediate range missiles. In addition, a $50 million subsidy to European research against tactical Soviet missiles was proposed. These items were viewed with skepticism by many in the United States who believed they were additional subsidies to NATO members who were already heavily subsidized by U.S. expenditures for the defense of NATO.[24]

At the same time, another reason for Allied involvement in SDI research appeared when it became apparent that many of the weapons developed for the SDI could also be used in conventional combat situations. For example, researchers on the rail gun at the University of Texas found that not only was the rail gun "directly comparable with the best conventional techniques for accelerating things at very high velocities. . . . [But] as a result of worrying about making [it] light enough to launch into space, it became light enough so that it became possible to think about putting it on vehicles."[25]

The use of other SDI technology in ground warfare was also suggested. Included were advanced lasers, the means of detecting Soviet ICBM's, and the use of discriminating, ultra accurate weapons.[26] Thus the combination of more favorable European attitudes toward SDI, the sizeable amount of U.S. R&D that had been offered to the Allies, and the appearance of an excellent rationale for European involvement in the program seemed to assure that the Allies would play a major role in SDI research and development.

Since these events, quite the reverse has occurred. As already noted, out of almost 2000 Request For Proposals (RFPs) connected with the SDI that were circulated in Britain in 1985, British industry was able to respond to less than 15.[27] The inability of Europe to compete with the U.S. on SDI-related technology caused the U.S. to start the European Architecture Study, whose main purpose was to shift some business to European Industry. However, the Europeans have still been thoroughly disappointed by both the low volume and low value of contracts for SDI research work. As of March, 1988, European companies had been awarded 80 SDI contracts

worth a total of $127.16 million and one British industrialist described the
U.K. contract amounts as 'peanuts.'[28] The Federal Republic of Germany
received the most money for research on the SDI, a total of $46.5 million
between October, 1985, and March, 1988. Over this same period, the U.K.
received $43.4 million; Belgium, $94,000; the Netherlands, $40,000; Italy,
$7.5 million; France, $6.2 million; and Canada, $1.07 million.[29]

Another obvious source of non-U.S. research on the SDI—Japan—has
had no involvement in the project. By March, 1988, Japanese Industry was
still waiting to get its first contract. Two reasons were cited for Japan's
total lack of participation: first, Japanese firms were divided in their interest
in doing SDI research, with many undecided about the value of the research,
and second, Japanese industry was waiting for the Japanese government
to respond to U.S. proposals for a theater anti-missile defense program for
the Asia-Pacific region.[30]

Additional programs of any larger magnitude are unlikely for either Japan
or the NATO Allies because in September, 1987, the U.S. Senate approved
the Glenn amendment to the budget to restrict Allied involvement in SDI.
The amendment exempts foreign countries that agree to pay a 'substantial
portion' of the total cost of a specific contract. A West German industrialist
called the U.S. action a "narrow, parochial approach" and one that was
"not in the spirit of cooperative defense research and certainly not in the
spirit of the [NATO] alliance."[31] The House had passed a similar measure
in May, 1987. It prohibited non-U.S. participation in SDI research and
development contracts unless the work cannot be done by a U.S. firm at
an equal or lower price.[32]

The story of non-U.S. R&D on the SDI points up several interesting facts
about the state of European defense technology. First, large portions of the
European defense industry were unable to respond to U.S. proposals for
research. Second, the Europeans exhibited more interest in a French proposal
that stressed commercial, not military technology. Third, the Allies in general
were upset about U.S. provisions to limit R&D unless they themselves agreed
to pay for some of the costs. In other words, they were not interested in
SDI research and development per se, instead they were interested in SDI
R&D that was subsidized by the United States. None of this bodes well for
the future of independent Allied R&D in the defense field and it has added
one more element to the general issue of burden-sharing between the U.S.
and the allies.

Burden-Sharing

'Burden-sharing' is the generic term for sharing the cost of defending
ourselves and our allies from Communist aggression. Most of this defense
involves NATO's role against the Warsaw Pact, but burden-sharing issues

can arise any time the United States and another country unite against a common threat. Thus, it is central to the issue of European efforts to reallocate economic resources to conventional defense after a nuclear accord has been signed or a strategic defense is developed.

At the heart of the burden-sharing debate is the simple economic concept of the subsidy. An American tourist who returns from Europe overwhelmed by the transportation system and generous social programs enjoyed by Europeans, and who asks why the United States does not have similar benefits, may begin to suspect that U.S. defense spending is providing a subsidy to European governments that allows more spending for non-defense programs. The businessman who sees the support provided by the Japanese government to its industrial sector, and who questions why the United States cannot afford similar programs, may similarly begin to suspect that U.S. defense spending is providing a subsidy to Japan which allows it to spend more on modernization of its industrial sector.

Deputy Secretary of Defense William Taft IV, speaking to a NATO transatlantic Conference in July, 1988, pointed out that the 14 European NATO nations have over 400 million people, 100 million more than the Soviet Union, and a Gross Domestic Product (GDP) exceeding $4 trillion, substantially higher than that of the Soviet Union. Yet, several NATO nations fund defense at nominal or near zero rates of growth.[33] A 1988 study by the Congressional Budget Office claimed that the European nations of the NATO alliance could save the United States as much as $16 billion a year in operating and construction costs simply by paying for some of the items done in the common defense[34] and Barry Carter claims that

> if the NATO allies and Japan accelerated their increases in defense spending to 4 percent per year versus the present average increase of about 2 percent per year, the United States could [have reduced] its planned growth in defense expenditures from the projected 7.2 percent over 1984–1988 to less than 6.5 percent. This would [have meant] a saving of about $60 billion in 1984 dollars for the five-year period. Annual increases in allied defense spending of 5 percent per year could save the United States about $90 billion.[35]

Defense analyst Leonard Sullivan Jr. says that what currently attracts so much attention to the burden-sharing debate is the powerful confluence of economic and defense issues that occurred in the late 1980's. First, there was the trillion dollar U.S. trade deficit. Then there was the Soviet-U.S. INF treaty and the hope that it would lead to further agreements to limit strategic arms. And then there were the academic arguments that the U.S. is declining as a power because of its attempts to handle too many world commitments.[36] Because of the reallocation of economic resources that might occur, these points have even more serious consequences for burdensharing in a world that enjoys either nuclear disarmament or an operable defense against strategic nuclear weapons.

The U.S. Department of Defense estimates that about 60 percent of the U.S. defense budget is allocated to NATO—roughly $171 billion in 1988. But British Defense Minister George Younger counters that while there is a need for improvement in some areas, "the size of the European contribution refutes the idea that the division of effort within NATO is fundamentally unequal." He cited a contribution of $110 billion per year, up 30 percent from 1971. The U.S. increases since 1971 have only been 12 percent.[37]

However, the Europeans generally claim that an accounting approach to burdensharing unfairly characterizes the size of their contribution since it does not take into account political costs of having a military draft in European countries, the need to host U.S. bases on their soil, the risk of a Soviet invasion, or the toll of hosting the training exercises that are a constant feature of life.[38] Lord Carrington, the NATO Secretary General, has said that burden-sharing "is not just a matter of mechanics and bookkeeping. French, Norwegian, Danish and British troops, for example, work smoothly together in exercises. The Alliance has not done so badly." He also stated that NATO members can spend less "with a prudent use of resources," and that burden-sharing "involves the whole question of the relationship between the United States and Europe in trade and trade deficits. There are wider economic issues as well to make the relationship between all the countries of the alliance more equitable."[39]

The Nunn Amendment (May, 1985) obligated the U.S. to fund parts of multilateral research programs with the Allies as part of a carrot and stick approach to try to get NATO members to spend more for defense. Twelve multinational research accords were signed in the first two years of the agreement, but doubts remain about whether the allies will live up to their financial commitments. Some nations are hesitant to take on new projects because of budget constraints and concerns over the health of domestic defense industries.[40] "The Europeans are uncomfortable with the idea of fencing money in a budget for a program or programs to be decided later," according to a NATO official. "Also, when you set aside money for a program in Europe you set it aside for three to five years. Europeans do not reopen the budget every year like we do."[41]

In addition, Rep. Pat Schroeder, D-CO, has questioned whether the U.S. can ever convince the European Allies to spend more "because it looks like they're kowtowing to the U.S. version of what the threat is."[42] Mostly in response to the growing U.S. political controversy surrounding burden-sharing, the NATO defense ministers ordered a complete review of the alliances' defense costs in May, 1988. The 12 European defense ministers had challenged U.S. criticisms on burden-sharing, noting that they provided the majority of the troops, tanks, artillery and combat aircraft in the Alliance.

They also pointed out that they contribute 65 percent of the major warships as well as providing all the land for training, military bases, and substantial support for the 326,000 military personnel stationed in Europe.[43]

Comparative Sacrifice:
The NATO Allies Versus the United States

According to the Organization for Economic Cooperation and Development (OECD), public expenditures, particularly for public welfare, have increased much faster than economic output in all major industrialized nations, including the United States.[44] But two events that occurred during the Reagan administration's first term added a new dimension to the burden-sharing problem. The first was the buildup of the U.S. defense establishment (that actually began during the last year of the Carter administration). This buildup caused huge budget increases for U.S. forces, and raised U.S. concerns over the contribution and commitment of all U.S. allies to the common defense effort. A second event, that unfortunately coincided with the first, was a serious global recession that severely decreased every country's ability to pay for defense and that accentuated the debate on whether government budgets should be devoted to military or social expenditures.

In the United States, the question of spending for military or social programs was answered by a clear shift to the military side. In NATO, whose countries were pressed harder by the recession than was the U.S., the reverse was often the case. There is no clear measure of the 'burden' that resulted from these decisions, but Figure 10.1 presents one way to view the situation. From these data, several things are apparent. First, although the total gross national product of the European allies is about 85 percent of that in the U.S., their defense spending is only about 47 percent of the U.S. amount. Second, while European expenditures for education are about what would be expected given the relative size of their GNP, the amount that these nations spend on public health is much higher than the U.S. amount. And third, Japanese performance in all sectors is about what one would expect given the size of their GNP (about 33 percent of the U.S. GNP), except for defense which, at about 1 percent of GNP and 5.5 percent of the amount the U.S. spends, even makes the lowest European spending look good.

At first glance, the fact that the United States is ranked so high in this type of comparison would seem to indicate that it is indeed carrying more than its share of the burden. However, such a conclusion presumes that the European NATO countries and Japan should spend their money in the same proportion that the U.S. does. There is also a serious problem with using the gross percent of GNP statistic to depict U.S. defense spending for NATO. When a European country spends money on defense, almost all

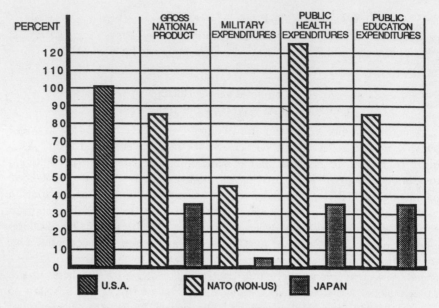

Figure 10.1: Measures of Burden-Sharing (1984 Data)
Source: Data are from the Institute for Peace and International
Security. Reprinted in Dan Beyers, "Diplomats Brush Off Criticism,
Insist Burden Sharing At 'Top of Agenda'," Defense News, March 21, 1988.

of that defense is allocated to the European region because that is where
the country is located. This is not the case with the United States where
defense spending supports a world-wide commitment. Therefore, if one
wants to calculate statistics based on percent of GDP, the relevant numbers
to compare are the amounts spent directly on the European NATO region.

At one time, it was thought, based solely on the cost of American forces
in Europe, that about 17 percent of the total U.S. defense budget was spent
on NATO. Studies done in 1984 by the Government Accounting Office and
by the Department of Defense both concluded that a much higher percent
of the total budget was spent (GAO said 56 percent, the Defense Department
said 58 percent) if the cost of all NATO backup forces was included.[45]
Thus, the amount actually spent in NATO is 58 percent of the 100 percent
reference bar in Figure 10.1, an amount that puts the U.S. ahead of, but
much closer to, the NATO partners.

Another indicator of burden-sharing, per capita defense expenditure, is
shown in Table 10.2. A 1988 study by the Defense Budget Project, while
acknowledging that the U.S. does spend more on defense (6.54 percent of
the GNP in 1986 as opposed to 3.66 percent for large NATO countries and
2.85 percent for small NATO countries) shows that the Allies are making

Table 10.2:   NATO Per Capita Defense Spending

Country	1960	1970	1980	1986
USA	930	1036	845	1120
Belgium	209	242	367	291
UK	375	346	437	503
Canada	292	227	232	212
Denmark	207	259	331	332
France	373	378	492	510
FRG	292	346	437	455
Greece	65	125	215	251
Italy	124	163	205	238
Luxembourg	74	71	146	154
Netherlands	258	316	364	371
Norway	184	317	401	511
Portugal	45	132	95	89
Turkey	27	31	40	53
Small States[1]	146	162	185	199
Large States[1]	291	309	393	426
TOTAL NATO[2]	506	560	528	654

All figures in constant 1986 dollars using NATO expenditures, 1986 deflators and exchange rates.

Note: Per capita statistics present only a general picture of relative spending over time due to fluctuations in exchange rates and population.
[1]Average per capita spending
[2]Defense spending for all of NATO divided by the population of NATO

Source: Leopold, George, "Study Rekindles Heated Burden-Sharing Debate, Challenges Congress' Assertions," *Defense News*, March 28, 1988, 13.

significant contributions and that their support has been more consistent than that of the U.S.

This view is further reinforced when one realizes that the use of per capita data again overstates U.S. spending on NATO. If the 58 percent figure is used to determine the actual amount of U.S. defense spending that is devoted to NATO, the per capita spending figure of $1120 from Table 10.2 is reduced to $650, a figure that is higher by about $100 to $200 than the major NATO countries. Some of the remaining difference can be accounted for by the fact that per capita statistics tend to penalize countries with large populations. While this measure does give an indication of the defense burden born by each citizen of a country, it, like the other two measures, is only a valid comparison for countries that are essentially the same in all other respects. None of these measures accounts for differences between countries such as geographic location, amount of industrialization, skill level of the citizens, historical perspective, potential level of contribution not linked to defense spending (ports, roads, rail facilities, etc.) and other similar indicators that may be critical in a future military action involving the European theater. In short, spending for defense measures input, not output and can only be regarded as a sign of commitment, not capability.

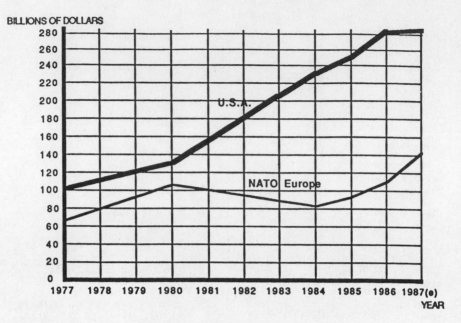

Figure 10.2:   U.S. and European Defense Spending Trends
Source: NATO Press Center.   Reprinted in Giovanni de Briganti,
"European Nations Spending Slide Shows Signs of Reversal," *Defense News*,
February 22, 1988.

Spending Trends—NATO

Another measure of burden-sharing is one that takes into account trends in defense spending instead of dealing with point indicators. The point indicators in the previous section give little sign that the United States has carried more than its share of NATO costs. However, the trends provide a different picture of what is currently happening. Figure 10.2 shows that the spending trends in both Europe and the United States were almost identical— until 1981. In 1981, a dramatic change occurred in European defense spending, and with this change came an increased interest in burden-sharing. Why NATO spending stagnated after 1980, in an era of vastly increased U.S. defense budgets, can best be explained in the context of the economic climate in the period 1981 through 1984.

With the onset of the global recession in 1981, the United States and the NATO European nations both had a choice to make: should shrinking resources be allocated to social or defense programs? The Reagan admin- istration had received a substantial election mandate to allocate these funds to defense—and it proceeded to do so. The European NATO partners had received no such mandate and, in addition, were more severely affected by the recession. When the U.S. pressed the Europeans for defense spending increases to match those in the United States, the result, as expressed by a senior official in the West German Defense Department was a feeling that "We can't be lectured on how to reduce social expenditures in favor of defense spending. We have to win our own elections and maintain social stability. We don't tell the U.S. what's good for Oregon, and they shouldn't tell us what's good for us."[46]

In response to economic problems and social pressures, the European NATO members lowered their spending to annual increases of roughly 1.5 percent and have maintained that lower level until 1987.[47] Whether 1987 really represents a change in the NATO spending trend shown in Figure 10.2 is open to conjecture:

- France's 1988 defense budget included a 3 percent increase to $29.4 billion. Of interest is the fact that about 33 percent of the total procurement accounts were for nuclear forces, an increase of 10 percent from 1986, and spending for space programs increased 80 percent.[48]
- The West German defense budget for 1988 grew only 1.5 percent. to $28.67 billion. The German Finance Minister Gerhard Stoltenberg said he had no idea where he would get the money for even the 1.5 percent increase along with the money he needed to pay for his country's contribution to increased European Community costs; the subsidies for steel, coal, shipbuilding, and agriculture, or to pay for planned income tax reform.[49]
- The British defense budget was forecast to show no growth and perhaps even decline in 1988.[50]
- The Norwegian defense budget dropped from a 3 percent to a 2 percent annual increase in 1988 because of economic difficulties. The 1988 budget was about $3 Billion, a figure that is about 10 percent of the total Norwegian budget.[51]

In sum, it is unclear that the Europeans have any desire or intent to significantly change their spending levels for defense. It is, however, clear that U.S. spending levels are falling. One result of this might be that the U.S. will have less reason to accuse the NATO allies of inequitable burden-sharing in the coming years, but more likely results will be a rapid deterioration of NATO conventional forces, increased U.S. pressure on the Allies to spend more on defense and further attempts to use nuclear weapons to make up for inferior conventional forces. Pressures on the Allies by the U.S. are unlikely to succeed because the U.S. and its allies have such different views of the world. As the *Defense News* stated

In dozens of private interviews . . . European government and industry officials made it clear that there is no money in their treasuries to pay substantially more NATO costs and that, in any event, there is little sympathy among their tax-paying publics to do so. . . . The great majority of European officials think their countries already are paying their share of NATO's costs. What many do not understand is the depth of American feeling about burden-sharing. America's economic relationship with Europe has changed radically and its defense relationship should reflect that fact. Making this change without damage to NATO will require compromise by all sides.[52]

Such a compromise would be difficult under the best of circumstances. It will be even more improbable if it is attempted at the same time that NATO is trying to accommodate the structural changes that would come with nuclear disarmament or an operable defense against strategic nuclear weapons—and the accompanying conventional buildup these changes would require.

Implications of the European Burden-Sharing Decision for the Use of Nuclear Weapons

In February, 1988, Richard Perle told a House Armed Services Committee panel that the Reagan Administration routinely prepared its reports on *Allied Contributions to the Common Defense* by "thinking of ways to put the best possible gloss on some pretty dismal figures."[53] The defense spending decision by the European NATO partners strained the alliance for two reasons. First, it gave rise to a great deal of political pressure in the United States to similarly reduce U.S. defense spending related to NATO. This pressure culminated in an effort by the U.S. Senate in June, 1984, to influence the European allies by attempting to withdraw as many as 90,000 U.S. troops from Europe.[54]

The second result of the NATO European member's decision was that after three years of this policy, NATO's conventional force strength was badly eroded and there was increasing concern that weakened conventional forces would leave the West with only a nuclear option if the Warsaw Pact attacked. David M. Abshire, the U.S. Ambassador to NATO, noted that "the new attention to conventional capabilities is directly related to fear of nuclear war. Some of this fear finds expression—wrongly, I believe—in calls for nuclear freezes or unilateral nuclear disarmament. Some of it is rooted— rightly—in anxieties that our deterrent depends more on nuclear weapons than it should."[55] And Barry Carter pointed out that "the Administration should try to use the strong popular sentiment that exists in many allied countries against nuclear weapons by better communicating the important point that *an enhanced conventional defense can raise the nuclear threshold*."[56]

In early December, 1984, the European NATO members agreed to increase the amounts being spent on defense. They approved a budget of $7.8 billion to upgrade airfield, port, pipeline and communication facilities in the following six years, West Germany extended its conscription period by three months, and eight or nine NATO members promised to increase defense expenditures by 3 percent in the future.[57] However, as Figure 10.2 shows, few significant steps were taken and the spending trend was not reversed. The $7.8 billion allocated to conventional forces was $1.2 billion less than defense experts estimated was needed to do the job[58] and this figure represented an increase in spending, before accounting for inflation, of less than 1.4 percent.

Thus, while there is little statistical support for the contention that the United States carried more than its share of the NATO burden prior to 1981, it is clear that the European countries made a conscious decision to lower defense spending in favor of maintaining social programs in the 1980's. Since the period of lower European defense spending coincided with the defense buildup in the U.S., and with the rise in the value of the dollar, it probably appears to be more serious, in monetary terms, than it actually is. But the result of that decision must now be remedied at a time when U.S. budgets are severely strained.

It is this decision, not the dollars involved, that raised serious questions about Europe's commitment to its own defense, and it is this decision that potentially increased the risk of nuclear war as the strength of NATO's conventional forces deteriorated. If, as GAO and Department of Defense reports have shown, roughly 56–58 percent of the U.S. defense budget continues to be spent on NATO-related items, it is hard to escape the conclusion that the U.S. cannot afford to show more interest in Europe's defense than that shown by the Europeans themselves. And if European defense spending continues to be sacrificed for social programs through the rest of the decade, the burden-sharing issue will dominate NATO relations in the 1990s and will be a destructive force within the alliance for years to come. Large U.S. deficits will clearly limit the United States' ability to maintain its defense and social spending in the future, and could easily force a decision by the United States to limit NATO spending and to fund other areas of higher national priority. Thus, the decision by the European allies has not only increased the likelihood of nuclear war, it may have also established an environment in which the Alliance is unable to respond to the costly conventional force restructuring required if nuclear weapons are removed from the NATO arena.

The Situation of the Allies—Conclusions

When discussing the attitudes and policies of our Allies, it is necessary to remember that:

- Economic self interest is a significant concern of the allies, just as economic self interest governs the actions of the United States. This means that allied economic interests may not coincide with those of the United States.
- The allies have a long history of arms manufacturing and sales, and a similar history of competing with one another in this field.
- While the allies are perfectly willing to sign defense accords with the United States, most do not view the U.S. or any other partner in NATO as a trustworthy source of conventional arms. For this reason, no ally is willing to depend solely on external sources for these arms. However, because of the expense of strategic arms and the restrictions inherent in the use of nuclear weapons, most allies are quite willing to allow the U.S. to provide strategic protection and deterrence, and they are generally willing to allow the U.S. to be the source of strategic weapons, should they be required.
- The allies have political agendas that are distinctly their own—both on international and local levels. These attitudes are often shaped by living in closer proximity to the Soviets than the U.S. and by the realization that Europe will be the battlefield in a conventional war with the USSR.
- The NATO allies have social agendas that preclude the amount of military spending the U.S. desires. This situation is unlikely to change significantly in the future, irrespective of statements by the NATO hierarchy about the future spending levels that the organization will achieve. As a result, U.S. responses to NATO spending decisions must ultimately be unilateral. While this is an uncomfortable position for any member of an alliance, the sooner the U.S. stops trying to change behaviors that are essentially fixed, the happier everyone will be.
- NATO is a good deal for the allies. This good deal operates on several levels. First, in the strategic sector, the U.S. foots almost the entire bill for creating deterrence and the protection it provides for all the allies. In a nuclear-free world, this expense would probably be shifted to the allies to the extent that they agreed to increase their conventional armaments. Second, on the conventional front, the U.S. participates heavily in conventional preparations for a war with the USSR in spite of the fact that the NATO allies are fully capable of carrying the entire burden for their defense. Thus, it is in the economic self interest of the allies to make sure that these alliances are perpetuated.

The European attitude in the 1980's toward the choice between defense and social spending makes burden-sharing a potent political issue. In the final analysis, this is a cost-benefit question. Does the U.S. get more from supporting the alliances it has established than it would get by walking out?

The answer to this question becomes less clear in a scenario where continued U.S. budget austerity causes a reordering of priorities.

It is doubtful that the U.S. can apply more pressure to NATO than it has in the recent past. How this situation would change in the face of a conventional buildup that accompanied a nuclear accord or an operational defense against strategic weapons is impossible to forecast. However, it comes down to a question of whether the U.S. is willing to maintain a rough approximation of the status quo—with the realization that we may continue to carry more than our share of the defense of NATO—to preserve the alliances we now have, or whether we should withdraw and spend the money elsewhere. Because the down-side risk of such a move is unacceptably high, it is reasonable to assume that the situation will remain essentially unchanged in the future.

Notes

1. Offsets include a range of industrial and commercial compensation practices required as a condition of purchase of military related exports (either Foreign Military Sales or commercial sales of defense articles and defense services) as defined by the Arms Export Control Act and the International Traffic in Arms Regulations. Offsets may include Coproduction, Licensed Production, Subcontractor Production, Overseas Investment, Technology Transfer, Direct Offsets, Evidence Accounts, Compensation or Buy Back, Barter, Counterpurchase, Switch Trading, Reverse Countertrade, Blocked Currency, Mandatory Offsets, Bilateral clearing Accounts, Best Effort Contracts and Additionality. For a complete discussion of the principles and practice of offsets, see Weida, William J., *Paying For Weapons: Politics and Economics of Countertrade and Offsets,* Frost and Sullivan, Inc., New York, 1986.

2. Silverberg, David, "U.S. Dominance of Markets Ending, Study Says," *Defense News,* February 29, 1988.

3. Silverberg, David, "Domestic Sources Reap Bulk of U.S. Prime Contracts," Note: Per capita statistics present only a general picture of relative spending over time due to fluctuations in exchange rates and population. *Defense News,* October 5, 1987, 15.

4. Conversation with Dexter Smith, Strategic Affairs Editor, *Defence,* November, 1985.

5. Directorate for International Acquisition, Office of the Under Secretary of Defense, (Research and Engineering), Department of Defense, 30 January, 1985.

6. A very rough calculation of the benefit to the United States of this trade imbalance could be done as follows:

U.S. Sales ($8177 million) − U.S. Purchases ($2034 million) = $6143 million net advantage

$6143 million × GNP Multiplier (2.5) = $15,358 million increase in GNP

$15,358 million × average tax rate (.25) = $3839 million increase in U.S. revenues.

7. Silverberg.

8. Andrews, Walter, "Pentagon Replaces Colt .45 With Beretta," *Washington Times,* January 15, 1985, 2.

9. "Europe does it the second-best way," *The Economist,* June 21, 1986, 21–23.

10. Ibid.

11. Fisette, Bob, "Incentives and Obstacles to EAC," *European Arms Cooperation Conference,* Airlie House, Virginia, April 21, 1987.

12. Beyers, Dan, "Understanding 'Codevelopment' Key to Allied Fighter Participation," *Defense News,* October 5, 1987, 17.

13. "Europe does it the second-best way."

14. Adams, Peter, "Europe Looks to 1993 and Unity," *Defense News,* July 25, 1988, pp. 1, 32.

15. Ibid.

16. Ibid.

17. Ibid.

18. Weeks, Albert, "Perceptions of benefits seen softening Western Europe's position on SDI," *Free Press International,* March 11, 1985.

19. Ibid.

20. Wolfe, Charles, Jr., "SDI Is No European Economic Elixir," *The Wall Street Journal,* October 23, 1985, 36.

21. Davidson, Ian, "Tonic that failed to give a lift," *Financial Times,* London, September 29, 1986.

22. See Fitussi, F.P., *Economic Benefits of ESA Contracts,* European Space agency, 1978 and Niederau, Goetz, *Economic Benefits of ESA Contracts,* European Space Agency, 1980.

23. Hudson, Richard L., and Gumbel, Peter, "Europe's High-Technology Eureka Project Is Beset by Squabbles, Inadequate Funding," *The Wall Street Journal,* November 5, 1985, 36.

24. Krauss, Melvin, and Fossedal, Gregory A., "Star Wars for the Allies, Usual Terms," *The Wall Street Journal,* May 8, 1986.

25. Wheeler, David L., "Scientists Refine for Battlefield Use a Weapon Designed for Star Wars," *The Chronicle of Higher Education,* January 21, 1987, 4, 5, 9.

26. Cohen, Sam, "Use Star Wars Weapons in ground wars," *The Wall Street Journal,* April 20, 1988.

27. Conversation with Dexter Smith, Strategic Affairs Editor, *Defence* in November, 1985.

28. de Briganti, Giovanni, "U.S. Exports Little Strategic Defense Work, Europeans Complain," *Defense News,* March 21, 1988, 10,16.

29. Gilmartin, Trish, "Federal Republic of Germany Tops Foreign Entities in Monies for SDI Research," *Defense News,* May 16, 1988, 9.

30. Sneider, Dan, "Japanese Progress on SDI Drags," *Defense News,* Mar 21, 1988.

31. Gilmartin, Trish, "Senate Moves to Restrict Allied Involvement in Star Wars Project," *Defense News,* September 21, 1987, 1.

32. "Defense Department Lists Protectionist Measures," *Defense News,* October 5, 1987, 16.

33. Briley, Harold, "Taft Urges European Burden Sharing," *Defense News,* July 25, 1988.

34. Adams, Peter, "European NATO Burden-Sharing Would Trim U.S. Alliance Costs," *Defense News,* May 16, 1988, 9.

35. Carter, Barry E., "Strengthening Our Conventional Forces," in *Rethinking Defense and Conventional Forces,* Center for National Policy, Washington, D.C., 1983, 26.

36. Beyers, Dan, "Arms Control, Economic Developments Stir Up Burden Debate," *Defense News,* May 2, 1988, 6.

37. Adams, Peter, "Deputy Secretary Taft Raises Burden-sharing Debate on Overseas Campaign," *Defense News,* May 30, 1988, 6.

38. Beyers, "Arms Control, Economic Developments Stir Up Burden Debate."

39. Adams, Peter, "European NATO Burden-Sharing Would Trim U.S. Alliance Costs," *Defense News,* May 16, 1988,9.

40. Beyers, Dan, "Uncertainty, Lethargy Dog Effort To Build NATO Arms Cooperation," *Defense News,* February 29, 1988, 12.

41. Ibid.

42. Adams, "Deputy Secretary Taft Raises Burden-sharing Debate on Overseas Campaign."

43. Briley, Harold, "NATO Ministers Call for Extensive Review of Western Alliance's Defense Costs," *Defense News,* May 30, 1988, 7.

44. "The Rise in Public Expenditure—How Much Further Can It Go?" *The OECD Observer,* May, 1978, 8.

45. "Burden Shared," *The Economist,* August 4, 1984, 38. It should be noted that these figures still do not include the contribution of U.S. Strategic Forces to the defense of NATO.

46. Thurow, Roger, "NATO's Economic Bind Restricts Its Defense Options," *Wall Street Journal,* June 5, 1984, 38.

47. de Briganti, Giovanni, "European Nations Spending Slide Shows Signs of Reversal," *Defense News,* February 22, 1988, 1,36.

48. de Briganti, Giovanni, "Giraud Asks 3 Percent MOD Budget Rise," *Defense News,* October 15, 1987, 1.

49. Thelen, Friedrich, "West German Defense Budget Grows Only 1.5 Percent," *Defense News,* July 6, 1987.

50. de Briganti, "European Nations Spending Slide Shows Signs of Reversal."

51. Erlander, Hans C., "Economy Forces Norway to Cut Defense," *Defense News,* June 6, 1988.

52. "The Real Burden of Burden Sharing," *Defense News,* July 4, 1988.

53. Beyers, Dan, "Correction of Burden-Sharing Reports Urged," *Defense News,* February 15, 1988, 9.

54. "Paying Up," *Time,* December 17, 1984, 58.

55. Abshire, David M., "NATO: Facing the Facts," *Washington Post,* December 31, 1984, 13.

56. Carter, 26.

57. Ibid, 13.

58. Drozdiak, William, "Conventional Buildup Troubling NATO," *Washington Post,* November 21, 1984, 9.

11

Nuclear Weapons and the Competition
for Soviet National Resources

Whether one believes that the United States builds forces to counter the Soviet threat or that the U.S. builds forces for other reasons and only uses the Soviet threat as a rationale, the size of the U. S. defense effort is linked, in large part, by the amount of Soviet military spending. Unfortunately, a similar linkage exists between U.S. defense expenditures and those in the Soviet Union. These linkages between U.S. spending and Soviet spending create a political requirement, particularly during buildups on either side, for evidence of increased spending by the opponent. And this, in turn, means that data on the Soviet military effort are seldom reported in an unbiased, academic manner in the U.S.—and vice versa.

The Soviet Union has been called 'an LDC with a nuclear bomb.' While this overstates the case, it does emphasize that the Soviets are far from being in the same economic league as the United States. For the Soviets, with a GNP of roughly 55 percent of the U.S., to match the military effort of the United States implies a tremendous economic and social strain on the Soviet people. In economic terms, the Soviet problem is centered around the concept of opportunity costs, and even after the gross inefficiencies inherent in the Soviet system are taken into account, the problems experienced by the Soviet Union provide an extreme example of the result of consistently shifting resources from nondefense to defense uses over an extended period of time.

Soviet Opportunity Costs

During testimony on the 1984 budget, Congressman Dicks, addressing Secretary of Defense Weinberger on the subject of Soviet military strength, stated ". . . when you look at this chart, apparently they [the Soviets] are getting a lot more for their ruble than we are for our dollar." Secretary Weinberger answered "They are, because they don't spend very much on quality of life. . . ."[1] Unfortunately, neither the question nor the response was correct. When all costs are considered, the Soviets pay more for defense than the United States because the real costs of defense are opportunity costs (what is given up by making an economic choice), and these costs are not shown in Soviet spending figures.

For example, stated U.S. costs will always be larger than stated Soviet costs for similar weapon systems because the opportunity costs of building a U.S. system are fully expressed through the bidding action of the free market. The Soviets use the best material and people for defense, and of those resources, they use the best for high technology strategic weapons and for their space effort. However, they have no way (or desire) to express these costs accurately in the Soviet budget.

There is some question as to whether the Soviets even know how much their defense is costing them. In addition to not accounting for the true costs of the resources they employ, the Soviets have used bad economic data (no inflation is 'possible' in a centrally planned economy, so none is recorded) for so many years that it is highly unlikely they could accurately calculate true expenditures for their own defense effort even if they decided to try to account for all opportunity costs. In a revealing comment on this possibility, Marshal of the USSR Sergei Akhromeyev said in 1988 that ". . . with growing openness in defense developments, the Soviet Union plans in the next few years to publish more detailed figures on its military budget. *But that will be possible only after a pricing reform has been carried out in our country.*"[2] (Author's italics.)

In addition, U.S. opportunity costs are lower than opportunity costs In the Soviet economy, partially because the U.S. GNP is larger, but mainly because the United States operates much closer to its production possibility frontier than the Soviets do to theirs. The Soviets operate so inefficiently, and get so little return from their available resources that the cost, in terms of other projects forgone, to build a new weapon is extremely high. This situation is further exacerbated when the weapon is technologically advanced and is in direct competition with projects needed to revitalize the Soviet economy. The U.S., on the other hand, has more available resources, and may not have to sacrifice nearly as much for the same weapon. To further complicate the issue, the cost of Soviet military personnel (at least, the drafted enlisted force) is understated and opportunity costs are again not correctly represented. The U.S. all-volunteer force has made personnel costs reflect the true burden on American society of maintaining the military.

A 1986 report by the CIA and DIA to the Joint Economic Committee of Congress attributed the poor economic growth in the Soviet Union since the 1950's to the defense burden.[3] and there are clear signs that the Soviets have begun to recognize this. G. Isaev stated in *Sovietskaya Rossiya* in 1984, that "It cannot be denied. Forced expenditures for defense do not allow us the means for the time being to improve our welfare to the extent we would like."[4] And the multiple reforms initiated by General Secretary Mikhail Gorbachev seem to further recognize this fact. The share of Soviet GNP devoted to defense (approximately 15 percent, compared to 7 percent for the U.S.) is higher than that of any other developed industrial society. It was probably higher in the early 1950's than in the later 1950's and 1960's, but it grew throughout the 1970's. No model has been able to link Soviet defense spending to any combination of U.S., Chinese, or NATO spending, and it also seems to have been totally independent of the performance of the Soviet economy.[5]

As Soviet military spending has grown faster than the economy as a whole, the opportunity cost of defense spending has become even higher. In 1982, Hopkins and Kennedy used optimal control theory to investigate the effect of defense and other factors on the Soviet economy. They found that in the 1980's the Soviets would not be able to maintain the same rate of consumption and defense as they did in the 1970's—but that they would be able to at least 'muddle through.' ('Muddle through' is defined arbitrarily as a 1 percent per capita rate of growth in consumption.)[6] Later work by both the CIA and DIA resulted in the assessment that

> competition for resources could be intense . . . for some basic materials and some intermediate goods, such as high-quality steel and microprocessors, and for skilled labor—resources traditionally supplied on a priority basis to military production. This competition could result in some tradeoffs at the margin between military and civilian production.[7]

The cost to the Soviet military and Soviet society of muddling through is high, but since direct figures for this burden are not available, it must be inferred from other indicators. For example, in the last decade Soviet infant mortality increased from 23/1000 to 40/1000 (there are no neonatal intensive care units in the Soviet Union). as life expectancy fell for Soviet men and women—an unprecedented occurrence in an industrialized country.[8] Over the same period, deaths from cardiovascular disease rose from 247/100,000 to 500+/100,000 (while they dropped in the United States by 23 percent).[9]

In the Soviet military, there are similar indications of deep underlying problems. Cockburn (1983) found that the design of many Soviet aircraft was deficient, tanks and other Soviet equipment were quite unreliable, troop morale was bad, alcoholism was extremely high, reserves were hard to mobilize, and Soviet equipment (with a few notable exceptions such as the AK47 rifle) was generally poor.[10] Similarly, Blacker (1983) found that Soviet weapons are generally inferior in quality and performance, Soviet troops are not well trained, and the Soviet army is rife with ethnic and language problems.[11] Further indications:

- One fourth of the Soviet's Northern Fleet submarines were not seaworthy in early 1985[12] and known Soviet nuclear submarine mishaps resulted in the loss or disabling of thirteen boats in the period 1967–1984.[13]
- Soviet soldiers, who are drafted and who receive low rates of pay ($10 per month), have generally low morale and very limited training. Among these soldiers, common diseases such as typhoid, cholera, hepatitis and influenza have become epidemic, and shortages of medical supplies require the reuse of items as common as hypodermic needles. Given the priority granted to the military, data such as these indicate that the situation for average civilians is even worse.[14]
- Soldiers are trained to perform only a single task, and they perform this job throughout their tour. Flexibility in the use of manpower is non-existent. In addition, live fire practices, flying time, and live missile firings are all extremely limited, making the actions of the military under actual combat conditions much harder to predict.[15]
- The Soviet officer corps is weakened by corruption and alcohol. Bribery appears to be a common method of passing inspections, getting promotions and easing the day-to-day military existence. It is noteworthy that corruption is worse in the inspection units and that the punishment for corruption is often light.[16]

As a result of these kinds of deficiencies, in October, 1988, the Kremlin publicly censured the Soviet Ministry of Defense citing "a serious concern . . . caused by the facts of evasion of military service, relations between servicemen which do not correspond to military regulations [i.e., bribery], cases of duty violations and accidents involving military equipment."[17]

Added to all these factors is the unreliable state of the Warsaw Pact allies. These countries are not modernizing their forces and, as a result, the Soviets have been forced to station more troops in Eastern Europe. Technologically advanced Soviet equipment such as the MiG 29 and the T-80 tank are no longer compatible with the Warsaw Pact's MiG 21's and its 30-year old T-54 tanks. In addition, the Pact countries are not politically reliable, particularly in a long war, and the Soviets have had to reorganize their divisions in the area to fight without the aid of the Warsaw Pact troops.[18]

Opportunity costs are also increasing because the composition and performance of the Soviet labor force which, due to changing birth rates and losses suffered during WWII, is assuming a non-Slavic makeup. This has seriously degraded productivity. For example, Hopkins and Kennedy (1982) determined that the relative efficiency of Slavs to non-Slavs was 1.27/1.[19] Among other things, these changes have decreased the number of draft-aged males available for service in the Soviet military to the level where, by 1987, the Soviet Union had to recruit 85 percent of all 18-year old males just to maintain its military forces at a constant present level. The decline in the labor pool has raised the opportunity costs of using men for military service so high that the Soviet government recently announced it would begin accepting women as 'volunteers' in the military.[20]

Given the serious economic bind these constraints create for the Soviets, it is interesting to speculate on possible methods of correcting these problems. There are several options, but from the Soviet viewpoint, all are unattractive and none hold the promise of increased resources for military use:

1. Raise GNP: this would require reduced military spending to spur investment in industry, a difficult step given the Soviet view of the world.
2. Revert to Stalinism: this is not really feasible given the current status of Soviet society and it is the reverse of the reforms instituted by Gorbachev.
3. Reform: decentralize, increase incentives and private production, and use the second economy. In a generic sense, this is what Gorbachev has attempted. However, such reforms have a great potential to undermine Soviet authority.
4. Use external adventures to ease political pressures at home: as the experience in Afghanistan demonstrates, this only increases economic pressures.[21]

In sum, it has cost the Soviets dearly to maintain and expand their military capability, particularly in those areas associated with high technology and strategic weapons. In the process, they have demonstrated a level of will and priority that is hard to ignore. This is a good indication that the theory that the United States can 'spend the Soviets under the table' in the arms race is simply wrong. If, due to the inability to account for opportunity costs, Soviet defense expenses are understated, and if, by any agreed measure, stated Soviet expenditures are at least roughly in parity with our own, then the true Soviet defense effort and its related burden on the Soviet economy must exceed that of the U.S. by a considerable margin.

Economic Implications of Allocating Resources to Soviet Defense Spending

The rapid economic growth of the Soviet Union between 1950 and 1975 was essentially a one-time phenomena achieved by extensively exploiting natural resources, by increasing inputs from under-utilized rural labor, and through the use of Western technology. Since 1975, Soviet economic growth has averaged less than 2 percent a year (1 percent per capita).[22] The slowdown in Soviet growth in the early 1980's may have been an attempt to catch their breath and increase efficiency, but it did not achieve the desired results because of shortages in energy and raw materials. This disrupted production, and industrial output fell even further until the decline in economic growth was partially arrested in 1983–84.[23]

When Gorbachev took power in 1985, he recognized that the Soviet Union was rapidly becoming an economic backwater because of its low economic growth. Soviet GNP was forecast to grow between 0 and 1 percent through the end of the century, with a number of Soviet scholars predicting negative economic growth. The Soviets had begun to lose significant ground to countries like Korea and Italy.[24] Thus, in the April, 1985, plenum, Gorbachev laid out a long term economic strategy that called for a sharp acceleration in national income growth.. To achieve this growth, near term plans stressed the 'human factor,' while long term strategy involved a restructuring and modernization of the entire economy.[25]

This caused a direct conflict with military spending plans in general and with specific attempts by the military to acquire technologically advanced strategic weapons. Instead, accelerated investment in capital stock and accelerated technical progress (in machine tool, computer, and instrument making electrical equipment) in the economy was stressed by Gorbachev. The progress envisioned by Gorbachev required unobtainable rates of growth in producer durables of over 15 percent per annum while a 1986 plan called for a 7.6 percent increase in capital investment, a rise in civilian machine building of 30 percent, a 31 percent rise in oil extraction, a 27 percent increase in coal production, and a 24 percent increase in electric power.[26] These plans proved to be highly unrealistic. In 1988, Robert Gates, Deputy Director of the Central Intelligence Agency claimed that "after three years of reform, restructuring and turmoil, there has been little, if any, slowing in the downward spiral of the Soviet economy."[27]

Economic Problems and Soviet Defense Spending

The record economic growth sought by Gorbachev requires machinery that must be produced in the Soviet machine building and metalworking sectors. These sectors are the primary source of military hardware production.[28] Thus, Gorbachev's plans call for direct competition between the defense and civilian sectors for goods and services. In the near term, the Soviet military is well positioned to accommodate shifts in resource demand and still contribute to the current Soviet order of battle because of the expansion and upgrading that took place in the military industries after 1975. But competition for resources will be intense in areas that require high quality metals, microprocessors, and skilled labor[29], and these are the specific sectors that produce technologically advanced weapons for both strategic and conventional use. In these areas, most experts agree that

Soviet industry is simply not ready to produce new generations of weapons like a Soviet version of the SDI.[30] To be able to do this, the Soviet defense sector would have to command enough resources that it would probably thwart plans to expand the civilian sector of the economy.

Thus, resource allocation in the high technology area will be a major test for Gorbachev's reforms. If economic reforms in the Soviet Union do not go well, Gorbachev will have to ask the military for additional resources at a time that the loss of those resources could have severe consequences for the defense establishment in the short run. On the other hand, if economic reform succeeds, the civilian side of the Soviet economy will be better able to support the long run needs of the military.

Soviet Strategic Forces and the Competition for Soviet Resources

The effect on the Soviet economy of building and maintaining the technologically advanced weapons in the Soviet strategic arsenal relates both to the numbers of these weapons and to the efforts that are made to develop new systems. Chapter 2 provides current, unbiased estimates of the size of Soviet strategic forces, and these numbers give an indication of the manner in which past decisions regarding competition between the civilian and defense sectors for resources with strategic weapon uses were made. How the Soviet Union will try to balance its perceived strategic weapon needs in the future with the recognition that diversion of these resources to defense may be particularly damaging to the Soviet economy is not clear. Soviet defense spending appears to have increased at about a 3 percent rate in 1986 and 1987, up from a 1.5–2 percent rate in the period 1961–1966. However, a Defense Policy Panel report notes that "Economic concerns, namely the need to shift resources from defense to civilian use, appear to be driving Gorbachev's efforts to move the Soviet military toward a smaller, more defensively oriented force structure."[31]

In addition, the military leadership appears to be in general agreement with the Soviet civilian leadership on strategic nuclear policy even though it still is not inclined to make concessions in conventional weapons.[32] This is curious because some aspects of the Soviet problem are similar to the European situation where a fundamental inability to fund both defense and non-defense at the desired levels has resulted in pressures for cuts in the defense sector. However, in Europe these cuts have made it more difficult to build conventional forces and to remove strategic weapons. In the Soviet Union, the response seems to be just the reverse, and this may be an indication of how great pressures on Soviet high technology are. For example, when he was asked if *perestroika* would cut defense costs, Marshall of the USSR, Sergei Akhromeyev indicated that it might because "Our current steps include *imparting our armed forces a non-offensive structure, limiting offensive weapons systems,* and somewhat lowering the scale of munitions manufacture."[33] (Author's italics.)

Future Soviet Weapons

In a step that further complicated the problem of allocating resources between its defense and non-defense sectors, in 1985 the Soviet Union embarked on an expensive 20-year cycle of defense policy and weapon development. This new cycle is typified by the 'high-tech' battlefield and it may see the Soviets begin to accept the Western view that conventional conflicts can remain non-nuclear.[34] The fourth generation Soviet fighter aircraft that are part of this cycle were demonstrated at the Farnsborough Air Show in 1988. But although the Soviets have demonstrated the ability to apply excellent high technology to limited numbers of weapons representing specific areas of interest, questions remain about Soviet competitiveness across the spectrum of areas that require modern defense technology.

[Mikhail Gorbachev] has inherited a non-competitive Soviet economy that is in a terrible state. A cumbersome system of central planning produces shoddy goods, and discourages any sort of creativity or technological innovation. The Soviet economy is simply incapable of participating in the high-tech, electronic age.[35]

In fact, a study by Amann, Cooper, and Davies, published in 1977, has concluded that there is no evidence that the technological gap between the USSR and the West was substantially reduced in the previous 20 years.[36]

Given these limitations, attempts by the Soviet Union to compete in high technology military systems, particularly at this critical time during initial efforts to rebuild the Soviet economy, entail tremendous opportunity costs. And even if these costs are accepted by the Soviet leadership, there is serious doubt that the Soviet Union can match Western technology at any cost. For example, although fourth generation Soviet fighters are now in production, they are about equal to the 1970's technology in the F-18A (based on the Farnsborough aircraft, the Soviet avionics are only of 1960's vintage). The U.S. already has prototype fighters that are a full generation ahead of the F-18A.

It is clear that the Soviets remain formidable adversaries. However, if the Soviets find they cannot compete technologically, they will be faced with a difficult and dangerous situation. Each day they will fall further behind the West, and their options will be extremely limited. Substituting quantity for quality will be less effective as U.S. technology improves, and quantity will also be limited by economic constraints. Buying weapons or components abroad is difficult at best, and impossible for those items that are most critical. When Epstein (1984) looked at all the problems facing the U.S.S.R.'s tactical air wings, he concluded that the Soviet threat was overstated. He also concluded that this may force the Soviets to behave in certain ways that are not to the advantage of the United States. In particular, Soviet uncertainty about their abilities is likely to lead to a 'short war' doctrine involving mass, surprise, and preemption.[37] All of this could leave the Soviet leadership in the position of either starting a war to preserve what advantage they currently have, or watching themselves slowly become less and less competitive. Such a doctrine would probably involve an early use of nuclear weapons.

Overcoming Soviet Resource Constraints
Through Theft of Technology

This chapter has centered on the Soviet dilemma of trying to allocate insufficient resources between military and civilian goods in the future when the cumulative effect of previous allocations has caused severe damage to the Soviet economy. If either U.S. defense expenditures or some other factor necessitates (in Soviet opinion) continued increases in defense spending, what will happen if the Soviet economy cannot respond? One solution to this problem is for the Soviets to acquire expensive technology from outside their economy by stealing it or by acquiring it at low cost from the West. One only has to look at the similarities between Soviet and U.S. aircraft to see how often this is done by the U.S.S.R. And since most desirable technology is also dual use, a purchase of civilian equipment from the West can also result in the acquisition of militarily useful technology.

Acquiring military equipment or technology in this manner may solve short-run resource allocation problems, but it may also create long run difficulties. When Spawr Optical Research, Inc. used falsified export documents to ship fifty high energy laser mirrors to West Germany, where the Soviets were able to complete the transfer to the U.S.S.R, the U.S. Air Force Weapons Laboratory Commander estimated that the acquisition saved the Soviets millions of dollars and almost 100 man years of research and development.[38] But even with 'reverse engineering,' the Soviets gained neither the ability to manufacture the mirrors nor the R&D knowledge to design them. Thus, a short-term savings in money and labor became a long-term dependency on western technology for a vital component of a weapon system—and when the supply of that critical system was cut off, R&D and manufacturing had to be accomplished anyway. In fact, the United States has used the problems associated with foreign sourcing (done legally) to justify its own policy of manufacturing indigenously every weapon component it acquires overseas.

While the Soviets have gained a tremendous amount through espionage and other methods of acquiring western technology, whether or not they were legal, this has only been a stopgap method of dealing with a structural problem that will require painful decisions about allocating Soviet resources. Clearly, the Soviets would have preferred to produce the foreign acquisitions necessitated by their economy's inability to support the military establishment. For example, the Soviets decided to buy personal computers abroad only after extensive efforts to produce the 'Agat'—a take off on the Apple II—failed.[39]

It is interesting to note that in the 1970s, the need for foreign exchange currency caused the Soviets to market many of the technologies in which they had a lead, in spite of the defense implications of this reverse flow to the West. Technology acquired by U.S. companies during this period was not in the form of purchased Soviet goods but rather, in the acquisition of manufacturing processes. This method of technology transfer avoids the problems just noted, and has enabled the U.S. to tap Soviet technology to develop improved aluminum castings, armored alloys, tank gun barrels, steel coatings, and microwave generation, all of which have obvious military applications.[40]

In sum, everyone agrees that the Soviet Union has embarked on a massive effort to acquire Western technology. While the West should try to stop this flow, it is important to remember that as long as the ability to manufacture goods is not acquired by the U.S.S.R., transferred technology creates dependencies and additional weaknesses that may adversely affect the Soviet defense effort, particularly in a prolonged war. For this reason, it must be assumed that the Soviets have been driven to this type of acquisition through economic necessity and that, given a healthy economy with adequate resources, they would prefer to produce indigenously those goods used by the Soviet military.

Concluding Thoughts on the Situation of the Soviet Union

The Soviets, by spending so much on their military establishment, have robbed the civilian economy of the resources necessary to produce healthy economic growth. And this, in turn, has resulted in an economy that is often unable to support Russian military requirements. These factors have created a very unstable situation that threatens the ability of the Soviets to compete in high-technology items and that, as a result, may lead to rash actions on the Soviets' part as their perceived dominance in many weapons begins to disappear.

It is probable that even with sufficient investment, sustained rates of economic growth in the soviet Union cannot be maintained without a reduction in the procurement of military hardware. As a result, the conflict between military and civilian production will become more intense in the next five years and the pressure on the technologically advanced sectors of the Soviet economy will be acute. Given this scenario, Soviet choices will be limited to either

1. holding defense spending at a constant growth rate of 2 percent per annum. Under the current scenario, this means that defense will take an ever larger share of Soviet GNP—just the reverse of what is needed to turn around the economy. Or
2. keeping the ratio of defense spending to the Soviet GNP at 12–14 percent. This will probably result in decreased budgets for the military and the need to make some very difficult decisions regarding modernization of the Soviet forces. At present, this is the likely choice, but because of the implications it has for the Soviet strategic forces, it will be difficult to implement without a comprehensive strategic weapons limitation agreement that can remove some of the pressure to develop high technology weapons.

Notes

1. "Testimony on the Defense Budget," Proceedings of the House Committee on Appropriations, U.S. House of Representatives, 1984, 406.

2. "Interview with Marshal of the USSR, Sergei Akhromeyev," Defense Science, October, 1988, 64.

3. "The Soviet Economy Under a New Leader," A Report to the Joint Economic Committee, U.S. Congress, Central Intelligence Agency and the Defense Intelligence Agency, March 19, 1986.

4. "Testimony on the Defense Budget," 28.

5. Becker, Abraham S., The Burden of Soviet Defense, RAND, R2752-AF, October, 1981, 1–72.

6. Hopkins, Mark M., and Kennedy, Michael, The Tradeoff Between Consumption and Military Expenditures For the Soviet Union During the 1980's, RAND, R-2972-NA, November, 1982, 1–65.

7. "The Soviet Economy Under a New Leader," i, ii.

8. CIA Data, 1985.

9. Knaus, William A., "Arms Spending and the Decline in Soviet Health," Washington Post, October 14, 1982, 19.

10. Cockburn, Andrew, The Threat: Inside the Soviet Military, Random House, New York, 1983, 1–338.

11. Blacker, Coit D., After Brezhnev, Georgetown Center For Strategic and International Studies, Washington, D.C., 1983.

12. Jane's Defence Weekly reported in "Some Soviet Subs Held Unseaworthy," Washington Times, March 13, 1985, 5.

13. Smith, Fredrick N., "USSR: Nuclear Submarines Problems Continue," *Defense and Foreign Affairs Daily,* January 23, 1985, 2.

14. Feshbach, Murray, in a report based on articles in Voyenno-Meditsinskiy Zhurnal and Tyl i Snabzheniye, reported in "Enemy for the Soviet Army: Rampant Disease," *New York Times,* April 15, 1985, 11.

15. Maze, Rick, "Soviets Pay Soldiers Less, Get Less, Say DoD Officials," *Navy Times,* October 8, 1984, 36.

16. Simis, Konstantin, "An Officer and a Crook: Ripping Off the Red Army," *Washington Post,* January 8, 1984, C1-C2.

17. "Kremlin blasts poor discipline," *The Gazette Telegraph,* October 15, 1988, A14.

18. Pincus, Walter, "Experts Tell of Soviet Woes," *Washington Post,* February 14, 1985, p. 23.

19. Hopkins and Kennedy, 1-65.

20. Doder, Dusko, "Soviets to Accept Women as 'Volunteers' in Military," *Washington Post,* April 1, 1985, 1.

21. Ulsamer, Edward, "Will Economic Weakness Increase Soviet Militancy?" *Air Force Magazine,* March, 1983, 40-47.

22. See Joint Economic Committee, *Soviet Economy in the 1980's: Problems and Prospects,* Part 1, Section III, 1982 and Rowen, Henry S. and Tremel, Vladimir G., "Gorbachev and the Ailing Russian Bear," *The Wall Street Journal,* April 21, 1986.

23. *The Effect of Defense Spending On the Soviet and U.S. Economies,* A Conference at Cornell University, April, 1987.

24. *Gorbachev's Modernization Program: A Status Report,* A Central Intelligence Agency report to the Joint Economic Committee, Washington, D.C., March 19, 1987, 1-2 and "The Soviet Economy Under a New Leader," 11-14.

25. "The Soviet Economy Under a New Leader," 1-10.

26. Rowen, Henry S., and Tremel, Vladimir G., "Gorbachev and the Ailing Russian Bear," *The Wall Street Journal,* April 21, 1986 and *Gorbachev's Modernization Program: A Status Report,* 5.

27. "Little Hope Seen For Soviet Economy," *The Gazette Telegraph,* October 15, 1988.

28. "The Soviet Economy Under a New Leader," 15-16.

29. Ibid., i, ii.

30. *Gorbachev's Modernization Program: A Status Report,* 4.

31. Adams, Peter, "Study: Soviet Buildup Persists Despite Economic Concerns," *Defense News,* September 19, 1988, 42, 43.

32. Ibid.

33. "Interview with Marshal of the USSR, Sergei Akhromeyev," *Defense Science,* October, 1988, 63.

34. Bodansky, Youssef, *Jane's Defence Weekly,* reported in: Weeks, Albert, "New Soviet Epoch of Defense Based on High-Tech, Seen Opening in '85," *FPI News Service,* March 4, 1985.

35. Bialer, Seweryn, "Will Russia Dare to Clean Up Its Economic Mess?" *Washington Post,* April 21, 1985, K-1.

36. Amann, R., Cooper, J. M., and Davies, R. W., eds., *The Technological Level of Soviet Industry,* Yale University Press, New Haven, Conn., 1977.

37. Epstein, Joshua M., *Measuring Military Power: The Soviet Air Threat to Europe,* Princeton University Press, Princeton, N.J., 1984, 1–288.

38. U.S. Congress, Senate, Permanent Subcommittee on Investigations of the Committee on Government Affairs, *Transfer of United States High Technology to the Soviet Union and Soviet Block Nations,* Hearings, 97th Congress, 2nd Session, Washington, Government Printing Office, 1982, 510, 517–524.

39. Sanger, David E., "The Russians Seek IBM Compatibility," *New York Times,* March 3, 1985, 22E.

40. Fialka, John J., "Technology Purchased From the Soviets Starts to Yield Military Uses," *Wall Street Journal,* April 24, 1985, 1.

12

Reallocating Strategic and Tactical Nuclear Weapon Resources to Non-Defense Applications—A U.S. Example

It is clear from the chapters that have preceded this that removing national resources from the production of nuclear weapons and strategic delivery systems will be difficult to do. While one might claim that all that is required is a signed disarmament treaty and an order from the government, the issues are really much more complex. If political and economic problems are not addressed at the start of a nuclear arms reduction process, there will be no disarmament agreement because it will have been stopped by elements within both negotiating countries. This chapter provides one method by which the economic issues surrounding nuclear weapon production might be addressed. Based on employment concerns alone, this method could be of use in the U.S., France, and the United Kingdom. In addition, it might also be used to preserve the organizational integrity and political power that will be important elements in nuclear disarmament in the Soviet Union.

The Difference Between Delivery System and Nuclear Warhead Production

Decisions to reallocate the resources used to produce strategic weapon systems must first consider the differences between the production of delivery systems and the production of nuclear warheads. In the first case, resources that are allocated to the production of strategic delivery systems are used by profit-making companies, and most of these resources have other uses. Profit-oriented companies that make strategic delivery systems would probably pursue other endeavors as soon as it becomes obvious that such systems could no longer be sold. This is not to imply that all (or even most) companies that make strategic delivery systems would survive a change to other kinds of production. Rather, it acknowledges that the market system and the profit motive will play a major role in this reallocation process.

247

A second case concerns the resources used to manufacture strategic or tactical nuclear warheads. The facilities involved in this production are so specialized and so highly contaminated that even converting the land on which the production plants reside to other uses is out of the question. Nor are the plants operated within a rational market system, so there is no incentive to switch production to achieve higher profits. In addition, while defense production facilities are normally built with the expectation that they will have a finite life and then be disposed of, the residents of the isolated regions that host nuclear production facilities, and the agencies that operate the plants, both tend to view them as being like the old arsenals—with all the permanence that implies. These unrealistic expectations create additional problems when plants become obsolete or when the output from the plants is no longer required.

Thus, although the primary purpose of defense-related projects should never be to provide employment, political reality dictates that sites like Hanford in Washington and Savannah River in South Carolina, both critical to the economy of an isolated region, must be treated in a manner that is sensitive to regional economic issues. For all these reasons, the conversion of nuclear production sites will be difficult, and nuclear waste management and storage probably present the only reasonable alternatives to nuclear weapon production. This kind of conversion has the added benefit of creating the long-term, stable federal presence required for regional economic health.

The following section presents two brief scenarios that might arise as a result from international agreements to limit the number of nuclear weapons, and a third scenario that concerns the conversion of nuclear production facilities that would be necessitated by the outcome of scenario 2. These scenarios could be faced by any of the nuclear powers. The specific reaction to any of the scenarios would obviously differ depending on which country is involved.

Scenario 1: Stopping or Limiting
Nuclear Warhead Production

This scenario would arise from an agreement to simply stop the production of new nuclear warheads or to limit the number of nuclear warheads to a fixed amount without additional agreements concerning the disposition of any or all the warheads that already exist. While such agreements are the least practical way of reducing the nuclear threat, they serve as a lower bound for potential treaties that might be negotiated in the future, and they bear some similarity to parts of the Strategic Arms Reduction Talks (START) agreement where, as Henry Kissinger has noted, "In START, unlike INF, the production lines for strategic weapons would remain open."[1]

In a scenario of this type, tritium is the key to determining what would be done in the nuclear industry. Tritium, which is currently used in nuclear warhead triggers, has a very short half life—10 years. This assures that production of tritium must continue as long as a stock of warheads is maintained. In addition, the next generation of strategic warheads, including those used on the Trident D-5 submarine launched ballistic missile (SLBM) and the MX will all be tritium-based to allow greater explosive yields.[2] This means that the inventory of warheads would have a relatively short half life in the future and that nuclear production facilities would have to remain essentially unchanged from their current status. In fact, it is likely that a number of new facilities, called New Production Reactors, would be built to accommodate the increased demand for tritium.

Under this scenario, there is also no reason to suspect that any important changes would take place in the industry that produces strategic weapons. Again, it would be likely that new contracts would be let and new facilities would be built to accommodate the increased need for efficiency that would arise if the number of weapons was constrained at a fixed amount. Thus, under this scenario, a lower bound is also set for the reallocation of national resources. Little or no change would occur from the situation that presently exists.

Scenario 2: Stopping Nuclear Warhead Production and Disposing of Existing Warheads

The 1988 INF agreement provides a partial model for this scenario. For the purposes of establishing an upper bound on the kinds of resource reallocation that might occur, we assume that an agreement stops all defense nuclear production and disposes of all warheads. In this case, neither the production of plutonium nor tritium would be necessary, and all defense nuclear production plants could be shut down.

In this scenario, the delivery systems for nuclear warheads may or may not be used in conventional roles. If they are altered slightly and then used as conventional weapons or space delivery vehicles, little or no change would take place in the industries producing delivery systems.[3] If they are not used, a massive move out of the production of strategic systems would occur, and the market system would largely govern how resources are reallocated. However, one can also assume that a number of industries would not survive and that defense industrial base and regional economic arguments would be used by special interest groups to attempt to preserve the employment associated with non-competitive industries. Scenario 3, and later chapters, provide a complete discussion of how this situation might ultimately evolve.

Within the nuclear warhead industry, this scenario would result in a complete cessation of work. Even though the nuclear weapon budget is a small part of the total defense budget, it comprises 65 percent of DOE funds[4] and stopping nuclear weapon production would effectively wipe out most of the Department of Energy and a number installations that have no other function or use. As a result, it would also deal a devastating economic blow to a number of regions of the country, particularly given the fact that these regions are likely to be geographically isolated.

A shift of military and civilian labor out of the strategic nuclear weapons fields will be easier or harder depending on how much transfer there is between the past occupation of the worker and the future choices. More recently trained individuals will probably move more easily than long-time employees. If the demand for military labor decreases at the same time—a likely scenario in a total disarmament and a far less likely scenario if a reduction in nuclear arms is accompanied by a large conventional buildup—the search for other jobs will be more difficult.[5] Any of these scenarios would be further complicated by the fact that there is already an employment problem in the nuclear engineering sector that stems from the decline of the civilian fission nuclear power industry.

As previously discussed, the supply of engineering and scientific labor has remained sufficient to satisfy demand over the last 15 years. However, the supply of skilled workers is critical in a number of areas, and if these individuals were willing to relocate, the cessation of nuclear weapon production could provide a ready source of workers. Companies engaged in construction, aerospace and defense contracting have complained about the lack of skilled machinists, electricians, masons, pipe fitters and welders.[6] These workers, who are employed by the nuclear industry in large numbers, would be readily absorbed by other, non-nuclear industries.

In addition to shifting labor resources, the question of the disposition of both the facilities and the sites associated with the production of strategic delivery systems and with defense nuclear production will also have to be addressed. This is the subject of the following scenario.

Scenario 3: Converting the Nuclear Weapon Industry to Other Production

The United States performed a massive conversion from a military to a civilian industrial base after WWII that involved changing from the production of conventional weapons to civilian goods. Boulding remarks that

> It is odd that [the Great Disarmament of 1945 and '46] has left so little impression the American consciousness. It was achieved with unemployment never rising above 3 percent and with astonishingly little dislocation. Its history

has never been properly written, but it is one of the most extraordinary episodes in all of economic history. Here is the transfer of almost a third of the economic activity of a large and very complex society from the war industry into civilian purposes. It is done in little over a year and with an incredibly small amount of disruption.[7]

The Soviet view of this process also stresses that based on historical precedent, conversion is possible without undue hardships to the country involved:

No doubt, the restructuring of military production involves certain difficulties of a technical, economic and social character. . . . [We believe] such difficulties can be overcome, that conversion is quite feasible and, moreover, will contribute to the common good. . . . The main difficulties involved in this restructuring are, in the final analysis, not technical and economic ones; rather they lie in the resistance to conversion on the part of reactionary and militaristic forces and above all the military-industrial complexes.[8]

However, as opposed to these views, there is no experience with converting nuclear facilities to other uses, and there is good reason to suspect that such efforts would be extremely difficult. In addition, there is little evidence to support the notion that producers of strategic delivery systems could easily engage in other kinds of production. A major difference between military and civilian projects and products is that the military project is not concerned with economic efficiency, it is concerned with performance at any cost. Another second difference may be one of product-life design. Products with nuclear warheads are obviously designed for one-time use only. Both of these differences create a production philosophy that is markedly different than that used for civilian goods, and in manufacturing, design follows philosophy.

Thus, one can assume that within the community of manufacturers of strategic delivery systems, being successful in the commercial market will require so many changes in attitudes about cost, reliability and marketing that very few industries will be able to make the transition. In fact, past attempts of defense contractors to diversify into commercial markets have usually been unsuccessful, and the normal case has been for movement to occur in the opposite direction. BMY, General Dynamics and Singer are all examples of companies that elected to become defense contractors when they could not compete in the civilian sector.[9]

This book has already discussed the likely outcome of this situation as regional interests seek to preserve inefficient, employment producing companies in their area. But it must be remembered that these are private companies, and while they may have ample reason to oppose certain elements of nuclear disarmament to preserve their share of defense contracts, in the end analysis, what happens to them if they are unable to compete in the civilian marketplace is of little concern to the federal government. Their resources will be transferred to other parts of the U.S. economy through the working of the market system, and if left to proceed on its own course, this transfer will take place with as much efficiency as possible given the circumstances.

This is quite different from the situation of the production facilities for nuclear warheads. First, although these plants are managed by private contractors, they are clearly government installations. Second, although the labor that operates the plants may be transferrable to other areas, the facilities and the land on which the nuclear production plants reside are so highly contaminated that they cannot be used for other kinds of production and are too dangerous to even be abandoned without constant, long term monitoring and upkeep. This effectively removes any chance for the resource market to become involved in the reallocation process. And third, these plants have been purposely located in isolated areas that have little other means of economic support. This creates both political problems and some degree of government obligation. All these factors indicate that while the reallocation of resources from the construction of strategic delivery systems to civilian uses will be governed by market forces, the reallocation of resources from nuclear warhead production must be managed in some other way. One way that a conversion of nuclear weapon production facilities could occur is suggested in the following section.

Converting from Nuclear Weapon Production to Hazardous Waste Management at Hanford, Washington

Speculation about the actual effects of stopping nuclear weapon production is not necessary because a real-life example of this scenario is available for study. When the Department of Energy (DOE) decided in mid-February, 1988, to mothball the Hanford N Reactor, which was dedicated to producing materials for nuclear warheads, this decision eliminated 6000–6500 direct jobs at Hanford by the end of 1995. Nine hundred workers were laid off by September 30, 1988 (300 of these workers were involved in safety enhancement and would have completed their jobs in any case). By September 30, 1989, another 2000 workers will be laid off, and from then until 1995, an additional 3000 to 3400 workers employed in related defense materials production will be released. The 6000 lost jobs represent almost 10 percent of the total employment in the Tri-cities area. This, and the fact that the area already had been hit by other large layoffs, provides an excellent example of the likely outcome stopping nuclear weapon production in an isolated area.

A Brief Economic History of the Hanford Region

The Hanford site occupies about 600 square miles in southeastern Washington. Hanford has produced nuclear materials (mostly plutonium) for defense uses since 1943, but it also produces electricity, does research, and handles waste management.[10] Three cities are adjacent to Hanford. Called the Tri-Cities area (Richland, Kennewick and Pasco), they form the second largest metropolitan area in the state of Washington. The Tri-Cities population was 150,100 in 1981, and about 340,000 people live within 80 km of the Hanford waste management area (1980 census).[11]

Benton and Franklin Counties comprise the general regional area affected by Hanford. Benton County had a 1987 population of 104,100, down 4.9 percent from 1980. Franklin County had 35,500, up 1.4 percent from 1980.[12] Benton County had a cumulative in-migration between 1970 and 1981 of 36,066. Its population increased 62 percent during this period. The population of Franklin county increased 36 percent over the same period.[13]

Between 1973 and 1981, economic and population growth in the Hanford region was caused primarily by the construction associated with the Washington Public Power Supply System (WPPSS) reactors. During this period, employment due to WPPSS increased at about 39 percent a year.[14] By 1983, total employment at the Hanford Site was about 10,300. The total population gain from 1970 to 1980 was 51,113, or about 55 percent. Net migration contributed to over 80 percent of Benton county's growth during this time.[15]

These migration patterns yielded a population multiplier that was calculated to be 1.2. In other words, every new job resulted in an increase in population of 1.2 persons. However, as a result of high unemployment levels in Benton and Franklin Counties, the December, 1987 Environmental Impact Statement (EIS) on defense nuclear waste disposal at Hanford lowered this multiplier to .75 until employment reached 1981 levels.[16] This multiplier was further degraded by the decision to mothball the N reactor at Hanford, and the potential for any in-migration in Benton and Franklin counties will remain low unless a massive construction phase is undertaken at Hanford.

The average monthly wage in Benton County in 1986 was $1890. In Franklin it was $1230. The Benton figure was the highest in the state of Washington, exceeding most other areas by $400–$500 per month. However, in another statistic that reflected the high levels of unemployment, per capita income in Benton County was about equal to that in the rest of the state.[17] Payroll statistics also demonstrated the dependence of the region on Hanford. 'Chemical and Allied Products' (the category in which nuclear workers fall) made up 12.4 percent of the total pay in the Tri-Cities region, and contract construction was 32.4 percent of all regional pay.[18] Ninety percent of the jobs in the industry services component of business services were in firms associated with Hanford.[19] All told, Hanford directly accounted for one third of all wages earned in Benton and Franklin Counties.[20]

Employment History in the Hanford Region

By 1981, the Tri-cities contained one of the most unique and highly skilled labor forces in the nation. Local industries employed over 3000 engineers, 740 scientists, 2240 technicians, and 260 computer specialists out of a work force of 11,880.[21] At the time that WPPSS mothballed one plant and terminated another in 1981, the two WPPSS reactors had been averaging 7290 on-site construction workers.[22] Employment declined in Benton and Franklin counties and out-migration started.

In spite of this, the region had started to undergo a gradual economic recovery by 1986, with employment growing at .6 percent a year. Various federally funded projects were proposed that could contribute to employment in the Tri-Cities, including a Basalt Waste Isolation Facility (WIPP) for disposing of commercially generated radioactive waste (peak construction work force of 1100) and expansion of dams on the Priest River and Wanapum Rapids (peak work force of 1100).[23]

Hanford DOE-related employment was about 14,500 prior to mothballing the N Reactor, and WPPSS employment was about 1500.[24] When the Hanford N Reactor was closed, its employment losses were in addition to 1200 jobs that were terminated when the Basalt Waste Isolation Project was cancelled in December, 1987. All of the WIPP losses will occur by September, 1989.[25] In March, 1988, unemployment rates in Benton County were 8.7 percent and in Franklin County they were 11.5 percent. Washington State unemployment in March was 7.3 percent.[26] The Tri-Cities had the following employment statistics in February, 1988:

- Labor force = 66,100
- Employment = 59,200
- Unemployment = 6,900 or 10.4 percent.[27]

A study by two Battelle researchers predicted that mothballing the N Reactor would result in a total loss of 13,200 jobs in the Hanford region by 1996, based on an employment multiplier of approximately 2.2. In other words, in the long run, every direct job at the Hanford Site created another 1.2 jobs in the region surrounding Hanford (the Benton and Franklin County areas). The 6000 direct jobs lost at Hanford due to the N Reactor closing would thus cause an additional loss to the region of approximately 7200 jobs.[28] Similarly, the 1200 jobs that were lost when the Basalt Waste Isolation Project was eliminated would cause the long run loss of another 1440 jobs in the Hanford region, yielding a total impact of 2440 jobs.

Nuclear Waste Disposal Options for the Hanford Site

In an effort to compensate for the crippling blow to the economy of the Tri-Cities region caused by the closure of the nuclear weapon production

Table 12.1:   Total Construction Employment

	FY89	FY90	FY91	FY92	FY93
Total Direct Employment:	198	254	440	761	1023
Total Regional Employment:	435	558	968	1674	2250

Source: *FY 1989 Congressional Budget Request*, Atomic Energy Defense Activities Construction Project Data Sheets, U.S. Department of Energy, Washington, D.C., February, 1988.

facility known as the N Reactor, both environmental and nuclear industry groups, as well as representatives of the state and local governments, proposed that the Hanford site be converted to a hazardous waste management facility. Hanford is ideally suited for waste management because of its large, federally controlled site, its location on a plateau well above groundwater where waste could not be reached by any postulated flood conditions, and its location in a region that is semi-arid with little or no water to infiltrate waste sites.[29]

Three different waste management proposals were made for the Hanford region. Since each waste management proposal has the potential for restoring some of the 6000–6500 direct jobs lost by closing the N Reactor, these proposals have been used to demonstrate how conversion from nuclear weapon construction might take place. In each case, the employment impact on the Hanford region has been calculated using the employment multiplier developed by the Battelle researchers and also using the Commerce Department's RIMS II input-output model[30] to determine job generation per million dollars spent in the region. In each case, assumptions concerning the proportion of the money budgeted for a facility that would actually be spent in the local area were made by reviewing the specific construction proposals. In addition to calculating direct employment at the Hanford Site that would result from the proposal, total regional employment has also been estimated.

Of the three general categories of nuclear waste disposal options suggested for the Hanford Site, the first was a group of 362 options proposed by DOE in its FY 1989 Congressional Budget Request.[31] These proposals would simply have cleaned up some existing waste sites at Hanford that violated federal standards. If all of these programs were approved and implemented on the schedules given in the Congressional Budget Request, the effect on direct employment at Hanford and on long run total employment in the Benton and Franklin Counties region would be those shown in Tables 12.1 and 12.1A.

A second group of options was proposed in the course of considering Hanford for selection as a waste management site where waste would be imported from outside the state of Washington, treated and stored.[32] This proposal contained a waste treatment and storage plan favored by the

Table 12.1A: Total Operating Employment

Total Direct Employment:	946
Total Regional Employment:	2082

Source: *FY 1989 Congressional Budget Request*, Atomic Energy Defense
Activities Construction Project Data Sheets, U.S. Department of Energy,
Washington, D.C., February, 1988.

environmental groups that involved vitrification (converting the waste to a
glass-like substance) and then burying the waste in stainless steel containers
deep underground. This is shown in Table 12.2 and is known as the Geological
Disposal Alternative. It has the disadvantage of being expensive, and the
advantages of being the safest and, in the context of conversion, generating
the most jobs. For comparison, a much lower cost alternative that only
involved stabilizing hazardous waste in double-walled storage tanks is also
included in Table 12.3.

A third group of options evolved from proposals made by DOE in a
report to Senator John Glenn as chair of the Committee on Governmental
Affairs concerning the total cost to completely clean up the Department of
Energy defense-related sites.[33] The options in the report to Senator Glenn
are only presented in a gross form, making both cost and employment
calculations more problematical. In addition, even though these options
concern the cleanup of waste problems at Hanford, they do not appear to
duplicate the proposals made in the Congressional Budget Request. The
following employment figures in Table 12.4 are likely for the programs
suggested specifically for the Hanford site.

Table 12.2:   High Employment Option: Geological Disposal Alternative

	FY89	FY90	FY91	FY92	FY93	FY94
Total Direct Employment:	0	2244	2697	2697	3447	3445
Total Regional Employment:	0	4937	5933	7583	7583	7579

Source: *Disposal of Hanford Defense High Level, Transuranic and Tank
Wastes*, DOE/EIS-0113, Vol. 1, U.S. Department of Energy, Washington,
D.C., December, 1987. In particular, Appendix K of this document
contains employment estimates for this table.

Table 12.3:   Low Employment Option: In-Place Stabilization and
Disposal Alternative

	FY89	FY90	FY91	FY92	FY93	FY94
Total Direct Employment:	218	267	156	510	526	526
Total Regional Employment:	480	587	343	1122	1157	1157

Source: *Disposal of Hanford Defense High Level, Transuranic and Tank
Wastes*, DOE/EIS-0113, Vol. 1, U.S. Department of Energy, Washington,
D.C., December, 1987. In particular, Appendix K of this document
contains employment estimates for this table.

Table 12.4: Employment from Defense Nuclear Waste Cleanup Programs

	FY89	FY90	FY91	FY92	FY93	FY94
Total Direct Employment:	675	788	1182	1351	1375	1284
Total Regional Employment:	1486	1725	2601	2973	3025	2826

Source: 1988 Report to the Committee on Governmental Affairs, *Environment, Safety and Health Report for the Department of Energy Defense Complex*, U.S. Department of Energy, Washington, D.C., July 1, 1988.

Externalities[34] That May Affect Regional Employment

The previous sections have discussed the direct jobs that would result from nuclear waste disposal activities and the additional jobs that the waste-related employment would spawn in the region surrounding Hanford. However, it would be remiss not to mention that facilities like Hanford that are heavily involved in producing and managing nuclear materials can also have a depressing effect on the regional economy that might be alleviated by stopping the production of nuclear materials. As the Environmental Impact Statement on disposal of defense nuclear wastes at Hanford notes,

Public perceptions of economic risks, of defense waste management program credibility, and of the attractiveness of this region to future growth and development are expected to be enhanced by the implementation of a defense waste disposal program.

Concern has been expressed with respect to other activities on the Hanford Site in regard to future land use, and possible effects on tourism; similar concerns can be anticipated with respect to disposal of Hanford wastes. . . . Past operations and waste disposal have made an irretrievable and irreversible commitment of major portions of the unconfined aquifer to waste management.[35]

Public awareness of the externalities associated with the nuclear industry was heightened in the aftermath of Chernobyl, and there is cynicism about the information produced by nuclear energy officials.[36] If conversion from nuclear production is to take place, new, non-nuclear industries will have to create an economic base to give long-term stability to the regional economy. In the past, such industries were not likely to move into an area with a facility like Hanford. Thus, although the Hanford Site was an important job creator for the Tri-Cities area, it is also an important inhibitor of non-nuclear related jobs.

While it is probably true that the use of Hanford for safe nuclear waste disposal will enhance its image as a potential site for non-nuclear industries, this will only be the case if the disposal methods chosen are the safest possible alternatives. Even then, the Tri-Cities area faces a major, uphill publicity battle if it tries to convert to a significant non-nuclear based economy.

Conclusion

Hanford provides an excellent example of the job losses that come from shutting down defense-related nuclear facilities and the potentially compensating employment gains that could come from using the site for nuclear waste management. In general, when evaluating options for converting from defense nuclear production to waste management, decision makers should:

1. Try to select an option or combination of options that maximizes public welfare benefits when all costs, including externalities, are considered.
2. Try to diversify the export base of the regional economy.

Therefore, if a choice is possible, an attempt should be made to maximize the long-term economic impact by favoring those options that are safest (to minimize externalities) and that have the highest long term operations employment. Vitrification and geologic disposal would seem to best satisfy both of these criteria.

As rough rules of thumb, waste facility construction provides about three times as many jobs as the activities required to operate the facilities after construction. Operating a vitrification and geological disposal process will provide more than twice as many long term jobs as the operation of conventional waste disposal facilities because both the glass making and the mining operations involve processes that are heavy employment generating activities. Using as a standard of comparison the job loss associated with the Hanford N Reactor, the programs requested by DOE in the Congressional Budget Request for 1989 have the potential of replacing as much as 18 percent of lost employment. The options suggested by DOE for Hanford, if it is converted to a nuclear waste management facility, could replace from 10 percent to over 50 percent of lost employment. And the waste cleanup programs mentioned in the report to Senator Glenn may have the potential of replacing up to 20 percent of the jobs lost.

When these activities are considered as possible substitutes for nuclear weapon manufacturing, one should remember that the key to economic growth and stability in a region is the *long term employment* that results from operating a project, not the short term boost to employment that comes from construction. This makes vitrification and geological disposal look particularly promising as conversion prospects.

Notes

1. Kissinger, Henry, quoted in the *Washington Post,* April 24, 1988.

2. Adams, Peter, "Board Plans Recommendations for Tritium Site," *Defense News,* June 6, 1988, 3.

3. For example, on September 5, 1988, a Titan II vehicle, originally designed as a strategic missile, was used to place an Air Force satellite in orbit. This missile was the first of 12 converted missiles ordered for this task.

4. Morrison, David C., "The Power Behind the Energy Department," *Long Island Newsday,* January 24, 1984. And *FY1989 Budget of the United States Government,* Executive Office of the President, Office of Management and Budget, Washington, D.C., 6f–68, 72.

5. See Reppy, Judith, "Conversion From Military R&D: Economic Aspects," 38th Pugwash Conference, Dagomys, USSR, 29 August-3 September, 1988, 8.

6. Hicks, Jonathan, "For the Skilled, Its a Seller's Market," *New York Times,* June 5, 1988.

7. Boulding, Kenneth E., "The Deadly Industry: War and the International System," in *Peace and the War Industry,* Kenneth E. Boulding, ed., Aldine Publishing Company, 1970, 3–5.

8. Bobrakov, Yuri, and Konobeyev, Vladimir, *Disarmament and Economics: Problems of Economic Restructuring,* Novosti Press Agency Publishing House, Moscow, 1983, 8–9.

9. For examples of this lack of success see: Weidenbaum, Murray L., "Industrial Adjustments to Military Shifts and Cutbacks," in *The Economic Consequences of Reduced Military Spending,* Bernard Udis, ed., Lexington Books, Lexington, MA, 1973, 253–287. and President's Economic Adjustment Committee and the Office of Economic Adjustment, OASD (MI&L), *Economic Adjustment/Conversion,* Department of Defense, Washington, D.C., 1985, Chapter 7.

10. *Disposal of Hanford Defense High Level, Transuranic and Tank Wastes,* DOE/ EIS-0113, Vol. 1, U.S. Department of Energy, Washington, D.C., December, 1987, 1.3.

11. Ibid., 4.44.

12. *Annual Demographic Information,* Washington State Employment Security Department, Seattle, Washington, July, 1987, 4.

13. Ibid., 7, 8.

14. *Disposal of Hanford Defense High Level, Transuranic and Tank Wastes,* K.8.

15. *Annual Planning Report, 1982, Richland-Kennewick-Pasco SMSA,* Washington State Employment Security, Seattle, Washington, 1982, 1, 5.

16. *Disposal of Hanford Defense High Level, Transuranic and Tank Wastes,* K.12.

17. *Annual Demographic Information,* 76, 81.

18. *Annual Planning Report, 1982, Richland-Kennewick-Pasco SMSA,* 15, 16.

19. Ibid., 21.

20. Scott, Michael J., and Belzer, David B., "Hanford, The N Reactor, and Washington's Economy: The Impacts of Permanent Closure," *The Northwest Environmental Journal,* vol. 4, no. 1, 138.

21. *Annual Planning Report, 1982, Richland-Kennewick-Pasco SMSA,* 10.

22. Ibid., 20.

23. *Disposal of Hanford Defense High Level, Transuranic and Tank Wastes*, K.9, 4.42.

24. Ibid., 4.42.

25. *Washington Labor Market*, Vol. 12, No. 2, Economic Analysis Branch, Washington State Employment Security, Seattle, Washington, February, 1988.

26. Ibid., 13.

27. Ibid., 14.

28. Scott and Belzer, "Hanford, The N Reactor, and Washington's Economy: The Impacts of Permanent Closure," 147–149.

29. *Disposal of Hanford Defense High Level, Transuranic and Tank Wastes*, 1.14.

30. *Regional Multipliers: A User Handbook for the Regional Input-Output Modeling System (RIMS II)*, U.S. Department of Commerce, Bureau of Economic Analysis, Washington, D.C., May, 1986.

31. *FY 1989 Congressional Budget Request*, Atomic Energy Defense Activities Construction Project Data Sheets, U.S. Department of Energy, Washington, D.C., February, 1988.

32. *Disposal of Hanford Defense High Level, Transuranic and Tank Wastes*. In particular, Appendix K of this document contains employment estimates for this proposal.

33. *Environment, Safety and Health Report for the Department of Energy Defense Complex*, U.S. Department of Energy, Washington, D.C., July 1, 1988.

34. Costs to the surrounding socioeconomic system that are not born by the entity that generates those costs—in this case, the Departments of Energy and Defense.

35. *Disposal of Hanford Defense High Level, Transuranic and Tank Wastes*, 3.51.

36. Schemann, Serge, "Chernobyl and the Europeans: Radiation and Doubts Linger," *The New York Times*, June 12, 1988.

PART FOUR

The Future: Nuclear Politics, Inertia and Alternatives

13

Nuclear Weapons and the Future
Strategic Position of the United States

The United States Looks Toward the Future

As the 21st century approaches, it is reasonable to expect that the United States will continue to upgrade its strategic forces, in spite of expected limits on the growth of defense budgets. The U.S. will also attempt to extend the 1987–88 successes in arms control by taking advantage of ongoing changes within the Soviet Union. Together, the United States and the Soviet Union may decide to address many of the nuclear dilemmas outlined in this book. By doing so, these two superpowers may reduce the demand for nuclear weapons and the risks of nuclear war.

In the 1990s, U.S. defense budgets will be shaped by three different factors. First, there is the immense momentum generated by programs started by the Reagan Administration over the past eight years. It would be very difficult to cancel these en masse, since vested interests in their continuation are likely to be both vocal and powerful in Congress and in the Bush Administration. Second, evolving technologies, probably most noticeable in the results to date of the Strategic Defense Initiative (SDI), new stealth aircraft (the B-2 bomber and the F-117A fighter), very accurate MIRVed ICBMs, and "smart" conventional weapons, will cause significant changes in U.S. warfighting capabilities over the next two decades. Third, and perhaps most important, new U.S. policy makers will develop their own view of threats to U.S. security, which will be modified by external events and by U.S. analysis of those events.

A central decision of the Reagan Administration was to modernize the U.S. military so that the Soviets could no longer count on a complacent adversary, and to organize and equip paramilitary and proxy forces to counterattack in Third World countries whenever and wherever it was considered necessary. Consequences of this new resolve included the SDI program, modernization of strategic nuclear forces, the deployment of Pershing II and GLCMs in Western Europe, the invasion of Grenada, and direct support for anti-Communist rebels in Afghanistan and Nicaragua. Foreign policy successes include the INF Treaty, the beginning of START talks, and the agreement by the Soviets to withdraw their forces from Afghanistan. However, these programs also generated substantial growth in U.S. defense budgets and contributed to federal budget deficits during the period 1981–88.

The U.S. military build-up of the Reagan years generated incentives for the Soviet Union to increase its defense spending to match the United States, a build-up that resulted in substantial pressures within the Soviet economy. The Reagan Administration felt that Soviet military modernization would raise the price that Soviets would have to pay on an internal basis, both in terms of the opportunity costs of resource use and in terms of increasing dissatisfaction of Soviet consumers. The idea was that the Soviet economy was so inefficient that eventually Soviet leaders would be forced to a guns or butter decision. The Reagan Administration has claimed, with some justification, that Mikhail Gorbachev's policies of perestroika (reconstruction) are a direct consequence of the Soviet military build-up.

On assuming office, the Bush administration found that budgetary pressures such as the Gramm-Rudman Act and the federal deficit severely limited U.S. military growth, at least in the near term. However, even within budgetary limits, allocations can vary dramatically, not only between the service branches, but within them. The Bush Administration has also inherited a series of ongoing negotiations, weapons decisions, and unresolved foreign policy questions. The administration must approach this near-term agenda with specific positions based on well-defined priorities and criteria. Thus, this chapter outlines the nature of the defense programs that are likely to be pursued by the United States under a constrained budget.

The Bush Administration will also be expected to relate the near-term agenda to a long-term vision of U.S. security. Without such a vision, decisions over the next four years may lack direction and coherence. With it, the administration may be able to build support, not only for its own defense initiatives, but for even more far-reaching steps by its successors. Thus, this chapter also provides some estimates of likely long-term U.S. positions, and attempts to predict the likely interaction of U.S.-Soviet relations.

The Reagan Legacy

The Reagan Administration euphoria over the INF Treaty and progress in the START negotiations was probably due to a belief that the Soviet Union is undergoing profound changes that will lead to continued improvements in U.S.-Soviet relations. President George Bush participated in the decision making process of the Reagan Administration, and he probably shares some of its world view and optimism.

The Reagan legacy has resulted in a dual policy prescription. First, the U.S. will probably continue military modernization programs, causing the

Soviets to follow, which in turn will impose high costs on the Soviet economy. This will put further pressure on the Soviet Union to alter its allocation of national resources to achieve the efficiency necessary to compete. Second, the U.S. will probably pursue a policy of continued arms control negotiations, particularly with regard to reductions in land-based ICBMs, conventional forces in Europe, and nuclear proliferation.

This dual-track policy will be difficult to implement. To secure funds from Congress and public support for military modernization, President Bush must portray the Soviets as a continuing major threat to U.S. security. To convince them of the wisdom of arms control, he must portray the Soviets as sincerely interested in mutual stability.

President Bush has inherited a Five-Year Defense Plan (FYDP) from the Reagan Administration. However, several sets of programs are open to modification: these include highly classified, or "black" programs, the continued development and possible deployment of ground-mobile ICBMs, and of course, the Strategic Defense Initiative (SDI).

Black programs were a significant element in the Reagan defense build-up. The administration's black programs included the development of a series of very secret technologies and weapons, including "stealth" bomber and fighter aircraft. The highly classified nature of these programs precluded both the usual public review and an unbiased compilation of cost projections by the Department of Defense and by Congress.

This situation is not altogether new. Throughout the late 1950s, the armed services, particularly the Air Force, were able to develop in secret a series of spectacular and very expensive new weapons (for example, the SR-71 reconnaissance aircraft, deployed in the early 1960s). At the time, the Office of the Secretary of Defense did not exercise its power to review and control such programs. But by the early 1960s, accelerating costs made this practice unacceptable, and Secretary of Defense Robert McNamara initiated severe reductions. The machinery that McNamara put into place continued to limit new black programs until Reagan took office in 1981.

Since 1981, black programs, including stealth bomber and fighter aircraft, have grown to account for a significant percentage of Air Force procurement. In addition, all of the armed services plan to include "stealth" features, called "low-observable technologies" in Pentagon jargon, in many of their 21st century weapons. Planning for such hardware is already the military's top growth business. If continued, stealth projects currently under way will cost nearly $200 billion over the next five years, one fourth of the cost of the major programs launched during the Reagan Administration.[1]

Some Pentagon planners are heralding a new military doctrine, called "competitive strategies", which rests, in part, upon the hope that the growing application of stealth technologies will force the Soviets into a debilitating spending binge to create new defenses against the nearly invisible stealth bomber (the B-2) and stealth fighter (the F-117A). This new doctrine has the tentative support of President Bush and key members of Congress. For example, Armed Services Committee Chairman Sam Nunn (Democrat, Georgia), predicts that "[the B-2] will render obsolete billions of dollars of Soviet investment in their current air defense and cause them to spend billions more in an attempt to cope."[2]

Yet for all of the promise of stealth technology that might be applied to everything from surface warships to helicopters, there are troubling questions about its performance and cost. Still years away from its first operational mission, the B-2 has already suffered delays because of design and technical problems. Its first flight was repeatedly delayed and the original cost estimate of $36.6 billion for a planned force of 132 bombers has already increased at least 16 percent, to $42.5 billion. Congressional auditors have said that years of inflation will put the eventual total at almost $70 billion, a cost of over $530 million per aircraft. This cost is roughly double the current cost of the latest existing bomber, the B-1B.[3] In spite of the error of comparing current dollars (1988) to inflated dollars (1990 and beyond), the Congressional auditors are probably correct that costs of this magnitude will make the B-2 a prime target for budget cutters desperately seeking ways to cope with the federal budget deficit.

While few in Congress are ready to go so far as to kill the B-2 program at this early stage, even some supporters are beginning to question an open-ended commitment to a $70 billion weapon system. Representative Dave McCurdy (Democrat, Oklahoma) said that even though Congress has provided funds thus far, "the B-2 is not a given," unless it measures up in a cost-benefit analysis. Another backer, Chairman Les Aspin (Democrat, Wisconsin) of the House Armed Services Committee, warns that peak funding demands for the B-2 and other long overdue strategic missile programs (including the rail-mobile MX and the mobile Small ICBM) will all come in the early 1990s, and cannot all be met. He wants to negotiate an early agreement with the Bush Administration on an overall strategic spending total for five to 10 years, with certain new major weapons bought one at a time. Such a plan might delay production of the B-2 for several years.[4]

Some opponents of the B-2 question not only its cost, but its mission. For example, the Federation of American Scientists, a group that seeks to curb nuclear arms, has concluded that the B-2 could only work if used in a preemptive strike mode, and this could be an incentive for the Soviets to strike first in a crisis situation. Advocates of the B-2 reject these views, saying that the B-2's radar-evading prowess will be useful in many types of bombing missions, and it is wise to keep a high technology manned bomber because it is the only kind of strategic nuclear weapon that can be recalled after launch. Other critics believe the real future of stealth technologies will be in unmanned vehicles. Some of these critics tend to support less expensive aircraft that would remain outside a defended airspace and would launch stealth technology cruise missiles. The only certainty at this point is that most of the debate concerning costs and the future of stealth and certain other technologies will take place within the "black" world, invisible to the public.[5]

SDI programs are different because they are highly visible, very political, and colored by ideology. President Reagan viewed SDI as a means of eliminating the nuclear threat. He also indicated that he believed its existence will increase the pace of social and economic modernization in the Soviet Union. For these reasons, the Reagan Administration laid out a very large SDI investment program, possibly at the expense of U.S. strategic offensive forces.

To some in Congress and to certain anti-nuclear groups, SDI is nonsense. They doubt that the nuclear threat can be eliminated, and they also see the current nuclear balance as a source of world stability. Some also view arms control as a way of reducing the cost of that stability, and they oppose SDI because of its costs and because it may eventually result in a U.S. violation of the ABM treaty.

It is worth pointing out that not all SDI opponents are Democrats or belong to anti-nuclear groups such as the Federation of American Scientists, the Union of Concerned Scientists, etc. Some Department of Defense officials oppose SDI because of its opportunity cost, both in terms of research and development and in terms of possible deployment. Continued research and eventual deployment would use up a substantial amount of a shrinking (or relatively static) defense budget, leaving less for other weapon systems, operations, and maintenance. The Navy is especially concerned about possible cuts in its planned 15 aircraft-carrier surface fleet, and the Army wants more money for conventional force upgrades, including tanks, helicopters, and "smart" weapons (precision-guided munitions, etc.).

After repeated shifts in its declared research focus, the SDI is now oriented toward producing a "Phase 1" defensive system for deployment in the mid-1990s. Phase 1 would be designed to defend ICBM silos, selected facilities for the National Command Authorities, certain strategic bomber bases, and other elements of U.S. retaliatory forces. The September, 1988, cost estimate for Phase 1 is $69 billion. Subsequent phases could extend the defense to include other military installations and selected industrial areas. According to some critics, continuous upgrades would also be necessary to keep pace with Soviet offensive reactions to U.S. defenses. In any case, the Bush Administration may be in a position to decide whether or not to proceed with Phase 1 of a ballistic missile defense in the early 1990s. A commitment to deploy Phase 1 would have a major impact on defense budgets well into the 21st century.

The desire to deploy a ballistic missile defense will be tempered by the desires to reduce the federal budget deficit and to implement new or more expensive social programs. Given the general aging of the U.S. population, social security programs may also continue to demand additional funds. Competition will also continue within a reduced (or static) defense budget. A Phase 1 deployment will compete with other major weapons programs, such as the B-2 and other stealth technology weapons, the rail-mobile MX, the Small ICBM, and the Trident submarine program.

It is clear that the Bush Administration cannot do everything in the near term, especially if President Bush lives up to his campaign promise of "no new taxes." A likely set of priorities will include modest increases in social spending (catastrophic health care is almost a certainty), a stretchout of the development of the B-2, deployment of the F-117A, possible deployment of the Small ICBM, and continued debate and research on a rail-mobile MX. The prospects for a clear decision to deploy a Phase 1 ballistic missile defense are not good, at least from the point of view of proponents. A likely SDI scenario would include continued research and possible deployment of less controversial (and less costly) components of a Phase 1 system. Such components might include various space-based sensors and possibly some terminal defenses for ICBM silos and other elements of U.S. strategic retaliatory forces. Closely related research on anti-satellite weapons will continue, and may include testing of prototype systems. However, a major deployment of operational anti-satellite weapons is unlikely for the near term, primarily due to costs and the technical problems of going from prototypes to a fully operational systems.

Other Defense Priorities

Since World War II, the United States has relied upon its technological superiority as a mainstay of its defense policy. Indeed, nuclear bombs were the high technology means of ending World War II on terms favorable to the United States and its allies. Recent examples such as the SDI, which is an effort to use high technology to solve the problem of defense against ballistic missiles, and stealth aircraft, may cause the Soviet Union to spend billions of rubles to upgrade their air defenses. However, in recent years, U.S. leadership in many defense technologies has decreased, and U.S. defense policy makers have become concerned about the condition of the U.S. defense industrial base.

Yet a 1988 Defense Science Board report indicated that there is a significant difference between what U.S. industry can do and what national security plans assume it can do. The report goes on to propose recommendations to shore up the sagging U.S. technological leadership, both in defense and in the global marketplace. Recommendations include a cabinet level council to monitor industrial capabilities and generate policy initiatives, and a role for the Secretary of Defense in integrating production surge capacity and planning into the weapon system acquisition process.[6]

Plants that produce plutonium, tritium, and other nuclear materials for warheads are key elements in the defense industrial base. The recent public debate about the safety of the Savannah River Plant and others in Colorado and Idaho put nuclear warhead production in the political spotlight. These plants, for the most part, are old and have, for a number of years, experienced serious safety problems. There is also the chronic problem of disposing of nuclear waste. The more serious problems of this industry will have to be at least addressed by the Bush Administration. As this book has explained, change will not occur without domestic political and economic costs, since these plants are important elements in certain local economies.

Another economic priority related to national defense is the U.S. position in the world economy. President Bush must deal with a Japan that is reasserting its economic (and political) power in East Asia. He must also deal with the European Economic Community, which taken as a whole, has an annual output of goods and services that exceeded $4.5 trillion in 1985— a total that is substantially larger than the gross domestic product of the United States ($3.9 trillion in 1985). He must also deal with rapidly developing Third World nations such as Brazil and India. A faltering Mexican economy is placing ever-increasing pressure on the United States. Potential future immigration into the U.S. from both Mexico and strife-torn Central America may place extreme pressure on the U.S southern border. Some observers believe that the relative decline of the United States in world trade, its chronic balance of trade deficit, and other international economic problems will eventually affect U.S. international political power, and eventually its military power. What President Bush does to alleviate U.S. international economic problems will set the course for key aspects of U.S. foreign policy well into the 21 century.

Notes

1. Friedman, N., "The Next President and Defense," *Defense Electronics,* November 1988, 73–74. Also see "The Brave New World of Stealth Warfare," *U.S. News and World Report,* November 28, 1988, 20–28.

2. "Fighting Smart, Not Rich," *U.S. News and World Report,* November 14, 1988, 24–25. Also see "The Brave New World of Stealth Warfare".

3. "The Brave New World of Stealth Warfare".

4. Ibid.

5. Ibid.

6. Pellerin, C., "Defense Science Board Urges Industrial Base Revamp," *Washington Technology,* November 3–16, 1988.

14

Nuclear Weapons and the Future Strategic Position of the European NATO Allies

The present position of all the NATO allies is one of great flux and uncertainty. Western democracies rely on frequent ratification of their actions by an electorate conditioned by the market system to expect rapid and successful solutions to everyday problems. For this reason, the western democracies are only well suited to pursue international policies that provide some sense that an issue can either be immediately resolved or be resolved in a reasonable amount of time. They are not well equipped to deal with the economic, political, and social stresses that come from living with a problem that seems to never be concluded.

The impact of the West's inability to take the "long view" cannot be underestimated when one discusses either conventional or nuclear deterrence of the Soviet Union or its allies. The very conditions that make deterrence work—the threat (never exercised) of actions whose outcome cannot be clearly specified—create an environment that promises no quick fixes and delivers no clear solutions. Instead, deterrence establishes a long-term stalemate whose only benefit, a conflict that did not happen, must be stated in the negative. This can cause 'psychological exhaustion' in an electorate that has grown weary of paying for things it cannot see, an exhaustion that can easily lead to the pursuit of alternatives that lower cost, irrespective of the outcome.

There is a distinct difference between a deterrent posture undertaken to keep a potential enemy from doing things that are so monstrous, in terms of one's culture or survival, that they cannot be tolerated, and a deterrent posture undertaken as an alternative to doing the painful economic, social or military things necessary to defend oneself. The first is an act of ultimate sacrifice to be used only in a time of ultimate danger, while the second is only an an attempt to avoid paying the true cost of defense. No matter what weapons one chooses, true deterrence—an act of the first kind—is always the safest posture one can take if conflict is to be avoided. Deterrent acts of the second kind carry with them more chance of conflict.

By 1988, the effect of 'psychological exhaustion' on many NATO allies was readily apparent. After the 1988 INF Treaty removed the threat of certain intermediate-range nuclear missiles from Europe, and after a series of apparently friendly and yet, completely innocuous statements by Soviet leaders removed some of the fear that had been a binding force on the alliance, members of NATO sensed that at last, a payoff may have arrived.

In the face of the certain knowledge that a buildup of conventional forces would be required to overcome the loss of nuclear weapons, the Federal Republic of Germany planned to cut its armored units by 33 percent and reduce its troops by 5 percent, the United States retired 16 frigates and decommissioned fighter wings, Denmark mothballed its largest warships, and the United Kingdom planned to withdraw some forces from Europe.[1] More than anything else, psychological exhaustion rooted in 35 years of attempting to maintain deterrence has influenced the position of the allies described in the following sections.

Historical Background

Prior to the Reagan Administration, there were three attempts by the U.S. and its allies to generate a credible conventional defense. The first, begun in 1950 as a result of the Korean war, took the form of a National Security Memorandum (NSC-68) that discussed the inadequacy of Western conventional forces and the economic weakness of Europe, but did not recommend any specific strategy for attacking either problem. The larger U.S. forces that would have been required by NSC-68 were reduced soon after the Korean War.[2]

A second effort started with the Kennedy Administration in 1961. This study accepted the 'containment doctrine' but was critical of the use of nuclear weapons and called for a new emphasis on conventional forces. The study identified probable theaters of conflict and eventually settled on a likely scenario involving the simultaneous occurrence of a major Soviet and Chinese attack and a smaller conflict with a country like Cuba. The result was the 'two-and-a-half war' strategy, and although the force requirements to support this contingency were developed, they were never purchased.[3]

The third effort took place during a review of U.S. foreign policy by the Nixon Administration in 1969. The new strategy eliminated the 2 1/2 war strategy and recommended flexible general purpose forces that could respond to either Soviet or Chinese attacks. Both the Ford and Carter Administrations went along with this view and attempted to structure their forces accordingly.[4]

In 1981, the Reagan Administration formulated a return to the containment doctrine that, in retrospect, was both ill-defined and overly ambitious. It simply claimed that "United States conventional forces, in conjunction with those of our allies, should be capable of putting at risk Soviet interests, including the Soviet homeland."[5] While this strategy incorporated most of the elements of containment, it did so in an open-ended manner that made it almost impossible to acquire the forces necessary to accomplish the strategy.

After the first years of the Reagan Administration, many observers began to realize that the containment model had already worked and that a world view centered on the Soviets was little help in dealing with many of the problems facing the U.S. in the 1980's. These problems promised to become increasingly important in the 1990's as third world countries attempted to deal with trade difficulties, poverty, and disease, and they manifested themselves in a growing pattern of international terrorism, strained political relationships with the third world and the richer Arab countries, and, when conditions became bad enough to be exploited by a superpower, 'surrogate wars'[6] that were held in isolated regions around the globe. Each of these was a threat to U.S. security, though it was clear that the USSR was not responsible for most of the fundamental problems that created these threats. This realization created a new definition of U.S. security that was far broader than a simplistic containment approach and that stressed economic and political issues as well as military conflicts.[7] This strategy de-emphasized the direct conflict between the U.S. and the USSR and, in the process, it tended to diminish, at least in the eyes of the United States, the importance of the the U.S. role in the European NATO region.

Nuclear Forces in NATO

Chapter 2 provides a complete list of the nuclear weapons possessed by both the NATO alliance and the Warsaw Pact, and Chapter 3 discusses the motivation for their acquisition by the NATO allies. In the final analysis, there is little to say about nuclear weapons in the context of NATO except that they provide a deterrent to war that is much cheaper to purchase and maintain than conventional forces, and that the use of nuclear weapons ties the United States firmly to the fate of the NATO allies. Although nuclear weapons are controversial among European groups that would like to ban the entire class of weapons, within the Alliance these weapons have not been nearly as controversial as conventional forces. There is a simple reason for this: the status of NATO's conventional forces and its ability to fight a conventional war will ultimately determine whether nuclear weapons will have to be used in Europe.

One might initially presume that the Europeans would be anxious to be rid of weapons that promise to devastate their homeland if they are used. But according to French defense expert Francois Heisbourg, many Europeans are worried that negotiations to limit nuclear arms are the "first step on a slippery slope to the denuclearlization of Europe, and therefore [could lead] to a decoupling [of United States and European relations]."[8] These worries stem partly from the fear that the Soviet Union would find it advantageous to attack Europe if it was not defended by the United States, and partly from the realization that the European countries would have to devote a much larger share of their resources to defense if nuclear weapons were no longer used and/or if the U.S. was not providing both military resources and strategic protection.

If U.S. nuclear weapons were removed from Europe, French and British nuclear forces would become critical to European nuclear deterrence. This would have a major impact on the relationship of France to the rest of NATO. There have already been proposals to include West Germany under the French nuclear umbrella.[9] On the other hand, Britain's defense establishment is in such dire economic straits that there is a serious possibility that it might have to sacrifice its nuclear forces to maintain a strong conventional presence in NATO.

European Responses to U.S. Nuclear Defenses

Defenses against nuclear weapons could have the same effect as banning those weapons by helping to insulate the United States from Soviet attack, and they have generally been viewed by the Europeans as one more blow to the status of the offensive nuclear deterrent. When the SDI was initially announced, European officials feared it

> would establish a defensive umbrella over the United States and eliminate any likelihood that the United States would respond with nuclear weapons to a conventional assault on Western Europe by Warsaw Pact forces. It would also greatly reduce the effectiveness of the British and French nuclear arsenals. . . .[10]

Like the NATO countries, the French were worried that the new technologies developed for the SDI would threaten "the stability—and thus peace—that has resulted so far from the invulnerability of the means of nuclear response."[11] In the end, when the European nations were faced with the uncertainty that SDI promised they preferred to remain with the status quo, even though it could be argued that their idea of 'invulnerability' was based on rather shaky assumptions concerning the likelihood of a preemptive Soviet strike.

The British tried to be supportive of the Reagan Administration, and were slow to express their misgivings. They agreed that SDI research and development were fine, but they made it clear that their approval did not extend to deployment or anything else that would violate the 1972 Anti-

Ballistic Missile Treaty. They also expressed concern that stability be maintained. As Sir Geoffry Howe explained,

> We must consider the potential consequences for [NATO]. We must be sure that the United States' nuclear guarantee to Europe will indeed be enhanced not at the end of the process, but from its very inception.[12]

Aside from European fears about the impact of SDI on the behavior of the U.S. in NATO, attitudes of many Europeans toward the system were also negative because SDI simply did not fit the defense needs of Europe. A strategic defense shield would rule out a limited nuclear response because the Soviets would have to launch an overwhelming attack to get a few warheads through. SDI also fed the European peace movement that sought to abolish nuclear weapons. Finally, the allies believed a total elimination of nuclear weapons would increase the risk of conventional war in Europe.[13]

In an effort to change this perception, the Reagan Administration offered a number of inducements to the allies. These have already been described in detail, but three things were important in changing the allied attitudes toward nuclear defense. The first was the realization that SDI research and development could provide valuable commercial and conventional weapon spinoffs. The second was the growing recognition that the 'umbrella' concept of the SDI, as originally envisioned, would not work, and that if any system ever was developed from SDI research and development, it would be of such limited capability that it would not have the detrimental effects on NATO that the allies once feared.

The third element was the European conclusion that one part of the SDI plan that called for a non-nuclear missile defense system for Europe might be feasible. The Europeans elected to participate in the development of this system because it would counter intermediate and short range non-nuclear missiles in their terminal phase of flight and defend particular geographic regions of Europe. It could also be ground based, could use a good deal of existing technology, and would benefit from the super-accurate munition research already being done in NATO. In addition, it could compliment conventional forces by destroying incoming Soviet missiles whose purpose was 'defense busting'; i.e., destroying NATO's military installations and supplies. As a curious adjunct, this decision broke NATO away from the 1972 ABM treaty by interpreting that document as prohibiting only defenses against nuclear missiles—even though one could not tell if an incoming medium or short range missile was nuclear or not. Thus, the current state of European efforts toward nuclear defense is expressed by this attempt to develop a system that will destroy incoming short and medium range nuclear weapons—by mistake.

Research for the SDI has already created new possibilities for NATO conventional forces. In essence, the SDI not only has the possibility of creating a defense against some nuclear weapons, its research also holds the promise for highly accurate conventional munitions and weapons that could replace nuclear arms on the conventional battlefield. For example, the rail gun is now light enough for use in conventional combat. In addition, kinetic energy devices launched from orbit could hit targets on earth, and the use of lasers against soft targets like command and control networks, power grids and ships is also very likely.[14]

Advanced technology will also allow sensors that can distinguish objects clearly enough that computers can perform 'image correlation' and identify targets that are to be attacked. These weapons could easily take the place of most 'brute force' nuclear warheads because they can be counted on to squarely hit their targets.[15] For example, in 1984 Army General John Wickam told the House Armed Services Committee that the U.S. was on the verge of technological breakthroughs that would allow enough accuracy in conventional munitions to give them the same effect as small nuclear warheads. Such weapons would include both long range missiles and computer guided warheads.[16] General Wickham went on to predict that these weapons would be available in five years. Difficulty in developing the required technology has delayed that date considerably, but these weapons still have a tremendous potential for conventional warfare.

Conventional Forces in NATO

A detailed list of the conventional forces in Europe is provided as an appendix to Chapter 2. However, there are several problems with conventional force comparisons in the European Theater. First, current NATO forces were structured in recognition of the nuclear deterrent provided both by the U.S. and some of the NATO allies and of the use of tactical nuclear weapons to make up for shortcomings in equipment or troops. By deploying conventional forces in this manner, the allies may have made nuclear war more likely, but they have also managed to reduce overall defense spending by relying on cheaper nuclear weapons. As a result, whether or not NATO conventional forces are numerically inferior to Warsaw Pact forces is largely irrelevant—if one presumes that a war in Europe would escalate into nuclear conflict almost immediately.

If, instead, one assumes that the war remains conventional for its entire duration, either due to restraint on the part of the combatants [an unlikely outcome], a complete nuclear disarmament, or an operable defense against strategic *and* tactical nuclear weapons [also an unlikely event], the situation changes dramatically. Now NATO forces must be structured to fight with only conventional means, a much more expensive option that will command a larger share of the resources of all the members of the Alliance. It is in this situation that conventional force comparisons between NATO and the Warsaw Pact become critical. And at this point, an additional problem arises.

NATO and Conventional Force Reduction Treaties

Since the mid-1970s, NATO and the Warsaw Pact have held Mutual and Balanced Force Reduction (MBFR) talks that have generally proved fruitless. During this period, the West concentrated on reducing the levels of military manpower, feeling that stability would result from cutting the number of troops on both sides in Europe. Recently, the attention of the West has shifted to the "forward deployment of conventional forces capable of rapid mobility and high firepower" that are possessed by the Pact. This is the area where statistics show the West to be furthest behind.[17]

The Allies have been slow to respond to the flurry of proposals for conventional arms control that accompanied Mr. Gorbachev's ascendency to power in the Soviet Union. Because of the cumbersome requirement to get all 16 NATO members to agree, one nation's objections can delay or doom any proposal. In 1988, the Soviets proposed an exchange of data on troop and equipment dispositions that could answer long-standing allied questions and enable some degree of real progress in conventional arms negotiations.[18]

The USSR may consider trading tanks for NATO dual purpose (both nuclear and conventional weapon capable) aircraft. This brings up a key question that the allies are unprepared to answer because of their uncertainty about the conventional balance of forces: what should NATO be willing to trade to get Warsaw Pact reductions? For example, James Thompson of RAND estimated that gaining stability could require the withdrawal of 'equivalent divisions' in a 5 to 1 ratio of Warsaw Pact to NATO divisions.[19] Such tradeoffs are unlikely to be acceptable because the Warsaw Pact's relative advantage over NATO lies in its ability to maintain large numbers of conventional forces in Europe. Any alteration of this advantage would require the Soviet Union and the Warsaw Pact to compete in other, less advantageous militarily areas, and this would result in tremendous opportunity costs. The implications of such competition are discussed in the chapter on competition for resources in the Soviet Union.

Alternative NATO Strategies

This chapter has pictured a NATO alliance troubled and uncertain both about its current position and its future. This is not to say that the alliance is too weak to function. Experts who reviewed the results of the *Reforger* exercise in September, 1987, found that should deterrence fail, the alliance could mobilize, deploy, reinforce and sustain combat in Europe and could hold and possibly break an invasion by the Warsaw Pact forces.[20]

However, the 'position of the allies' that this chapter bears as a title does not exist as a single, definitive statement. It is more correct to speak of what the position of the European members of NATO would be under alternative future scenarios. This section suggests a number of alternative strategies that might be adopted as NATO attempts to cope with the problems it now faces. Any of these strategies will have to be able to counter a Soviet doctrine that holds the following major tenants:[21]

- Numbers count to achieve quantitative superiority.
- Escalation is likely to include the use of chemical or nuclear weapons.
- Surprise, cover and deception are critical to the chances for success.
- There is a distinction between tactical, operational and strategic operations.
- If deterrence breaks down, victory for the USSR is possible.
- It pays to strike first to generate shock among enemy troops.
- The only sound military doctrine is offensive, not defensive.

Ambassador David M. Abshire has called NATO's strategy in the early 1980s a 'Grand Strategy' and he claimed that the NATO alliance was the first great alliance to ever have a deterrent strategy. This strategy was based on flexible response and forward defense, and it required "a credible capability and determination to use nuclear weapons, if necessary" as well as requiring that the Alliance be able to defend itself with conventional forces should deterrence fail.[22] NATO's forward defense incorporated an effort to defend the Federal Republic of Germany at or near its eastern borders. However, this part of the strategy is relatively inflexible and it could be exploited by the Soviet's ability to break through with specially trained units.

A second part of NATO's strategy is the Follow On Forces Attack (FOFA) that would be mounted against the second echelon of the Warsaw Pact invasion force. Unfortunately, technology has not progressed to the point of being able to ensure the success of this part of the strategy and the detection devices necessary for it to function are extremely expensive.[23] In addition, this part of the strategy concentrates on Warsaw Pact forces that are far from the front line and not as great a threat as the invading forces.[24] Strategists have also pointed out that this type of operation shifts one's thinking from the defensive to offensive, attack-oriented aims.

These elements of strategy are then augmented by the use of tactical nuclear weapons to overcome numerical deficiencies in the NATO forces. The Europeans have historically been afraid that shifting too much emphasis to conventional deterrence could tempt the Soviet Union to think that it could launch a limited assault without fear of nuclear reprisal.[25] However, it is clear that the SDI, the INF treaty, and the economic and political conditions of the allies in the 1980s have all created an environment that will require changes in NATO strategies if the alliance is to successfully cope with conditions in the 1990s and beyond. All or part of the six alternatives that follow may be incorporated into NATO's new strategy.

Alternative 1: The U.S. Disengagement Strategy

At least a decade would be required to implement the gradual disengagement of the U.S. from NATO. This strategy would be based on the assumption that the deterrence that is lost would have cost the U.S. more than the losses it would sustain in the future because it withdrew. Disengagement would proceed at a deliberate pace with constant consultations. The allies would be encouraged to develop sufficient conventional force capabilities and the U.S. would devise nuclear doctrines that more clearly decoupled it from the defense of Europe.[26]

Alternative 2: Reducing the Role of Nuclear Deterrence in NATO

In a report to the House Foreign Affairs Committee, *Challenges to NATO's Consensus: West European Attitudes and U.S. Policy*, it was suggested that NATO should reduce the role of nuclear deterrence in its strategy and compensate for the loss of nuclear weapons by reorganizing its defense forces into lighter, smaller, more mobile units. At the same time, it should shift defense funds from expensive offense-oriented systems such as tanks and fighter bombers to less expensive weapons like antitank and antiaircraft systems.[27]

Alternative 3: A Coalition Strategy

Ambassador Robert Komer has suggested that a balanced, coalition approach to conventional forces would allow the NATO allies to get their forces cheaply enough that they could afford a sufficient number to fight a conventional war in Europe. This strategy would replace the current balanced national force concept, allowing each NATO member to contribute those forces it can add with most efficiency. Conventional forces would be related to the strategy designed to best preserve NATO's interests and would exhibit greater readiness, mobility and forward deployment.[28]

Alternative 4: Defense Cooperation

This long standing proposal starts with the creation of a multinational combat unit (in this case, Franco-German) as a first step toward closer military relations in Europe, a concept that goes back to the European

Defense Community proposed by the French in 1954. Later, in 1963, France and Germany agreed on defense cooperation, but this was ruled out when the French withdrew from NATO in 1966. The concept now calls for a joint command under a French general, and for the French nuclear umbrella to encompass the Federal Republic of Germany.[29]

In 1988 the Italians and the Germans agreed to establish a joint working group on military cooperation following the Franco-German model.[30] And a 1988 report from the North Atlantic Assembly included a special European combat division as part of a wide ranging plan for defense cooperation. It also recommended the formation of a European defense market, annual assessments of the threats to the alliance, establishment of a common Research and Development fund for new weapons, establishment of a NATO working group to handle out-of-area situations like the Gulf, and stopping the requirement for U.S. compensation for bases on European soil.[31]

A 1986 Independent European Programme Group (IEPG) paper on defense cooperation also recommended new centralized structures to make sure that weapon programs are not duplicated and that Europe gets the most from its defense R&D money. This paper suggested a central R&D agency modelled after the European Space Agency, and recommended fixed price contracts for all stages of projects including development, and information sharing by the European nations about long term and immediate equipment needs.[32]

Alternative 5: Competitive Strategies

This was an idea of Secretary of Defense Weinberger in 1986 that was later adopted by Secretary of Defense Carlucci. This strategy seeks to pit NATO strengths against Warsaw Pact weaknesses. The 1988 competitive strategies report lists available, proven technologies for near term use in NATO. These include microcircuitry, precision guidance systems, intelligence fusion, saturation of enemy command and control systems, low observable stealth technology, fuel-air explosives, decoys, and survivable command, control, communication, and intelligence.[33] This strategy incorporates a high technology approach that gets defense efficiently by using only those things that NATO already has to exploit Soviet weaknesses.

Alternative 6: Resource Strategy

This strategy capitalizes on the sum of the potential of the NATO members to run the alliance efficiently. Arms cooperation in the development and production of conventional weapons, enhanced by a balanced flow of trade between NATO and the U.S. are elements of this plan. In addition, cooperative R&D would be done by all the NATO countries. As envisioned by Ambassador David Abshire, this strategy would rest on a three part framework:

1. A Dynamic Military Appreciation unit would group together the various mechanisms for evaluating the Warsaw Pact threat and generate one comprehensive assessment each year that the allies could consider before deciding how to redress weaknesses.
2. A Conceptual Military Framework would establish priorities and relationships among the latest NATO military concepts.
3. A NATO Resources Strategy would match each member nation's industrial capability and economic conditions with the conceptual framework to channel NATO's resources to the highest priority items.[34]

Conclusion

NATO is in a period of change that will have a significant impact on its ability to survive as a viable alliance into the next century. As it emerges from this period, the strategy it employs will undoubtedly have concepts from a number of the alternatives in the previous section. This strategy will also reflect the economic realities of the various countries in NATO and hence, it will be the major determinant of NATO's demand for nuclear weapons.

Given the movement toward an economically unified Europe, it is likely that any future NATO strategy will also have many of the elements found in the defense cooperation strategy. If this transpires, it could mean an economically and defensively unified Europe and it could create a more efficient and streamlined NATO defense establishment that could afford conventional arms and hence, is less dependent on nuclear weapons. This would give the Soviet Union some pause to consider as it contemplates its own future defense spending as well as future spending for the Warsaw Pact.

Notes

1. "The Cold War Is Not Over," *Defense News,* May 2, 1988, 22.
2. This section draws heavily from Kaufmann, William W., *Planning Conventional Forces: 1950–80,* The Brookings Institution, Washington, D.C., 1982.
3. Ibid.
4. Ibid.
5. Halloran, Richard, "Pentagon Draws Up First Strategy For Fighting a Long Nuclear War," *New York Times,* May 30, 1982, 1.
6. These wars are fought in and by third countries where each side represents the interests of a major power. Thus, the major powers can contest the control of an area without becoming directly involved with one another and risking a nuclear war.

7. For a good explanation of how the current U.S. strategy is developing, see Mossberg, Walter S., and Walcott, John, "U.S. Redefines Policy on Security to Place Less Stress on Soviets," *Wall Street Journal,* August 11, 1988, 1, 12.

8. Beyers, Dan, "Europeans Search For New Defense Relationship," *Defense News,* July 20, 1988, 1, 36.

9. Ibid.

10. Hoagland, Jim, "'Star Wars' Plan Worries Envoy," *Washington Post,* October 30, 1984, 21.

11. Greyelin, Philip, "France and Star Wars," *Washington Post,* January 28, 1985, 11.

12. Pond, Elizabeth, "Britain Voices Europe's Qualms About US Strategic Defense Plans," *Christian Science Monitor,* March 18, 1985, 15.

13. Salkowski, Charlotte, "Guaging effect of SDI on Geneva talks," *Christian Science Monitor,* April 4, 1985, 3.

14. Knickerbocker, Brad, "'Star Wars' defense may lead to space-based offense," *Christian Science Monitor,* January 23, 1985, 1.

15. Keyworth, George, "Supersmart weapons—alternative to nukes," *Washington Times,* October 19, 1984, 6-b.

16. Andrews, Walter, "Non-nuclear superbombs seen ready in five years," *Washington Times,* February 7, 1985, 1.

17. Hunter, Robert, "Conventional Arms: NATO Faces Tough Issues," *Defense News,* April 11, 1988, 27, 28.

18. Fialka, John, "NATO is Showing Strain as It Confronts Gorbachev's Disarming Arms-Curb Ideas," *Wall Street Journal,* July 14, 1988, 23.

19. Hunter, Robert, "Conventional Arms: NATO Faces Tough Issues," *Defense News,* April 11, 1988, 27, 28.

20. Middleton, Drew, "An Assessment of the NATO Alliances Strength," *Defense News,* October, 26, 1987.

21. Lambeth, Benjamin, *How To think about Soviet Military Doctrine,* a paper presented at a seminar on Soviet Military Doctrine, Harvard University, February 13, 1978, 2.

22. Abshire, David M., "NATO: Honing the Grand Strategy," *Wall Street Journal,* September 12, 1984.

23. Middleton, Drew, "An Assessment of the NATO Alliances Strength," *Defense News,* October, 26, 1987.

24. Gordon, Michael R., "NATO's High-Tech Defensive Strategy Draws Fire From Within the Alliance," *National Journal,* December 15, 1984, 2394–2396.

25. Drozdiak, William, "NATO Weighs Nonnuclear Strategies," *Washington Post,* September 26, 1983.

26. Ravenal, Earl, "Reconsider Defense Commitment to Europe," *Oakland Tribune,* April 24, 1984.

27. Adams, Peter, "Allies Face Tough Choices in Nuclear Umbrella Shuts," *Defense News,* June 8, 1987, 1, 56.

28. Komer, Robert, "Future of U.S. Conventional Forces: A Coalition Approach," *Rethinking Defense and Conventional Forces,* Center for National Policy, Washington, D.C., 1983, 43–52.

29. Hunter, Robert E., "France, Germany Moving Toward Military Cooperation," *Army Times,* July 6, 1987.

30. Rossi, Sergio, "Countries Work Toward Defense Cooperation," *Defense News,* May 16, 1988.

31. Beyers, Dan, "Report Says Europe Can Play Larger NATO Role," *Defense News,* April 25, 1988, 1, 36.

32. "NATO: Outdated by 2000?" *Defense News,* July 25, 1988.

33. Amouyal, Barbara, "Pentagon Concept Fortifies NATO Superiority, Exploits Warsaw Pact Weaknesses," *Defense News,* August 1, 1988, 8.

34. Abshire, David M., "The Atlantic Alliance: The Development of a Resource Strategy," *Signal,* October, 1984, 23.

15

Nuclear Weapons and the Future Strategic Position of the Soviet Union

Soviet Perspectives

There are great hopes among NATO nations that the changes taking place in the Soviet Union will result in significant decreases in both tension and nuclear arms. Much of this hope is the result of the extensive public relations efforts of Soviet General Secretary Mikhail Gorbachev. In 1986, Gorbachev declared that "in the military sphere, we intend to act in such a way as to give nobody grounds for fears, even imagined ones, about their security."[1] However, history provides the United States and its NATO allies with ample reason for caution. Previous Soviet leaders have made similar statements, but events in Hungary (1956), Berlin (1949 and 1961), Cuba (1962), Czechoslovakia (1968), and Afghanistan (1979) tended to shock Western policy makers back to a more cautious stance.

Although Gorbachev's pronouncements and his actions on the INF Treaty and strategic arms reduction negotiations have given cause for cautious optimism with regard to future negotiations, it is obvious that Soviet leaders, will only agree to reductions that are in the best interests of the Soviet Union. To anticipate the likely outcomes of future negotiations, the reader must understand the incentives that motivate Soviet negotiators. Thus, this chapter focuses on the position of the Soviet Union with regard to the strategic nuclear balance, the role of conventional forces, and the likely Soviet agenda in future arms control negotiations.

Glasnost and Perestroika

According to the Soviet Union, the fundamental changes are along the following lines:

- Soviet military doctrine now has a purely 'defensive' character. Evidence of change cited by both the Soviet and the Western press includes the

Gorbachev initiatives concerning INF reductions in Europe and the 1988 U.S.-Soviet strategic arms reduction talks. Statements along these lines were also made by a spokesperson from the Soviet Academy of Science: "Our military doctrine, as already pointed out, carries a defensive character, with the aim of guarding the gains of socialism."[2]

- The Soviet government has increased its emphasis on raising the standard of living of the Soviet people at the expense of the production and maintenance of military forces. As evidence of this new emphasis, the Soviet press has cited among the glasnost (openness) and perestroika (reconstruction) policies of Gorbachev those policies that are intended to provide incentives for factory managers and workers to increase both the quality and quantity of consumer goods.

On the other hand, glasnost has stripped away much of the cloak of mystery that past Soviet leaders have used to hide Soviet weaknesses from the outside world. For example, the anger that large numbers of Estonians, Armenians, and Azerbaijanis expressed so openly in 1988 and 1989 has revealed the extent of unrest occurring on the fringes of the Soviet 'empire.'

To satisfy increasing demands for consumer goods, Gorbachev has little choice but to attempt fundamental reforms of the inefficient Soviet economy. The only other viable alternative is repression of dissent with force, something that Gorbachev has become increasingly reluctant to do. Gorbachev's problem is that economic reforms and efficiency cannot be instituted with military force; indeed, military force would be counter-productive.

Perspectives on Soviet Military Doctrine and Force Structure

If fundamental changes are indeed taking place in Soviet policies, particularly those that affect relations with the West, then these changes should begin to be evident in changes to Soviet military doctrine and force structure. However, with regard to military doctrine, a book written in 1987 for use by Soviet military officers points out that military doctrine has two sides: the political and the military-technical. According to the book, only the political side is 'defensive.' With regard to force structure, the Soviets began in 1987-88 to reduce their INF forces in Europe, and they have also removed Soviet troops from Afghanistan. However, they have increased the funding for the development of anti-satellite and anti-ballistic missile systems, including the development of both kinetic energy and directed energy weapons. They have also continued to improve their MIRVed nuclear warheads for their ICBMs and SLBMs, and they have continued to upgrade the nuclear warfighting capabilities of Warsaw Pact air and ground forces in Central Europe.[3]

This apparent difference between the political and military-technical sides of Soviet military doctrine is, however, consistent with past Soviet behavior in issues that have involved Soviet national security and worldwide political interests. For example, the 'police action' in Hungary (1956), the invasion of Czechoslovakia (1968), and the invasion of Afghanistan (1979) were all considered by the Soviets to be defensive with respect to the political side of military doctrine. Even the placement of nuclear-armed missiles in Cuba in 1962 was termed, by the Soviet press, as 'defensive'.

From the Soviet perspective, the actions of the United States continue to appear to be threatening. In 1986, Soviet Marshal Ogarkov pointed out that:

We know, for example, that the United States built the world's first atomic bomb in 1945 and proceeded to use it to threaten the Soviet Union, which did not develop a similar weapon until four years later. What is more, the United States was the first to test an even more powerful hydrogen bomb in 1952, while the USSR followed suit in 1953. The Americans were also the first to build nuclear-powered submarines armed with ballistic missiles in 1960, while the USSR followed suit in 1967. . . . This list of strategic weapons could go on and on.[4]

Based on Soviet press releases (Pravda), the Soviet government also regards the Reagan administration Strategic Defense Initiative as part of a U.S. plan to negate Soviet retaliatory forces and move the U.S. toward a first strike capability. Four days after President Reagan's 1983 SDI speech, then Soviet President Andropov denounced Reagan's proposal to develop new types of ballistic missile defense systems. Andropov said the idea of strategic defensive measures might seem attractive to the uninformed, but:

In fact, the strategic offensive forces of the United States will continue to be developed and upgraded at full tilt and along quite a definite line at that, namely that of acquiring a nuclear first strike capability. Under these conditions, the intention to secure itself the possibility of destroying, with the help of the ABM defenses, the corresponding strategic systems of the other side, that is, of rendering it unable to deal a retaliatory strike, is a bid to disarm the Soviet Union in the face of the U.S. nuclear threat.[5]

This theme has been reiterated vigorously and persistently ever since by Soviet newspaper commentators, scientists, diplomats, and by General Secretary Gorbachev.

From the Soviet point of view, much depends on what the United States chooses to protect with ballistic missile defense forces. For example, if the U.S. protects its urban populations and not its strategic nuclear forces, the Soviets would probably perceive this a first strike posture by the United

States, because the U.S. would have an incentive to launch its unprotected nuclear forces before the Soviets could destroy them on the ground, and then ride out a ragged Soviet retaliatory attack on protected U.S. cities. On the other hand, if the United States protected its strategic nuclear forces and not its urban populations, the Soviets would probably not perceive this as a U.S. first strike posture (in spite of Soviet rhetoric). Since U.S. strategic forces would be protected, the U.S. would have no incentive to launch its strategic forces first to avoid destruction. In addition, U.S. cities would remain vulnerable to a Soviet retaliatory strike.

In spite of Soviet public relations efforts to impress the general public on both sides, there is as yet little change in Soviet military doctrine and force structure. The Soviets have continued to expand and modernize nuclear forces, ballistic missile defenses, and conventional forces. Since the U.S. is also expanding and modernizing, the current structure of 'deterrence' clearly provides substantial incentives for both nations to continue the arms race.

Economic Incentives for Arms Limitations
and Force Reductions

There is support for the view that the Soviets are dismayed by the fact that the Reagan administration has followed a policy of modernization of forces in areas where the U.S. has the advantages of superior technologies and funding. If the Soviets continue to follow suit, as they have for previous U.S. buildups, enormous pressures will be generated within the Soviet economy. The current U.S. build-up of high-technology weapons, particularly those in the anti-satellite and anti-ballistic missile categories, has the potential to cost more in terms resources than any military build-up in history. Thus, a natural Soviet response to the U.S. build-up is to eliminate, by negotiations, a race they can neither afford nor win. Following this line of argument, the Gorbachev initiatives in Europe, Afghanistan, and even glasnost, may be Soviet attempts to appear less of a threat to the West and to reduce the incentives for the U.S. to continue its build-up of high-technology weapons.

The Soviets also have strong incentives to reduce NATO nuclear weapons in Europe. NATO has always been a nuclear-armed alliance because of the Soviet advantage in conventional forces. Britain's Prime Minister Thatcher and France's President Mitterrand both made statements in 1988 that indicated they recognize the dangers of a conventional force build-up in Europe and, in particular, the resource costs of such a build-up to the Europeans. In this sense, the continued deployment of nuclear weapons can be viewed as a relatively cheap means of maintaining the East-West balance of power.[6]

In spite of their motives, the Soviet approach under Gorbachev does offer some hope for a easing of East-West tensions, particularly in Europe. Both sides would benefit by a reduction in military expenditures because the resources that are currently being devoted to defense could be used for non-defense purposes. However, it is also clear that the Soviets should prefer that the United States posture itself for an arms race in which the Soviets have the advantage, namely, a conventional arms build-up in Europe. Further reductions in nuclear weapons, particularly in Europe, will make this situation difficult to avoid unless the Soviets actually make good on the 1989 Gorbachev proposals to reduce conventional arms.

An Agenda for Negotiations

As the 21st century approaches, NATO and Warsaw Pact leaders will inherit a series of ongoing negotiations, weapons decisions, and other unresolved questions involving the nuclear arms race. Western nations can expect the Soviet Union to approach negotiations based on well-defined priorities and criteria. As always, the Soviets will attempt to form agreements that foster their vision of long-term Soviet security and economic progress. The Soviet agenda for negotiations will probably include: tactical nuclear forces in Europe; strategic nuclear weapons; ballistic missile defenses; nuclear proliferation, and strengthening bilateral and multilateral arms control institutions.

Negotiations on the reduction of conventional forces in Europe will begin in earnest in 1989, and will include forces located in the area from the Atlantic to the Urals. Participants in the talks will include all of the NATO allies, including France, and all seven members of the Warsaw Pact.

According to Soviet leaders, there is an approximate equilibrium between the forces of the two alliances. The Warsaw Pact has more ground forces, while the U.S. and its allies have more combat aircraft and naval armaments. Over all, however, a rough parity exists. According to Sergei Akhromeyev, Marshal of the Soviet Union, "our approach to such cuts proceeds from the existence of an approximate military balance between the Warsaw Pact and NATO. There are, of course, asymmetries in individual types of weaponry, but they do not upset the general parity."[7]

On the other side, the NATO allies have a concept of developing parity at lower levels with regard to ground forces, particularly with regard to tanks and artillery. However, if NATO decides to ask for an equal ceiling in main battle tanks between the two alliances at 20,000 tanks per alliance, this would mean a total NATO reduction of about 4,250 tanks, and a total Warsaw Pact reduction of about 32,000. If carried out, this reduction would eliminate a very large portion of the Warsaw Pact ground forces in the Atlantic-to-the Urals area. The asymmetries are similar with respect to artillery. Clearly, a NATO call for tank and artillery parity would be hard to achieve unless the Soviets were willing to accept deep cuts in their forces. An approach more acceptable to the Soviets appears to be to seek such parity in Central Europe (Denmark, the Benelux countries, West Germany, East Germany, Czechoslovakia, Poland, Hungary, and the Western Military Districts of the Soviet Union), with accompanying commitments not to increase forces in the remaining Atlantic-to-the-Urals area.

For NATO, it would not make sense to permit the Soviet Union to reduce obsolescent tanks in its many reserve divisions, while NATO forces, primarily in West Germany, reduced modern tanks from their lesser number of active-duty units. On the other hand, the Soviets can be expected to propose this type of agreement, since tanks and artillery units are the mainstay of their conventional forces on the Central Front.

The Soviets can also be expected to propose linking reductions in tanks and artillery with reductions in fighter-bombers, helicopters, ground anti-tank units, naval forces, and especially tactical nuclear weapons. With the exception of nuclear-capable artillery, NATO obviously can be expected to have strong reservations about including these weapons in any force reduction agreement. The Soviets, on the other hand, might repeat the successful tactics employed during the INF negotiations: an offer to reduce tactical nuclear weapons to zero, backed by strong appeals to Western public opinion.

The Strategic Arms Reduction Talks (START), now under negotiation, has the potential to reduce certain U.S. and Soviet strategic nuclear weapons by a large fraction; for example, a stated U.S. goal is to cut the number of Soviet ICBMs by half. In particular, the U.S. can be expected to propose reductions in Soviet SS-X-24 rail-mobile and SS-25 road-mobile ICBMs, as well as silo-based ICBMs.

However, the Soviets can be expected to link any such reductions to reductions in U.S. air and sea launched cruise missiles as well as U.S. ICBMs, particularly silo-based U.S. MX missiles that have up to 10 MIRVed warheads. A possible common ground could be reductions in the more vulnerable U.S. and Soviet silo-based ICBMs and possible limitations on the number of warheads that can be carried by ground-mobile ICBMs. If such a common ground exists, the Soviets would retain an advantage in mobile ICBM forces, and the U.S. would have an incentive to deploy road mobile, single warhead Small ICBMs and possibly to continue efforts to develop rail-mobile MXs with fewer MIRVed warheads per missile. The Soviets can also be expected to push for limitations on nuclear tests and flight tests of new generation, highly accurate, MIRVed warhead ICBMs, areas of development where the U.S. has technological advantages.

With the probable exception of the Krasnoyarsk phased-array radar, the Soviets appear to be complying with the letter of the 1972 Anti-Ballistic Missile (ABM) Treaty. This treaty bans the additional development, testing, and deployment of ABM systems by the Soviet Union and the United States. Under the treaty, the Soviets have been allowed to keep their ABM system deployed around Moscow. The United States gave up the right to keep the Safeguard ABM System originally deployed in North Dakota.[8]

For the future, the Soviets are unlikely to be the first to openly break the ABM Treaty, because it is in their interest to maintain a treaty that inhibits U.S. development and deployment of sophisticated ballistic missile defenses. However, the Soviets have anticipated possible U.S. deployment of SDI systems by continuing to upgrade their system of phased-array radars that could provide a basis for ground-based terminal ballistic missile defenses for substantial portions of Soviet territory. They have also continued to upgrade the capabilities of their GALOSH and GAZELLE ABM missiles, and to test their SA-X-12B and SA-10 surface-to-air missiles in a possible ABM mode. The pace of Soviet development of these systems will depend on what the United States does with regard to a possible Phase I deployment of a ballistic missile defense under the SDI program. Clearly, the 'star wars' race is one in which the U.S. has the technological and economic advantages and, as stated earlier, the Soviets would prefer to negotiate rather than to participate in a race they cannot win.

Like the United States, the Soviet Union has a vested interest in limiting the proliferation of nuclear weapons. The current Nuclear Non-Proliferation Treaty (1968, 137 members, including the United States and the Soviet Union) bans the transfer of nuclear weapons and technologies to nations that do not have nuclear weapons. It also requires those nations that have nuclear weapons to provide safeguards with regard to research and weapon production facilities and to negotiate, reduce and eventually eliminate nuclear arsenals. Other agreements that limit proliferation include the Treaty of Tlatelolco (1967, 25 nations), the Antarctic Treaty (1959, 35 nations), the Outer Space Treaty (1967, 95 nations), the Seabed Treaty (1971, 82 nations), and more recently, the South Pacific Nuclear Free Zone Treaty (1985, 9 nations).

While it is unlikely that the either the United States or the Soviet Union will ever agree to completely eliminate their own nuclear arsenals, there are incentives on both sides to limit the availability of nuclear weapons to nations that do not currently have them, particularly non-aligned nations. Key areas of interest to the Soviets include the Middle East, Southern Asia, and Africa.

The Outer Space Treaty bans nuclear weapons in space, including space-based ballistic missile defense weapons that carry nuclear warheads. In addition to ballistic missile defense, the treaty bans the deployment of satellites with space-to-ground nuclear weapons. Such weapons are of deep concern to the Soviets, since the U.S. has a substantial lead in sensors, computers, and other technologies that would be necessary for accurate delivery of space-based warheads.

If the U.S. ever deployed nuclear warheads in space, the Soviets could be expected to react vigorously, even to the point of declaring that such weapons are a direct threat to Soviet sovereignty. Such a declaration could be followed by demands for the elimination of such weapons or the Soviets would possibly attempt to destroy them. Clearly, the Soviets have a strong incentive to maintain and strengthen the Outer Space Treaty, and this provides a possible avenue for fruitful future negotiations with the United States.

On the other hand, both the Soviet Union and the United States rely heavily on satellites as essential 'eyes and ears' for military intelligence activities. Both also depend to a certain extent on satellites for global communications and navigation, although the United States has invested substantially more in such systems compared to the Soviet Union. Thus, both nations have an interest in banning anti-satellite weapons that would threaten such systems.

However, since the early 1970s, both nations have had programs to develop and deploy anti-satellite weapons, and both have incipient capabilities, particularly against low earth orbit satellites. New weapons under development by both sides include kinetic kill weapons and ground-based lasers. Whether or not the Soviet Union or the United States has an advantage in this area of arms race competition is not publicly known. Thus, it is difficult to assess whether or not the Soviets would seriously consider reducing or eliminating their anti-satellite capabilities. Since the United States depends more heavily on satellites than the Soviets, it would seem that the Soviets would take a hard line in any future negotiations to eliminate anti-satellite weapons.

In summary, Soviet leaders have strong incentives to negotiate on areas of military competition where the United States has technological and economic advantages. While this Soviet position will result in their earnest participation in negotiations during the 1990s, the United States should proceed with caution. Based on the history of U.S.-Soviet relations and the current strategic balance, it is clear that the Soviet Union will continue to pose the major threat to U.S. security for the foreseeable future.

Notes

1. Scott, W., "Another Look at the USSR's Defensive Doctrine," *Air Force Magazine,* March 1988, 48–52.

2. See "Interview with Marshal of the USSR Sergei Akhromeyev," *Defense Science Magazine,* October 1988, 63–66, to catch the flavor of recent press interviews with Soviet leaders with regard to Soviet military doctrine.

3. Scott.

4. Ibid.

5. Carter, A., and Schwartz, D., *Ballistic Missile Defense,* The Brookings Institution, Washington, DC, 1984, 324.

6. Sources include: Various *Time Magazine* articles, October 1987-March 1988, and various television news broadcasts over the same period.

7. "Interview with Marshal of the USSR Sergei Akhromeyev."

8. The U.S. did keep the Perimeter Acquisition Radar Characterization System (PARCS), which originally served Safeguard as an acquisition radar. The single-faced PARCS is rapidly approaching obsolescence, and will probably either be substantially modernized or replaced during the 1990s.

16

Arms Control

Reducing the number of nuclear weapons and ending the arms race between the United States and the Soviet Union are so critical to the survival of both nations that hundreds of books and articles have been written on the subject. It is not the purpose of this chapter to either duplicate or encapsulate those efforts. Rather, this chapter will first extend the argument, made by Graham Allison in 1974, that instead of being a simplistic action-reaction process between the U.S. and the USSR, the arms race is the result of extremely complex acts, the motivations for which are often internal. Following this general discussion, likely specific aspects of future arms control negotiations will be summarized.

Previous chapters in this book have described the internal and external motivations in both the United States and the NATO alliance for the production and deployment of nuclear weapons. They have also described the results of this production by noting the tremendous inventories of strategic weapons that have accumulated on both sides. The issues in this chapter concern how internal economic motivations have affected past attempts to achieve arms control, and how they are likely to shape future attempts to reduce the number of strategic weapons and eventually stop the arms race. The reader is notified in advance that no specific actions involving either the use of strategic weapon contracts to stimulate regional economies or a choice by Alliance partners of nuclear weapons to reduce defense costs can be directly linked to specific lost opportunities for arms control. However, it is important to recognize that these kinds of decisions have direct implications for the arms race that will make arms control easier or more difficult to achieve. Thus, achieving arms control may often be affected as much by internal issues as it is by external factors.

Deterrence and the Arms Race

The relationship between the concept of deterrence and the fact of the arms race is not easy to define. The arms race is quantifiable. Deterrence is not. The arms race has specific costs and less specific benefits, while the cost required to create a satisfactory level of deterrence is unknown and the main benefit of deterrence (peace, or at least, the absence of nuclear war) is quite apparent. The reason these two concepts are difficult to link together can best be found in the basic nature of deterrence itself. As Boulding has noted,

the international system is the major part of the total social system where threat predominates as a social organizer. . . . The international system is characterized primarily by deterrence (that is, a threat-counterthreat system). 'If you do something nasty to me, I will do something nasty to you.' . . . The main difficulty with the threat system is that it is most effective when the threats are not carried out (that is, when they are credible enough to influence behavior), but unless they are occasionally carried out they cease to be credible. The carrying out of a threat, though, is often more costly to the threatener than it is to the victim. This makes the whole economics of the threat system very peculiar.[1]

In addition, attempts to link deterrence directly to the arms race usually force one to view deterrence in terms of offensive destruction and to ignore defensive systems that could also reduce the risk of war.[2]

Thus, although both the strategic arms race and the efforts to achieve strategic arms control affect deterrence, the relationship is not direct. Instead, it is most satisfactorily viewed as a condition that results from changes in a 'perceived balance' of arms that arise from alterations of arms race and arms control variables. This is a critical point because only by changing variables that affect either the arms race or arms control can major structural changes in deterrence be realized. If one can adequately specify the major variables involved in producing or controlling arms, the 'perceived balance' that results in deterrence is easier to understand.

The Causes of the Arms Race

The arms race provides the need for arms control, and the basic tool for explaining the arms race has usually been an action-reaction hypothesis where Soviet or U.S. actions trigger reactions from the other side that, in turn, result in an endless chain of further responses. Secretary of Defense Robert McNamara discussed the elements of this philosophy in a 1967 speech:

What is essential to understand is that the Soviet Union and the United States mutually influence one another's strategic plans. Whatever be their intention, whatever be our intentions, actions—or even realistically potential actions— on either side relating to the build-up of nuclear forces, be they either offensive or defensive weapons, necessarily trigger reactions on the other side. It is precisely this action-reaction phenomenon that fuels the arms race.[3]

In *The Dynamics of the Arms Race,* George Rathjens expanded on the basic action-reaction hypothesis by adding the concept of uncertainty, noting that "action reaction phenomenon, stimulated in most cases by uncertainty about an adversary's intentions and capabilities, characterizes the dynamics of the arms race."[4] Among other causes, uncertainty about capabilities is a direct result of building the weapons that create nuclear deterrence because these weapons cannot be tested or displayed under realistic combat conditions. As previous chapters in this book have noted, it is these weapons—which lack both standards for success and specific quantity requirements—that are the ideal instruments for regional economic stimulation.

However, the action-reaction hypothesis is too simplistic to account for the fact that the lead times necessary to create new strategic weapons are extremely long, and the uncertainty associated with the process is very high because it stresses responses to what opponents *have done.* Clearly, to be prepared for the worst plausible case, the appropriate response is to react to what an opponent *might do.*[5] While this establishes a need to modify the basic arms race hypothesis to account for a more complicated set of conditions, it also acknowledges the existence of an environment that generates strategic weapons in response to uncertain military requirements—weapons whose construction is ideally suited for regional economic stimulation because the political support generated in those regions will be critical for the weapon's survival in the absence of specific military requirements.

After considering the complications to the simple arms race scenario, Graham Allison established the basic proposition that "the nature of the interaction between U.S. and Soviet strategic forces is extraordinarily more complex than the action-reaction hypothesis implies and . . . this interaction is currently not well understood by American officials and analysts."[6] Allison went on to note that a multitude of factors govern the decision to deploy a weapon, and a substantial number of these are driven by bureaucratic, political, and organizational elements. In particular, he noted that "the story . . . presented here suggests a picture of the arms race less as tightly coupled reactions to specific actions, and more as *a general competition in which motivation for particular actions is predominantly internal.* (Author's italics.)[7]

Previous chapters of this book have described many of these internal factors in detail and have demonstrated that they are often economic in nature. The end result, as Allison states it, is that "controlling strategic arms is harder than we usually think it is."[8]

Allison's proposition that the essential cause of an arms race is the interaction between the military programs of adversaries is all one must accept to create a causal link between the final difficulties in achieving arms control and initial attempts to stimulate a region's economy through pork barrel spending for weapons. As military programs are increased through attempts to funnel procurement funds to specific regions of the United States, this *internal* process generates additional weapons that stimulate the arms race. This is particularly true for strategic weapons because these programs are the instrument of choice for allocating defense funds to various regions in the United States. The expenditures to build these weapons, which arise from an internal decision to respond to political, bureaucratic, organizational or economic needs, are often defended by referring to external threats that have grown as the Soviets attempt to counter the systems that are being developed. A similar chain of events, that has its origin in internal Soviet decisions to build a system to satisfy political, bureaucratic or organizational needs, can just as easily be assumed, and it will result in an eventual response from the United States. The only difference between the two starting points is that there is no evidence that the Soviet Union constructs weapons to provide regional economic stimulation, and there is ample evidence that the United States does.

Viewing this process, Jerome Kahan wrote:

> Even within the nonrational framework of bureaucratic models, an interplay between U.S. and Soviet strategic postures exists. For one thing, organizations and officials pressing for programs that serve their narrow self-interests may use the adversary's programs and policies as arguments to strengthen their position—a pattern of action emphasized by advocates of the bureaucratic model approach. It is far more difficult for policymakers to succeed in controlling weapon programs that have gained technological or economic momentum if the programs can be justified as necessary to match or counter an adversary's program. Consequently, one nation's strategic programs—whether the outcome of rational debate or blind bureaucratic forces—can affect the weapon decision process in another nation and generate a series of arms buildups on both sides.[9]

Thus, in those instances where strategic weapons are built or retained in the armed forces primarily to assure the flow of federal money and jobs to one or more regions of the country, these programs must be viewed as internally motivated causes of the strategic arms race and, as such, as being in fundamental opposition to the goals of the U.S. arms control effort. This could imply that residents of regions whose economies depend on defense spending for strategic systems may either realize that opposing arms control is in their economic self-interest or recognize that the programs they seek to enhance their economic viability will weaken the prospects for arms control. However, it is more likely that residents of these regions have little or no understanding that the strategic weapon programs they seek could counter arms control efforts. In fact, since people generally recognize that arms control is desirable (in December, 1987, 80 percent of the general public favored arms control[10]), the failure to connect arms control and regional economic initiatives could account for actions on the part of the residents of these regions that seem irrational.

The Rationale for Arms Control

Three main reasons are generally cited for arms control:

1. Effective arms control should make nuclear war less likely.
2. Effective arms control would help to limit the damage should nuclear war occur.
3. Arms control should allow the major powers to reduce defense expenditures for strategic weapons.

These three reasons each offer long term benefits. However, the short-term rationale for arms control is usually much more mundane. Recent arms control efforts on the part of the United States have been attributed, in part, to President Reagan's desire to have his presidency viewed favorably by future historians. And the Soviets have been motivated by the need to reallocate scarce resources from defense uses to other areas in order to accomplish economic reforms.[11] Thus, internal motivations not only drive an important part of the arms race, they also play a large part in establishing a climate where arms control can succeed.

Beyond these generalizations, it is difficult to specify the benefits that are likely to flow from arms control. For example, the primary function of arms control negotiations is to remove sources of military instability. But if conventional weapon and manpower issues are not addressed, a greater level of instability may actually be created. And, due to the indirect link between arms control and deterrence, attempts to promote arms control may be harmed by weapon programs that enhance deterrence—as was the case when the cruise missile threatened arms control talks at the same time that it enhanced stability.[12]

As a result, there has been considerable skepticism on the part of many observers of the arms control movement about the usefulness of efforts to limit the numbers of arms. Sources of this skepticism are varied, but they provide a composite picture of the difficulties involved in maintaining both a satisfactory level of deterrence and an appropriate international presence while, at the same time, attempting to stop the arms race. Skepticism has generally been caused by:[13]

1. The evidence of both improvement and expansion of Soviet strategic forces in spite of statements by the Soviet leadership about their peaceful intentions.
2. The question of whether arms control agreements are possible with a regime as repressive as the Soviet regime.
3. The fact that while common assumptions about the use of nuclear weapons may be necessary to reach an agreement on their control, the Soviets do not seem to have the same assumptions as we do.
4. The fact that the U.S. appears to some to be less secure now than it was when arms control negotiations were first undertaken.
5. The evidence that while arms control negotiations may not only have failed to remedy some acute military problems in the NATO alliance, they may also have impeded their solution.
6. The feeling on the part of some that it is unwise to give up any control over the future of military plans and projects—even though arms control presumes some loss of control.
7. The problem of new technologies and weapons that constantly confound efforts to control arms.

For reasons such as these, after the approval of the INF treaty Senator Dan Quayle, the ranking Republican on the Senate Armed Services Committee, urged that

1. the agreement not set a verification precedent for strategic arms control.
2. future agreements should not limit NATO deployment of long-range air and sea launched non-nuclear deep strike weapons.
3. the agreement not serve as an excuse to avoid strengthening NATO's air defenses.[14]

In spite of these doubts, an arms control bureaucracy established during the Carter years remained firmly entrenched in the 1980s, surviving even the early period of the Reagan Administration when attitudes toward arms control ranged from benign neglect to outright hostility. In 1979, a National Security Affairs Conference identified four facets of modern arms control efforts that helped shape the policies of both the Carter and Reagan administrations and that will have a lasting effect on arms control in the future:[15]

1. Arms Control has become a permanent diplomatic institution.
2. Defense planning and arms control appear to proceed down disconnected tracks.

3. Arms control negotiations cause serious problems between U.S. government agencies if, as happened during the Carter Administration, the bureaucratic strength of the Arms Control and Disarmament Agency (ACDA) drives the Pentagon into a defensive posture.
4. Arms control is generally defined as a civilian process and as such, it often suffers from a lack of military participation.

The problems, limitations and doubts concerning arms control have made what would initially appear to be a universally desirable policy very susceptible to political manipulation by groups of various ideological persuasions. This, in turn, has resulted in a loss of central direction for the arms control effort and, as is likely to happen when a piecemeal approach is used to solve any complicated problem, it has created opportunities for doing everything from building to destroying weapons while claiming that each action has furthered the cause of limiting arms. Thus, internally motivated weapon systems such as the SDI and the MX missile can be claimed to advance the cause of arms control by "showing we are tough on defense" or because they "provide a bargaining chip" even though their most likely effect will be to further increase the arms race.

For example, Secretary of Defense Caspar Weinberger claimed in 1984 in reference to the SDI that

Not only can the Strategic Defense Initiative strengthen deterrence but it can also enhance the opportunity for arms reductions. Strategic defense can . . . enhance arms control by devaluing nuclear ballistic missiles, which will create powerful incentives for sharp reductions in their numbers—reductions that would enhance the security of the United States, its allies, and the Soviet Union.[16]

The counter to this view was that the SDI might prevent an arms limitations treaty primarily because it created suspicion that the U.S. was searching for a unilateral advantage in strategic weapons. This made an accumulation of Soviet arms likely as the USSR attempted to swamp the SDI.[17] In 1985 President Reagan added further weight to this concept by conceding that "If someone was developing such a defensive system and going to couple it with their own nuclear weapons yes, that could put them in a position where they might be more likely to dare a first strike."[18]

Very early in the development of the SDI it was reported that the Soviets were well aware of the schedule and economic implications of Star Wars and they thought the U.S. could probably succeed with the system. They also viewed it as an integral part of our first strike capability—something that one presumes would have made them likely to respond in some way. In addition, the Soviets had a history of fielding systems that were not yet operational and then perfecting them in the field.[19] The GALOSH missile defense system around Moscow is a good example of this, and it would clearly make the Soviets think that the U.S. might be doing the same thing with the SDI. In the logical conclusion of this chain of events, the Soviets claimed in March, 1985, that the SDI would cause them to build up their own arms and that this would be part of the "action and reaction which is well familiar to you."[20]

Arms Control and NATO Defense Planning

In addition to the problems with the control of strategic weapons, there are serious problems with arms control and tactical nuclear weapons in Europe. Since neither the U.S. nor its allies have a theory of theater nuclear force use in the European land battle, it is impossible to derive defensible military requirements for either nuclear or conventional weapons in any scenario that may require either a mix of both forces or a transition from one type of force to the other.[21] For this reason, the National Security Affairs Conference reached the conclusion that "NATO does not have an agreed vision of a nuclear land battle, which is one reason, a major reason, why it is extraordinarily difficult for NATO to decide upon its military requirements for theater nuclear forces—unlike the Soviet Union, for example."[22]

In addition, because neither the U.S. nor its allies have ever used nuclear weapons in a NATO tactical or theater mode, none of the allies has any experience or perspective on how these weapons will actually affect the course of a battle. The result is that no one knows exactly how many conventional forces have actually been replaced by nuclear weapons or, in the case of a decision not to use nuclear weapons, how many conventional forces would be required to compensate for their loss. This ambiguity has the effect of stymieing both disarmament negotiations and attempts to plan for disarmament, and again, it creates an environment where the requirements for weapons are so inexact that almost any system can be justified. As this book has already pointed out, such loose requirements are well suited for construction of a weapon whose primary purpose is regional economic stimulation.

The lack of planning for the use of nuclear arms in the European NATO region, coupled with the fact that the NATO countries do not want to make the transition to totally conventional forces because of the increased costs it would levy on them, has created a two-faced approach to arms control by the NATO allies. For example, after asking the U.S. to put the Pershing II missile in Europe, many of the Allies tried to appease their political parties on the left by claiming that the U.S. was not doing enough on arms control. However, when the U.S. came close to achieving an agreement with the

Soviet Union in Reykjavik in 1986, the NATO allies were almost universally opposed to the U.S. efforts.[23] This opposition clearly has its roots in factors that are primarily internal and generally economic in nature. These factors represented distinctly European concerns and hence, were not given enough weight by the U.S. negotiators to satisfy the NATO allies.

After Reykjavik, the allies took immediate steps to rectify this situation, and as the *Financial Times* of London noted, "as a result of the complaints by the European allies that Mr. Reagan did not take their interests sufficiently into account in Iceland, the Nato arms control negotiating stance has been clarified and refined to an unprecedented degree. *That is a factor which should prevent unwarranted illusions about what could be achieved at another summit.*"[24] (Author's italics.)

One obvious way for the Allies to solve the dilemma represented by the conflict between their internal desires to cut defense spending and the likely outcome of any broad agreement to limit nuclear weapons would be to engage the Soviets in Strategic Arms Reduction Talks (START) to limit conventional as well as nuclear arms. However, for some of the reasons already cited in this section, the Allies have been unable to agree on exactly what kind of imbalance currently exists in conventional forces between NATO and the Warsaw Pact.[25] Such a determination will obviously have to be made before any negotiations to alter force structure can be undertaken.

The use of sea and air launched cruise missiles has been suggested by a number of political leaders to establish a nuclear shield that would replace the forces lost in the INF agreement.[26] However, the fact that sea-launched cruise missiles may be better suited to a surprise attack than the intermediate range missile they replace[27] means that the underlying objective of arms control may once again be subverted by a chain of events that finds its origin in the internal economic interests of the allies.

The Likely Shape of Future Arms Control Negotiations

If significant reductions in strategic nuclear weapons are achieved, the composition of the remaining nuclear forces must be carefully crafted so that neither side can achieve a military advantage in launching a first strike. Ensuring the survivability of remaining weapons is crucial, so as to not create a 'use or lose' situation, i.e., during a crisis, neither side should have the incentive to launch vulnerable weapons before they are destroyed by the other side.

The main outline of a START agreement has already been publicly discussed by both sides. The treaty would limit strategic delivery vehicles (ballistic missiles, bombers, etc.) as well as nuclear warheads. From the U.S. point of view, a likely major achievement would be a reduction in the numbers of Soviet SS-18s, a silo-based missile that can carry up to 10

MIRVed warheads. The U.S. will also probably continue to press for reductions in Soviet multiple warhead rail-mobile ICBMs (SS-X-24s), although success in this endeavor will probably be limited. If the Soviets refuse to eliminate or at least reduce their rail-mobile SS-X-24s (up to 10 warheads) and road-mobile SS-25s (a single warhead missile), the U.S. will have strong incentives to deploy rail-mobile MXs and road-mobile Small ICBMs.

From the U.S. point of view, START negotiations will include discussions of the following topics:

1. Reductions in the number of multiple warhead missiles: Such reductions would be designed to encourage a shift toward single-warhead missiles, and to reduce the incentives of both countries to mount a first strike.
2. Deployment of single-warhead ground-mobile missiles: Mobile missiles are inherently more survivable than missiles deployed in fixed silos. Thus, the deployment of such missiles would tend to reduce the incentive for the other side to mount a first strike against a highly survivable mobile missile force.
3. Limits on sea-launched cruise missiles (SLCMs): These difficult-to-verify weapons are being deployed by both sides in submarines and surface ships. SLCMs can carry both conventional and nuclear warheads. Such missiles are not subject to any current arms control restrictions. However, the U.S. is likely to resist Soviet efforts to limit them, because of the U.S. technological lead and because SLCMs are a major weapon for U.S. power projection to various regions of the world.
4. Limits on missile modernization: Discussions with regard to testing new multiple warhead missiles and maneuvering warheads will likely take place. However, the U.S. will likely remain cool toward Soviet attempts to limit testing in technologies where the U.S. has the advantage.
5. An agreement to continue discussions: The initial START agreement will leave both superpowers with nuclear arsenals far exceeding the levels necessary for minimum deterrence. Both the United States and the Soviet Union are likely to agree to continued START discussions, with the objective of further reductions. A possible future scenario would involve reductions to a relatively low number of nuclear weapons, which could include ballistic missile defenses to make them highly survivable.

The Reagan Administration's aggressive pursuit of SDI has been a major element of the U.S. domestic debate on arms control and a cause of great concern on the part of the Soviet Union. For a while, the Soviets insisted on a mutual U.S.-Soviet commitment to continued adherence to the ABM Treaty as a precondition of the Strategic Arms Reduction Treaty (START), while the U.S. insisted on keeping a free hand to proceed with SDI. That the START negotiations are proceeding without such a public precondition on the part of the United States has taken some of the force out of the arguments of domestic SDI critics, who are now dwelling on the cost issue.

In 1985, the Reagan Administration announced that it was considering a new interpretation of the ABM Treaty. This new interpretation was designed to allow extensive testing of space-based ballistic missile defense weapons. If put into practice, critics say that such testing would in effect nullify the treaty. The Reagan Administration backed off from any immediate space-based testing to de-fuse the storm of criticism (both domestic and foreign) that resulted from the announcement. As a result, the decision on whether to test space-based SDI weapons such as Zenith Star (a space-based laser) was deferred to the Bush Administration.

Thus, the Bush Administration will have to deal with the issue of the ABM Treaty in conjunction with its decisions concerning the future of certain SDI programs. One possible approach would be to negotiate 'threshold limits' on various performance characteristics of potential space weapons. For example, limits could be placed on weapons that would restrict their effective use to anti-ballistic missile defense, i.e., they would not have the capability to attack ground-based facilities in either the United States or the Soviet Union. For example, such limits could eliminate the deployment of space-based weapons that carry nuclear warheads. While the U.S. would probably agree to certain limits on weapons capabilities, it would probably not accept limitations on space-based sensors, since they are not threats in themselves, and could have beneficial applications for surveillance and attack warning.

The U.S. is likely to be willing to negotiate limits on the deployment of anti-satellite weapons, which are not restricted by any current treaty. An agreement on such weapons would probably benefit the U.S. as much if not more than the Soviet Union, since the U.S. is much more dependent on space-based assets for communications, surveillance, attack warning, and attack assessment. However, the U.S. will probably push for an agreement that would allow both sides to continue research and to develop prototype anti-satellite systems.

The U.S. agenda for negotiations with the Soviets will include more than strategic weapons and SDI. Other topics will probably include conventional forces in Europe, nuclear proliferation, and strengthening bilateral and multilateral arms control institutions.

Talks on conventional forces in Europe will begin in 1989. These talks will cover NATO and Warsaw Pact forces from the Atlantic to the Urals. The U.S. delegation will participate with other NATO allies, including France, in discussions with all seven members of the Warsaw Pact. The U.S. can be expected to push for parity in ground forces at lower levels. Tanks, artillery, and troop numbers will be of particular interest, since the Warsaw

Pact has a numerical superiority in each of these areas. However, the Soviets can be expected to propose reductions in attack helicopters and certain naval forces, which are areas of NATO superiority.[28]

The Soviets will probably push for additional reductions in tactical nuclear weapons. However, the NATO allies will probably be reluctant to agree to reductions in addition to those agreed to under the INF treaty, without corresponding reductions in the Soviet conventional forces that tactical nuclear weapons are designed to counter.

On the other hand, the U.S. may be more flexible in this area than in previous years because of recent U.S. advances in precision-guided warheads. Such warheads are extremely accurate, and they permit the destruction of targets with conventional warheads that previously required nuclear warheads. If the U.S. desires to negotiate with the Soviets on this basis, it will have to convince its NATO allies that precision-guided conventional warheads are suitable substitutes for tactical nuclear warheads. Further, the U.S. may have to promise that the technologies for precision-guided warheads will be made available to its allies prior to any agreement with the Warsaw Pact. This approach would involve technology transfer issues in addition to force reduction issues.

In general, the Bush Administration can be expected to proceed cautiously with regard to further reductions in strategic and tactical nuclear weapons. Successes will probably be announced with regard to START, and possibly with regard to extensions or clarifications of the ABM Treaty. However, initiatives for additional arms reductions appear more likely to come from the the Soviet Union. This situation is clearly consistent with the goals of U.S. policy under the Reagan Administration, which include forcing the Soviet Union into a high technology competition that they can ill afford. Thus, from an economic standpoint, the Soviets have a greater incentive to negotiate than the United States.

However, the United States, the Soviet Union, the United Kingdom, France, and China all have an interest in extending the provisions of the Nuclear NonProliferation Treaty in 1995 and also promoting other treaties that inhibit the development or deployment of nuclear weapons by nations that do not now admit to having such weapons. The United States can also be expected to continue its efforts to strengthen existing treaties that prohibit the transfer of nuclear weapons technologies. In spite of U.S. rhetoric concerning the capabilities of the United Nations, one approach would be for the U.S. to attempt to strengthen the position of the International Atomic Energy Agency (IAEA). The U.S. can also be expected to push for limitations on the availability of relatively cheap delivery systems, such as short and medium range missiles with nuclear warhead capabilities.

Whether or not the U.S. is successful in these efforts will depend to a large extent on whether or not it can convince its allies not to sell nuclear power generation plants and other nuclear materials when it becomes clear that these items may be used to further the development of nuclear warheads. However, the U.S. has not been very successful in its previous efforts to reduce the worldwide trade in nuclear materials, and there is little reason to expect that it will be successful in the future, at least in the short term. External factors will probably continue to drive the development of further restrictions in this area. Events that might galvanize world opinion to support new or more stringent treaties could include the explosion of a nuclear device by South Africa, Israel, Pakistan, or some other near-nuclear nation.

Conclusion

This chapter has demonstrated that the internal motivations for the arms race and for opposing certain aspects of arms control are sufficiently strong that they cannot be ignored in either the United States or Europe when arms control agreements are sought. However, since the goals of the groups who have these motivations are so different from those whose objective is arms control, it is not clear that one can sufficiently overcome the objections of the internally motivated group without either offering substitute programs for those that are lost through arms control or, in the case of the European allies, providing some method of reducing the cost of conventional forces to a level that corresponds with budget realities for those countries.

Dealing with the internal motivations of the European allies requires the recognition that because the allies are unlikely to change their funding levels to any significant degree, either the United States will have to supply the additional conventional forces required after a strategic arms limitation treaty or an agreement to limit conventional forces will have to be negotiated at the same time that further limitations to the number of strategic weapons are pursued. Constraints on the U.S. defense budget make the latter alternative the only acceptable course of action, and this means that in the future, failure to generate a conventional arms agreement with the Soviets is likely to result in the concurrent failure of strategic arms talks.

For those objections to arms control that primarily concern regional economic interests, it is important to remember that building strategic weapons only to destroy them later (the case of the INF) has much different implications for regional economic stimulation, for the defense budget, and for the defense industrial base than does outlawing a class of weapons before it is built—as might be the case with the certain elements of the SDI, nerve gasses and biological warfare. There is a fundamental contradiction between trying to keep the defense industrial base strong and diversified and then not building a weapon or a class of weapon systems because such an arms control decision not only removes the weapon, it removes the capability to build it at any time in the future. However, this decision also never allows the weapon to become established as an economic necessity in a region and thus it avoids the inertia that builds around a system that has a major regional presence. On the other hand, if a weapon is built and then destroyed later, not only is it possible to use the weapon for regional economic stimulation during its construction, it is also possible to have a substantial capability to rebuild the weapon in the future if that is required. In this case, the economic inertia in the region that builds the weapon may become so large that cancelling the system is extremely difficult.

There are two alternatives that have an excellent potential for use as substitutes for strategic weapon construction programs in such a situation. If the system to be cancelled has large numbers of delivery vehicles whose construction is economically important to a region, it is possible that the defense facilities located there could be converted to conventional weapon production. This would probably require retooling, but it would also allow the production facility to continue to produce the same generic product, and it probably would still be able to satisfy some requirements of the defense industrial base. Such a production shift is much more likely to succeed than an attempt to convert the facility to some type of civilian production. Alternatively, if the regional defense production that needs to be replaced involves the manufacture of nuclear weapons, only converting the production site to hazardous waste management has the potential to overcome some of the regional economic concerns. However, such a conversion should preserve most of the jobs and economic input in the region.

In either case, it should be possible to adequately address economic concerns that form important internal motivations for strategic weapon production and, in so doing, to allow a reasonable arms control effort to proceed with as much support as possible.

Notes

1. Boulding, Kenneth E., "The Deadly Industry: War and the International System," in *Peace and the War Industry,* Kenneth E. Boulding, ed., Aldine Publishing Company, 1970, 10–11.

2. Wallcott, John, "Approach to Arms Control Combines Missile Reductions, Work on Defense," *The Wall Street Journal,* October 20, 1986, 28.

3. McNamara, Robert, An Address to the Publishers and Editors of United Press International, reprinted in *Department of State Bulletin,* October 9, 1967, 443–451.

4. Rathgens, George, "The Dynamics of the Arms Race," *Scientific American,* April, 1969, 24.

5. Allison, Graham T., "What Fuels the Arms Race?" in *Contrasting Approaches to Strategic Arms Control,* Robert L. Pfaltzgraff, ed., Lexington Books, D.C. Heath and Company, 1974., reprinted in Chapter 5, *Arms Control: The Cooperative Pursuit of Security,* Pergammon Press, New York, N.Y., 1985, 465–466.

6. Ibid., 463.

7. Ibid., 474.

8. Ibid., 475.

9. Kahan, Jerome, *Security in the Nuclear Age: Developing U.S. Strategic Arms Policy,* The Brookings Institution, Washington, D.C., 1975, reprinted in Chapter 5, *Arms Control: The Cooperative Pursuit of Security,* Pergammon Press, New York, N.Y., 1985, 395.

10. Seib, Gerald F., "Arms-Treaty Backers Fear Senate Changes, Not Outright Defeat," *The Wall Street Journal,* December 9, 1987, 1.

11. "The prospect for arms talks," *Financial Times,* London, December 29, 1986.

12. Burt, Richard, "Defense Policy and Arms Control," in *Continuity and Change in the Eighties and Beyond,* Proceedings of the National Security Affairs Conference, National Defense University, Washington, D.C., 23–25 July, 1979, 16–18.

13. "Introductory Essay," *Arms Control: The Cooperative Pursuit of Security,* Pergammon Press, New York, N.Y., 1985, 384–392.

14. Quayle, Dan, "After INF Treaty, Avoid These Things," *Defense News,* October 26, 1987, 24.

15. *Continuity and Change in the Eighties and Beyond,* 5–7.

16. Weinberger, Caspar, Remarks to the Town Hall of California, Los Angeles, California, October 24, 1984.

17. "Panel: 'Star Wars' prevents arms pact," *The Gazette Telegraph,* Colorado Springs, Colorado, November 27, 1984, 2.

18. Earle, Ralph, "Summit Big on Image, Not Substance," *Defense News,* June 13, 1988, 36.

19. Judge, John F., "The Strategic Defense Initiative and Arms Control," *Defense Electronics,* March, 1985, 96–101.

20. Oberdorfer, Don, and Pincus, Walter, "'Star Wars' Will Trigger Arms Buildup, Soviet Warns," *Washington Post,* March 6, 1985, 1.

21. *Continuity and Change in the Eighties and Beyond,* 8.

22. Ibid., 9.

23. "Europe vs. Arms Control," *The Wall Street Journal,* October 24, 1986, 24.

24. "The prospect for arms talks."

25. Pohling-Brown, Pamela, "NATO Faces Choice Between Conventional, Nuclear Reduction Focus," *Defense News,* December 7, 1987, 10.

26. Adams, Peter, "Nunn: U.S. Must Keep Longer Range Missiles," *Defense News,* May 23, 1988, 1–36.

27. "Slickums," *Scientific American,* June, 1988, 20.

28. Union of Concerned Scientists, *Presidential Priorities,* 1988, 25–33.

17

Finding Strategies to Deal with the Nuclear Weapon Dilemma

Defining the Problem

In many ways, nuclear weapons have begun to outlive their time and place in U.S. strategy. Other weapons have experienced this phenomena, but nuclear arms have spawned both a mindset and a dedicated production sector that will make their passage from the U.S. arms inventory particularly difficult and prolonged. For this reason, the inevitable movement of the U.S. and other countries beyond nuclear deterrence will be a painful and tumultuous experience, accompanied by problems that can only be overcome if policy makers and citizens alike understand the factors that led to the present world situation.

It is important to remember that the U.S. did not start out to use nuclear weapons in a deterrent role. The United States resorted to the use of nuclear weapons at a time when its leaders felt that other alternatives for defeating Japan carried an unacceptably high price in U.S. lives. Thus, the age of nuclear weapons was born out of a desire to end a conflict that the U.S. had not initiated—and to end it with as little loss of U.S. life as possible. While the U.S. decision to trade the lives of Japanese civilians for those of American military personnel in such an indiscriminate manner will be debated for centuries to come, there is no question that this decision had unintended consequences. Had these been fully understood, they might have altered that first decision to use nuclear weapons.

The same factors that allowed nuclear weapons to function in their initial role became the rationale for their use as a deterrent. They were terrible, indiscriminate weapons that would cause any adversary to carefully weigh the costs of military adventures and, as a pleasant coincidence, their huge destructive power fitted nicely with the inaccuracy of the weapons systems that would deliver them. Through it all, there is only one indisputable fact about the period of nuclear deterrence—it worked. There was no armed conflict between the major powers while nuclear deterrence was the national policy of the U.S. and the Soviet Union.

However, as increasingly rapid, accurate and efficient methods were developed to deliver nuclear weapons, the condition that had dominated the first decision to use these arms—the agonizing, careful decision to employ the weapon—became less and less possible. By the 1970s the U.S. and the Soviet Union found themselves in a position where the use of nuclear weapons was becoming almost automatic. Both countries soon found this condition to be untenable.

In the 1970s the U.S. and the Soviet Union, as well as the NATO allies, began to encounter an additional problem. This was the rising cost of weapons, a cost that accelerated as the technological level of arms increased. These costs make it more difficult for every country to maintain armed forces, but they have affected various countries in differing ways with respect to the use of nuclear weapons. For some, rising defense costs have made nuclear weapons a more desirable alternative because of the relative cheapness of these weapons when they are compared to similar amounts of conventional forces. For others, rising costs of maintaining the technology inherent in advanced strategic nuclear weapons have provided an additional reason to reduce the number of nuclear arms.

While the growing accuracy of conventional munitions and the present movement by the U.S. and the Soviet Union toward limited nuclear disarmament both indicate that nuclear weapons are slowly becoming obsolete, the question of how to safely disengage from the current reliance on these arms remains. It is at this juncture that the demand and incentives for— and alternatives to—nuclear weapons discussed in this book become important. Moving beyond deterrence must start *within* the United States and the Soviet Union, not as an externally generated agreement between the two states. To facilitate this process, the following steps are suggested.

First, it should be recognized that the accumulation of nuclear arms is a symptom, not a cause of the fundamental defense problems faced by the US. Recent cuts in the U.S. budget have emphasized the problems this country faces when allocating resources to the strategic and non-nuclear elements of defense. In addition, these problems have been worsened by past allocative decisions, and they indicate that the United States must develop a 'grand strategy' that will allow all aspects of economic and defense strength to be used as efficiently as possible in the defense of the nation.

One way to approach these problems is to start from the premises that the U.S. cannot adequately predict the future for specific, long range military or economic planning, and that the U.S. economy contains mechanisms to allocate resources to every national priority in the most efficient way. This implies a need for a flexible and diversified economy to support future defense requirements, and leads one to consider the factors that affect the ability of the U.S. economy to efficiently allocate national resources. This ability depends directly on the constraints placed on the economic allocation process. Unless constraints are realistic, resource allocations are altered in a perverse way and reasonable economic tradeoffs are impossible.

If reasonable constraints are used when the U.S. allocates resources to each sector of the economy, it should be possible to develop a national strategy that will allow the economy to be a major factor in the defense of the nation.[1] If, instead, perverse constraints preclude legitimate allocation of resources to some sectors of the economy, the result will be a weakened, less flexible economy that supports neither defense nor non-defense requirements.

Economic Strategies

Economic strategies determine the various ways in which national resources can be used and thus, they link economic and military objectives. In this sense, economic policy is defense policy. The reasons the U.S. builds weapons the way it does, and our decisions to use either nuclear or non-nuclear weapons, preclude certain strategies to allocate resources to defense.[2] In addition, the difficulty of accurately forecasting future events makes developing specific long and short-term economic strategies an exercise in futility.

This puts a premium on maintaining a flexible, powerful economy that allows the United States to quickly change course to take advantage of new developments. The objective of a comprehensive national defense strategy must be to make the economy an effective instrument of any *likely* defense requirement. This can occur in two modes:

- An active mode where economic policy is used as a weapon. Such strategies involve sanctions, economic warfare, import and export restrictions, asset freezes, and other means of exerting economic pressure. Only buying (importing) and financial power are required to implement these strategies, but such uses of economic power have generally been ineffective because they lacked the support of allies or other exporters.[3] In the past, active economic policies have often further alienated the target country and isolated that country's economy from American influence.
- A passive mode where the economy provides a support structure for defense efforts. This mode offers the indigenous ability to serve a diverse set of defense needs where:
  1. research, scientific, and engineering ability must be available upon demand.
  2. industrial capacity must be able to serve current defense production requirements.

3. productive capacity must be available in the specialty, normal, and surge modes required to support the defense establishment in each of its likely future roles.
4. funds must be generated to support both defense and those assistance and investment requirements that can decrease the need for defense.

Developing and maintaining these capabilities may compete with other defense requirements for national resources. In addition, there is often no clear choice between defense and non-defense spending because decisions to build or preserve an economic base to support defense may affect both areas. For example, a decision to strengthen the general economy may provide future flexibility and capacity in all sectors. As such, this decision represents a choice with long run implications for both defense and non-defense capabilities.

Resource Allocation Problems Associated with Defense Spending for Nuclear Weapons

There are several obvious connections between the strength of the economy and the defense of the nation. First, the economy provides the productive base for the manufacture of defense goods. Second, the economy generates taxes that provide funds for defense. And third, the economy provides a foundation of technology upon which future defense efforts depend.

Ideally, defense spending should follow a realistic and comprehensive defense strategy. Competing projects should be evaluated by how they contribute to the strategy, and money should be allocated accordingly. However, this is possible only when spending priorities are defined. Spending on nuclear weapons only to show a 'commitment' to some political entity such as NATO, or to provide economic support to some region of the United States, provides little indication of priorities. Similarly, assuming a Soviet threat so large that any amount of spending is justified renders priorities useless and generates a strategy that requires an infinite amount of resources.

The objective of an optimal resource allocation strategy is to balance resource allocations between nuclear and non-nuclear uses within the defense establishment and, in a larger context, between defense and non-defense uses. Since perfection is impossible, the actual allocative process will always be degraded to some degree, with the output of the process altered more or less substantially depending on the constraints that are applied. If these constraints are perverse, resource allocations will also be perverse. Thus, the constraints themselves must be the primary focus of any debate about resource allocation.

Constraints generated by the political nature of the allocation process usually reflect short-term objectives. In fact, it is commonly claimed that short-term needs are so pressing that resource allocations cannot be altered to achieve long range objectives. However, this does not justify short range allocations that degrade long range prospects. A strong economy will provide the flexibility to allow a transition from cheaper nuclear weapons to more expensive conventional forces without creating immediate hardships on the general population. While the U.S. should always pay for defense as it is used, in a strong economy this transition could be made with limited impact on the allocation of other resources.

Constructing Economic Strategies
That Can Support Likely Future Requirements
for Nuclear and Non-Nuclear Forces

The variability of the environment in which defense operates prohibits a single strategy to maximize the effectiveness of long and short term defense efforts. However, efficient economic strategies for a variety of defense scenarios can still be developed, and the economy will allocate resources efficiently to both defense and non-defense needs if reasonable constraints are used in the allocation process.

What measure should determine the 'reasonableness' of economic constraints? As a general rule, a constraint that preemptively rules out resource allocation to some defense or non-defense use is unreasonable because such a constraint makes cost benefit analysis meaningless.[4] When reasonable constraints allow all possible solutions to a problem to be considered, and when defense spending competes with non-defense spending in a process that recognizes the true costs and benefits of each, the resulting allocation will be in the best interests of both the economy and the defense effort.

When resources allocations are made in such a manner, the remainder of the allocative process becomes relevant. Short-term costs and benefits to the economy and to defense may now be compared to long term costs and benefits, and allocative decisions can contribute to both long and short term strengths. An efficient allocation of resources can then be made at each of the three levels of the decision process. Each step is possible if the economy accurately weighs the economic tradeoffs between nuclear and non-nuclear defense spending and the more general split between defense and non-defense spending.

To accurately reflect the tradeoff between these differing allocations, the nation must pay for defense when defense is purchased and it must reduce the consumption of non-defense goods, if necessary, to free increased resources for defense. The consumption sacrifice necessary to attain a given level of defense spending is directly related to the strength and capability of the economy. It is therefore obvious that a strong economy will make the decisions involved with any level of defense spending easier.

General Policies to Reduce the Need
for Nuclear Weapons

U.S. policy should stress stability in both a national and an international context as well as a slow, continued improvement in economic growth. This can be accomplished through two broad categories of strategies:

1. *National strategies that have favorable international economic effects.* These include a reduction of the U.S. national debt to put less pressure on international interest rates, continued efforts to fight any form of trade protectionism, the pursuit of policies that assure a reliable flow of energy resources from Southwest Asia, and the continued protection of world sea lanes to ensure the safe transit of trade.
2. *National strategies for aid and assistance.* On a bilateral basis, these strategies promote technology transfer to industrialized countries and technical assistance to the LDCs, the use of offsets and countertrade to build local industrial capabilities, adherence to the two-way street in arms deals with NATO, cooperative weapon development programs with our industrialized allies and coproduction programs designed to accommodate the varying needs of participants, security assistance to maintain stability in the LDCs, economic assistance to those allies where the marginal effect of such aid will be the greatest, and efforts to foster private investment in LDCs through incentives and insurance for the risk involved. On a multilateral basis these strategies include the support and use of the IMF and World Bank Facilities to enhance currency stability and to provide financial assistance, the support of those Regional Development Banks that operate effectively, and the support of interest rate reductions and easier terms on international debt held by LDCs.

Most of these strategies represent small dollar programs with potentially high marginal benefits. Each contributes to international economic growth and stability at a cost that is relatively small compared to the military expenditure required to counter the threat created if growth and stability are not present.

Strategies for Redirecting Defense Spending
to Provide Additional Efficiency and
a Reduced Use of Nuclear Weapons

Redirecting defense spending within an austere budget will require a careful rethinking of constraints applied to past resource allocations to defense. A review of the logic behind the defense budget cuts that started in 1987 indicates that this has not happened. As retired Admiral James Watkins noted, "too many people are getting strategy and tactical deployment of forces mixed up" in attempts to reduce the budget.[5] Defense spending must reflect a strategy that maximizes both economic and military strength at the lowest possible cost. Such a strategy will not result unless the Department of Defense prioritizes all military programs, independent of the service to which they belong, to ensure that every program funded by a service is more critical than *any* program that is cut. In addition, the following alternatives should be considered.

Get Help from U.S. Allies

The NATO allies have always differed from U.S. views on spending for defense and social needs. This view diverged even further from the U.S. over the last ten years, and while the U.S. spent 7.4 percent of its GDP on defense in 1986 and Great Britain spent 5.2 percent the remainder of the NATO allies and Japan only spent from 1.0 percent to 3.4 percent of their GDPs on defense.[6] The unwillingness of these countries to increase their defense spending is due, in part, to a shortage of discretionary funds for defense.[7] This shortage, when coupled with the allies' nondefense spending priorities, created the depressed defense spending evident in the 1980s.

How the burden of defense is divided between the allies is an issue that complicates possible reallocations of resources between nuclear and non-nuclear forces. As long as the United States provides nuclear deterrence to subsidize allied defenses, the allies have less incentive to share the expenses of defending NATO. This would not be troublesome if our allies made the same spending choices we made. But when the United States sacrifices social spending objectives to maintain its presence overseas, and when our allies continue to spend proportionately more for social programs, areas of unequal support in our alliances present opportunities to redirect our resources.

In NATO, cuts in nuclear forces by the United States are likely to increase the cost of defense. This could further strain the alliance unless an acceptable way of providing some tangible evidence of a U.S. commitment to NATO can be demonstrated. The cheapest way to show this commitment is to leave U.S. troops in Europe while cutting other expenses as much as possible. In Japan, where the barrier to defense spending is more psychological, Japan should pick up part of U.S. aid and assistance to the LDCs in return for continued U.S. involvement in its defense.

Reduce the Worldwide Defense Commitments
of the United States

There is strong evidence that the United States could defend its essential security with fewer forces. Unfortunately, comparisons between commitments and forces are meaningless unless the commitments are subject to a process that evaluates the impact of each additional commitment on other defense and nondefense goals. Thus, although a reduced U.S. force structure could probably serve U.S. commitments adequately, a firm statement of our national strategy and an analysis of the economic, political and defense impact of reduced or altered commitments would be necessary before reallocations between nuclear and non-nuclear forces are possible.

Cut and Stretch the Procurement of Defense Systems

This approach was suggested by William Kauffman in 1984, and some of Kauffman's cuts, along with many others developed by the Department of Defense, were employed in the FY1988 and FY1989 budget reductions.[8] However, Kauffman's suggestions clearly demonstrated the weaknesses that arise from a failure to adequately consider the marginal benefits from alternative resource allocations. For example, Kauffman concentrated so heavily on strategic systems that many felt he 'gutted' the strategic forces— and he did so without providing a clear picture of the the conventional forces that might be required to replace the decreased strategic forces.

Unfortunately, most 1988 budget reduction measures taken by the Department of Defense, particularly in the area of manpower reductions and across-the-board cuts, also appear to suffer from a failure to consider marginal costs and benefits. In fact, most of these reductions will make it more difficult to redirect US forces from nuclear to non-nuclear status. Neither Kauffman's suggestions nor the cuts employed by the Department of Defense were guided by a statement of comprehensive national strategy. As a result, it is difficult to guess how full implementation of either the actual or proposed cuts will affect defense and non-defense sectors.

Reduce Defense Waste, Fraud and Abuse

Reducing the amount of defense money wasted on shoddy military goods, lack of coordination between the armed services, and general malfeasance in government and defense industries will be essential when restricted future defense funds must support more expensive non-nuclear forces. Savings may result from greater competition for defense contracts, and from a reduction in the use of defense contracts for regional economic gain. However, if all problems associated with waste, fraud and abuse are corrected, only a small amount of additional resources will be realized.

More important will be efforts to assure that fraudulent contracting, coupled with political pressure, does not prevent resources from being redirected to new, non-nuclear defense systems. Waste and coordination problems can be solved whether or not a cohesive national defense strategy is developed, but a critical issue remains: it does no good to produce a weapon as cheaply as possible if that weapon is not needed in the first place. The lack of a cohesive strategy will ensure that political pressure continues to result in suboptimal weapon choices.

Freeze or Cap the Defense Budget

These actions portray the most likely future for the defense budget in the 1990s. By limiting the amount available for defense, they may force the Department of Defense to allocate its remaining funds more efficiently. However, a common response to a freeze or cap is to apply it to each budget element. This completely subverts the tradeoffs that must be made when an organization is restructuring its force composition during a period of tight budgets. Thus, freezing or capping will allocate defense funds appropriately only if one assumes that the Department of Defense can efficiently allocate its own resources. And this presumes that the DoD is in receipt of unambiguous and reasonable instructions from the Executive branch concerning the makeup and use of defense forces.

Cut Operations, Maintenance and Personnel Costs

These cuts were proposed in November, 1988 by former Undersecretary of Defense Fred Iklé. They are attractive because they are felt immediately, they preserve inventories of weapons (although, with reduced maintenance, the condition of those inventories is open to question), and they do not affect weapon programs that transfer large amounts of money and jobs into the Congressional districts. However, cuts in operations, maintenance and personnel have disastrous effects if they occur without the guidance of a national strategy. For example, recent manpower cuts have been taken in the face of a proposed Intermediate Nuclear Forces agreement that will almost certainly result in a requirement for increased conventional forces. And cutting operations and maintenance funds will degrade the ability of the remaining conventional military forces to operate effectively.

Mechanisms

The efficient allocation of national resources is too important to be left to the partisan processes that have increasingly dominated the last thirty years. Many years ago, a similar realization regarding the management of the nation's currency was partially responsible for the creation of the Federal Reserve System. The Federal Reserve Board, which has its own budget, consults with Congress and is legally independent of the executive branch of government. While the significance of the Federal Reserve's independence should not be exaggerated,[9] perhaps an organization similar to the Fed could form a high-level, non-partisan group that evaluates how the entire U.S.

stock of resources can be used most efficiently to enhance our national strength and long term viability.

Such a plan would still allow the Department of Defense to make the lower level allocation decisions that it is best qualified to handle. But it would place the general resource allocations now made by the Congress and the President in the hands of an impartial office whose only charter was to use national resources as efficiently as possible. This office should not prohibit a President from making defense decisions as the Commander in Chief. Instead, it should define the defense and non-defense resources available to the President, and it should clearly describe the additional short and long run costs associated with using those resources in other than an efficient manner.

Conclusion

During the 1980s, defense spending for both strategic and conventional weapons increased dramatically, Social Security and Medicare spending also increased, and most other government programs received decreased funding. During this same period, net interest on government debt more than doubled. Among these spending categories, defense was different in one major respect: money was spent for defense in response to a *perceived* military threat to the United States. This perception was held, in different forms, by a majority of the people in the United States in 1980. But public support for defense spending has eroded continuously from its high point in January, 1981, and budget problems have multiplied.

The erosion of public support can be linked to an ambivalence about defense spending that stems from an inability to connect the resources committed to defense to clear national goals. This has been particulary evident in the area of spending for strategic systems and it has recently become a major factor in the criticisms of spending for strategic defense. The Department of Defense now finds itself locked into long term contracts for the purchase of major weapon systems while it is forced to cut increasingly important operations and maintenance functions. This situation emphasizes the importance of restructuring defense spending to avoid the boom and bust cycles of the last twenty years. To accomplish this, resources allocated to defense must be better balanced between investment and operations, and decisions to use U.S. national resources for defense or non-defense purposes must clearly reflect the needs of the entire nation.

This means that hard allocative decisions must be made when resources are spent for either defense or non-defense goods. These decisions must not be delayed, abrogated in favor of political gains, or subverted by unrealistic assessments of needs and threats. In the case of national defense, the surest way to accomplish this is to pay, with decreased consumption, for defense when it is purchased.

Notes

1. Reasonable constraints make the tradeoffs inherent in defense spending apparent by lowering consumption to pay for defense when defense is purchased. For example, war bonds perform this function while also alerting the holders of the bonds to the eventual requirement that they be redeemed. Even though defense purchases that are financed through a general expansion of the national debt must also be repaid in the future, a comparable reduction in consumption does not occur, and the requirement for repayment of the debt is not as apparent.

2. These reasons create U.S. requirements for accuracy and operator survivability based on technological advantage. See Weida, W.J., and Gertcher, F.L., "Military Weapon Systems Expenditures and Risk: Theory and Evidence," *International Journal of Social Economics,* London, August, 1982.

3. An obvious exception was the use of U.S. economic power instead of military power to attempt to unseat General Noriega of Panama in March, 1988. However, this was possible only because of Panama's almost total dependence on the U.S. financial sector and even then, the effort failed.

4. For example, unreasonable constraints would include a) assigning an infinite value to the Soviet threat, b) assuming complete and total disarmament in the current world environment, c) spending for either defense or non-defense to show commitment, i.e., in a manner where only the amounts spent, not the results achieved, are important.

5. Starr, Barbara and Adams, Peter, "Deficit Reduction Deal Looms Large Over Pentagon, Its Budget," *Defense News,* Vol. 3, No. 7, February 15, 1988.

6. Nelson, Mark M., "Cash-Strapped NATO Members Grapple With Waste," *Wall Street Journal,* August 6, 1987 and International Institute for Strategic Studies and OECD estimates.

7. Chase Econometrics Conference, Mayflower Hotel, Washington, D.C., September 18, 1984.

8. Kauffman, William W., "Spending for a Sound Defense: Alternatives to the Reagan Military Budget," *The Committee for National Security,* March 22, 1984.

9. Buchanan, James M., "Easy Budgets and Tight Money," *Lloyds Bank Review,* April, 1962, 17–30.

APPENDIX 1:
The Case of Defense Spending
in Colorado Springs, Colorado

The reasons that a community chooses to make its economy more dependent on military spending are never simple or well defined. While each attempt to secure federal funding is usually viewed as an isolated, often opportunistic occurrence, there are usually deeply rooted structural reasons for a decision to use defense spending the boost the economy of a region. These reasons are normally of two general types: a) those arising from economic weaknesses that have existed since the inception of the specific regional economy and b) those that have arisen more recently because of changing economic or technological conditions.

More specifically, a region's economy may become dependent on military spending if the industries in the region are suppliers to the military and if the military takes such a large percentage of the output of these industries that they would have difficulty compensating for a cutback in military spending. In such a case, the *internal*[1] economy of the region may be well developed, but its narrow focus on military goods leaves it susceptible to external spending shifts. The regions that host the aerospace industries in California are an example of this situation.

A region's economy may also become dependent on military spending if the region has never developed an internal economy or if the industries on which the region once relied for its internal economy have failed. In either case, the result of the federal (defense) spending on such a region is to provide an external source of economic stimulation that supplants the internal economy. The following case studies a community that typifies this situation. It demonstrates the difficulties that are encountered when, due to a change in defense strategy, such a community has to be 'weaned away' from a major source of its economic strength—particularly if the lack of economic alternatives that originally motivated that community to use defense spending to boost its economy still persists.

Background and History

Colorado Springs, Colorado, started its existence in 1870 as a fairly typical western town. Its founders hoped that Colorado Springs would be a successful land development, but when enough customers did not show up, the organizers of the little community began to actively cultivate the early tourist trade. In this endeavor, Colorado Springs had definite advantages—beautiful scenery, mild climate, and low humidity. The latter attribute made the town a natural location for tuberculosis sanitariums, and these, coupled with a growing tourist trade and a small amount of agriculture formed the basis of Colorado Springs' economy. As the city grew, Colorado Springs also served as a local financial center for some of the mining and railroad construction that accompanied the gold rush in the Rocky Mountains.

While its location made Colorado Springs ideal for tourists, it proved to be a negative factor in the development of a strong local economy. Fifty miles to the north, Denver was already a economic center when Colorado Springs was founded. As the main departure point for people going to the mining communities in the mountains, and as the reception point for the products of those mines, Denver developed a large number of finished goods industries that served the needs of a region that stretched from Salt Lake City, Utah, to Albuquerque, New Mexico. Pueblo, Colorado, fifty miles south of Colorado Springs, became the center for coal and steel production because it was located close to the coal mines of Huerfano County. Colorado Springs, whose needs for both semi-finished and finished goods were satisfied by its neighbors to the north and south, developed no industrial base.

As the years passed, Colorado Springs gradually lost the tuberculosis sanitarium business to advances in medicine, and Colorado mining dried up as demand dropped and the mines played out. The city did not develop an internal economy to replace these sectors, relying instead on growth in tourism and agriculture and a slow but steady stream of new citizens to keep it afloat. Thus, the economic base of the community stagnated until the start of World War II.

Using Spending for Conventional Military Forces to Spur Regional Growth

By 1940, WWII was causing a major exodus from the Pikes Peak region as residents left to take high paying jobs in defense industries. Without an industrial base of its own, Colorado Springs could not participate in this booming wartime economy. Hundreds of homes were on the market at a fraction of their real value, and many businesses were boarded up in the downtown area.[2] Civic leaders, who were searching for a way to stop the economic and human losses the community was experiencing, realized that Colorado Springs had a resource that would be ideal for military training in the huge parcels of poor land surrounding the city.

Thus, in 1940 Colorado Springs set out to try to persuade the Congress and the Defense Department to build the first military installation in the region. In an effort that would become a model for many future attempts to secure military spending, Colorado Springs acquired 35,000 acres of land that it offered to the U.S. Government as a home for the proposed facility, and it dispatched two leading citizens to lobby Congress for a small ($1 million) Army base.[3] The city was successful beyond its wildest dreams, and in 1941 the Army announced that it would spend $30 million to build Camp Carson (later to become Fort Carson) as a home for the 30,000 men of the 89th Division.[4]

The economic impact of this decision on Colorado Springs (whose population was only 35,000 in 1941) was huge. This impact was further magnified when, in 1948, the Air Force created Peterson Field—a small, but fairly stable Air Force installation on the eastern edge of the city. By 1949, military payrolls at the two installations resulted in a direct injection of $5 million per month into the economy of Colorado Springs.[5]

Colorado Springs found its new military installations to be such an excellent source of external funding that there was little reason to worry about its continuing failure to develop an internal economy. In addition, the bases provided a degree of economic stability and a potential for economic growth that the community had never known in the past. Meanwhile, the military people stationed in Colorado Springs were usually impressed by the little community and its climate, and they began to retire in Colorado Springs in increasing numbers.

In 1950, the Congressional action that had separated the Air Force from the Army had created a requirement for a new military academy. At an estimated price of $200 million, the new Air Force Academy was actively sought by four hundred cities in 44 states and, almost on a whim, Colorado Springs joined in the competition.[6] However, Colorado Spring's efforts quickly intensified as community leaders recognized the potential economic impact of the new academy.

The national search for a location for the Academy was narrowed to three sites, one of which was just outside Colorado Springs. As had been done in the case of Fort Carson, Colorado Springs civic leaders combined active lobbying with a proposal that included an offer of over 17,500 acres of land along the base of the Rampart Range. This proposal, coupled with the region's excellent flying weather (flying was presumed to be a major part of the new academy's curriculum) and the community's favorable attitude toward military people carried the day. On June 24, 1954, it was announced that the academy would be built outside Colorado Springs, and by 1958 the first cadets moved into the new facilities.[7] Colorado Springs had gained another dependable source of external funding that further substituted for an internally developed economy.

About the same time as the Air Force Academy started in Colorado Springs, the North American Air Defense Command (NORAD) was formed from the old Air Defense Command and a similar group of Canadian resources. This new command controlled the U.S. response to various strategic nuclear threats, and it was located in a huge facility carved out of the inside of Cheyenne Mountain, to the west of Colorado Springs. As was the case with the other military bases secured by Colorado Springs, NORAD was a significant source of federal injections. And although NORAD was not a stable training base in the mold of Fort Carson and Air Force Academy, it was tied forever to the Pike's Peak region by its expensive and unique facilities.

By 1970, only 30 years had elapsed since the first attempt to secure a small military installation to boost the economy of Colorado Springs. During this period, the effect on Colorado Springs had been dramatic. The population of the city had risen from 35,000 to 151,000, and injections from military sources ($295 million) accounted for 55 percent of the region's total income. In the same year, industrial income was $188 million and income from tourism was $72 million.[8]

Almost everyone assumed that the economic future of the city was assured, but no one closely analyzed the unique factors that had created the successes they observed. Each of the military installations that had located in Colorado Springs had required only an initial political effort to attract. Further 'political maintenance' was not required because:

- Each was funded and constructed immediately after the approval process was concluded.
- Each (with the initial exception of Peterson Field) required such a large investment in land and facilities that removing the installation in the future was out of the question.
- All were associated with conventional weapons or with stable training and operations, and each was linked to a firm, long-standing military mission that had wide, bipartisan political support.

Also overlooked was the fact that because of the stability possessed by each of these installations, most of the economic growth over the previous thirty years had occurred with the *addition* of military facilities, not because of the growth of existing installations.[9] As a result, no thought was given to how economic growth based on federal spending could be sustained if new facilities were not added, even though it was obvious, based on geographic constraints alone, that this would eventually have to be the case.

Economic Problems in Colorado Springs

The manner in which military installations accumulated in Colorado Springs (one every five to six years) tended to emulate the kind of economic growth one would anticipate from a booming internal economy. From 1950 to 1965 the city of Colorado Springs doubled in size, increasing from a population of 45,000 to 91,500 people. And from 1965 to 1980, the city began to look like a boom town as it tripled in size to 260,000 people, recording growth rates of 9 to 11 percent in the process.[10]

One side effect of the rapid increase in population was the creation of a real estate sector that rapidly became a major part of the city's economy. This sector required substantial population growth rates in Colorado Springs to stay healthy and this, in turn, implied either a booming economy or the continual addition of new military facilities. The lack of high population growth rates is a relatively minor problem in most cities and is even regarded as being desirable in many 'planned communities.' But real estate interests had become so entrenched in Colorado Springs that they were in a position to lobby for high growth simply to support their own economic interests.

However, by the early 1970s, growth slowed to about 4 percent a year. There were several reasons for this. The end of the Vietnam war in the mid-1970s caused a reduction in troop strength at Fort Carson and decreased spending at the other military bases. This caused a consequent loss of revenue for Colorado Springs. The end of the war also signaled the end of the construction of new military bases that had provided increasing levels of federal injections and rapid growth in the local economy.

Thus, when the energy crises of 1972 resulted in a moratorium on natural gas hookups for homes, the already weakened Colorado Springs home construction industry collapsed in a manner that closely paralleled the dark days of 1940. And while the inflation of the late 1970s allowed a temporary recovery, the high interest rates of the early 1980s caused a second collapse of the real estate market. Without compensating inputs from an internal economy to cushion these blows, the business cycles caused by reduced federal injections and the volatile real estate market were so severe that they threatened the well-being of the entire city.

Using Spending for Strategic Military Forces to Spur Regional Growth

These experiences finally convinced a number of civic leaders of the folly of trying to run the economy of a major city on a mix of external sources and real estate construction. The city clearly could not hope to continually acquire additional military bases to provide the growth necessary to support either its economy or its real estate industry. As a result, the city began to actively search for 'clean' industries that could move to Colorado Springs and begin to establish a larger internal economy. Based on the few electronics plants it had already attracted and on its low humidity, the city decided to recruit heavily in the electronics industry and specifically, in the area of microchip production.

While this campaign was a success, and a number of electronic and microchip manufacturers moved their factories to Colorado Springs, civic leaders overlooked the fact that most electronic industries were heavily dependent, either directly or indirectly, on defense business. And in a significant departure from the past, the health of these industries was linked closely to military spending for strategic and space systems, not conventional forces. As civic leaders talked about becoming a second 'Silicon Valley' and even about enticing industries from California to move to Colorado, a mix of technological and trade factors caused the U.S. electronics and microchip industries to go into serious decline, and Colorado Springs was once again trying to find a way to get its economy growing.

Colorado Springs had always created the growth it needed in times like these by securing yet another military installation. This had not been possible in the late 1970s, but in 1984 the chance to acquire part of the facilities for the new Strategic Defense Initiative arose—a possibility of gaining one more military base and one more spurt of growth for a city that had always relied on military spending to solve its economic problems.

The SDI and Colorado Springs

The previous sections of this case have covered the development of structural factors in Colorado Springs that created an inertia for continued federal money from military projects to keep the city's economy running. Obviously, politicians from the Colorado Springs area were aware of this inertia, and while they were anxious to act as representatives of the people, they were also quick to realize that delivering new money greatly enhanced their chances of being elected. This was particularly true as the developers and other real estate interests gained control of the Colorado Springs city government. This group badly needed high rates of growth in Colorado Springs to keep the real estate industry healthy.

On November 30, 1984, shortly after President Reagan's announcement proclaiming the Strategic Defense Initiative, a unified command was formed to manage military

Table A1.1: Military Spending in Colorado Springs and Denver in 1983
and 1986 (millions of current year dollars)

	1983	1986
Colorado Springs Area		
Payroll	750	879
Prime Contracts	250	434
Total	1000	1313
Denver Area		
Payroll	450	530
Prime Contracts	675	1266
Total	1125	1796

Source: Economic Analysis Division, Office of the Director of Program
Analysis and Evaluation, *The Geographic Distribution of Potential
Defense Expenditures*, 1984 and 1987.

efforts in space. The U.S. Space Command had been actively promoted by U.S.
Representative Ken Kramer of Colorado Springs[11] who, not surprisingly, also favored
locating the command headquarters in Colorado Springs. By December, 1984, Colorado
Springs had been named as the home of the new command and of the $1.2 billion
Consolidated Space Operations Center (CSOC) that would house it.[12] Press reports
noted that "capturing the Space Command was a coup for the city, which expects
huge gains in employment, business activity and national prestige. Land prices are
skyrocketing."[13]

Coincident with this announcement, the Air Force decided to merge its missile,
air and space warning roles at the North American Air Defense Command. This
necessitated accelerating the schedule for making more than $1 billion in improvements
by NORAD to the Cheyenne Mountain complex, and it provided the appearance of
a further economic boost to Colorado Springs, even though the money involved
would have been spent anyway.[14]

During this period, the effects of the Reagan defense buildup were reflected in
the nature of defense spending in Colorado Springs. The city had always hosted
military bases with large payrolls and fairly constant missions, a factor that contributed
an unusual amount of stability to an economy so dependent on external resources.
Table A1.1 shows the difference between the military spending involved in the
Colorado Springs economy and that usually found in an area with a healthy internal
economy (Denver is used as an example) where most spending goes for manufacturing
contracts.

When military contracts are involved, a manufacturing economy is usually quite
volatile. Note that in the three years of the Reagan buildup covered in Table A1.1,
military spending in Colorado Springs increased by 31 percent while in the Denver
area military spending increased by 60 percent. Of course, spending decreases can
occur just as quickly when military budgets are constrained, but decreases are far
less likely in payroll accounts than they are in purchasing. Because the Reagan
buildup was so heavily oriented toward equipment purchases, the split between
military payroll and prime contracts in Colorado Springs went from about 75/25 in
1983 to 67/33 in 1986. During this same period, the split in Denver went from
about 40/60 in 1983 and 30/70 in 1986.

However, by attempting to capture the SDI, the city of Colorado Springs had unknowingly embarked on a course that marked a significant departure from its past efforts to acquire military installations. Because the SDI was a strategic system with with a less firmly defined military mission, and because it lacked bipartisan political support, it would require not only an initial effort to secure, but continual, intense 'political maintenance' to assure that funding levels were maintained. Colorado Springs was not used to waging this kind of political effort and as a result, it assumed that—as had been the case with all previous military installations built in the city—the initial announcements about the SDI were sufficient to assure its construction. Instead, the city soon found itself receiving lots of political statements but few actual defense dollars.

By 1986, Colorado Springs thought it was well on the way to establishing itself as the center for SDI in the United States. This was aided by the fact that 1986 was an election year, and local politicians were anxious to deliver new federal spending before the voting began. Colorado Springs was engaged in a three-way competition with Pueblo, Colorado and Ft. Belvoir, Virginia, for a SDI research facility, and political writers speculated on whether Rep. Mike Strang, R-CO would be helped by an award to Pueblo or whether Rep. Ken Kramer, R-CO would benefit from the selection of Colorado Springs. Commenting on the criteria for the selection, Rep. Strang noted that "there are other strategic criteria [for the selection]—and we don't know what they are. . . ."[15]

As the hype surrounding the construction of SDI-related facilities grew, a group of civic leaders and developers from Colorado Springs traveled to Houston to explore parallels and note future problems Colorado Springs might expect. Houston was eight times the size of Colorado Springs, but this trip made good press and it helped to create the impression that Colorado Springs was going to be a military Space Center just like Houston. One group of developers also circulated a forecast that 82,000 people would be living in the immediate area around CSOC by the year 2000. While this forecast was patently ridiculous, it received a great deal of attention from members of the community.[16]

At approximately the same time, the Colorado Springs city planning office and its forecaster, Tony Roso, estimated that SDI spending would create only 9000 jobs in the El Paso County area by the year 2000, or an average of about 600 jobs a year.[17] An independent, confirming study yielded similar, but slightly higher figures. These more conservative forecasts indicated considerably less population growth from new jobs associated with the SDI facilities.[18] Then, on June 25, 1986, retired General James Hill (the new head of the U.S. Space Foundation, a space lobbying group, and the president of one of the largest real estate development firms in Colorado Springs) announced that the National Test Bed for the Strategic Defense Initiative would be built in Colorado Springs. The test bed was expected to cost $80 million, and it was expected to employ 2500 people when completed.[19]

Other Economic Factors

Announcements of new projects scheduled to be constructed in Colorado Springs were an almost weekly occurrence, but a disquieting parallel trend was developing.

The Colorado Springs economy was doing very poorly and it continued to show signs of weakness. There were several reasons for this. First, though many facilities connected with the SDI had been designated for Colorado Springs, little money was actually being spent in the community. Second, although Colorado Springs lagged behind the trends in the national economy, it had been caught in the same economic slump as the rest of the midwest. Third, developers who had anticipated a rush to Colorado Springs because of the SDI program were finding that the expected boom was not occurring and they could no longer afford to carry the financing for the land they had purchased. And fourth, and perhaps most disappointing, the electronic and microchip industries Colorado Springs had relied on to build a solid internal economy continued to suffer.

Commenting on the fact that Colorado Springs experienced over 1,200 layoffs in the high technology electronics industry in 1986, and that it had created only 2,700 new jobs in 1986 compared to 7,200 in 1985 and 11,600 in 1984, an economist for a major regional bank pointed out that "Colorado Springs is becoming more and more a one-industry town. That has always been true, but with all of the new facilities, it is now more dependent on the military."[20] One reason for this assessment was that Colorado Springs had also experienced 1,484 new hires in some of its high technology companies during 1986[21], but there were significant differences in the kinds of products these companies made. The layoffs had, for the most part, occurred in companies that dealt with the private sector. The hiring had occurred in companies that sold defense goods. Thus, Colorado Springs' plan to establish an internally driven economy was instead, developing yet another sector that depended on military spending for strategic and space systems. This difference was critical because by 1986 Colorado Springs found that spending on new military projects was drying up. In December, 1986, it was revealed that the Shuttle Planning and Operations Complex part of the CSOC would not be funded, causing a 'loss' to the community of $25 million in 1987 and a potential loss of 900 jobs.[22]

Colorado Springs ended 1986 on a depressed note. Unemployment had risen to 7.9 percent and retail sales increased the smallest amount in a decade.[23] The construction industry was weak, with nonresidential contracts down 73 percent from the previous December and home contracts down 56 percent over the same period.[24] Worse, civic leaders could suggest no course of action to remedy the situation aside from the old standby—increased defense spending. The 1988 defense budget had $150 million worth of projects for Colorado Springs, with SDI-related activities heading the list. However, in November, 1986, the city's advocate for SDI-related construction, Representative Ken Kramer, was defeated in his bid for the Senate, and within the next month Senator John Glenn, D-Ohio, began attempts to move the SDI test bed facility slated for Colorado Springs to Ohio.[25]

After Rep. Kramer was defeated in his bid for the Senate, he was immediately hired as a lobbyist by Aries Properties, a large Colorado Springs developer. Frank Aries had purchased most of the land on the east side of Colorado Springs, and he stood to gain the greatest profit from increased spending at the CSOC. Aries said his firm needed Kramer to help maintain the government's interest in financing the facility and noted that "naturally, we have a lot of stake in what's going on there."[26] Aries also expressed his concern that no one is adequately protecting the city's interests. That was vividly illustrated when the Shuttle Operations and Planning Complex (SOPC), under construction at Falcon Air Station, was deleted from the 1988 and '89 federal budgets. And, he added SOPC was just an indication that we need some representation. I don't feel Colorado Springs has that today.[27]

Frank Aries had correctly identified the issue for Colorado Springs. If the city was going to run its economy on federal money connected to strategic systems, it was going to have to change its approach from the way it secured military spending in the past. It now had to have someone in Washington who was continually dedicated to pursuing its interests and who, if necessary, could work to mold national spending priorities to fit the economic needs of the region. This became an even bigger issue as the SDI tried to expand its national political base to keep the program alive. More states needed to receive SDI contracts to generate additional support for the program, but spreading the contracts worked to the disadvantage of Colorado Springs.

While Senator Glenn continued his fight to move the Test Bed facility to Ohio[28], the House Armed Services Committee killed all funding for the facility in the 1988 budget.[29] And with new federal spending stagnating, Colorado Spring's economy continued to falter. Unemployment climbed to 10 percent as new workers moved to Colorado Springs based on the news of the SDI and then found that the economy was not growing fast enough to absorb them.[30] Finally, in a bit of ironic news, the Government Accounting Office confirmed that Falcon Air Force Station was the best site for the SDI test bed—even though funds for the facility were still not included in the defense budget.[31]

Thus, Colorado Springs found itself in an economic 'coffin corner'. It had no alternative but to continue to pursue new defense spending from the SDI, even though the likelihood of significant new spending was becoming less and less. Of course, it was precisely because it had no alternative that Colorado Springs elected this course of action in the first place, and the availability of alternatives had not improved as the economy faltered. The *inertia* for defense spending was so entrenched in the economy of Colorado Springs that the city, its leadership, and its representatives in Washington were committed to support the SDI at any price—not because of SDI's promise as a weapon, but because the health of the region's economy was at stake.

Conclusion

This case has studied the creation of economic inertia for defense spending in a community. Inertia started when the community failed to develop an internal economy and found that defense money was an easy substitute. Colorado Springs' fortuitous ability to secure a number of stable military training and command bases early in its history created a dependence on continually securing new bases to promote the growth required to sustain its economy in general and its construction industry in particular. This was a game that could not continue, based on space constraints alone, and whose rules changed significantly when the city elected to try to attain a politically justified strategic system instead of the conventional and training facilities it had sought in the past.

However, the inertia created by Colorado Springs' reliance on military spending established an atmosphere that allowed it to be sucked into what was, in retrospect, a highly speculative military project in the hopes that it would provide the stimulation for rapid future growth. It is interesting to note that as things began to turn sour, the easiest remedies, and the courses of action that continued to hold everyone's attention, always involved the politics of securing more military spending. At no time during this process was any question asked except whether the project, whatever it was, would bring additional jobs and money to the city.

Notes

1. This is the economy that is based on local production of goods and services.

2. Sprague, Marshall, *Newport in the Rockies,* The Swallow Press, Inc., Chicago, Illinois, 1971, 309–310.

3. Sprague, 310. It is worth noting that the community's aspirations were limited. It hoped to secure a small Army post that would result in federal spending of $1 million or so.

4. Ibid., 310–311.

5. Ibid., 311–312.

6. Ibid., 312.

7. Ibid., 312–313.

8. Ibid., 313.

9. All of the facilities located around Colorado Springs except for Fort Carson were remarkably stable in size and number of personnel. And even in the case of Fort Carson, only the transient element of the base varied greatly over this period.

10. Data provided in 1986 by the City Planning Office, Colorado Springs, Colorado.

11. "Space Command Welcome," *Gazette Telegraph,* Colorado Springs, Colorado, December 9, 1984.

12. Readers who are interested in regional economic impacts should always view announced spending on military projects with caution. These figures give the total amounts of money to be spent *nationwide over the number of years* it will take to complete a given project. Thus, to claim that Colorado Springs would immediately benefit from the total expenditure listed for CSOC is wrong on two counts. First, this money will be spent over a number of years. And second, much of it will be spent for equipment that is imported into Colorado and bolted to the floor at the Consolidated Space Operations Center. To claim that money spent for this equipment will provide local economic stimulus is similar to assigning the economic impact of the entire value of a tank to the community adjacent to the Army base where the tank is located. It should be noted, however, that in the case of Colorado Springs the entire figure of $1.2 billion was the one most commonly used when discussing the local impact of CSOC.

13. Reid, T.R., "Welcoming Weapons in Space," *Philadelphia Inquirer,* December 9, 1984, 6F.

14. Covault, Craig, "Space Command, NORAD Merging Missile, Air and Space Warning Roles," *Aviation Week and Space Technology,* February 11, 1985, 60–62.

15. Haddow, Ellen, "Aide: Star Wars plan would boost Strang," *Rocky Mountain News,* Denver, Colorado, May 31, 1986, 10.

16. Given an average family size, this would assume about 33,000 jobs if there was only one wage earner per family. With an employment participation rate of about 65 percent (the national average) this forecast would assume about 53,000 jobs. More reliable forecasts by the city planner anticipated the creation of a total of 77,000 jobs in the entire Pikes Peak region by the year 2000. If the developers' forecast was correct, 70 percent of all people who were newly employed in the Pikes Peak region by the year 2000 would have to live around the CSOC.

17. Cotten, Teri, "Space centers offer two cities link to the future," *Gazette Telegraph,* Colorado Springs, Colorado, June 8, 1986.

18. Ibid. Roso's forecasts and his comments about the developer's forecast were to cost him his job by early 1987.

19. Bobbit, Stephen, and Hill: "Springs to get Star Wars site," *Rocky Mountain News,* Denver, Colorado, June 25, 1986, 6.

20. Heilman, Wayne, "Military cavalry for business," *Gazette Telegraph,* Colorado Springs, Colorado, December 2, 1986.

21. Mahoney, Jerry, "Don't be blue, employment statistics tell high-tech industry," *Gazette Telegraph,* Colorado Springs, Colorado, January 4, 1987.

22. McMillin, Sue, "Tight money may ground shuttle complex," *Gazette Telegraph,* Colorado Springs, Colorado, December 6, 1986. The project was finally completely scrapped on January 29, 1987 by Secretary of Defense Weinberger who decided, instead, to buy more missiles. Colorado Senator Tim Wirth pledged to make Secretary Weinberger change his mind, saying "I will make certain that Colorado Springs and Colorado get their fair share of federal dollars." See: Yack, Patrick, "Pentagon scraps Springs shuttle complex," *Denver Post,* Denver, Colorado, January 30, 1987, B1.

23. Heilman, Wayne, and Mahoney, Jerry, "Area economists discuss outlook," *Gazette Telegraph,* Colorado Springs, Colorado, January 11, 1987, E1.

24. "Construction contracts up in U.S., down in area," *Gazette Telegraph,* Colorado Springs, Colorado, January 30, 1987.

25. McMillin, Sue, "SDI site tops list for local projects," *Gazette Telegraph,* Colorado Springs, Colorado, December 6, 1986.

26. Delaney, Ted, "Kramer to lobby for Springs developer," *Denver Post,* Denver, Colorado, March 6, 1987, 4A.

27. Bird, Julie, "Kramer to lobby for Aries, firm says," *Gazette Telegraph,* Colorado Springs, Colorado, March 6, 1987.

28. McMillin, Sue, "SDI fight continues, Wirth tries to mend rift," *Gazette Telegraph,* Colorado Springs, Colorado, March 27, 1987.

29. "House panel kills Reagan's SDI request," *Gazette Telegraph,* Colorado Springs, Colorado, April 9, 1987, 1.

30. Mahoney, Jerry, "Springs unemployment rate hits 10 percent," *Gazette Telegraph,* Colorado Springs, Colorado, May 8, 1987, F1.

31. Dolan Jack, "Falcon favored," *Gazette Telegraph,* Colorado Springs, Colorado, May 20, 1987, B1.

BIBLIOGRAPHY

Abshire, David M., "The Atlantic Alliance: The Development of a Resource Strategy," *Signal,* October, 1984.

‾‾‾‾‾. "NATO: Facing the Facts," *Washington Post,* December 31, 1984.

‾‾‾‾‾. "NATO: Honing the Grand Strategy," *Wall Street Journal,* September 12, 1984.

Adams, Peter, "Air Force, Navy Vie for Targets Under START Warhead Limits," *Defense News,* June 13, 1988.

‾‾‾‾‾. "Allies Face Tough Choices if Nuclear Umbrella Shuts," *Defense News,* June 8, 1987.

‾‾‾‾‾. "Board Plans Recommendations for Tritium Site," *Defense News,* June 6, 1988.

‾‾‾‾‾. "Congress at Odds with DoD on Military Balance," *Defense News,* September 5, 1988.

‾‾‾‾‾. "Deputy Secretary Taft Raises Burden-sharing Debate on Overseas Campaign," *Defense News,* May 30, 1988.

‾‾‾‾‾. "Europe Looks to 1993 and Unity," *Defense News,* July 25, 1988.

‾‾‾‾‾. "European NATO Burden-Sharing Would Trim U.S. Alliance Costs," *Defense News,* May 16, 1988.

‾‾‾‾‾. "Nunn: U.S. Must Keep Longer Range Missiles," *Defense News,* May 23, 1988.

‾‾‾‾‾. "Study: Soviet Buildup Persists Despite Economic Concerns," *Defense News,* September 19, 1988.

‾‾‾‾‾. "U.S. Eyes Non-Nuclear Strategic Missile Class," *Defense News,* August 31, 1987.

‾‾‾‾‾. "U.S. Senate Endorses INF Treaty After Conservatives Give Up Fight," *Defense News,* May 30, 1988.

Aerospace Industries Association of America, Inc., *Aerospace Facts and Figures 1984–85,* published by Aviation Week and Space Technology, Washington, DC, 1984.

Air Force Association, "Soviet Theater Estimates, October 1987," *Air Force Magazine,* March 1988.

‾‾‾‾‾. "The Military Balance 1985/86," *Air Force Magazine,* February 1986.

Allison, Graham T., "What Fuels the Arms Race?" in *Contrasting Approaches to Strategic arms Control,* Robert L. Pfaltzgraff, ed., Lexington Books, D.C. Heath and Company, 1974., reprinted in Chapter 5, *Arms Control: The Cooperative Pursuit of Security,* Pergammon Press, New York, N.Y., 1985.

Amann, R., Cooper, J. M., and Davies, R. W., eds., *The Technological Level of Soviet Industry,* Yale University Press, New Haven, Conn., 1977.

Amouyal, Barbara, "Pentagon Concept Fortifies NATO Superiority, Exploits Warsaw Pact Weaknesses," *Defense News,* August 1, 1988.

Andrews, Walter, "Non-nuclear superbombs seen ready in five years," *Washington Times,* February 7, 1985.

————. "Pentagon Replaces Colt .45 With Beretta," *Washington Times,* January 15, 1985.

Annual Demographic Information, Washington State Employment Security Department, Seattle, Washington, July, 1987.

Annual Planning Report, 1982, Richland-Kennewick-Pasco SMSA, Washington State Employment Security, Seattle, Washington, 1982.

Arkin, W.M., and Fieldhouse, R.W., *Nuclear Battlefields: Global Links in the Arms Race,* Ballinger Publishing Company, Cambridge, MA, 1985.

"Assignment of Ground Forces of the United States to Duty in the European Area," *Senate Hearings,* 82 Congress, 2 Session, U.S. Government Printing Office, Washington, DC, 1951.

Aviation Week Staff, "Strategic Defense Initiative Blueprint for a Layered Defense," *Aviation Week Magazine,* New York, November 23, 1987.

Banks, A., *Political Handbook of the World,* CSA Publications, Bighamton, NY, 1986.

Barker, Rocky, "Andrus Is Pleased With Cleanup Plan," *The Post Register,* Idaho Falls, Idaho, August 30, 1987.

————. "DOE Sets 2 More Hearings," *The Post Register,* Idaho Falls, Idaho, March 25, 1988.

————. "State Asks For Oversight Panel," *The Post Register,* Idaho Falls, Idaho, March 27, 1988.

————. "Texan Says SIS Should Be Scuttled," *The Post Register,* Idaho Falls, Idaho, March 28, 1988.

Barnet, Richard J., "Rethinking National Strategy," *The New Yorker,* March 21, 1988.

Bass, G., Jenkins, B., et al., *Options for U.S. Policy on Terrorism,* RAND, Santa Monica, CA, July 1981.

"Battle of the Bean Counters," *Time,* June 15, 1987.

Becker, Abraham S., *The Burden of Soviet Defense,* RAND, R-2752AF, October, 1981.

Beres, L.R., *Terrorism and Global Security: The Nuclear Threat,* Westview Press, Boulder, CO, 1979.

Bethe, H., Garwin, R., Gottfried, K., and Kendall, H., "Space Based Ballistic Missile Defense," *Scientific American,* New York, October 1984.

Beyers, Dan, "Arms Control, Economic Developments Stir Up Burden Debate," *Defense News,* May 2, 1988.

————. "B-52 Could Get New Lease on Life as Alternative to Newer, More Costly Planes," *Defense News,* May 2, 1988.

————. "Correction of Burden-Sharing Reports Urged," *Defense News,* February 15, 1988.

————. "Europeans Search For New Defense Relationship," *Defense News,* July 20, 1988.

_____. "New Priorities Plan May Cost Navy," *Defense News*, February 29, 1988.

_____. "Report Says Europe Can Play Larger NATO Role," *Defense News*, April 25, 1988.

_____. "Uncertainty, Lethargy Dog Effort To Build NATO Arms Cooperation," *Defense News*, February 29, 1988.

_____. "Understanding 'Codevelopment' Key to Allied Fighter Participation," *Defense News*, October 5, 1987.

Bialer, Seweryn, "Will Russia Dare to Clean Up Its Economic Mess?" *Washington Post*, April 21, 1985.

Biddle, Wayne, "Star Wars Conflict of Interest Seen," *New York Times*, April 30, 1985.

_____. "Study Says Plan to Reduce Nuclear Weapons May Save $30 Billion," *New York Times*, March 27, 1984.

Bird, Julie, "Kramer to lobby for Aries, firm says," *Gazette Telegraph*, Colorado Springs, Colorado, March 6, 1987.

Blacker, Coit D., *After Brezhnev*, Georgetown Center For Strategic and International Studies, Washington, D.C., 1983.

Blair, Bruce, *Strategic Command and Control: Redefining the Nuclear Threat*, The Brookings Institution, Washington, D.C., 1985.

Blueprint for Tomorrow (Executive Brochure), U.S. Air Force, Aeronautical Systems Division, Wright-Patterson AFB, Ohio, 1985.

Bobbit, Stephen, "Hill: Springs to get Star Wars site," *Rocky Mountain News*, Denver, Colorado, June 25, 1986.

Bobrakov, Yuri, and Konobeyev, Vladimir, *Disarmament and Economics: Problems of Economic Restructuring*, Novosti Press Agency Publishing House, Moscow, 1983.

Bodansky, Youssef, *Jane's Defence Weekly*, reported in: Weeks, Albert, "New Soviet Epoch of Defense Based on High-Tech, Seen Opening in '85," *FPI News Service*, March 4, 1985.

Boulding, Kenneth E., "The Deadly Industry: War and the International System," in *Peace and the War Industry*, Kenneth E. Boulding, ed., Aldine Publishing Company, 1970.

Boutacoff, D., "Backscatter Radar Extends Early Warning Times," *Defense Electronics Magazine*, Volume 17, Number 5, May 1985.

Briley, Harold, "NATO Ministers Call for Extensive Review of Western Alliance's Defense Costs," *Defense News*, May 30, 1988.

_____. "Taft Urges European Burden Sharing," *Defense News*, July 25, 1988.

Buchanan, James M., "Easy Budgets and Tight Money," *Lloyds Bank Review*, April, 1962.

Budget of the United States Government, FY 1988 and FY 1989, U.S. Government Printing Office, Washington, DC, 1987–88.

Builder, C., and Graubard, M., *The International Law of Armed Conflict: Implications for the Concept of Mutual Assured Destruction*, RAND, Santa Monica, CA, January, 1982.

"Burden Shared," *The Economist*, August 4, 1984.

Burt, Richard, "Defense Policy and Arms Control," in *Continuity and Change in the Eighties and Beyond*, Proceedings of the National Security Affairs Conference, National Defense University, Washington, D.C., 23–25 July, 1979.

"California's Second Look at its Defense Dollars," *U.S. News and World Report*, February 25, 1985.

Campbell, C., *Nuclear Facts: A Guide to Nuclear Weapon Systems and Strategy*, The Hamlyn Publishing Group, Limited, New York, 1984.

Canan, James, *War in Space*, Harper and Row Publishers, New York, 1982.

Carlson, Eugene, "Economists See Difficult Days Ahead For West and Midwest," *The Wall Street Journal*, September 30, 1986.

Carlucci, F., *Annual Report to the Congress, Fiscal Year 1989*, U.S. Government Printing Office, Washington DC, February 11, 1988.

————. *Soviet Military Power: An Assessment of the Threat 1988*, U.S. Government Printing Office, Washington, DC, April 1988.

Carney, Larry, "Army Fears Loss of $3 Billion and 10,000 Troops in Huge Budget Shift to Shore Up Navy Firepower," *Defense News*, June 13, 1988.

Carter A., and Schwartz, D., *Ballistic Missile Defense*, Brookings Institution, Washington, DC, 1984.

Carter, A., Steinbruner, J., and Zraket, C., *Managing Nuclear Operations*, The Brookings Institution, Washington, DC, 1987.

Carter, Barry E., "Strengthening Our Conventional Forces," in *Rethinking Defense and Conventional Forces*, Center for National Policy, Washington, D.C., 1983.

Chalmers, Malcolm, and Unterseher, Lutz, *International Security*, Summer, 1988.

"Chamber Panel Sensitive to SIS Impacts," *The Post Register*, Idaho Falls, Idaho, August 16, 1987.

Chant, C., and Hogg, I., *Nuclear War in the 1980's?* Harper and Row Publishers, New York, 1983.

Churchill, W., *Triumph and Tragedy*, Houghton Mifflin Press, Boston, MA, 1953.

Clayton, James L., *Does Defense Beggar Welfare?* Agenda Paper No. 9, National Strategy Information Center, New York, 1979.

Cockburn, Andrew, *The Threat: Inside the Soviet Military*, Random House, New York, 1983.

Cohen, Sam, "Use Star Wars Weapons in ground wars," *The Wall Street Journal*, April 20, 1988.

Conference on Improving National Security by Strengthening the Defense Industrial Base, Harvard University, May 10–12, 1982.

Congressional Quarterly, Inc., *The Nuclear Age: Power, Proliferation and the Arms Race*, Washington DC, 1984.

"Construction contracts up in U.S., down in area," *Gazette Telegraph*, Colorado Springs, Colorado, January 30, 1987.

"Construction Project Data Sheets," *FY 1989 OMB Budget Request—Atomic Energy Defense Activities*, U.S. Department of Energy, Washington, D.C., May, 1987.

Cotten, Teri, "Space centers offer two cities link to the future," *Gazette Telegraph*, Colorado Springs, Colorado, June 8, 1986.

Covault, Craig, "Space Command, NORAD Merging Missile, Air and Space Warning Roles," *Aviation Week and Space Technology*, February 11, 1985.

Cushman, John H. Jr., "Shortage To Hurt S.D.I., Study Says," *New York Times,* June 12, 1988.

"Cuts in Component Size Shrink Cost Estimates for Star Wars," *GazetteTelegraph,* October 24, 1988.

Data Resources, Inc./McGraw Hill, "Defense Spending and Jobs," *Defense Economics Research Report,* Vol. II, No.11, November, 1982.

Davidson, Ian, "Tonic that failed to give a lift," *Financial Times,* London, September 29, 1986.

Davies, John, "Calif. Urged to Wage 'Economic War'," *Journal of Commerce,* April 12, 1985.

de Briganti, Giovanni, "European Nations Spending Slide Shows Signs of Reversal," *Defense News,* February 22, 1988.

_____ . "Giraud Asks 3 Percent MOD Budget Rise," *Defense News,* October 15, 1987.

_____ . "U.S. Exports Little Strategic Defense Work, Europeans Complain," *Defense News,* March 21, 1988.

Dean, Jonathan, *Watershed in Europe,* published under the auspices of the Union of Concerned Scientists, Lexington Books, Lexington, MA, 1987.

"Defense Department Lists Protectionist Measures," *Defense News,* October 5, 1987.

Defense Financial and Investment Review, U.S. Department of Defense, Washington, D.C., June, 1985.

Degenhardt, H. and Day, A.J., eds., *Treaties and Alliances of the World,* 4th ed., Gale Research Company, Detroit, 1986.

Delaney, Ted, "Kramer to lobby for Springs developer," *The Denver Post,* Denver, Colorado, March 6, 1987.

Denton, Herbert, "Reagan Cooly Received on Midwest Swing," *Washington Post,* October 5, 1982.

Disposal of Hanford Defense High Level, Transuranic and Tank Wastes, DOE/EIS-0113, Vol. 1, U.S. Department of Energy, Washington, D.C., December, 1987.

Doder, Dusko, "Soviets to Accept Women as 'Volunteers' in Military," *Washington Post,* April 1, 1985.

"DOE chief: Waste plant No. 1 priority," *The Idaho Statesman,* Boise, Idaho, July 20, 1988.

Dolan Jack, "Falcon favored," *Gazette Telegraph,* Colorado Springs, Colorado, May 20, 1987.

Draft Environmental Impact Statement—Special Isotope Separation Project, DOE/EIS-0136, Idaho National Engineering Laboratory, U.S. Department of Energy, Idaho Operations Office, Idaho Falls, Idaho, February, 1988.

Drozdiak, William, "Conventional Buildup Troubling NATO," *Washington Post,* November 21, 1984.

_____ . "NATO Weighs Nonnuclear Strategies," *Washington Post,* September 26, 1983.

Dunn, L., *Controlling the Bomb: Nuclear Proliferation in the 1980s,* Yale University Press, New Haven, CT, 1982.

Dyson, Freeman., *Weapons and Hope,* Harper and Row Publishers, New York.

Earle, Ralph, "Summit Big on Image, Not Substance," *Defense News,* June 13, 1988.

Economic Report of the President, Government Printing Office, Washington, D.C., 1978.

"Economist: SIS job numbers misleading," *The Post Register,* Idaho Falls, Idaho, April 17, 1988, Twin Falls, Idaho, *Times News,* April 16, 1988.

Environment, Safety and Health Report for the Department of Energy Defense Complex, U.S. Department of Energy, Washington, D.C., July 1, 1988.

Epstein, Joshua M., *Measuring Military Power: The Soviet Air Threat to Europe,* Princeton University Press, Princeton, N.J., 1984.

Erlander, Hans C., "Economy Forces Norway to Cut Defense," *Defense News,* June 6, 1988.

"Europe does it the second-best way," *The Economist,* June 21, 1986.

"Europe vs. Arms Control," *The Wall Street Journal,* October 24, 1986.

Feshbach, Murray, in a report based on articles in Voyenno-Meditsinskiy Zhurnal and Tyl i Snabzheniye, reported in "Enemy for the Soviet Army: Rampant Disease," *New York Times,* April 15, 1985.

Fialka, John J., "Technology Purchased From the Soviets Starts to Yield Military Uses," *Wall Street Journal,* April 24, 1985.

————. "NATO is Showing Strain as It Confronts Gorbachev's Disarming Arms-Curb Ideas," *Wall Street Journal,* July 14, 1988.

"Fighting Smart, Not Rich," *U.S. News and World Report,* November 14, 1988.

Fisette, Bob, "Incentives and Obstacles to EAC," *European Arms Cooperation Conference,* Airlie House, Virginia, April 21, 1987.

Fitussi, F.P., *Economic Benefits of ESA Contracts,* European Space agency, 1978.

"Focus: Air Force to Test OTH-B Against Small Targets," *Defense Electronics Magazine,* Volume 19, Number 9, September 1987.

Friedman, N. "The Next President and Defense," *Defense Electronics,* November 1988.

FY1989 Budget of the United States Government, Executive Office of the President, Office of Management and Budget, Washington, D.C.

FY 1989 Congressional Budget Request, Atomic Energy Defense Activities Construction Project Data Sheets, U.S. Department of Energy, Washington, D.C., February, 1988.

Gertcher, F., and Kroncke, G.T., *U.S. Aerospace Industry Space Launch Vehicle Production,* a Preliminary Report for the National Defense University by R&D Associates, RDA-TR-301200, Colorado Springs, Colorado, December 1985.

Gilmartin, Trish, "10-Year Cost of SDI Could Rise to $452 Billion," *Defense News,* June 6, 1988.

————. "Federal Republic of Germany Tops Foreign Entities in Monies for SDI Research," *Defense News,* May 16, 1988.

————. "Firms Scrap for Key SDI Job as Defense Alters Bid Rules," *Defense News,* August 24, 1987.

————. "Pentagon Doubles Price of Phase One Strategic Defense Scheme," *Defense News,* March 14, 1988.

————. "SDI Organization Announces Availability of Technology for Private Applications," *Defense News,* November 2, 1987.

————. "Senate Moves to Restrict Allied Involvement in Star Wars Project," *Defense News,* September 21, 1987.

Glenn, John, Thomas J. O'Brien, and Donald M. Kerr, Acting Assistant Secretary for Defense Programs, Department of Energy, *Hearings,* March 23, 1978.

Gorbachev's Modernization Program: A Status Report, A Central Intelligence Agency report to the Joint Economic Committee, Washington, D.C., March 19, 1987.

Gordon, Michael R., "NATO's High-Tech Defensive Strategy Draws Fire From Within the Alliance," *National Journal,* December 15, 1984.

Gowing, M., *Britain and Atomic Energy, 1939–1945,* MacMillian, London, 1964.

Greider, William, "Birds of a Feather: Hawks and Doves Flock Together for Defense Dollars," *Milwaukee Journal,* August 12, 1984.

Greyelin, Philip, "France and Star Wars," *Washington Post,* January 28, 1985.

Gumble, B., "Air Force Upgrading Defenses at NORAD," *Defense Electronics Magazine,* Volume 17, Number 8, August 1985.

Haddow, Ellen, "Aide: Star Wars plan would boost Strang," *Rocky Mountain News,* Denver, Colorado, May 31, 1986.

Hager, Jan, a contractor for the SIS speaking in: Brugger, Brad, "SIS Would Open New World For Technology Transfer," *Idaho State Journal,* Pocatello, Idaho, January 13, 1988.

Halloran, Richard, "Pentagon Draws Up First Strategy For Fighting a Long Nuclear War," *New York Times,* May 30, 1982.

Hansen, James H., "Countering NATO's New Weapons—Soviet concepts for War In Europe," *International Defense Review,* Volume 17, no. 11/1984.

"Hard Military Choices," *New York Times,* May 28, 1985.

Hatfield, Mark O., *The Plutonium Cushion—A Report On U.S. Defense Plutonium Needs And The Hanford N Reactor,* October, 1987.

Heilman, Wayne, "Military cavalry for business," *Gazette Telegraph,* Colorado Springs, Colorado, December 2, 1986.

Heilman, Wayne, and Mahoney, Jerry, "Area economists discuss outlook," *Gazette Telegraph,* Colorado Springs, Colorado, January 11, 1987.

Hicks, Jonathan, "For the Skilled, It's a Seller's Market," *New York Times,* June 5, 1988.

Hildebrandt, Gregory, *Capital Valuation of Military Equipment,* RAND, R-3212, January, 1985.

Hoagland, Jim, "'Star Wars' Plan Worries Envoy," *Washington Post,* October 30, 1984.

Hoffman, B., *Terrorism in the United States and the Potential Threat to Nuclear Facilities,* Rand Corporation, R-3351-DOE, January 1986.

Hoffman, C.A., G.R. Wells, R.D. Balsley, and J.H. Davis, *Socioeconomic Impacts of the Idaho National Engineering Laboratory,* Idaho State University, Center for Business Research and Services, Pocatello, Idaho,1986.

Hollaway, David, *The Soviet Union and the Arms Race,* 2nd. ed., Yale University Press, New Haven, Conn. 1984.

Hopkins, Mark M., and Kennedy, Michael, *The Tradeoff Between Consumption and Military Expenditures For the Soviet Union During the 1980's,* RAND, R-2972-NA, November, 1982.

House Appropriations Committee, *FY1985 Hearings for the FY1985 Energy and Water Development Appropriations,* Part 4.

"House panel kills Reagan's SDI request," *Gazette Telegraph,* Colorado Springs, Colorado, April 9, 1987.

Hudson, Richard L., and Gumbel, Peter, "Europe's High-Technology Eureka Project Is Beset by Squabbles, Inadequate Funding," *The Wall Street Journal,* November 5, 1985.

Hunter, Robert E., "France, Germany Moving Toward Military Cooperation," *Army Times,* July 6, 1987.

———. "Conventional Arms: NATO Faces Tough Issues," *Defense News,* April 11, 1988.

Huntington, S., *The Common Defence: Strategic Programs in National Politics,* Columbia University Press, New York, 1961.

Hyland, W.G., *Soviet-American Relations: A New Cold War?* RAND, Santa Monica, CA, May 1981.

Institute for Peace and International Security. Reprinted in Beyers, Dan, "U.S. Diplomats Brush Off Criticism, Insist Burden Sharing at 'top of Agenda'," *Defense News,* March 21, 1988.

"Interview with Marshal of the USSR Sergei Akhromeyev," *Defense Science Magazine,* October 1988.

"Introductory Essay," *Arms Control: The Cooperative Pursuit of Security,* Pergammon Press, New York, N.Y., 1985.

Jane's Defence Weekly reported in "Some Soviet Subs Held Unseaworthy," *Washington Times,* March 13, 1985.

Jenkins, B.M., "A Strategy for Combating Terrorism," *an occasional paper, RAND,* Santa Monica, CA, May 1981.

Joint Economic Committee, *Soviet Economy in the 1980's: Problems and Prospects,* Part 1, Section III, 1982.

Judge, John F., "The Strategic Defense Initiative and Arms Control," *Defense Electronics,* March, 1985.

Kahan, Jerome, *Security in the Nuclear Age: Developing U.S. Strategic Arms Policy,* The Brookings Institution, Washington, D.C., 1975, reprinted in Chapter 5, *Arms Control: The Cooperative Pursuit of Security,* Pergammon Press, New York, N.Y., 1985.

Kauffman, William W., "Spending for a Sound Defense: Alternatives to the Reagan Military Budget," *The Committee for National Security,* March 22, 1984.

———. *Planning Conventional Forces: 1950–80,* The Brookings Institution, Washington, D.C., 1982.

Keaney, Thomas A., *Strategic Bombers and Conventional Weapons,* Monograph 84–4, The National Defense University, Washington, D.C., 1984.

Kelly, G., "The Political Background of the French A-Bomb," *Orbis,* vol. 4, Fall, 1960.

Keyworth, George, "Supersmart weapons—alternative to nukes," *Washington Times,* October 19, 1984.

Kissinger, Henry, *Washington Post,* April 24, 1988.

Klare, Michael, "Defense budget hides as much as it reveals about true nuclear spending," *Oakland Tribune,* April 29, 1984.

Knaus, William A., "Arms Spending and the Decline in Soviet Health," *Washington Post,* October 14, 1982.

Knickerbocker, Brad, "'Star Wars' defense may lead to space-based offense," *Christian Science Monitor*, January 23, 1985.

Kohl, W., *French Nuclear Diplomacy*, Princeton University, Press, Princeton, NJ, 1971.

Komer, Robert, "Future of U.S. Conventional Forces: A Coalition Approach," *Rethinking Defense and Conventional Forces*, Center for National Policy, Washington, D.C., 1983.

Krauss, Melvin, and Fossedal, Gregory A., "Star Wars for the Allies, Usual Terms," *The Wall Street Journal*, May 8, 1986.

"Kremlin blasts poor discipline," *The Gazette Telegraph*, October 15, 1988.

"Labs Struggle to Promote Spin-offs," *Science*, No. 240, May 13, 1988.

Lakos, A., *Interational Terrorism: A Bibliography*, Westview Press, Boulder, Colorado, 1986.

Lambeth, Benjamin, *How To think about Soviet Military Doctrine*, a paper presented at at seminar on Soviet Military Doctrine, Harvard University, February 13, 1978.

Lambeth, Benjamin, and Lewis, Kevin, *Likely Soviet Responses to the SDI*, Rand Corporation, 1988.

"Laser Isotope Separation of Uranium," and "Laser Isotope Separation of Plutonium," *Energy and Technology Review*, UCRL-52000-87-7, July, 1987.

Leites, Nathan, *Soviet Style in War*, RAND, Santa Monica, CA, 1982.

Leopold, George, "Study Concludes Pentagon's R&D Cuts Threaten U.S. Microwave Industry," *Defense News*, August 24, 1987.

_____ . "Study Rekindles Heated Burden-Sharing Debate, Challenges Congress' Assertions," *Defense News*, March 28, 1988.

Life Guard Idaho, a publication of The Snake River Alliance, July, 1987.

"Little Hope Seen For Soviet Economy," *The Gazette Telegraph*, October 15, 1988.

Luttwak, Edward N., *Strategy: The Logic of War and Peace*, The Belknap Press of Harvard University Press, Cambridge, Massachusets, 1987.

Mahoney, Jerry, "Don't be blue, employment statistics tell high-tech industry," *Gazette Telegraph*, Colorado Springs, Colorado, January 4, 1987.

_____ . "Springs unemployment rate hits 10%," *Gazette Telegraph*, Colorado Springs, Colorado, May 8, 1987.

Malloy, Chuck, "Not all 'good' GOPers for SIS," *The Post Register*, Idaho Falls, Idaho, May 22, 1988.

_____ . "Stallings Links SIS with START Talks," *The Post Register*, Idaho Falls, Idaho, April 17, 1988.

Marwah, O., "India's Nuclear and Space Programs: Intent and Policy," *International Security*, vol. 2, Fall, 1977.

Maze, Rick, "Soviets Pay Soldiers Less, Get Less, Say DoD Officials," *Navy Times*, October 8, 1984.

Mazour, A. G., *Russia: Tsarist and Communist*, Van Nostrand Company, Inc., Princeton, NJ, 1962.

McMillan, Sue, An Address to the Publishers and Editors of United Press International, reprinted in *Department of State Bulletin*, October 9, 1967.

_____ . "Revised Missile Defense Plan Is Unveiled Before Congress," *Gazette Telegraph*, Colorado Springs, Colorado, October 7, 1988.

_____ . "SDI fight continues, Wirth tries to mend rift," *Gazette Telegraph*, Colorado Springs, Colorado, March 27, 1987.

_____ . "SDI site tops list for local projects," *Gazette Telegraph*, Colorado Springs, Colorado, December 6, 1986.

_____ . "Tight money may ground shuttle complex," *Gazette Telegraph*, Colorado Springs, Colorado, December 6, 1986.

Middleton, Drew, "An Assessment of the NATO Alliances Strength," *Defense News*, October, 26, 1987.

Molero, Joe, "Foreign Technology and Local Innovations: Some Lessons Learned from Spanish Defense Industry Experience," in *The Relations Between Defence and Civil Technologies*, Philip Gemmett and Judith Reppy, eds., Dordrecht: Kluwer, 1988.

Morrison, David C. "The Power Behind the Energy Department," *Long Island Newsday*, January 24, 1984.

Mossberg, Walter S., and Walcott, John, "U.S. Redefines Policy on Security to Place Less Stress on Soviets," *Wall Street Journal*, August 11, 1988.

Muscatine, Alison, "Computer Bid Fails," *Washington Post*, November 15, 1984.

Nacht, M., *The Age of Vulnerability: Threats to the Nuclear Stalemate*, The Brookings Institution, Washington, DC, 1985.

National Academy of Sciences, *Nuclear Arms Control: Background and Issues*, National Academy Press, Washington DC, 1985.

"NATO Arms Dispute Left Unresolved," *Gazette Telegraph*, March 4, 1988.

NATO Press Center, Reprinted in de Briganti, Giovanni, "European Nations Spending Slide Shows Signs of Reversal," *Defense News*, February 22, 1988.

"NATO: Outdated by 2000?" *Defense News*, July 25, 1988.

Nelson, Mark M., "Cash-Strapped NATO Members Grapple With Waste," *Wall Street Journal*, August 6, 1987.

New York Times News Service, "Star Wars Laser Testing Underway," *Gazette Telegraph*, January 3, 1988.

Niederau, Goetz, *Economic Benefits of ESA Contracts*, European Space Agency, 1980.

"No Reaganomics," *The Economist*, February 11, 1984.

"NORAD Profile," *Defense Electronics Magazine*, August 1985, Volume 17, Number 8.

North American Aerospace Defense Command, *Pocket Information Handbook*, prepared by the Directorate of Cost and Management Analysis, DCS Comptroller, Peterson Air Force Base, Colorado Springs, CO, October 1984.

Oberdorfer, Don, and Pincus, Walter, "'Star Wars' Will Trigger Arms Buildup, Soviet Warns," *Washington Post*, March 6, 1985.

Office of Management and Budget, *Budget of the United States Government FY 1988*, U.S. Government Printing Office, Washington, DC, 1987.

_____ . *Budget of the United States Government, FY 1989*, U.S. Government Printing Office, Washington DC, 1988.

Ofte, Don, INEL manager in Malloy, Chuck, "Ofte predicts INEL job rate to stay stable," *The Post Register*, Idaho Falls, Idaho, Jan 6, 1988.

"Organization of the Soviet Armed Forces," *Air Force Magazine*, Air Force Association, March 1988.

Osgood, R.E., *NATO: The Entangling Alliance*, University of Chicago Press, Chicago, IL, 1962.

———— . *The Case for the MLF: A Critical Evaluation*, Washington Center of Foreign Policy, Washington, DC, 1964.

"Panel: 'Star Wars' prevents arms pact," *The Gazette Telegraph*, Colorado Springs, Colorado, November 27, 1984.

"Paying Up," *Time*, December 17, 1984, 58.

Payne, K., *Laser Weapons in Space: Policy and Doctrine*, Westview Replica edition, Boulder, CO, August 1983.

Pechman, Joseph A., ed., *Setting National Priorities: The 1979 Budget*, The Brookings Institution, Washington, D.C., 1978.

Pellerin, C., "Defense Science Board Urges Industrial Base Revamp," *Washington Technology*, November 3–16, 1988.

"Pentagon sours on 'Star Wars'," *Gazette Telegraph*, Colorado Springs, Colorado, April 3, 1988.

Pierre, A. J., *Nuclear Politics: the British Experience with an Independent Strategic Force, 1939–70*, Oxford University Press, London, 1972.

Pincus, Walter, "Experts Tell of Soviet Woes," *Washington Post*, February 14, 1985.

Podhoretz, "The Present Danger," *Commentary*, Volume 69, No. 3., March 1980.

Pohling-Brown, Pamela, "NATO Faces Choice Between Conventional, Nuclear Reduction Focus," *Defense News*, December 7, 1987.

Polsky, Debra, "DoD Readies $700 Million Conventional Arms Effort," *Defense News*, December 21, 1987.

Pond, Elizabeth, "Britain Voices Europe's Qualms About U.S. Strategic Defense Plans," *Christian Science Monitor*, March 18, 1985.

Pratter, Mark, "'Winds of change' buffet senior senator," *The Post Register*, Idaho Falls, Idaho, July 31, 1988.

President's Economic Adjustment Committee and the Office of Economic Adjustment, OASD(MI&L), *Economic Adjustment/Conversion*, Department of Defense, Washington, D.C., 1985.

Quandt, W., *Decade of Decisions: American Policy Toward the Arab-Israeli Conflict 1967–76*, University of California Press, 1977.

Quayle, Dan, "After INF Treaty, Avoid These Things," *Defense News*, October 26, 1987.

Quester, G., *Nuclear Diplomacy: The First Twenty-Five Years*, Dunellen, New York, 1970.

Ramo, Simon, *The Bulletin of the Atomic Scientists*, October, 1981.

Rathgens, George, "The Dynamics of the Arms Race," *Scientific American*, April, 1969.

Ravenal, Earl, "Reconsider Defense Commitment to Europe," *Oakland Tribune*, April 24, 1984.

Raytheon Advertisement, *Defense Electronics Magazine*, Volume 19, Number 9, September 1987.

"Reagan, Gorbachev Plan to Hold Summit," *Gazette-Telegraph*, Colorado Springs, CO, September 19, 1987.

Reese, Michael, and McAlevey, Peter, "'Aerospace Valley' Takes Off," *Newsweek*, July 15, 1985.

Regional Multipliers: A User Handbook for the Regional Input-Output Modeling System (RIMS II), U.S. Department of Commerce, Bureau of Economic Analysis, Washington, D.C., May, 1986.

Reich, Robert B., "High Tech, A Subsidiary of Pentagon Inc.," *New York Times*, May 29, 1985.

Reid, T.R., "Welcoming Weapons in Space," *Philadelphia Inquirer*, December 9, 1984.

"Report Urges that Pentagon Pay for Its Nuclear Warheads," *New York Times*, July 17, 1975.

Reppy, Judith, "Conversion From Military R&D: Economic Aspects," *38th Pugwash Conference*, Dagomys, USSR, 29 August–3 September, 1988.

Rossi, Sergio, "Countries Work Toward Defense Cooperation," *Defense News*, May 16, 1988.

Rowen, Henry S., and Tremel, Vladimir G., "Gorbachev and the Ailing Russian Bear," *The Wall Street Journal*, April 21, 1986.

Ryan, Bill, "SDI: A Boost for the Technology Battle," *Defense News*, August 10, 1987.

Salkowski, Charlotte, "Guaging effect of SDI on Geneva talks," *Christian Science Monitor*, April 4, 1985.

Sanger, David E., "The Russians Seek IBM Compatibility," *New York Times*, March 3, 1985.

Scheinman, L., *Atomic Energy Policy in France Under the Fourth Republic*, Princeton University Press, Princeton, NJ, 1965.

Schemann, Serge, "Chernobyl and the Europeans: Radiation and Doubts Linger," *The New York Times*, June 12, 1988.

Schlesinger, James R., "Debunking the Myth of Decline," *The New York Times Magazine*, June 19, 1988.

Schwartz, D. N., *NATO's Nuclear Dilemmas*, Brookings Institution, Washington, DC, 1983.

Scott, Michael J., and Belzer, David B., "Hanford, The N Reactor, and Washington's Economy: The Impacts of Permanent Closure," *The Northwest Environmental Journal*, vol. 4, no. 1.

Scott, W., "Another Look at the USSR's Defensive Doctrine," *Air Force Magazine*, March 1988.

Seib, Gerald F., "Arms-Treaty Backers Fear Senate Changes, Not Outright Defeat," *The Wall Street Journal*, December 9, 1987.

————. "Defense Buildup Threatens Long-Term Economic Growth, House Report Asserts," *Wall Street Journal*, April 24, 1984.

Silverberg, David, "Domestic Sources Reap Bulk of U.S. Prime Contracts," *Defense News*, October 5, 1987.

————. "U.S. Dominance of Markets Ending, Study Says," *Defense News*, February 29, 1988.

Simis, Konstantin, "An Officer and a Crook: Ripping Off the Red Army," *Washington Post*, January 8, 1984.

Sivard, R.L., *World Military and Social Expenditures 1987–88*, published under the auspices of the Union of Concerned Scientists, World Priorities, Inc., Washington, D.C., 1987.

"Slickums," *Scientific American,* June, 1988.

Sloss, L., "The Strategist Perspective," in *Ballistic Missile Defense,* Carter, A., and Schwartz, D., ed., The Brookings Institution, Washington, D.C. 1984.

Smith, Fredrick N., "USSR: Nuclear Submarines Problems Continue," *Defense and Foreign Affairs Daily,* January 23, 1985.

Sneider, Dan, "Japanese Progress on SDI Drags," *Defense News,* Mar 21, 1988.

"Space Based Surveillance," *Defense Electronics Magazine,* Volume 19, Number 9, September 1987.

"Space Command Welcome," *Gazette Telegraph,* Colorado Springs, Colorado, December 9, 1984.

Sprague, Marshall, *Newport in the Rockies,* The Swallow Press, Inc., Chicago, Illinois, 1971.

"Star Wars, SDI: The Grand Experiment," *IEEE Spectrum,* September 1985.

Starr, Barbara, and Adams, Peter, "Deficit Reduction Deal Looms Large Over Pentagon, Its Budget," *Defense News,* Vol. 3, No. 7, February 15, 1988.

Stevenson, Richard W., "The Big Push for Pentagon Dollars," *New York Times,* July 5, 1987.

"Study Cites Cost of Closing Reactor," *The Post Register,* Idaho Falls, Idaho, September 2, 1987.

Teller, Edward, and Sagan, Carl, "Pros and Cons of Strategic Defense," *Discovery Magazine,* September 1985.

"Testimony on the Defense Budget," *Proceedings of the House Committee on Appropriations,* U.S. House of Representatives, 1984.

"The Brave New World of Stealth Warfare," *U.S. News and World Report,* November 28, 1988.

"The Cold War Is Not Over," *Defense News,* May 2, 1988.

The Defense Monitor, Vol. XII, No. 7, Center for Defense Information, Washington, D.C., 1983.

The Effect of Defense Spending On the Soviet and U.S. Economies, A Conference at Cornell University, April, 1987.

The Impact of Defense Spending on Nondefense Engineering Labor Markets, A Report to the National Academy of Engineering by the Panel on Engineering Labor Markets, Office of Scientific and Engineering Personnel, National Research Council, National Academy Press, Washington, D.C., 1986.

"The prospect for arms talks," *Financial Times,* London, December 29, 1986.

"The Real Burden of Burden Sharing," *Defense News,* July 4, 1988.

"The Rise in Public Expenditure—How Much Further Can It Go?" *The OECD Observer,* May, 1978.

The Significance of Divergent U.S./USSR Military Expenditures, RAND, N-1000-AF, February, 1979.

"The Soviet Economy Under a New Leader," *A Report to the Joint Economic Committee, U.S. Congress,* Central Intelligence Agency and the Defense Intelligence Agency, March 19, 1986.

Thelen, Friedrich, "West German Defense Budget Grows Only 1.5 Percent," *Defense News,* July 6, 1987.

Thomas, Bill, "Military Spinoffs, Engines of Change," *Best of Business Quarterly,* Spring, 1988.

Thompson, Mark, "Research, development for defense takes beating," *Gazette Telegraph,* Colorado Springs, Colorado, April 3, 1988.

Thurow, Roger, "NATO's Economic Bind Restricts Its Defense Options," *Wall Street Journal,* June 5, 1984.

TMI-4/Rev. 0/2-17-88, Lawrence Livermore National Laboratory and Westinghouse, Inc., February 17, 1988.

Trego, Lamar, Westinghouse Idaho Nuclear Co., in: Fields, Dave, "Proposed center could lure SIS spinoffs to area," *The Post Register,* Idaho Falls, Idaho, Dec 10, 1987.

U.S. Arms Control and Disarmament Agency, *World Military Expenditures and Arms Transfers 1985,* ACDA Publication 123, Washington, DC, August 1985.

U.S Congress, House Committee on Armed Services, *The Ailing Defense Industrial Base: Unready for Crisis,* a report of the Defense Industrial Base Panel, U.S. Government Printing Office, Washington, D.C., December 31, 1980.

U.S. Congress, Senate, Permanent Subcommittee on Investigations of the Committee on Government Affairs, *Transfer of United States High Technology to the Soviet Union and Soviet Block Nations,* Hearings, 97th Congress, 2nd Session, Washington, Government Printing Office, 1982.

U.S. Department of Commerce, *U.S. Industrial Outlook,* U.S. Government Printing Office, Washington, DC, January 1987.

Ulsamer, Edward, "Will Economic Weakness Increase Soviet Militancy?" *Air Force Magazine,* March, 1983.

Union of Concerned Scientists, "Antisatellite Weapons," *Briefing Paper,* 1985.

Union of Concerned Scientists, *Presidential Priorities,* 1988.

Wallcott, John, "Approach to Arms Control Combines Missile Reductions, Work on Defense," *The Wall Street Journal,* October 20, 1986.

Washburn, D., and Gertcher, F., *The Strategic Defense Initiative: Background, Transition and Strategy Evolution,* RDA-TR-180072-007, for Air Force Space Command, December 1984.

Washington Labor Market, Vol. 12, No. 2, Economic Analysis Branch, Washington State Employment Security, Seattle, Washington, February, 1988.

"Weapons Production More Than Jobs, Payroll, Economy," *The Post Register,* Idaho Falls, Idaho, August 10, 1987.

Weeks, Albert, "Perceptions of benefits seen softening Western Europe's position on SDI," *Free Press International,* March 11, 1985.

Weida, William J., *Paying For Weapons: Politics and Economics of Countertrade and Offsets,* Frost and Sullivan, Inc., New York, 1986.

————. Testimony at the hearings on the Special Isotope Separation Project, Idaho Falls, Idaho, March 25, 1988.

Weida, W., and Gertcher, F., *The Political Economy of National Defense,* Westview Press, Boulder, Colorado, 1987.

————. "Military Weapon Systems Expenditures and Risk: Theory and Evidence," *International Journal of Social Economics,* London, August, 1982.

Weidenbaum, Murray L., "Industrial Adjustments to Military Shifts and Cutbacks," *The Economic Consequences of Reduced Military Spending,* Bernard Udis, ed., Lexington Books, Lexington, MA, 1973.

Weinberger, Caspar W., *Annual Report to the Congress, Fiscal Year 1984,* U.S. Government Printing Office, Washington, D.C., January, 1983.

———— . *Annual Report to the Congress, Fiscal Year 1985,* U.S. Government Printing Office, Washington, D.C., January 1984.

———— . *Annual Report to the Congress,* Fiscal Year 1988, U.S. Government Printing Office, Washington, D.C., January, 1987.

———— . Remarks to the Town Hall of California, Los Angeles, California, October 24, 1984.

———— . *Soviet Military Power,* U.S. Government Printing Office, Washington, D.C., March 1983.

———— . *Soviet Military Power,* U.S. Government Printing Office, Washington, D.C., March, 1987.

Wheeler, David L., "Scientists Refine for Battlefield Use a Weapon Designed for Star Wars," *The Chronicle of Higher Education,* January 21, 1987.

Wolfe, Charles, Jr., "SDI Is No European Economic Elixir," *The Wall Street Journal,* October 23, 1985.

Yack, Patrick, "Pentagon scraps Springs shuttle complex," *The Denver Post,* Denver, Colorado, January 30, 1987.

Yegorov, et al., *Soviet Military Thought,* No. 2., Moscow, 1973.

INDEX